# INTRODUCTION

## TO

# COMPUTER

# LITERACY

**Helene G. Kershner**

State University of New York at Buffalo

D. C. HEATH AND COMPANY

Lexington, Massachusetts    Toronto

Acquisitions Editor: George Lobell
Developmental Editor: Ann Hall
Production Editor: Andrea Cava
Designer: Cornelia L. Boynton
Production Coordinator: Lisa Arcese
Photo Researcher: Martha L. Shethar
Text Permission Editor: Margaret Roll
Cover: Joanna Steinkeller

Published simultaneously in Canada.

Printed in the United States of America.

International Standard Book Number: 0-669-09560-5

Library of Congress Catalog Card Number: 89-84258

10  9  8  7  6  5  4  3  2  1

This text is dedicated to Josh and Libby,

without whose love and attention

this book would have taken half the time,

and to Bruce,

whose love made all this possible.

# Preface

Computers have become an essential part of our daily lives. We often use them without even knowing we are doing so. Yet, knowing how to get cash from an automatic teller machine or how to program a VCR does not require an understanding of how computers work. To fully tap a computer's resources, it is important to understand how its components work together to store and process information. To be effective users, students must understand the potential and limitations of the hardware, the process of problem solving, the capabilities of today's software, and much more.

*Introduction to Computer Literacy* is designed to meet this need. The purpose of this book is to make students literate in all aspects of computers and, by so doing, make them comfortable in the computer age. By introducing the student to the hardware, software, and vocabulary of computers, the mystery of computers is removed. All major types of computers, from microcomputers to mainframes, from laptops to supercomputers, are discussed. Comprehensive coverage of common applications the student will encounter, including word processors, spreadsheets, data bases, and graphics packages, both IBM and Macintosh versions, are also covered. The information presented provides students with an essential understanding of computers and their uses while establishing a firm foundation for further study.

## TEXT CONTENT AND ORGANIZATION

To meet the needs of both students and instructors, careful consideration has been given to the content and organization of *Introduction to Computer Literacy*. Topic selection, readability, flexibility of presentation, pedagogical structure, and supporting materials have been specifically designed to assist both student and instructor in achieving student computer literacy.

### Variety

The table of contents provides a glimpse of the many topics covered. Beginning with an overview and a brief history of computers, the book deals with both the computer hardware and the applications software that transforms the machine into a tool for problem solving. The text develops for the student the problem-solving technique of designing algorithms. This top-down technique is not only applicable to the design of programs but to solving problems in general. The text directly applies this approach to applications software such as spreadsheets and data base systems.

All chapters are designed to give the student a solid grounding in the uses and potential of computers. The increasingly important area of computer communications and networking is given extensive coverage, with practical examples including E-mail and on-line information services as well as academic and business networks. The often-neglected topic of ethical use of the computer is discussed throughout the text, with an emphasis on the individual's responsibility for ethical use. Discussions include criminal use of the computer and the computer's impact on personal privacy. Additional topics covered include programming languages and the very practical issue of how to buy computers and software.

## Flexibility

An important feature of any text is how well it can be adapted to meet the needs of various instructors in different courses. This text uses a generic approach to software. Computer screen examples are drawn from the most popular packages, but discussion is not limited to specific packages. This text's flexibility makes it ideal as a core text or, when paired with the Heath *Software Guides* or with the Heath Laboratory Course Series, as part of a lecture/lab sequence. After Chapter 1, "An Overview of Computers," the chapters may be covered in order or rearranged to conform to the various needs of almost all instructors.

## Readability

Written in a clear, engaging style, this text makes sometimes-difficult concepts understandable to students. Realistic, practical examples are used extensively. The reading level has been carefully monitored by the editors, course instructors, and reviewers. The material has been widely classroom tested.

## Chapter Preview

Because repetition is one of the keys to learning, each chapter begins with a preview telling the student the main topics that will be presented.

## Examples

To demonstrate to the students that computers are approachable, nonthreatening tools, the examples in the text are drawn from situations students typically experience in everyday life.

## Boxed Features

"On Line" boxes provide a glimpse of how computers solve problems and meet needs in the real world. Demonstrating that computers are a vital part of everyday life, the articles reflect current technology and issues of common interest.

## Design and Illustrations

Textbooks that are well designed and contain ample illustrations hold the student's interest. Illustrations, including photographs and line art, are used liberally in this text. High-resolution pictures of computer screens and program examples prepare the student for data displays encountered when working with the computer. A section with color photographs enhances the presentation of key subjects.

## End-of-Chapter Material

Carefully graded review materials are provided at the end of each chapter to reinforce understanding. A comprehensive, yet concise summary reviews the major points discussed in each chapter. "Key Words" lists include important terms, with page references, that appear in boldface type in the chapter. "Test Your Knowledge" questions help the student recall the details just presented, and "Expand Your Knowledge" questions challenge the student to apply the facts to realistic situations. The exercises stress hands-on experience to reinforce the learning process.

## Glossary and Index

A complete glossary includes clear definitions for the boldface terms in the text and chapter references. In addition, a comprehensive index provides a handy reference for both student and instructor.

## SUPPLEMENTS

Extensive packages of software and programming supplements are offered with the text to help both student and instructor cover the material. Each supplement has been prepared by experienced teacher/authors.

### Software Supplements

The Heath *Software Guides* and the new Heath Laboratory Course Series will teach the student to start using applications packages productively. Most of the popular applications packages are included in the series, and many of the manuals are available with software. A listing of the Heath Laboratory Course Series, which is also available, appears on the back cover of this text.

### Programming Supplements

For courses with a programming language component, comprehensive programming supplements are available. The supplements are offered free or at a reduced rate to adopters.

- *An Introduction to Structured Microsoft BASIC Programming* by Thomas W. Doyle and Jeremy I. Clark.
- *Programming in Pascal* and *Programming in Pascal with an Early Introduction to Procedures* by Nell Dale, The University of Texas at Austin
- *Modula-2: A Complete Guide* by K. N. King, Georgia State University
- *Pascal on Videotape* by Nell Dale, The University of Texas at Austin

### Instructor's Supplements

The supplements designed for instructors include an Instructor's Guide and computerized testing for the IBM PC.

- *Instructor's Guide.* The Instructor's Guide includes a wealth of materials for busy instructors. For each chapter, learning objectives, a chapter overview, annotated lecture outlines, answers to text questions, additional classroom and lecture materials, transparency masters, and test items are provided.
- *HeathTest Plus.* HeathTest Plus, a computerized test generator for microcomputers, is also available. Instructors can produce chapter tests, midterms, and final exams easily and accurately. The instructor can also edit existing questions or add new ones as desired, or preview questions on screen and add them to the test with a single keystroke.

## ACKNOWLEDGMENTS

A book such as this is not produced in a vacuum. Ideas, thoughts, and perspective require a supportive and stimulating environment. A special debt is owed to Kulbir Arora for his contribution of the assembly language and LISP programs. Barbara Sherman's general support and help with the revision of the data base chapter is gratefully acknowledged. Thanks go to Patricia J. Eberlein, former chairman of computer science at the State University of New York at Buffalo, for urging me to begin this endeavor. Thank you also to Jeff Kushner of Pennsylvania State University–Behrend College for his strong support during this project.

I would like to thank my colleagues who reviewed the manuscript including Harvey Blessing, Essex Community College; Walter Bremer, California Polytechnic State University; Alice Cimpkins, Paine College; Richard Dillman, Western Maryland College; Diane Drozd, College of DuPage; Peter Frey, Northwestern University; Cindy Hanchey, Oklahoma Baptist University; Grace Hertlein, California State University–Chico; Lindsay Hess, Montana College of Mineral Science & Technology; Gerald Isaacs, Carroll College; Betty Jehn, University of Dayton; Russel Lee, Allan Hancock College; Antonio M. Lopez, Jr., Loyola University; William Pritchard, University of South Florida; and Paul W. Ross, Millersville University.

Special thanks go to Ann Hall, developmental editor, for her organization and direction on this project.

Above all, two people must be thanked. To David C. Brown at the University of Wisconsin–Madison goes my heartfelt appreciation for reading every word, making corrections where needed, and listening to my frustration when writing became difficult. I also must thank my husband, Bruce. Not only did his support at home allow me the time I needed to craft this text, but without his daily support and editorial skills this text would not have been possible. He read each chapter as it came off the printer, corrected my spelling, edited the text, and then willingly reread it in its next iteration before any material was ever sent to D. C. Heath. This text was clearly a family project.

H.G.K.

## ABOUT THE AUTHOR

Helene G. Kershner is the assistant chairman of computer science at the State University of New York at Buffalo. She is an award-winning teacher, recognized for her ability to make complex concepts understandable. During her fifteen years as a teacher and administrator, she has developed a strong appreciation for the needs and concerns of the nontechnical computer user. In addition to teaching, she oversees the instructional laboratories that are used to introduce computing to more than 700 students each semester. She has appeared on radio and television and has given numerous workshops and talks on computer literacy, the importance of computers, and computer science as a discipline. Helene Kershner received her B.A. in mathematics from Queens College and her M.S.E. in computer and information systems from the University of Pennsylvania and completed advanced graduate work in educational psychology at the University of Connecticut–Storrs. Before coming to the State University of New York at Buffalo, she was the departmental administrator for computer science at the University of Wisconsin–Madison.

# Brief Contents

1   An Overview of Computers   1

2   The History of Computers   31

3   The Central Processing Unit   69

4   External Memory   89

5   Input and Output   111

6   Designing Algorithms   155

7   Processing a Program   177

8   Programming Languages   199

9   Introduction to Applications Software   221

10   Word Processing   249

11   Spreadsheets   275

12   Data Bases   303

13   Computer Graphics   327

14   Computer Communications and Networking   349

15   Evaluating Computers and Software   375

16   Issues and Responsibilities   393

    Photo Credits   411

    Glossary   413

    Index   427

# Contents

## 1    An Overview of Computers    1

Understanding the Machine  2

*On Line: Pay That Ticket! 3*  •  Data Versus Information  3  •  The "Basic"
Computer  5  •  Instructing the Machine  7

The Binary Machine—Bits and Bytes  7

Different Goals, Different Machines  9

Digital Computers  9  •  Analog Computers  9  •  Hybrid Computers  9  •
Special-Purpose Computers  11  •  General-Purpose Computers  11

Machines and Their Size  11

Microcomputers  14  •  Minicomputers  19  •  Workstations  21  •
Mainframes  23  •  Supercomputers  24

Summary  27

Key Words  •  Test Your Knowledge  •  Expand Your Knowledge

## 2    The History of Computers    31

The Development of Computing Machines  32

The Pre-Computer Age  32

The Abacus  32  •  Oughtred's Slide Rule  33  •  Pascal's Calculator  33  •
*On Line: The Slide Rule's Downward Slide  34*  •  Leibniz's Multiplier  35

Programming and Expanding the Machine  35

Jacquard's Loom  36  •  Charles Babbage  36  •  Hollerith's Census
Machine  40  •  Burroughs' Adding and Listing Machine  41

The Computer Age  43

Atanasoff's ABC  44  •  Germany's Wartime Computer  44  •  England's
Wartime Computer  45  •  America's Wartime Computer Research  45  •
Von Neumann's Logical Computer  48

A Computer Geneology  52

First-Generation Computers (1951–1958)  53  •  Second-Generation Computers
(1959–1964)  53  •  Third-Generation Computers (1965–early 1970s)  55  •
Fourth-Generation Computers (early 1970s–present)  58

The Rise of the Microcomputer  60

Computers from a Kit  60  •  The Birth of the Personal Computer  60  •  Toward
a User-Friendly Machine  62  •  *On Line: The Computer Museum  63*

Beyond the Fourth Generation  63

Summary  64

Key Words  •  Test Your Knowledge  •  Expand Your Knowledge


**3**     **The Central Processing Unit**                                  **69**

The Central Processing Unit (CPU)  70

The Arithmetic and Logic Unit  71  •  The Control Unit  72  •  Registers  72  •
Memory  73

Coding Information  73

*On Line: The NeXT Computer  74*  •  EBCDIC  75  •  ASCII  75  •  Parity  77

Addresses: Locating Information  78

Executing Instructions  79

Primary Memory  80

Magnetic Core Memory  80  •  Semiconductor Memory  80  •  RAM and ROM  82

New and Changing Technologies  83

Bubble Memory  83  •  Biological Chips  84  •  Parallel Processing  84

Summary  85

Key Words  •  Test Your Knowledge  •  Expand Your Knowledge

## 4  External Memory                                                89

Organizing Information  90

Sequential File Organization  91  •  Direct Access File Organization  91  •  Indexed File Organization  91

Paper Media  91

Magnetic Tape  93

Data Organization  93

Magnetic Disks  95

Data Organization  97

Floppy Disks  99

Winchester Disks  99

The Bernoulli Box  101

Backup  102

Future Technologies  102

Optical Memory  102  •  Perpendicular Recording  103  •  Superconductors  104  •  *On Line: Superconductor Breakthroughs 105*

Summary  106

    Key Words  •  Test Your Knowledge  •  Expand Your Knowledge

## 5  Input and Output                                              111

Dedicated Input Devices  112

    Keyboards  113  •  Input Alternatives  115

Dedicated Output Devices  122

    Soft Copy: Monitors  122  •  Hard Copy: Printers and Plotters  123

The Terminal: An Input/Output Device  132

Specialized Technologies  134

    *On Line: Are VDTs a Health Threat?  135*  •  The Voice as Input  136  •  Voice
Synthesis as Output  139  •  Print Recognition Technology  140

Combination Systems  144

    The Automated Cash Register  145  •  Automated Teller Machines  147  •  The
Automated Post Office  150

Summary  151

    Key Words  •  Test Your Knowledge  •  Expand Your Knowledge

## 6  Designing Algorithms                                         155

Problem Solving  156

    What Is an Algorithm?  158  •  Why Program?  158

Flowchart Versus Outline  159

Choosing a Plan  159

Top-Down Analysis  160

Problem-Solving Steps  161

Define the Problem  161  •  Define the Output  161  •  Define the Input  162  •
Define the Initial Algorithm  162  •  Refine the Algorithm  163  •  Define the
Program  163

Sample Problems and Solutions  164

Example One  164  •  Example Two  166

Summary  173

Key Words  •  Test Your Knowledge  •  Expand Your Knowledge

## 7  Processing a Program                                177

Files  178

Translating Programs  179

*On Line: The History of the Bug  181*

Executing Programs  185

Debugging  190

Hand Simulation  191  •  Intermediate Results  192

Testing  192

Summary  196

Key Words  •  Test Your Knowledge  •  Expand Your Knowledge

## 8  Programming Languages                               199

Types of Computer Languages  201

Machine Language  201  •  Assembly Language  202  •  High-Level
Languages  203  •  Natural Language Processing  204

Choosing a Computer Language 205

Common Languages 206
FORTRAN 206 • BASIC 207 • Pascal 209

Other Popular High-Level Languages 212
ALGOL 212 • COBOL 212 • LISP 212 • LOGO 213

Languages Gaining in Popularity 213
Ada 214 • C 214 • Modula-2 214

Summary 215
*On Line: Selecting a Programming Language the Easy Way 216*
Key Words • Test Your Knowledge • Expand Your Knowledge

## 9  Introduction to Applications Software       221

Types of Software 222

Applications Software 223
Specialized Applications Software 224 • General-Purpose Applications
Software 231 • *On Line: St. Silicon's Hospital Makes House Calls 237*

Expert Systems 238

Our Changing Libraries 239

Software Integration 241
Integrated Environments 241 • Integrated Packages 243 • Package
Integrators 244 • Families of Software 245

Summary 245
Key Words • Test Your Knowledge • Expand Your Knowledge

## 10  Word Processing                                                    249

Changing the Way We Write  250

What Can a Word Processor Do?  251

Word Processing Hardware  251

Keyboard  251  •  Display Screen  251  •  Printer  252

Types of Word Processing Programs  252

Text Editor/Text Formatter  253  •  What You See Is What You Get (WYSIWYG)  254

How Does Word Processing Work?  254

Entering Text  255  •  Editing Text  256

Text Formatting  259

Page Layout  261  •  Character Adjustment  262

Advanced Features  263

Search and Replace  263  •  Moving Blocks of Text  264  •  Additional Capabilities  264  •  *On Line: Hypertext—A New Way of Reading  266*

Desktop Publishing  267

Problems and Pitfalls  268

Editing Problems  269  •  Search and Replace  269  •  Spelling Checkers  270  •  Loss of Text  270  •  Special Effects  270

Summary  271

Key Words  •  Test Your Knowledge  •  Expand Your Knowledge

## 11  Spreadsheets                                                       275

What Is an Electronic Spreadsheet?  276

Common Spreadsheet Features  277

Planning a Spreadsheet  280

    *On Line: Spreadsheets and Tax Returns  282*

Building a Spreadsheet  282

    Design the Spreadsheet  283  •  Enter the Data  284  •  Save the Data  285

What If  287

Programming Tools  290

    Inserting and Deleting  290  •  Copying Cells  290  •  Formatting Data  292  •
    Mathematical Functions  292

Pitfalls, Problems, and Solutions  295

Summary  297

    Key Words  •  Test Your Knowledge  •  Expand Your Knowledge


**12   Data Bases**                                                        **303**

What Is a Data Base?  304

    Paper Data Bases  305  •  Modern Data Base Systems  306  •  Microcomputer
    Data Base Systems  306

Steps in Getting Started  308

    *On Line: Putting the Byte on Crime  309*

The Data Base in Use  309

    Creating a Data Base  310  •  Searching and Sorting  311  •  Changing a Data
    Base  314  •  Generating Reports  316

Complex Searches and Sorts  316

Using Multiple Files  319

Advanced Features  320

Pitfalls, Problems, and Solutions  321

Improving Sorting Speed  321  •  Maintaining Data Integrity  321  •  Avoiding Deletion Errors  321  •  Avoiding Data Loss  322

Data Base Machines  323

Summary  324

Key Words  •  Test Your Knowledge  •  Expand Your Knowledge

## 13  Computer Graphics                                327

Creating Images  328

Hardware  329

Boards and Monitors  329  •  Graphics Input Devices  331  •  Graphics Output Devices  333

Software  334

Analysis Graphics  335  •  Presentation Graphics  336  •  Computer-Aided Design  339  •  *On Line: CAD in Crystal  341*  •  Creative Graphics  342

The Computer as an Artistic Medium  343

Summary  345

Key Words  •  Test Your Knowledge  •  Expand Your Knowledge

## 14  Computer Communications and Networking     349

Making the Connection  351

Modems  352  •  Channels  353

Communication Media  355

Twisted-Pair Copper Wire  355  •  Coaxial Cable  355  •  Microwave Signals  356  •  Fiber Optic Cable  357

Software 358

Protocols 358 • Microcomputer Software 359

Networking 359

Early Connections 360 • Local Area Networks 361 • Wide Area
Networks 361 • Bulletin Boards 362 • Academic Computer Networks 363
• *On Line: "Talking" Over E-Mail 364* • Corporate/Business Networks 366 •
Information Networks 368

Summary 370

Key Words • Test Your Knowledge • Expand Your Knowledge

**15**   Evaluating Computers and Software                           **375**

Buying a Computer—Know Your Needs 376

Steps in Purchasing a Computer 377 • Purchase Sources 382 • *On Line:
Computers for Cadets 384*

Protecting Your Purchase 385

Surge Protectors 385 • Insurance Riders 386

Buying Software 386

Necessary Software 386 • Steps for Purchasing Software 387

Learning and Support 389

Documentation 389 • Information and Self-Education 389 • Courses and
Training 389 • User Groups 390

Summary 391

Key Words • Test Your Knowledge • Expand Your Knowledge

**16** Issues and Responsibilities 393

Computers, An Agent of Change  394

Computers and Crime  395

Hacking  397
  *On Line: Computer Viruses Can Make You Sick  399*

Theft, Piracy, and Plagiarism  400
  Protecting Intellectual Property  400  •  Plagiarism  401

Privacy  403

Computer Matching  406

Summary  408
  Key Words  •  Test Your Knowledge  •  Expand Your Knowledge

**Photo Credits  411**

**Glossary  413**

**Index  427**

# Introduction to Computer Literacy

# 1

# An Overview of Computers

**Chapter Outline**

Understanding the Machine
    Data Versus Information • The "Basic" Computer • Instructing the
    Machine

The Binary Machine—Bits and Bytes

Different Goals, Different Machines
    Digital Computers • Analog Computers • Hybrid Computers •
    Special-Purpose Computers • General-Purpose Computers

Machines and Their Size
    Microcomputers (Home Computers; Personal Computers;
    Portable Computers) • Minicomputers • Workstations •
    Mainframes • Supercomputers

Computers have become an essential part of our lives. We find them in our cars, our markets, and our schools. They are almost everywhere and affect nearly everything we do. Yet, most of us have no idea *what* they do and even less of an idea how they work. The study of computers, like any other field, has a language all its own. This is not surprising. Talking with a car mechanic is often like conversing in a foreign language. We expect to understand what the car mechanic is saying, but most often that is not the case. Talking to a doctor is even more like a visit to an exotic country. The physician discusses our medical problems, but to the average person, the words and procedures might just as well be a foreign language.

Learning about computers can be equally confusing and difficult until you know the jargon, the vocabulary. When working with computers, common words such as data, bug, or bit take on unique meanings. Some computer jargon, such as input, network, and down, has become part of our everyday language.

This text intends to familiarize you with the concepts upon which computers are based as well as the vocabulary used. When you have completed this text, computers will be familiar territory, not a foreign country. You will understand how the components that make up the computer work and how computers are changing the world. In addition, you will understand how programs are written and how they are used. You will speak the language of computers and be comfortable with these machines.

After studying this chapter, you will be able to:

- Understand the difference between data and information.
- Identify the basic components of all computer systems.
- Understand the binary number system, bits, bytes, and words.
- Distinguish between digital and analog computers.
- Identify the different classes of computers.
- Distinguish between microcomputers, minicomputers, and mainframes.
- Understand how workstations, superminis, and supercomputers are complicating the classification system used to describe computers.

## UNDERSTANDING THE MACHINE

To understand how computers work, we must start with the basic vocabulary. We need to comprehend the language being "spoken" before we can even begin to understand the machine. The first computer-related words to learn focus on what the computer does. We have heard that computers "crunch numbers." What computers really do—and just about the only thing they do—is *process*

# *On Line*

## PAY THAT TICKET!

Parking tickets are something to be avoided. When they can't be avoided, however, tens of thousands of people try something else—they simply ignore them.

The result is that states, municipalities, and universities find they have thousands of unpaid parking tickets each year and overcrowded traffic courts.

Microcomputers are coming to the rescue, however. One of the newest devices in the police officer's arsenal is the automated ticketwriter. An officer keys the critical information into a hand-held ticket-writing device. The device prints out a summons to be placed on the offending car's windshield and enters the license plate number and other crucial information into the system's memory. A data base of outstanding fines is also stored in the system's memory. The newly entered license number is automatically matched against licenses in the data base. If the ticketed car has other unpaid fines, the officer can have the car towed or immobilized.

A more complex version of this system is being found with increasing frequency mounted between the driver and passenger seats of patrol cars. Officers can enter a vehicle's description or license plate number and learn whether it was reported as stolen, has outstanding fines, or whether the owner is wanted for a crime. Appropriate action can then be taken.

Computerized ticket writers and in-car computer systems are aiding the police in locating lawbreakers. They are also giving a boost to towing companies and manufacturers of car immobilization devices. While it may not be possible to avoid all parking tickets, computers may make it impossible to avoid paying the associated fines.

*Source*: "Computers for Catching Scofflaws," *The New York Times*, July 6, 1986, p. F 13.

*data*. In this chapter we will discuss the meaning of these two words. Then we will see how computers do their work—and do it very well indeed.

### Data Versus Information

In common speech, the words *data* and *information* are used interchangeably. However, these terms have very different meanings. In everyday conversation these differences are not too important, but for computers this difference is critical.

**Data** are raw facts. Raw facts can be collected from any number of sources. For example, every 10 years the U.S. Census Bureau collects facts, such as the number of bathrooms, the ages of family members, and the first names of the children in America's households. Taken alone, these facts are not informative. It is impossible to draw meaningful conclusions about anything from this collection of data.

**Information**, on the other hand, is the result of data that has been transformed. The data has been changed in some ways so that meaningful conclusions can be drawn. For example, it is interesting to know that *J* names, such as Jeremy, Jennifer, and Joshua, are very popular among the children of the baby-boom generation, or that the average American family today has 1.5 children. This is information.

Why is the difference between data and information so important for computers? Computers have become the agents that transform data into information. The computer is used to collect, organize, sort, and transform raw facts into meaningful information from which logical conclusions can be drawn. For example, when registering for college, the following 10 students indicated their grade level:

| | |
|---|---|
| Penny Lofers | Freshman |
| Frank N. Stein | Freshman |
| Inna Pickle | Freshman |
| Sandy Beaches | Sophomore |
| Phil Errupp | Freshman |
| Polly Nomial | Junior |
| Said A. Mint | Sophomore |
| Telly Graham | Freshman |
| Willie Maykill | Senior |
| Senior Itis | Freshman |

In its current form we can draw few conclusions from this data. However, if we organize the data alphabetically we can easily find the status of an individual. Furthermore, if we sort the data by academic year we can make inferences about these students.

| | |
|---|---|
| Phil Errupp | Freshman |
| Telly Graham | Freshman |
| Senior Itis | Freshman |
| Penny Lofers | Freshman |
| Inna Pickle | Freshman |
| Frank N. Stein | Freshman |
| Sandy Beaches | Sophomore |
| Said A. Mint | Sophomore |
| Polly Nomial | Junior |
| Willie Maykitt | Senior |

We can conclude that most of these students are Freshmen, but all classes are represented.

Computers, therefore, are data transformers. They assist us in organizing raw facts so that meaningful conclusions can be drawn from them.

## The "Basic" Computer

In order to explain the actual work—processing—done by a computer, we must first look at the parts that make up every computer. All computers, from the smallest home computer to the largest supercomputer used by the military, are made up of the same basic components (see Figure 1.1).

**Input** represents the starting data, the raw facts, that are entered into the computer. The *processor,* or **CPU** for **Central Processing Unit**, is the data transformer. Inside the CPU, electronic circuits change the initial data in some way. Often, input data are combined with other data in the CPU to produce information. All computer processors have some **memory**, or **storage**. These are special electronic circuits that store data and the results of processing that will be needed later. Memory functions as an electronic storage cabinet. Information isn't useful if no one knows about it. **Output** is the result of processing. The ways in which we use the information produced by a computer depend on the form of the output. The form of the output depends, in turn, on the output device we use.

Computers also need additional storage if people are to use them as effective tools. Notice that the storage box in our diagram is outside the processor. Here, storage represents memory added onto the computer. This added memory makes it possible for the computer to remember and retrieve large amounts of both data and information. For example, census data can be stored in this additional memory. So can the instructions that will analyze the data and the results of that analysis. Such storage devices supplement the relatively small amount of memory built into the processor.

All computers have all of these components. However, the components are designed differently in different computers, as Figure 1.2 shows.

**Figure 1.1**        Simplified "General" All-Purpose Computer.

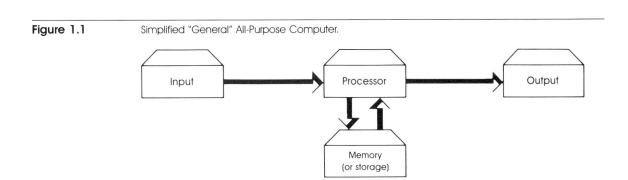

**Figure 1.2**          (a) The Apple Macintosh Microcomputer and (b) The CDC Supercomputer. All computers have similar components, although the design and power can differ markedly.

(a)

(b)

## Instructing the Machine

How is the initial data changed into output? The computer will only do what it is told. It must be given instructions because it cannot do anything on its own. In a sense, computers need directions. They need to follow these directions carefully, making all the correct turns and looking for all the appropriate landmarks, in order to arrive at the destination and produce the required output.

More specifically, a program is used to transform data. A **program** is the step-by-step set of instructions in a language understandable to the computer that directs the computer to perform specific tasks (transform facts) and to solve specific problems (create information). Programs used for problem solving or that direct the operations of the machine (coordinate its many parts) are called **software**. **Hardware**, on the other hand, is the set of physical components that combine to make up the computer. Just as a stereo system is made up of components, including the turntable and speakers, so a computer is made up of components, including the monitor, keyboard, and perhaps a printer.

Despite all the jargon, we must keep one thing in mind: a computer is a machine. It is a tool designed to assist people in solving problems. *Computers do not think.* They do exactly and only what they are told. They are not psychic, they cannot figure out what you meant or what you implied. They only follow the specific instructions they are given. *They do what you say, not what you mean.*

Computers can do some amazing things and accomplish a considerable amount of processing, however. Computers are used in sorting, comparing, listing, updating, ordering, calculating, and much more. By doing such lower-level processing, they free us to do more complex tasks.

So far, we have learned the difference between data and information and have looked at the main parts of every computer. Now we will learn some computer jargon relating to *how* a computer stores information.

## THE BINARY MACHINE—BITS AND BYTES

Computers don't really understand the data and instructions we put into them. All they really understand is two states: on or off. We can talk about the *on* state as being positive, or existing in the presence of electric current. We can talk about the *off* state as being negative, or existing in the absence of electric current.

These two electronic states are numerically represented as 1's (on, positive, electrical current present) and 0's (off, negative, no current). These two states can be represented in the base 2, or **binary number system**. In this system, combinations of 1 and 0 are used to represent all numbers, letters, and special characters.

Most of us learned arithmetic and process mathematical data in the decimal number system, or base 10. It seems reasonable to assume that our decimal system developed from our 10 fingers. The decimal system uses 10 unique symbols, or digits: 0, 1, 2, 3, 4, 5, 6, 7, 8, 9. All the remaining numbers in the decimal system are combinations of these 10 unique symbols.

When we enter numbers into a computer we do so in the decimal system. In order for these numbers to be used by the computer they must be converted into binary form, however. Using the short table that follows we see how the decimal number 5 is translated into its binary equivalent, 101.

| Decimal | Binary |
|---------|--------|
| 0 | 000 |
| 1 | 001 |
| 2 | 010 |
| 3 | 011 |
| 4 | 100 |
| * 5 | 101 |
| 6 | 110 |
| 7 | 111 |

Each 0 or 1 in the binary system is called a **bit** (for Binary digIT) when used with computers. The bit forms the simplest unit of data stored in the computer's memory. A single bit, though, does not tell a computer very much. By combining bits into groups, we can represent more complex things. A **byte** is a group of bits (usually eight). Each byte represents one character of data, such as a number, letter, or special symbol (%, $, and so on). Numbers, letters, and special symbols are the forms *we* use to represent information.

A computer "word" is the number of bits that can be processed at one time by the CPU. An 8-bit computer has a word length of a single character. The Apple IIGS is an 8-bit computer. The word length of a 16-bit machine is two characters or bytes. IBM PC-class machines are 16-bit machines. A 16-bit machine will process twice as much information over a fixed period of time as an 8-bit machine. Other computers use word lengths of 32 and 64 bits and process information significantly faster than 8- or 16-bit machines. The Apple Macintosh is a 32-bit machine.

Computers are frequently described in terms of the amount of memory that is associated with their processors. Computer memory is measured by the number of bytes it contains. This is usually expressed in terms of K bytes or kilobytes. K is often used to mean 1000 bytes, although technically it is equal to 1024 bytes. For example, the once-popular Commodore 64 had a 64K memory. IBM PCs often come with 640K and the Apple Macintosh II comes with 1 Megabyte (1000K bytes or 1 million bytes). This list could go on and on.

While all computers have great similarities, they are not all the same. Such terms as *digital* and *analog, mini, mainframe,* and *micro* are also part of today's computer vocabulary. All of these terms describe different kinds of machines. Let us look at these machines and examine how they differ.

## DIFFERENT GOALS, DIFFERENT MACHINES

There are two basic categories of computers. The two designs reflect two different ways we can look at or analyze our world. When we gather data for input to a computer we can represent mathematical values obtained by simply counting, such as the number of students or change from a dollar, or we can use continuous direct measurement, such as in gauging voltage, car speed, or body temperature.

### Digital Computers

The computers described throughout this text are **digital computers** and are by far the most popular and common of all computing devices. They assist in problem solving by organizing data into countable units or digits; that is, combinations of zeros and ones.

Digital computers have large and easily expandable memory capacity. By storing the programs and data in memory they are capable of solving many different kinds of problems. Digital computers are very flexible machines.

### Analog Computers

**Analog computers** operate with quantities such as voltage, pressure, and rotation. Since the input data of analog computers are directly measured in the real world, they are used to simulate or model problems. In analog computers the program is built directly into the hardware. Since processing a new program requires rewiring the machine, they are less flexible than digital machines.

The difference between analog and digital devices can be seen in the following example. A traditional watch is an analog device. The circular dial represents an hour, and the movement of the hands simulates the passage of time. The time of day must be approximated by reading the position of the hands. With a digital watch, however, the time of day is accurately expressed as a number of digits. The digits themselves can represent many things. When they appear in a clock we interpret them as representing time.

### Hybrid Computers

**Hybrid computers** are combination machines. The input/output design of analog computers is combined with the digital computer's ability to store instructions and perform highly accurate mathematical calculations. Examples of hybrid machines include those used in air traffic control and hospital intensive care units (ICUs). In an ICU for example, a patient's heart rate, temperature, blood pressure, and other vital signs are measured using analog devices. These direct measurements are converted into numeric quantities and are used as input to a

**Figure 1.3**    The Special-Purpose Computer: Special-purpose computers are designed to solve a single problem, such as (a) this Boeing navigational computer and (b) this NASA computer system used in space shuttle flights.

(a)

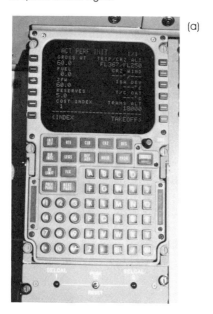

(b)

digital computer, which continually checks them against established standards and issues a warning if dangerous readings occur.

### Special-Purpose Computers

**Special-purpose computers** are designed to solve specific problems. The program instructions are built directly into the computer's hardware. For this reason, special-purpose computers are said to be **preprogrammed**. If the special-purpose machine is an analog device, the layout and organization of the computer components comprise the program. If it is a digital device, the instructions are built directly into the processor (see Chapter 3). Such computers, whether analog or digital, can only do what their hardware or built-in instructions tell them to do (see Figure 1.3).

Special-purpose computers are used for both trivial and critical purposes. Examples are blood analysis devices, automobile cruise controls, video arcade games, dishwasher and microwave memory panels, and navigational controls on spacecraft. Video arcade games use digital computers, while cruise controls are analog devices.

### General-Purpose Computers

**General-purpose computers** are designed to solve a variety of problems. They are not preprogrammed. These machines are flexible, so the same hardware can receive instructions of many kinds and be used to solve different problems (see Figure 1.4).

In general, most digital computers are general-purpose machines, while most analog computers are used as single-purpose machines. We must be careful with generalizations, however, because both digital and analog computers are used in other ways as well.

## MACHINES AND THEIR SIZE

Today's digital computers vary in cost, size, computing power, and speed. They perform a vast array of tasks, from monitoring patient health and supporting humans in space to providing entertainment and remembering dishwasher settings (see Figure 1.5).

Miniaturized computers can be as small as your fingernail. Such tiny computers are found in car engines, dishwashers, and microwave ovens. At the other extreme, room-size supercomputers are used to control and simulate space flights, in nuclear research, and to forecast the weather nationwide or even

**Figure 1.4**    General-Purpose Computers: These flexible machines include (a) microcomputers such as the IBM Personal System/2 Model 50 and (b) mainframe computers such as the IBM 3090/600E.

(a)

(b)

**Figure 1.5**     Computers in Household Equipment: Many appliances now have built-in microprocessors to control their operation and ease troubleshooting for repair.

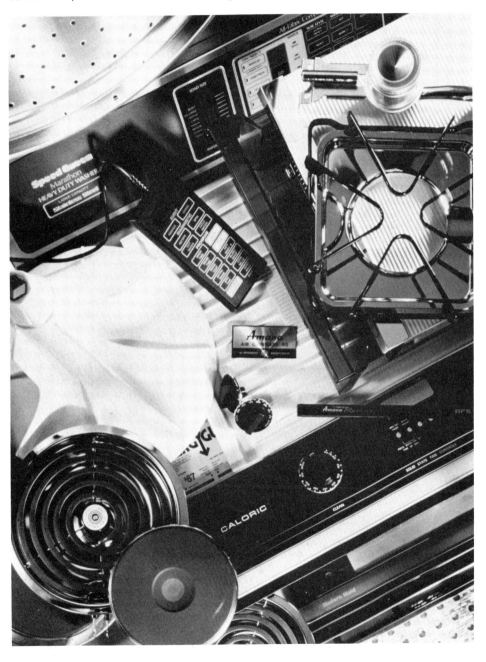

worldwide. As computers of various sizes were developed over the last decade, the following three logical groups became apparent:

*MICROCOMPUTERS*
relatively small
inexpensive ($500–$15,000)
single user
microprocessor based

*MINICOMPUTERS*
middle sized
medium priced ($15,000–$500,000)
multiple users (2–40 users at once)
multiprocessor based

*MAINFRAMES*
large to very large
very expensive (more than $500,000)
multiple users (more than 40 users at once)
multiprocessor based

It really is quite fortunate (although confusing) that the world of computers is not static. Despite our desire to categorize computers, they cannot be divided into clear-cut groups. At best, terms such as *micro, mini,* and *mainframe* can be used only as general guidelines. It is obvious that microcomputers are slower, smaller, and less expensive than minicomputers and mainframes. However, where one class of machine ends and another begins is increasingly difficult to distinguish. The rest of this chapter will examine various types of computers, from microcomputers to supercomputers, exploring their differences and similarities.

## Microcomputers

**Microcomputers**, or **micros**, are often called computers on a chip. The CPU of these machines is a **microprocessor**. This is a tiny processor designed to fit on a single chip smaller than a fingernail (see Figure 1.6).

However, micros consist of more than just processors, as Figure 1.7 shows. They require input devices, so a keyboard is usually added. Since they need a way to communicate their results to us (output), a special monitor or a standard TV and often a printer are added.

Floppy disk drives usually are attached to microcomputers as external memory. Hard disks are increasingly available for micros at affordable prices. As microcomputer users have become more sophisticated, using more complex programs and analyzing more data, they have demanded machines with more and

**Figure 1.6**   The Microprocessor: A powerful device in a tiny package, all of the electrical connections of this Motorola MC68020 microprocessor are etched onto a chip of silicon.

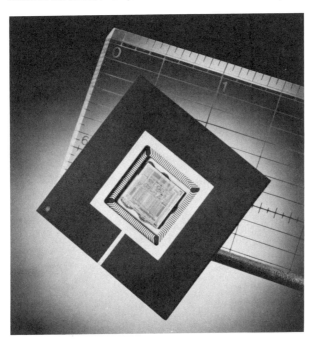

**Figure 1.7**   A Computer System: The microprocessor chip is part of a complete system with input and output devices.

Input device                    Microprocessor                    Output devices

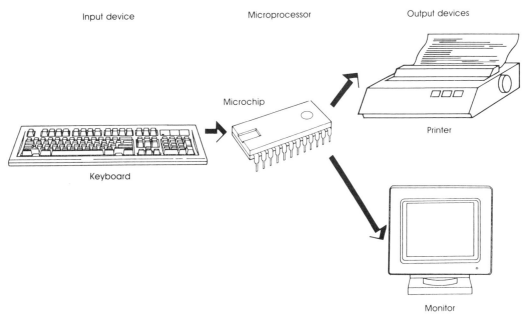

Microchip

Keyboard

Printer

Monitor

15

more internal memory. Today's micros, such as those in Figure 1.8, provide space to expand the machine's internal memory and add communication devices.

Microcomputers come in 8-bit (Apple IIGS), 16-bit (IBM PC), and 32-bit

---

**Figure 1.8**     Powerful Microcomputers: (a) The IBM Personal System/2 model 80 and (b) the Apple Macintosh II are powerful and flexible computers whose speed and power rival yesterday's room-sized machines.

(a)

(b)

(Apple Macintosh and IBM Personal System/2) varieties, depending upon the design of the microprocessor chip that forms the machine's core. The amount of memory and complexity of add-ons cause micros to vary widely in capabilities and price. Some very simple micros cost $500 or less, while sophisticated and complicated setups can cost as much as $15,000.

Since the core of the microcomputer is the size of your fingernail, manufacturers have designed micros to fit the needs and wants of their users. Within the major category of micro, several subgroups can be identified.

**Home Computers**   **Home computers** are micros that have been designed for use in the home. The basic form (a keyboard and microprocessor attached to the family television or color monitor) is relatively inexpensive. Home computers often have a disk drive and printer attached.

On most home machines, the available software dictates the machine's use. Entertainment packages ranging from video arcade-style games to interactive fiction games such as Space Quest are very popular.

Software is available to assist in maintaining family finances and printing greeting cards and posters. Word processing programs and printers are replacing the standard typewriter, and data base programs and computer files help organize family records. Income tax, check balancing, and investment programs are becoming increasingly popular. Learning games that reinforce math and reading skills have also found widespread acceptance.

Increasingly, children are learning and using the computer languages BASIC and LOGO to write their own programs and design their own games on home machines. At the same time they are learning skills that will prove invaluable in the future (see Figure 1.9).

**Personal Computers**   The term *personal computer,* or *PC,* was coined by IBM to describe its single-user microcomputer. As with other words that originated as brand names, such as Kleenex for tissues or Xerox for photocopier, **personal computer**, or **PC**, has come to refer to a flexible and memory-rich microcomputer. Personal computers are relatively inexpensive, single-user machines most often found in business settings. Increasingly, they are used in the home as extensions of the modern office, but once home they are used by the entire family. They are used to solve far more sophisticated problems than those solved by their less expensive home-computer cousins. Personal computers usually include additional internal memory, often as high as 1 Megabit, one or more floppy disk drives, and possibly a hard disk. Personal computers have 80-column monitors and at least one printer attached.

**Portable Computers**   **Portable computers** are complete microcomputers that are designed to be easily carried from place to place. They may be as large as a suitcase or small enough to fit in your pocket. Essentially, portable computers come in three varieties:

**Figure 1.9**          Home Computing: Games, personal financial planning, as well as educational use continue to
fuel sales of microcomputers such as this Apple IIGS.

- *Hand-held portables.* Battery-powered computers, **hand-held portables**
  are tiny and light. They have limited memory, although BASIC is usually built in. Cassette tapes are used to store data. They look very much
  like hand calculators, with tiny keys not designed for typing, and have a
  one-line display (see Figure 1.10). Despite their small size, peripheral
  devices such as printers and modems are available.

- *Laptop portables.* Small enough to fit comfortably into a briefcase, **laptop
  portables** have a typewriter-sized keyboard and a monitor (see Figure
  1.11). They have larger internal memories than their hand-held brothers
  and more peripheral devices are available, including floppy disk drives.

- *Desktop portables.* The **desktop portable** is essentially a personal computer designed to fit into a small suitcase (see Figure 1.12). Just as a
  portable typewriter can perform the basic tasks of a desktop typewriter,
  full-sized portables can mimic standard desktop microcomputers in
  their capabilities. In some cases, the only difference between the desktop
  model and the portable is the smaller size of the portable's monitor and
  a slightly smaller keyboard.

**Figure 1.10**     Hand-Held Portable Computer by Radio Shack.

Portable computers are "go anywhere" machines, allowing people the flexibility of taking their computers wherever they go. Now, computing can be done in the office, on the road, or at home. Portables allow for on-site data collection and analysis. Portability can be a real advantage in our fast-paced world.

### Minicomputers

In the late 1960s, Digital Equipment Corp. (DEC) marketed a new line of computers that differed significantly from earlier machines. They were called **minicomputers** or just **minis** because they were smaller, less sophisticated, and much less expensive than existing standards (mainframes).

Today's minis range in price from $15,000 to $500,000 and are usually 32-bit machines. Early models were 16-bit machines. They serve a portion of the computer market, mostly businesses that do not require the speed or immense storage capacity of a mainframe but require more computer power than the small, single-user micro can provide. Minicomputers are **multiuser** machines, which are computers that serve two or more users. Minis serve between 2 and 40 peo-

**Figure** 1.11          Laptop Computer by Toshiba.

**Figure** 1.12          Compaq Desktop Portable.

ple at one time, each with his or her own monitor and keyboard. They can handle large, complex programs and can support many sophisticated computer languages. Significant amounts of external memory can be attached.

With advances in computer technology and a rapid decline in the price of hardware, the minicomputer industry is increasingly being squeezed by its mainframe and micro competitors. As microcomputer companies add features and memory to their machines, minicomputer companies are forced to do the same. The result produces minicomputers that look more and more like mainframes. A number of computer manufacturers, such as Digital Equipment Corp., Prime, and Hewlett-Packard, produce computers that are classed as **superminis**, (extra-powerful minicomputers) and are hardly distinguishable in their abilities from other manufacturers' mainframes (see Figure 1.13).

## Workstations

When applied to computers, the term *workstation* unfortunately has more than one meaning, two of which we will discuss here. First, the most popular use of

---

**Figure 1.13**    Minicomputers and Superminicomputers: Ideal for medium-sized firms and scientific and engineering applications, minis and superminis such as these from Digital Equipment Corp. offer flexibility rivaling more expensive mainframe computers.

the word and the way it is commonly used in businesses and offices defines a **workstation** as the physical layout of furniture and computer equipment designed to make using computers both comfortable and efficient.

Such a workstation includes a personal computer placed at a height that is appropriate for comfortable use, a printer, and desk space (often at a different height) for preparing documents. In addition, the computer that makes up the workstation is generally part of a group of interconnected yet independent com-

**Figure 1.14**      Networked Computer Workstations: Operator comfort and the ability to communicate with other users or a larger computer have made this concept popular.

puters called a *local area network (LAN)*, which will be discussed further in Chapter 14. The connected equipment is directly wired together (hard-wired) within a restricted location, usually a building or group of buildings located close to one another (see Figure 1.14).

In this environment, the personal computer is usually connected to a larger machine. Such an arrangement allows individuals to take advantage of a variety of machines. The specialized, user-friendly software available for personal computers is accessible, as is the superior storage and calculating capacity of larger computers. Of equal importance, individuals are not isolated. They are interconnected with one another and can communicate using **electronic mail**, or **E-mail**, in which computer users exchange electronic messages that are temporarily stored on the machine. Electronic mail will be discussed in greater detail in Chapter 14. The users also have access to files stored on the larger machines. From their own desks, individual users can tap into large data bases, transfer files to other users, and work with large programs or data sets not compatible with small machines.

Increasingly, a second type of computer workstation is gaining popularity. This **workstation** is a highly sophisticated desktop minicomputer including a large graphics monitor, a pointing device (such as a mouse), and software that enables its user to run several programs at the same time (see Figure 1.15). Such systems are used in environments where processing power is a critical consideration. As with the business workstation described previously, this system is usually networked to other computers so that data and information can be shared.

The large screen can be divided into a number of sections, or **windows**, each of which displays a different computer process. Some systems are so sophisticated that different windows can actually display operations occurring on different machines.

These systems range in price from $5000 to $65,000. As the price of such systems decreases, they are likely to replace the personal computers used in the workstation environment described earlier in this section.

## Mainframes

In general, **mainframes** are large, very fast 32- to 64-bit multiuser machines (see Figure 1.16). They are generally used in environments with large, centralized processing needs, such as large business organizations, and for research and development. They can service more than 40 users at the same time. For example, using automated teller machines, bank customers can make bank transactions simultaneously in dozens of locations.

Mainframes process at speeds greater than 10 million instructions per second and cost more than $500,000. They are designed to support complex input/output systems. The CPU is usually a **multiprocessor**, designed so that multiple tasks can be performed simultaneously. Mainframes are designed to support massive amounts of internal and external storage. The availability of specialized

**Figure 1.15**    The Workstation: More powerful than a microcomputer but requiring little more space, the Sun Microsystem workstation is becoming more popular.

hardware and software makes mainframes ideal for the solution of complex problems that involve vast amounts of mathematical manipulations, or **number crunching**.

Common applications include data processing by large department store chains, income tax processing by the Internal Revenue Service, information storage and retrieval by colleges and universities, and manufacturing control and forecasting.

Some mainframes, such as ENCORE's Multimax, are parallel machines. These machines contain multiple CPUs and associated memory that can process instructions simultaneously.

### Supercomputers

As the complexity of our problems grew, so computers have grown to assist in solving them. Today, computers are being developed that dwarf the standard mainframes in terms of speed. These ultra-fast computers, or **supercomputers**,

**Figure 1.16**   The Mainframe Computer: Ideal for the needs of a large firm or government agency, mainframe computers such as this IBM 3090/600E are capable of processing enormous amounts of data.

are designed to process hundreds of millions of instructions per second and store and retrieve millions of data items (see Figure 1.17).

Some supercomputers are parallel machines that process hundreds of instructions simultaneously. Others process instructions at incredible speeds. Supercomputers service hundreds of users and cost millions of dollars to operate. American and Japanese computer manufacturers are currently locked in a battle to dominate the supercomputer market.

In the United States a number of companies, such as Cray Research Inc. (Cray-2 and Cray X-MP2) and Control Data Corp. (CYBER-205), currently market supercomputers. At present, supercomputers have been purchased by governments, large research universities, corporate think tanks, and industries to solve complex problems involving massive mathematical calculations. Aircraft design, oil and mineral exploration, long-range weather forecasting, computer circuit design and research, and the development and implementation of ideas such as space and laser weapons ("Star-Wars") all require the computing power of supercomputers.

The demand for these powerful machines has grown dramatically in the last few years. Researchers nationwide increasingly require access to supercomputers

**Figure 1.17**    The Supercomputer: The complex calculations and numerous variables involved in weather forecasting, aircraft design, and space exploration require ultrafast machines such as this Cray Y-MP supercomputer.

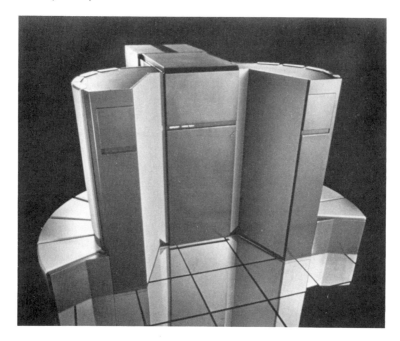

for their work. Unfortunately, these machines are not only incredibly expensive to purchase, they are also very expensive and difficult to manage and operate. In an effort to make such facilities available to all the nation's researchers, the National Science Foundation (NSF) is building a network of interconnected supercomputers called NSFnet, which will be discussed further in Chapter 14. The computers are located in centers across the country. By linking universities, government agencies, and research corporations in such a network, super-computer facilities can be available to all who need them and data and ideas can be shared as well.

We have seen that learning about computers requires an understanding of computer jargon. In addition, computers, like people, come in different shapes and sizes. The capacity of the computer to store and process information is re-flected in its use. Computers are used just about everywhere; from intensive care units to spacecraft, from the entertainment industry to the weather service. De-spite outward differences, they all require a processor, memory, and input/out-put devices to communicate with people. Furthermore, regardless of how com-plex the problem they are solving, they still follow the instructions given by people. If computers seem to have the capacity to change the world it is because they are the unique handiwork of humans.

## SUMMARY

Computers process data. Data are raw facts collected from any number of sources. When data have been changed so that meaningful conclusions can be drawn, the result is information.

All computers have four basic components: an input device, a processor, memory, and an output device. Input represents the starting data, the raw facts that are entered into the computer. The processor is the electronic circuitry that changes the initial data in some way to produce information. Memory is the special electronic circuitry that stores data, instructions, and the results of processing. Output is the result of processing presented to people.

A program is the step-by-step set of instructions, written in a computer language, that directs the computer to perform specific tasks and solve specific problems. Programs used for problem solving or directing the operations of the machine are called software. The physical components that combine to make up the computer are hardware.

All data and instructions used by a computer must be converted to the electronic states of on and off. These two states can be represented by the 1's and 0's of the base 2, or binary number system. Combinations of these two digits represent all numbers, letters, and special characters. Each 1 or 0 is called a bit and forms the simplest unit of data stored in the computer's memory. A byte is a group of bits representing a character of data. A word is the number of bits that can be processed at once. Computers are frequently described in terms of the amount of memory that is associated with their processors. Computer memory is represented in terms of K (approximately 1000) bytes.

There are two basic categories of computers. Digital computers use mathematical values obtained by counting for input. Analog computers use continuous direct measurement of such things as voltage and temperature as input. Hybrid computers combine the input/output design of analog computers with the ability to store instructions and perform highly accurate calculations found in digital machines. Special-purpose computers are designed to solve specific problems, while general-purpose machines are used to solve a variety of problems.

Digital computers come in a wide variety of sizes, costs, and computing capacity. Microcomputers are single-user machines based on the microprocessor. Microcomputers come in 8-, 16-, and 32-bit varieties. They range in price from $500 to $15,000. Microcomputers designed for use in the home are often called home computers, while those frequently found in businesses and offices are called personal computers. Portable computers are complete microcomputers that can be easily carried from place to place.

Minicomputers are multiuser systems designed to serve those organizations that do not require the speed or immense storage capacity of a mainframe but cannot be served by the small, single-user micro. Such computers are usually 32-bit machines and range in price from $15,000 to $50,000.

When used in most business environments, the term *workstation* refers to the physical layout of furniture and computer equipment designed to make using computers comfortable and efficient. However, a workstation also can refer to a highly sophisticated desktop minicomputer. Such a machine includes a large graphic monitor, pointing device, and software that enables it to run several programs at once and display each simultaneously in different windows on the monitor. These workstations range in price from $5000 to $65,000.

Mainframes are large, very fast, 32- to 64-bit multiuser computers costing more than $500,000. They are designed to support complex input/output systems and process millions of instructions per second. The largest of these machines, called supercomputers, are designed to process hundreds of millions of instructions per second and store and retrieve millions of data items.

## Key Words

As an extra review of the chapter, try defining the following terms. If you have trouble with any of them, refer to the page number listed.

analog computer  *(9)*
binary number system  *(7)*
bit  *(8)*
byte  *(8)*
central processing unit (CPU)  *(5)*
data  *(3)*
desktop portable  *(18)*
digital computer  *(9)*
electronic mail (E-mail)  *(23)*
general-purpose computer  *(11)*
hand-held portable  *(18)*
hardware  *(7)*
home computer  *(17)*
hybrid computer  *(9)*
information  *(4)*
input  *(5)*
laptop portable  *(18)*
mainframe  *(23)*

memory (storage)  *(5)*
microcomputer (micros)  *(14)*
microprocessor  *(14)*
minicomputer (minis)  *(19)*
multiprocessor  *(23)*
multiuser  *(19)*
number crunching  *(24)*
output  *(5)*
personal computer (PC)  *(17)*
portable computer  *(17)*
preprogrammed  *(11)*
program  *(7)*
software  *(7)*
special-purpose computer  *(11)*
supercomputer  *(24)*
supermini  *(21)*
window  *(23)*
workstation  *(22, 23)*

## Test Your Knowledge

1. Explain the difference between data and information.

2. List the four components that make up all computers. Explain the function of each component.

3. What is a program?

4. What is the difference between hardware and software?

5. Why must all data and instructions be converted to binary before they can be understood by the computer?

6. How do bits, bytes, and words differ?

7. What is a megabyte?

8. Describe the differences between the input used in analog and digital computers.

9. What is a hybrid computer?

10. Define *preprogrammed* and explain how such programming is applied to a special-purpose computer.

11. Describe a microcomputer.

12. How does a home computer differ from a personal computer?

13. Identify the three kinds of portable computers. How are they different?

14. Describe a minicomputer.

15. How is a supermini similar to and different from other minicomputers?

16. A workstation can mean two different things. Describe the office workstation. Describe the desktop workstation.

17. Describe a mainframe.

18. How do mainframes and supercomputers differ?

19. Explain number crunching.

20. What is NSFnet?

## Expand Your Knowledge

1. Go to your campus computing center and find out what kinds of computers (micros, mainframes, etc.) are available for student use on your campus. Make a list of these machines and their locations. How does a student get access to these machines? Who are they manufactured by?

2. Find out if your college has a discount purchase arrangement with microcomputer manufacturers. If so, what machines are available at a discount? How do students take advantage of these discounts? How much is the discount? If students have problems with machines purchased under this discount program, whom do they contact?

3. Using the pattern of binary and decimal digits displayed in this chapter, write out the binary equivalent of the decimal numbers 9 through 16.

4. When designing an office workstation, ergonomics is the key. What does ergonomics mean? Talk with friends and family members who work in an office. What factors do they consider important in a workstation? Look into a few offices on campus that have computers. Have the factors you identified been considered? If not, find out why.

5. A number of microcomputer manufacturers including IBM and Apple have developed machines they consider workstations. Go to a computer store and find out how such systems differ from standard micros. Who is expected to purchase these machines? What kind of specialized software is available on these systems?

# 2

# The History of Computers

**Chapter Outline**

The Development of Computing Machines

The Pre-Computer Age
   The Abacus • Oughtred's Slide Rule • Pascal's Calculator •
   Leibniz's Multiplier

Programming and Expanding the Machine
   Jacquard's Loom • Charles Babbage • Hollerith's Census Machine •
   Burroughs' Adding and Listing Machine

The Computer Age
   Atanasoff's ABC • Germany's Wartime Computer •
   England's Wartime Computer • America's Wartime Computer Research
   (Harvard Mark I; ENIAC) • Von Neumann's Logical Computer
   (EDSAC; EDVAC; UNIVAC I; IBM 650)

A Computer Geneology
   First-Generation Computers (1951–1958) • Second-Generation
   Computers (1959–1964) • Third-Generation Computers (1965–early
   1970s) • Fourth-Generation Computers (early 1970s–present)

The Rise of the Microcomputer
   Computers from a Kit • The Birth of the Personal Computer • Toward
   a User-Friendly Machine

Beyond the Fourth Generation

## THE DEVELOPMENT OF COMPUTING MACHINES

No invention springs forth from the human mind fully formed. Technological advances are the result of an evolving process. Existing products are continually being improved. The computer is an example of one such product. Since our prehistoric ancestors first stood upright, people have needed counting tools. The computer is an incredibly fast counting device with a long history.

Since the computer is a machine, it would be easy to focus on the technological changes alone that eventually produced it. However, machines are the physical results of the ideas, needs, and fascinations of people. This chapter looks at the people and ideas, as well as the machines, that in combination led to the development of the modern computer.

After studying this chapter, you will be able to:

- Trace the development of early calculating devices.

- Recognize the individuals who invented computing devices.

- Understand the theoretical contributions of Babbage and von Neumann.

- Explain the evolution of computers and the high-tech industry.

- Identify and analyze the characteristics of the computer generations.

- Trace the development of microcomputers.

## THE PRE-COMPUTER AGE

Our earliest ancestors used their fingers and toes as counting aids. It was not long before these built-in human tools gave way to more expandable devices. Groups of tiny stones or knots tied in strings became early counting devices. Counting evolved into mathematics. The ancient Egyptians and Aztecs used complex calculations to design and build their pyramids. The Phoenicians employed mathematics to keep track of their vast commercial activities and to navigate the seas.

### The Abacus

As the world became more complex, the use of mathematics increased. Calculations needed to be performed accurately and quickly. The earliest calculating device, the **abacus**, has seen approximately 7000 years of continuous use. While its invention is credited to the Chinese (the ancient Orient) around 5000 B.C., different forms of this device were also used in ancient Babylon, Rome, and Japan.

Calculations on the abacus are performed by manipulating strings of beads. With the abacus, still commonly used in China, adept users can perform calculations with remarkable speed. The abacus is a fast, inexpensive, highly portable non-electronic calculator (see Figure 2.1).

## Oughtred's Slide Rule

Many centuries passed, and in 1621 an English cleric and mathematician named William Oughtred invented the **slide rule**. A slide rule consists of two movable rulers fixed so that one will slide against the other (see Figure 2.2). Both rules are marked so that the distances of the marking from the ends are mathematically proportional. Oughtred's device was very popular, since it was accurate, easy to use, and inexpensive to make. It continued to be widely used until the 1970s when, unlike the abacus, it was replaced almost overnight by the hand calculator.

## Pascal's Calculator

In 1642, a Frenchman named Blaise Pascal, then 19 years old, invented what is often considered the first adding machine (see Figure 2.3). Pascal would later

**Figure 2.1**    The Abacus: A fast, inexpensive, and ancient calculating device.

**Figure 2.2**    The Slide Rule: Sales of this popular calculating device ended almost overnight with the advent of inexpensive hand-held electronic calculators.

# On Line

## THE SLIDE RULE'S DOWNWARD SLIDE

Until the 1970s, it was easy to spot engineering students on college campuses. The engineers were ones with a 12-to-18 inch scabbard hanging from their belts. At a moment's notice, they would pull their slide rule from its case with a swoosh and begin solving mathematical problems.

Before 1972, the slide rule was a mainstay in science and engineering classrooms. Carefully crafted models made of mahogany were available for around $100. Then the death knell sounded. In 1972, Hewlett-Packard released the HP35 hand-held calculator. Even at the asking price of $395, the HP35 was so easy to use that demand outpaced availability. Within a month Texas Instruments released the SR-10, which sold for less than $150 and could perform most of the slide rule's mathematical functions.

By 1976 most slide rule companies had ended production. Only one company continues to produce a small number of slide rules annually, priced between $10 and $25 each. A year later the hand-held calculator had completely replaced the slide rule. Technology had killed the slide rule almost overnight.

Some scientists and engineers continue to use their slide rules because for them it's second nature. They can't imagine using anything else. Some feel that students who use calculators are taking the easy way out and performing calculations without understanding the underlying mathematical principles. Some of these concerns are valid. Calculators are so easy to use that they can provide a false sense of security. Students need to scrutinize their work. An answer displayed by a calculator is not guaranteed to be correct.

Keep in mind that both the slide rule and the calculator are operated by people. They are only as accurate as the people using them.

*Source:* David Gates and Frank Bruns, "Sliding Towards Oblivion," *Newsweek,* July 23, 1984 p. 11A.

became a noted mathematician and a computer language would bear his name. One historical legend tells us that Pascal invented the device to assist his father, a tax collector, with the time-consuming task of adding and subtracting long columns of numbers. The device consisted of a series of gears or wheels moved with a pointed object. The basic functions of modern adding machines were found in Pascal's model. His invention, known as the Pascaline, had the following features:

- The *carry* (in addition) and the *borrow* (in subtraction) were performed automatically.

- Subtraction was performed by reversing the gears.

- Multiplication and division were performed as a series of repeated additions or subtractions.

**Figure 2.3**          Blaise Pascal and his calculator, the Pascaline.

Unfortunately, building Pascal's machines required a higher level of technical expertise than was generally available in his day. The calculators broke easily due to poorly cut gears. As a result, only eight of the approximately 50 calculators Pascal had built survived.

### Leibniz's Multiplier

In 1673, the German Baron Gottfried Wilhelm von Leibniz expanded upon Pascal's calculator and produced a machine that could multiply and divide. Leibniz's multiplier contained features found in modern calculators. Notably, all the digits of a number could be entered at once. As with Pascal's device, the limits of technical engineering continued to influence computer history. Leibniz's invention also broke easily due to poorly tooled parts (see Figure 2.4).

## PROGRAMMING AND EXPANDING THE MACHINE

The signposts of computer history mark ideas as well as physical inventions. The Industrial Revolution of the 1800s saw an incredible chain of evolving ideas and devices. Inventors often get their ideas from unlikely places, and out of the weaving loom came ideas critical to the development of modern computers.

**Figure 2.4**        Gottfried Wilhelm von Leibniz and his calculator.

### Jacquard's Loom

In 1804, a Frenchman named Joseph Jacquard invented an attachment to the mechanical loom for weaving cloth. Jacquard recognized that the design found in woven cloth followed a fixed, repetitive pattern (a program). By punching holes at specific intervals in cards attached to the loom, he was able to control the threads reproducing the desired pattern. Jacquard's improved loom automated the weaving industry, revolutionizing the way cloth was produced (see Figure 2.5).

### Charles Babbage

If punched cards could be used to store information and instructions for one device, it was only a matter of time before they were put to similar use in other devices.

Charles Babbage, a wealthy, eccentric British mathematician and inventor, is often considered the father of modern computers. Disturbed by the inaccuracies he found in the hand-calculated mathematical tables that scientists of his day used, he designed a machine to accurately and automatically calculate these tables.

**Figure 2.5**        Joseph Jacquard and his loom.

In 1822, he presented a paper to the Royal Astronomical Society proposing to build such a machine. The Difference Engine, as this device was called, was named after the method Babbage used to perform the calculations (Figure 2.6a). The British government was convinced that the accurate calculations produced by this machine would be a great help in navigation and ballistics. Armed with a government grant that was one of the first research grants, Babbage hired the finest tool makers to build his machine.

**Figure 2.6**          (a) Babbage's Difference Engine: a special-purpose calculating machine and (b) Babbage's Analytical Engine: a more sophisticated, general-purpose computing device.

(a)

(b)

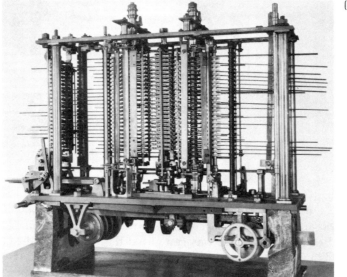

Although a scale model was built, difficulties between Babbage and the craftsmen over precision and design prevented the Difference Engine from being completed. As with Pascal and Leibniz before him, Babbage found the engineering techniques of the day inadequate. To complicate matters further, Babbage lost interest in the project when he became intrigued with more complex ideas. Babbage was not discouraged by his failure to complete the Difference Engine. The British government, however, held a different view and refused to fund his next project.

In 1833, Babbage designed a steam-powered device he called the Analytical Engine (Figure 2.6b). While the Difference Engine was a special-purpose machine that could perform specific calculations, his Analytical Engine was a far more sophisticated, general-purpose computing device. It included five of the key components that form the basis of modern computers:

1. *An input device* using punched cards that contained instructions and data.

2. *A processor* or calculator, called a *mill,* where all calculations were performed.

3. *A memory unit,* called a *store,* where data and intermediate calculations could be stored.

4. *A control unit* that controlled the sequence in which operations were performed.

5. *An output device.*

Babbage's input device incorporated the idea of punched cards invented by Jacquard for his loom. Babbage had the active support of Lady Ada Augusta, the Countess of Lovelace and daughter of poet Lord Byron (see Figure 2.7). Not only was she a gifted mathematician who saw the machine's potential, she was also Babbage's friend, providing the support he needed to continue his work. She contributed by developing the problem-solving instructions the engine would follow when doing calculations. Since she developed sample programs for the Analytical Engine, she is often referred to as history's first programmer. The programming language Ada is named after her. Ada Lovelace published notes discussing her work on the Analytical Engine. In them she remarked, "We may say most aptly that the Analytical Engine weaves algebraic patterns just as the Jacquard-loom weaves flowers and leaves."

While Babbage never lived to see the Analytical Engine built, it was a prototype for current computers. Using modern engineering techniques and Babbage's plans, his son built a successful electrical version of the Analytical Engine.

The Industrial Revolution radically altered the way people lived and worked in the world. People moved from farms and villages to the cities. Mechanization and industrialization changed the farms and created factories. The steam engine made long-distance transportation possible. Populations grew and businesses and governments found they needed to process information more rapidly. Hand

**Figure 2.7**          Lady Ada Augusta, the Countess of Lovelace, the first programmer and Babbage's co-worker.

calculations could simply not keep pace. Information processing needed to be mechanized.

## Hollerith's Census Machine

The U.S. Constitution requires that a census be taken every 10 years. The 1880 census, complicated by a rapid increase in the population due to immigration, took almost eight years to complete. The Census Bureau recognized that dramatic changes were needed if the 1890 census was to be completed before 1900.

Tabulations could not be performed by hand. To stimulate the invention of a machine to tabulate census data, the Census Bureau ran a contest seeking devices. The winner would be awarded the contract to tabulate the 1890 census. The contest's winner was Dr. Herman Hollerith, a Census Bureau employee, who developed a machine that automated the tabulating process. Hollerith's 1887 Census Machine combined electricity with Jacquard's method of storing information on punched cards (see Figure 2.8). Holes representing census information were punched in stiff paper cards and rods were passed through the holes. This completed electric circuits, causing clock-like devices (electro-magnetic counters) to advance and tabulate the information on the card.

The punched cards used by Hollerith measured 3 1/4-by-6 5/8 inches. This odd size is exactly that of the 1890 U.S. one dollar bill. Some historians believe that Hollerith chose this size because people were familiar with it. Current computer cards are approximately the size of Hollerith's original. Using Hollerith's machine, the data from the 1890 census was completely tabulated in less than three years.

Recognizing the immense commercial potential of his machine, Hollerith left the Census Bureau to found the Tabulating Machine Company. The company tabulated the 1900 census as well, but its largest client was the fast-expanding railroad industry. Hollerith's machine was used to keep track of the passengers and goods moved by the railroad. In 1911, the Tabulating Machine Company merged with a number of other companies to become the Computing, Tabulating, and Recording Company (CTR). In 1924, five years before Hollerith's death, CTR changed its name to International Business Machines, or IBM. The company at that time was under the leadership of Thomas Watson.

In preparation for the 1910 census, John Powers, an engineer and inventor who was employed by the Census Bureau, developed an automatic card-punching machine along with a variation of Hollerith's tabulating machine. Powers' machines further reduced the time required to tabulate census data. Like Hollerith before him, Powers recognized the value of his equipment and left the Census Bureau to start his own company. This company was awarded the contract to tabulate the 1910 census. Powers' company was later purchased by Remington Rand Corporation, which eventually became UNISYS. As one might expect, Hollerith and Powers were not alone in recognizing the demand for calculating devices.

## Burroughs' Adding and Listing Machine

In the latter half of the 1800s, the U.S. Patent Office did a booming business in desktop calculating devices. The most famous of these was patented in 1888 by William Burroughs. Burroughs invented the first adding and listing machine. His machine differed from others of his day by the addition of a device that printed out the numbers entered into the machine and the calculated results.

**Figure 2.8**    (a) Hollerith's Tabulating Machine combined Jacquard's method of storing information on (b) punched cards with electricity.

**Figure 2.9**     The Burroughs Adding and Listing Machine and William Seward Burroughs.

The calculator had a full numeric keyboard and was operated by a hand crank (see Figure 2.9). Burroughs founded the corporation that bears his name.

## THE COMPUTER AGE

The increasing complexity of the devices and systems just discussed improved the efficiency of processing information in the sciences and business. The next major wave of development in computing devices was spurred and funded by the World War II efforts of Britian, Germany, and the United States. However, research was headed toward the development of such machines even without the war.

During the late 1930s, scientists and engineers in all three countries began building digital computers. Computer technology was heavily influenced by the communications industry. As scientists tinkered with components while building their machines, they debated the comparative values of different types of hardware. The debate centered around the machines' internal components. Should the reliable electromagnetic relays found in telephone systems be used or the newer electronic relays called vacuum tubes? Vacuum tubes operated hundreds of times faster than electromagnetic telephone relays, but they were not as reliable. Vacuum tubes were also more expensive and required huge amounts of electricity to operate.

### Atanasoff's ABC

In the late 1930s, John V. Atanasoff and some of his graduate students at Iowa State University began working on a computing machine. Atanasoff designed a memory drum and arithmetic unit. In 1942, with the help of a student named Clifford Berry, a prototype of this special-purpose machine was built. It was called ABC (Atanasoff-Berry Computer). The ABC used vacuum tubes for internal components and punched cards for input. While a full-scale version of the computer was never assembled, the discoveries made by Atanasoff were incorporated into later machines (see Figure 2.10).

As the war intensified, scientific interaction decreased due to wartime security. Scientific teams made similar discoveries independently as a result.

### Germany's Wartime Computer

As Atanasoff was developing the ABC, a German named Konrad Zuse started building computer components in his parents' kitchen. Since the cost of elec-

---

**Figure 2.10**     John V. Atanasoff and The Atanasoff-Berry Computer.

tronic relays (vacuum tubes) was prohibitive, Zuse designed his machine around electomagnetic relays used in telephone systems.

In the early 1940s, Zuse sought support from Hitler's government based on the promise his device held for the war effort. Zuse's request was initially refused since the German government believed that the war was essentially over. In late 1943, however, the German government reconsidered and began to support Zuse's project. As German scientists worked on the development of missiles, Zuse's project was seen as leading to a quick, reliable, accurate means of calculating the paths of these missiles. While prototypes were built, most of the plans and hardware were destroyed in the Allied bombings. Some consider the 1941 prototype to be the first computer.

### England's Wartime Computer

In the early 1940s, weak and isolated England stood against the powerful German war machine. What the British lacked in military power, however, they made up for in sheer willpower and military research. For example, radar was invented to provide an early-warning system for the Royal Air Force. To assist the British military in analyzing information gathered about the German war effort, COLOSSUS was developed with the help of mathematician Alan Turing (see Figure 2.11). In December, 1943, under total secrecy, COLOSSUS became the first practical, single-purpose electronic computer.

It was a room-sized machine, designed exclusively to break German codes. While much of the research into COLOSSUS is still clouded in the secrecy of Britain's Official Secrets Act, it is known that more than 1800 vacuum tubes were used and paper tape acted as input. Ten machines were built and were invaluable to the Allied war effort. While historians agree that COLOSSUS was one of the first digital machines, it was designed to solve a specific problem. It could not solve other problems without major alterations to its design.

### America's Wartime Computer Research

Unlike England, the United States did not have the German army sitting on its front steps. As a result, America's wartime computer effort moved at a slower pace and was more diverse.

**Harvard Mark I**    Prior to the war, Harvard professor Howard H. Aiken developed the plans for a general-purpose computer (see Figure 2.12). Aiken realized that such a machine would require very strong financial backing. The story is told that Aiken approached Thomas J. Watson, the ruler of IBM, who made a snap decision to back Aiken's research and invest $1 million. When the United States' war effort began, the Aiken-IBM computer became a secret U.S. Navy project.

**Figure 2.11** Alan Turing, a developer of COLOSSUS.

**Figure 2.12** The Harvard Mark I computer.

In late 1943, the Harvard Mark I developed by Aiken came into being. Although Aiken did not know of Babbage's work, the Mark I contained many of the features Babbage had included in his Analytical Engine. Aiken's machine used electromagnetic telephone relays, choosing reliability over speed. The Harvard Mark I received instructions via punched paper tape and could perform addition or subtraction in 0.3 second. The Harvard Mark I did not have a memory, however. It was extremely noisy and slow compared to other machines of the period such as COLOSSUS and was not particularly reliable despite its use of telephone relays. These relays made it so noisy that people remarked that it was "like listening to a roomful of old ladies knitting away with steel needles." After the war, IBM mounted a publicity campaign with the Harvard Mark I, which made IBM a powerful name in the growing computer industry.

**ENIAC**    During the war, John W. Mauchly and J. Presper Eckert Jr. at the University of Pennsylvania's Moore School of Electrical Engineering, in association with the U.S. government's Aberdeen Proving Ground, began development of a general-purpose electronic computer. In 1946, ENIAC (Electronic Numerical Integrator and Calculator) was unveiled (see Figure 2.13).

**Figure 2.13**    J. Presper Eckert, Jr. (left) and John W. Mauchley (center) with their ENIAC computer.

While based in part on the earlier ABC machine, ENIAC was larger in scale and complexity than anything Atanasoff imagined. More than 18,000 vacuum tubes were used as internal components in this room-sized computer. ENIAC had independent circuits for storing numbers and program instructions. Several mathematical operations could be performed at once. By modern standards it had a very limited storage capacity of only 20 10-digit numbers. However, when compared with the Harvard Mark I, limited memory is significantly better than no memory. ENIAC did not store instructions as modern computers can. Instead, each new program required rewiring of its program circuits. It could multiply two numbers in 0.003 second.

The major drawback of the ENIAC was its insatiable appetite for electrical power to activate its 18,000 vacuum tubes. Some people claimed that whenever ENIAC was turned on, all the lights in Philadelphia dimmed. These tubes also generated tremendous heat, which caused them to burn out rapidly. In addition, ENIAC was difficult and time-consuming to program, since each new program required a complete rewiring of the program circuitry.

## Von Neumann's Logical Computer

Research continued at the Moore School and around the world. In 1944, John von Neumann added his talents to the ENIAC team. Even before ENIAC was completed, scientists recognized its limitations and set out to design a machine that was easier to program, more powerful, and compact at the same time (see Figure 2.14).

Von Neumann was a mathematician, not an engineer like Mauchly and Eckert. As such, he dealt with ideas and not the reality or limitations of technology. As a result, he was able to develop the logical framework around which computers have been built.

Von Neumann developed the concept of storing a program in the computer's memory, called the *stored program concept*. Before this, all computers, including Babbage's Analytical Engine, stored only the numbers with which they worked. The program to process these numbers was part of the circuitry. Each new program required that the computer be rewired.

Von Neumann's theory converted each program instruction into a numeric code. These codes, which were binary digits, could be stored directly in the computer's memory as if they were data. Von Neumann also reorganized the hardware of the computer. Rather than being a single, powerful unit, von Neumann's computer was broken into components. Each of these components performed a specific task and could be called upon repeatedly to perform its function.

The six components of von Neumann's theoretical computer bear a remarkable resemblance to the basic components found in Babbage's Analytical Engine. The components were:

1. *An arithmetic unit* for basic computation.

**Figure 2.14**    John von Neumann, a mathematician, developed the logical framework of computers.

2. *A logic unit* where decisions and comparisons could be performed.

3. *An input device* designed to accept coded instructions and numeric data.

4. *A memory unit* for storing instructions and data.

5. *A control unit* for interpreting the coded instructions and controlling the flow of data.

6. *An output unit* to communicate the results.

Von Neumann's theories, presented in lectures and papers, were well received. A number of stored-program computers were built around his design.

**EDSAC**    After attending von Neumann's lectures at the Moore School, Maurice Wilkes and his associates completed EDSAC (Electronic Delay Storage Automatic Calculator) at Cambridge University in England in 1949. This was the first computer to incorporate the stored-program idea. EDSAC used letters as input and converted them to binary digits. In addition, the EDSAC group created a library of small programs that could be used by the machine when problem solving.

**EDVAC**    While the British were working on EDSAC, von Neumann and Moore School engineers were developing EDVAC (Electronic Delay Variable Automatic Computer). It was a stored-program machine that used a unique code of zeros and ones developed for it by von Neumann. EDVAC's hardware directly reflected the distinct components he described.

The money-making potential of these early computers was not lost on their inventors. Computers quickly moved out of the laboratories and into big business.

Eckert and Mauchly left the Moore School for private enterprise, taking many of the ideas behind ENIAC and EDVAC with them. They founded Eckert-Mauchly Computing Corporation (EMCC). Low on capital, EMCC struggled for a number of years in an attempt to build and market the Universal Automatic Computer or UNIVAC, a commercial version of ENIAC. In 1950, just as John Power's company before it, EMCC was purchased by Remington Rand. A sound financial base for the development of the UNIVAC I was assured.

**Figure 2.15**    UNIVAC I: CBS News used the UNIVAC I to predict the election of Dwight Eisenhower in 1952. Newsman Walter Cronkite (right) and other CBS staff members are shown with the computer.

**UNIVAC I**    In 1951, the first UNIVAC I was delivered to the U.S. Census Bureau to assist in compiling the 1950 census data. UNIVAC I, containing only 5000 vacuum tubes, was relatively compact when compared with ENIAC. It was a stored-program machine and revolutionary in its use of a magnetizable tape, similar to audio tape, for input and output. It could read 7200 digits per second. The UNIVAC I was the first computer designed and marketed for business computing rather than military or research use. In 1952, CBS News used a UNIVAC I to predict the election of Dwight Eisenhower over Adlai Stevenson and ushered the computer age into America's living rooms (see Figure 2.15).

**IBM 650**    During this time, IBM was not sitting idly by. Thomas Watson, Jr. recognized the potential business demand for computers and convinced his father to put money into computer research (see Figure 2.16). IBM set out to build a relatively inexpensive business computer.

**Figure 2.16**    Thomas J. Watson, Jr.

**Figure 2.17**     The IBM 650: Designed for the business community, the IBM 650 started the company on its road to success.

In late 1954, IBM began selling a computer designed specifically for the business community. Like the UNIVAC I, it was a stored-program, vacuum tube machine. IBM executives expected to produce 50 of these IBM 650's (see Figure 2.17). Much to their surprise, they sold more than 1000. IBM's experience in selling typewriters helped sell computers. The company emphasized customer service along with research and development when selling its machines. As a result, IBM became the undisputed leader in the computer industry, a position it continues to hold even today.

## A COMPUTER GENEALOGY

Research into newer, faster, smaller computers did not stop with UNIVAC I or the IBM 650. Computer components have decreased in size since the 1950s, while remaining basically faithful to John von Neumann's ideas.

Computer generations, like human generations, are marked by the "birth" of new family members. Each new computer generation has distinguished itself from its predecessor by a further miniaturization of the machine's internal components.

### First-Generation Computers (1951–1958)

First-generation computers were epitomized by the UNIVAC I and the IBM 650. Remington Rand (UNIVAC) and IBM were by no means the only computer companies of the period, however. Honeywell, Burroughs, General Electric, and others also built first-generation machines.

What is a first-generation computer? First-generation computers have several characteristics: They used vacuum tube technology. Input and output of data and instructions were done using punched cards, although some machines, such as the UNIVAC I, used magnetic tape. While these machines were programmable; that is, stored-program machines, their use of numeric codes called machine language (see Chapter 8) made programming them very time-consuming. Computer memory consisted of magnetic core (see Chapter 3), which continued to be popular for 20 years.

As with anything truly new, first-generation machines were beset by problems, which were solved by the advancing technology of the next generations. These first computers were room-sized monsters with huge price tags. Their thousands of vacuum tubes generated tremendous heat, frequently resulting in blown tubes. Since tube burnout made the machines unreliable, keeping these monsters cool became a major engineering effort. First-generation machines also were energy hungry, since massive amounts of electricity were required to power the thousands of vacuum tubes. The focus of the research efforts that created the next generation of machines was on finding a device that would make vacuum tubes obsolete.

### Second-Generation Computers (1959–1964)

In 1948, John Bardeen, Walter Brattain, and William Shockley, working at Bell Labs, invented the transistor (see Figure 2.18). In 1956, they were awarded the Nobel Prize in Physics for their efforts. Transistors were being produced in volume at relatively low cost by 1959.

A **transistor** is a tiny electronic switch. It relays electronic messages, yet it is built as a solid unit with no moving parts **(solid state)**. The first transistors were approximately 1/100th the size of a vacuum tube.

The second computer generation saw the replacement of vacuum tubes by transistors. These new machines were at once smaller, faster, and more reliable than first-generation machines (see Figure 2.19). Second-generation computers used solid-state technology, which required no warmup time and eliminated troublesome tube burnout. They were also more rugged and energy efficient. In these newer and more powerful computers, machine language was replaced by the easier-to-program *assembly language*. Instructions were coded as letters, such as *A* for ADD or *L* for LOAD. Further developments resulted in English-like languages, such as FORTRAN (FORmula TRANslation) and COBOL (COmmon Business-Oriented Language). Programming languages are explained more fully in Chapter 8.

**Figure 2.18**     (a) John Bardeen, William Shockley, and Walter Brattain (left to right) invented the transistor in 1948.
(b) The first transistors (left) were about 1/100th the size of a vacuum tube.

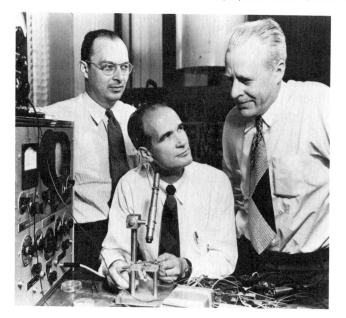

**Figure 2.19**     Second-generation computers such as this IBM 1401 used transistors instead of vacuum tubes.

Miniaturization continued. In the early 1960s, when IBM announced its revolutionary computer family—the IBM System/360—the third generation of computers was born. The generations of computer development are depicted in Figure 2.20.

### Third-Generation Computers (1965–early 1970s)

In the IBM System/360, transistors had been reduced in size so that hundreds of them could be embedded in small pieces, or chips, of silicon (see Figure 2.21). By etching these tiny silicon chips with the appropriate electronic circuitry, a new, miniaturized solid-state technology of **integrated circuits (IC)** was formed.

---

**Figure 2.20**      Generations of Computers.

*First-Generation Computers* (1951–1958)
- vacuum tube technology
- punched card or magnetic tape
- machine language
- magnetic core
- examples: UNIVAC I, IBM 650

*Second-Generation Computers* (1959–1964)
- transistor
- solid-state technology
- punched card or magnetic tape
- assembly language and some high-level languages
- magnetic core
- examples: IBM 1401, GE 235

*Third-Generation Computers* (1965–early 1970s)
- integrated circuit (IC) technology
- silicon chips
- large-scale integration (LSI)
- punched cards, magnetic tape, magnetic disks
- magnetic core, some semiconductor memory
- examples: IBM System/360, DEC PDP 8

*Fourth-Generation Computers* (early 1970s–present)
- very large-scale integration (VLSI)
- microprocessor chip
- magnetic disks, floppy disks, etc.
- high-level languages
- user-friendly software
- semiconductor memory
- examples: IBM SYSTEM/370, DEC VAX 11/785, Apple Macintosh

**Figure 2.21**  (a) Much smaller than vacuum tubes, (b) silicon chips in this IBM/360 could hold hundreds of electronic circuits.

(a)

(b)

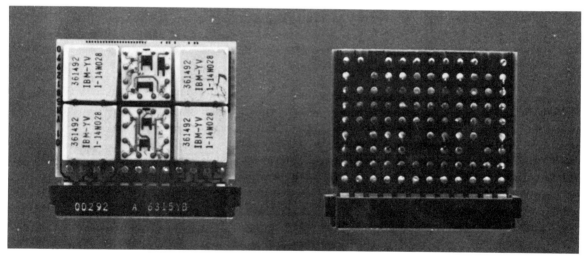

While integrated circuit technology was invented at Bell Labs as early as 1955, little use was made of it until IBM took the plunge and designed an entire machine around it.

Third-generation computers were smaller and even more reliable than their second-generation parents. With the significant reduction in size and raw materials came a significant reduction in power usage and an astronomical reduction in cost. Now, small and middle-sized companies and organizations could afford computers. Digital Equipment Corp. designed a line of minicomputers to suit the needs of these smaller organizations.

Throughout the third generation, the number of circuits squeezed onto chips grew from approximately 1000 per chip in 1965 to more than 15,000 by the early 1970s. This circuit squeezing is called **large-scale integration (LSI)**. Large-scale integration not only reduced machine size, but improved the computer's speed (the time involved in solving problems) by reducing the distance current had to travel. The result was that computers were more powerful and less expensive (see Figure 2.22).

The computer industry was evolving in other ways during the third generation. IBM lead the way. In addition to building cheaper, faster computers, IBM developed new and improved storage and input/output devices (peripheral devices) designed specifically for the business market. The IBM System/360 advertised 40 add-on devices. It came in a variety of models, each designed to serve

**Figure 2.22**    Smaller and more reliable, third-generation computers such as this Digital Equipment Corp. 8800 were also less costly.

different segments of the business community. Other manufacturers followed suit. A wide range of programming languages and prewritten software packages made third-generation machines more usable than earlier machines. Computers began to revolutionize business and industry.

### Fourth-Generation Computers
### (early 1970s–present)

In the fourth generation, as more and more circuits continued to be packed onto chips, technology moved from large-scale integration to **very large-scale integra-**

---

**Figure 2.23**    Hundreds of thousands of transistors and circuits are now packed onto silicon chips such as this Motorola MC88200.

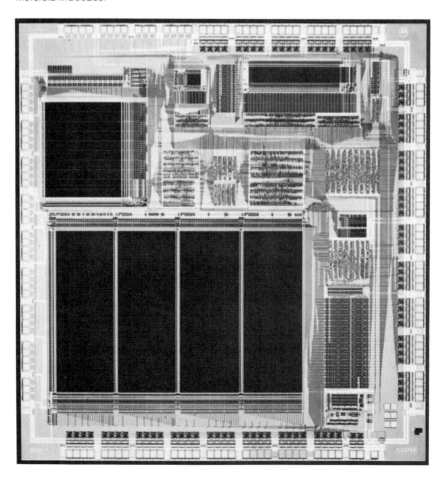

tion (VLSI). With this, hundreds of thousands of transistors and circuits are now being packed onto silicon chips (see Figure 2.23). Along with this incredible reduction in size came a computer with an entirely new design.

In the early 1970s an Intel Corp. engineer named Ted Hoff conceived of the microprocessor, or computer on a chip. As we stated in Chapter 1, a microprocessor chip is a central processing unit (CPU) condensed onto a single chip. Computers could now fit anywhere, since the entire CPU was no larger than a fingernail. With this microprocessor chip, the desktop microcomputer was born.

In addition to developing a highly compact CPU, peripheral devices were designed to make computers easier to use. Improved devices included compact storage devices (floppy disks), color graphic screens, and a wide variety of pointing devices (mouse). In addition to the development of small desktop computers, the fourth generation also saw the development of supercomputers. Using VLSI design, supercomputers have vast storage and processing capacity. Such machines are used to perform complex mathematical tasks. Compact chip technology also brought about the development of parallel computers. These computers use multiple processors working simultaneously to solve problems.

Hardware advances were followed closely by a software explosion. Prewritten software is now available for all sizes of machines. Packages for micros make up the largest segment of this multi-billion dollar industry (see Figure 2.24).

**Figure 2.24**    Microcomputer software makes up the largest segment of the software industry.

## THE RISE OF THE MICROCOMPUTER

In barely 50 years, the computer revolution has changed the way we live. The microcomputer, often considered the leading edge of this revolution, is much younger, however. Its birth is marked from the invention of the microprocessor. The microcomputer revolution began in the early 1970s when Intel Corp. successfully marketed the first microprocessor chip.

### Computers from a Kit

The microprocessor chip made it possible to design and build a computer small enough to sit on a desk and fit in a small box. In 1975, the first personal computer was advertised in *Popular Electronics* magazine by Ed Roberts. The Altair 8800 was an 8-bit, $400 microcomputer designed for the hobbyist and available only in kit form. The buyer had to put it together. The Altair 8800 was a huge success—hundreds were sold.

Success bred competition. Steven Jobs and Stephen Wozniak, working out of Jobs' garage, created and released the Apple I in 1976. The 8-bit Apple I was designed with the non-hobbyist in mind. It was easy to use, easy to assemble, and inexpensive. The first Apple showed there was a strong market for assembled machines, so in 1977 Jobs and Wozniak released an improved, fully assembled version, the Apple II.

### The Birth of the Personal Computer

Jobs and Wozniak understood that the future of their creations would depend on the tasks the machines could be made to do. Since they were essentially computer designers, they encouraged other companies to develop software and accessory hardware, such as printers and tape and disk drives, that would work with their machines. In 1979, the first business accounting software package, VisiCalc (VISIble CALCulator), was released commercially. VisiCalc was written and designed on an Apple II. Sales of both products skyrocketed because most purchasers bought them together. Meanwhile, dozens of other companies, including Radio Shack (Tandy), Atari, and Commodore, had entered the microcomputer market.

The infant microcomputer industry was dominated by companies as new as the products they sold. In 1981 all that changed. IBM, the world's largest manufacturer of computer hardware, released its 16-bit microcomputer, called simply the PC (Personal Computer). Breaking its historical pattern of developing and marketing only its own hardware and software products, IBM followed Apple's lead and encouraged other companies to develop software and accessory hardware for the IBM PC. In less than two years, IBM was the dominant force in the microcomputer market. Even now, it is unclear whether it was the superior design of the PC or simply IBM's reputation for reliability that sold its machines.

IBM's success had two significant effects. Almost immediately, IBM became the "standard" machine for which software and accessory hardware were designed. Competitors started building microcomputers that could do most of what an IBM PC could do. Such machines were called **compatibles**. They are able to run much of the extensive software designed for the IBM PC (see Figure 2.25). Some of these microcomputers went even further. They were virtual look-alikes, or **clones**, of the IBM PC. Clones and compatibles of the IBM PC are quite attractive to customers, since they usually cost less than IBM's product. Legally, IBM's competitors cannot build exact duplicates of IBM PCs. So, each of the compatibles or clones differ from IBM PCs in some way. Standard equipment on such machines often includes graphics monitors, additional internal memory, and redesigned microprocessor chips that work faster than those built into the IBM PC.

The IBM PC and later related models, such as the IBM XT and IBM AT, are all based on 16-bit chips from Intel. The compatibles are also based on Intel

**Figure 2.25**          Compatibles: IBM-compatible computers such as this Compaq Deskpro 386/20e use the same software and have most of the capabilities of the IBM PC.

microprocessors, which are inexpensive and readily available. Some compatibles, such as AT&T's 6300, have improved IBM's hardware design.

### Toward a User-Friendly Machine

In 1984, Apple responded to IBM's dominance by releasing the Macintosh (see Figure 2.26). This was a 32-bit machine designed for the unsophisticated user and advertised as the computer "for the rest of us." It featured on-screen pictures called **icons** to represent common computer tasks. The user pointed to an icon with a special pointing device called a mouse, which will be more fully explained in Chapter 5. Many people found this an easy and enjoyable way to start using a computer.

In 1987, both IBM and Apple released new microcomputer systems. The IBM Personal System/2 and Apple Macintosh II are powerful machines designed to run much of the existing software developed for earlier models, as well as new and improved applications packages. Despite differences in design and operation, both systems include many similar features such as screens for color graphics, mice, and compact storage devices.

**Figure 2.26**    The Macintosh: Apple Computer released the Macintosh in 1984 in response to IBM's domination of the microcomputer market.

# On Line

## THE COMPUTER MUSEUM

In a refurbished warehouse on Museum Wharf in downtown Boston stands the world's only computer museum. While it specializes in devices less than 50 years old, the technological changes in computers and computing devices over that period have been dramatic.

Exhibits span the computer's history from first-generation vacuum tube devices of monstrous proportions to fourth-generation microcomputers. Displays include computers used in business and the military as well as personal machines. Visitors can try their hand at flying a plane on a computer-based flight simulator or they can explore computer art and animation. Physical devices that no longer exist have been preserved on film. Whenever possible, the computers have been repaired and they remain operational.

The microcomputer gallery includes examples of the earliest micros, such as the Altair 8800, which was built from a kit, and the Commodore PET. Current models are also displayed. Visitors can explore paint packages and computer graphics. They can experiment with machines that talk and others that understand the spoken word.

The Computer Museum provides a hands-on learning environment. Visitors are encouraged to touch, examine, and experiment with the computers around them.

## BEYOND THE FOURTH GENERATION

What will fifth-generation computers be like? Not having a crystal ball, it is impossible to say with any certainty. Judging from current research in the United States and Japan, the next generation of computers is likely to have common features. They may be:

1. *More compact.* Their hardware will be more compact, based on "super chips" composed of thousands of already compact, smaller chips linked together.

2. *Faster.* They will operate and calculate hundreds if not thousands of times faster than current machines. Computers are likely to move away from the von Neumann model of processing information one piece at a time. Instead they will incorporate multiple processors working together, or parallel processing. On such machines each processor will be able to solve different parts of a problem independently.

3. *Smarter.* These machines will be considerably more "intelligent" than modern computers. Computer programs designed to make decisions in a

human-like fashion will be more capable of assisting people in decision making.

4. *Friendlier.* Software will make these new computers even more user-friendly. In other words, people will find computers easier to use and operate because the software will require less technical expertise.

5. *Closer to natural language.* Software will make greater use of natural or spoken language.

Computers, whatever their form, will link our homes with all kinds of services, from banking and shopping to education and entertainment. Our offices will become increasingly "paperless," and more and more people will work from home by dialing into the office.

While the computer in its present form is only 50 years old, two things should be clear. First, people have been engaged in the increasingly complex development of computing devices for hundreds if not thousands of years. Second, the computers available 20 years from now are likely to be as radically different from the machines in popular use today as the Apple Macintosh is from ENIAC.

## SUMMARY

The earliest computing tool was the abacus, which uses strings of beads to perform computations. The 1600s saw the development of many calculating devices. The slide rule, using specially marked rulers, was introduced in 1621 and continued in popular use until the 1970s. Blaise Pascal invented a mechanical calculator in 1642 and Gottfried Leibniz introduced a multiplier in 1673.

The Industrial Revolution not only produced greatly improved calculating devices, but began the process of designing machines that were programmable. Jacquard's use of punched cards to store the pattern woven in cloth directly influenced the designers of calculating devices. In 1833, Charles Babbage's Analytical Engine was designed. It was a complete computer containing punched card input, an output device, a processor, and memory. While this machine was not completed in Babbage's lifetime, his ideas assisted future scientists.

In the 1800s, computing devices found practical applications. Herman Hollerith invented a Census Machine that assisted in tabulating the 1890 and 1900 census. The railroad industry used it to keep track of passengers and goods shipped. William Burroughs' 1888 invention of an adding/listing machine found widespread application.

The pattern of devices from the 1600s through the early 1900s leads directly to the development of calculating machines that contained memory and were programmable. The research environment of World War II hastened the development of computing machines, including the ABC, Harvard Mark I, and ENIAC.

Recognizing the faults found in these machines, John von Neumann devised a means of storing program instructions in memory using numeric (binary) codes. His theoretical machine consisted of single function components, which still form the basis for today's machines. Von Neumann's ideas were first implemented in the EDSAC (1949) and EDVAC (1951) computers. Because of the commercial viability of these new machines, the UNIVAC I and IBM 650 were introduced in the early 1950s.

From the 1950s to the present, computer hardware changed very rapidly. Hardware and software advances mark the computer generations. First-generation computers used vacuum-tube technology and were programmed in machine language. The transistor marks the transition into the second computer generation. Transistors made computers smaller and more reliable. While assembly language was popular, both FORTRAN and COBOL were created during the second generation.

Miniaturization packed hundreds of transistors on a tiny silicon chip, bringing about the third computer generation. A wide variety of devices were invented that could be added to computers, making them easier to use. English-like programming languages and prewritten packages were the popular software. The fourth generation found manufacturers squeezing all of the components found in a CPU onto a single chip (microprocessor). Fourth-generation machines come in a vast array of sizes. Prewritten software has made these machines available to all of us.

Microprocessor-based microcomputers first became available in the early 1970s in kit form. In 1977, Steven Jobs and Stephen Wozniak released the Apple II, the first fully assembled microcomputer. Packaged software such as VisiCalc made microcomputers useful without a programming background. In 1981, IBM released its Personal Computer (PC) and encouraged other hardware and software manufacturers to develop products that could be used with it. In a short period of time, it was the industry standard. Apple's 1984 Macintosh featured a pointing device called a mouse and icons representing common computer tasks, making it easy to use. Both IBM and Apple released new computers in 1987 that feature color graphic displays, mice, and compact memory.

## Key Words

As an extra review of the chapter, try defining the following terms. If you have trouble with any of them, refer to the page number listed.

| | |
|---|---|
| abacus *(32)* | large-scale integration (LSI) *(57)* |
| clones *(61)* | slide rule *(33)* |
| compatibles *(61)* | solid state *(53)* |
| icons *(62)* | transistor *(53)* |
| integrated circuits *(55)* | very large-scale integration (VLSI) *(58)* |

## Test Your Knowledge

1. Explain briefly how the abacus works.

2. How do Pascal's calculator and Leibniz's multiplier differ?

3. What contribution did Jacquard's loom make toward the development of computers?

4. Why is Charles Babbage called the father of the modern computer?

5. Why is Ada Lovelace called the first programmer?

6. What was the Census Machine? Why was it important?

7. What was COLOSSUS? What did it do?

8. Why is the Harvard Mark I not considered a complete computer?

9. John von Neumann revolutionized the way computers' work. Explain his two major contributions.

10. How did ENIAC differ from EDVAC?

11. The UNIVAC I and IBM 650 were both important computer firsts. Explain this statement.

12. List the basic features of first-generation computers.

13. List the basic features of second-generation computers.

14. List the basic features of third-generation computers.

15. What distinguishes fourth-generation machines from those built in the third generation?

16. How did the Apple II differ from the Apple I?

17. What company coined the term *personal computer?* How is the PC different from the Apple II?

18. What are compatibles?

19. What are the basic differences between the Macintosh and the PC?

20. What features do IBM's Personal System/2 and the Macintosh II share?

## Expand Your Knowledge

1. Locate either a slide rule or an abacus. Learn how it works. Demonstrate its use to your class.

2. Write a three-page paper on Napier's "bones." They are considered a precursor to the slide rule. Include what the bones were and how they worked. Use at least two sources.

3. Reseach the Atanasoff versus ENIAC case. Write a short (three to five page) paper indicating your feeling about this question: Should ENIAC have been patented? Support your viewpoint. Use at least three sources of information.

4. Admiral Grace Hopper made critical contributions to the development of second-generation computers. Write a brief three-page paper describing her contributions.

5. What is Japan's Fifth-Generation Project? Write a short (three to five page) paper on this project. Use at least three sources of information.

6. Go to a local computer store and compare the IBM Personal System/2 with the Macintosh II. Identify key similarities and differences. Include a list of prices. If money were not an issue, which machine would you buy? Defend your position.

# 3

# The Central Processing Unit

## Chapter Outline

The Central Processing Unit (CPU)
> The Arithmetic and Logic Unit • The Control Unit • Registers • Memory

Coding Information
> EBCDIC • ASCII • Parity (Odd and Even Parity)

Addresses: Locating Information

Executing Instructions

Primary Memory
> Magnetic Core Memory • Semiconductor Memory • RAM and ROM

New and Changing Technologies
> Bubble Memory • Biological Chips • Parallel Processing

For many people, the computer is like a magician's "black box," an incredible machine that works mysteriously. For these individuals, what happens to data inside the computer is of no consequence. All that matters is that the results are consistent and accurate. If we opened this black box and found mice running around inside touching levers and pushing buttons, that would be fine. The process is less important than the results.

Many of us relate to our cars in the same way. We care only that when we turn the key the car starts. Although a car or a computer can be operated with such limited knowledge, when we think this way we are unable to handle or avoid problems. Driving and maintaining a car require some knowledge of how a car operates. It is important to understand that the muffler is part of the exhaust system, that the radiator assists in cooling the engine, and that the lights and starter require a working battery. In a similar way, to remove the mystery of the computer it is important to understand how the components work together to effectively store and process information. With such knowledge, we can better understand what the computer can and cannot do. An uninformed driver cannot effectively discuss the safety features of cars, and an uninformed computer user cannot effectively understand the power of computers.

After studying this chapter, you will be able to:

- Understand the components of the CPU.

- Explain the relationship between primary memory and the CPU.

- Illustrate how data is stored and addressed in memory.

- Relate the steps involved in executing instructions.

- Understand how EBCDIC and ASCII are used.

- Demonstrate the use of parity bits for error checking.

- Identify the basic types of primary memory.

- Relate the differences between RAM and ROM.

- Discuss new CPU and primary memory technologies.

## THE CENTRAL PROCESSING UNIT (CPU)

We mentioned in Chapter 1 that all computers, regardless of their size, cost, or manufacturer, have four basic components: input devices, a processor, memory, and output devices.

The "brains," or processor, of the computer consists of the central processing unit (CPU) and the primary memory associated with it (see Figure 3.1). The CPU, you will recall, is the electronic circuitry responsible for interpreting programs and issuing instructions to the rest of the machine so that the necessary operations will be carried out. The CPU has two components, the arithmetic and logic unit and the control unit.

**Figure 3.1**     General "All Purpose" Computer.

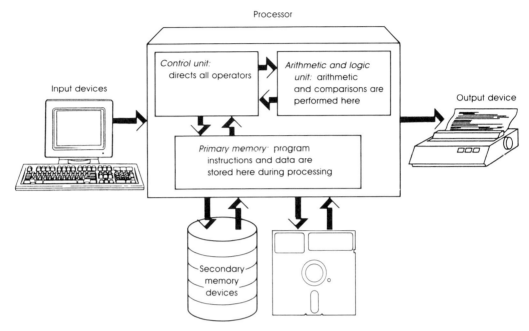

## The Arithmetic and Logic Unit

Computers are very fast calculating devices, and the **arithmetic and logic unit (ALU)** performs these calculations. The ALU has two functions. First, its circuitry is responsible for performing the arithmetic operations of addition, subtraction, multiplication, and division. Second, it can make simple "decisions" by choosing between two alternatives. In choosing, the computer uses the mathematical operations of less than (<), greater than (>), and equal to (=). When making decisions, the computer can be thought of as using an extremely exacting scale, as represented in Figure 3.2. By balancing two values, a computer can decide if one number is greater than another or if they are exactly the same.

Computers are more precise than people. When comparing the numbers 8.999999999 and 9 we would recognize them as essentially the same. To a computer, they are distinctly different. Numbers that are *essentially* the same are *not* equal.

$$8.999999999 < 9$$

Mathematical comparisons containing less than, greater than, and equal to are called *logical* operations resulting in the component's name. Computers can be designed to perform more complex comparisons, such as greater than or equal to, by combining the standard operations.

**Figure 3.2**    Logical Comparisons Using a Scale.

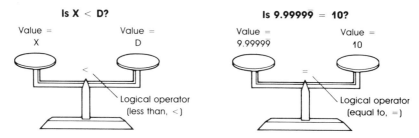

## The Control Unit

While the arithmetic and logic unit is responsible for mathematical calculations and comparisons, the **control unit** is the computer's internal police officer. This CPU component maintains order and controls all the internal activities of the machine. The control unit sends out electronic signals directing the computer to perform specific tasks. Information is moved between memory and the CPU, the ALU is activated, data is received from input devices, and information is sent to output devices. The control unit manages the flow of data throughout the machine based on the instructions it receives from programs. No instructions are processed by the control unit. Rather, it directs other parts of the computer to perform their functions in a specific order, at a specific time.

## Registers

The CPU contains a small number of very fast memory devices called **registers**. Each register temporarily holds a data item, an instruction, or a piece of information about to be transferred between the control unit and the ALU or processed by the ALU. The CPU can only process one instruction or use one item of data at a time. Registers are designed to hold the necessary information. Registers also hold the intermediate values used in calculations and comparisons. The final results of computations made by the CPU are transferred from registers to primary memory. To facilitate processing, the following registers are used by the CPU:

- *Accumulator.* This register holds the result of the operations performed by the ALU.

- *Storage register.* This register holds information just received from internal memory or just processed by the ALU and about to be sent to internal memory.

- *Address register.* This register holds the location of data about to be transferred from internal memory.

- *General-purpose register.* This register can store data, addresses, or instructions.

## Memory

While primary memory is not technically a part of the CPU, it stores the data and instructions required during processing. Without memory, the CPU could not effectively perform its duties. As shown in Figure 3.1, computers use two forms of memory: primary memory, directly associated with the CPU, and secondary memory, which will be discussed in Chapter 4. The name *primary memory* was not chosen casually. *Primary* means first; therefore, primary memory is the machine's first memory and its most important. It is designed for high-speed and easy access. However, data and program instructions are only temporarily stored in primary memory. As long as a program or file is being processed or worked on, it resides in primary memory. Information that is not being used is stored outside the CPU.

Both primary memory and the memory not associated with the CPU go under a host of different names. The common names used by primary memory are:

> primary memory or primary storage
> hard memory (hard-wired, built-in)
> main memory
> internal memory
> core memory

The names given to the memory outside the CPU are:

> auxiliary memory or auxiliary storage
> secondary memory or secondary storage
> mass storage
> external memory or external storage

## CODING INFORMATION

As indicated in Chapter 1, computers do not understand words or decimal system numbers. All data and instructions must be converted to binary digits (bits), combinations of zeros and ones, to be understood by the machine. People, however, are not machines. For people to use data, it needs to be organized so conclusions can be drawn and decisions made. No matter how effective our computers are, people ultimately have to do the organizing. Not only do we break down facts into data so they can be fed into a computer, but by writing programs we guide the computer in organizing the data to suit our needs.

# On Line

## THE NEXT COMPUTER

Without a crystal ball, few people would try to predict what computers will be like in the 1990s. In October of 1988, however, Steven Jobs did just that. He introduced a computer he calls "the machine for the 90s."

Jobs is a cofounder of Apple Computer. In 1985, he was pressured to leave Apple, where he had been the moving force behind the development of the Apple II and the Macintosh. Jobs started a new computer company called NeXT and began working on his computer vision of the future.

The NeXT machine, fondly called The Cube, is a workstation with a CPU based on the newest, state-of-the-art Motorola 68030 microprocessor chip. Added to this are a high-speed math chip to help process decimals and specially designed VLSI chips to control input and output. Primary memory consists of eight megabytes, or 8 million bytes of RAM. (IBM PCs and compatibles rarely contain more than 640K, or 640,000 bytes of primary memory.)

The Cube's mass storage device is a computer first: an erasable, removable, replaceable *optical* disk capable of storing 256 megabytes of data (see Chapter 4). This is the equivalent of more than 300 floppy disks.

All this power is housed in a one foot by one foot cube designed to sit on the floor or on a nearby shelf. The Cube is connected to a keyboard by a long cable. The full-featured keyboard contains a numeric keypad, cursor control keys, volume controls for the computer's stereo sound system, brightness control keys for the monitor, and the on-off switch. The cube controls a 17-inch high-resolution monitor and a mouse.

Impressive in-house developed software accompanies The Cube's dramatic hardware.

The NeXT computer uses the UNIX operating system, which is currently the system of choice among colleges, universities, and research organizations. Many people find UNIX hard to use, however. For this reason, Jobs created a Macintosh-like graphic interface that makes UNIX more user-friendly. Applications software includes a word processor, a personal data base, the Sound and Music Kit, an electronic (including voice) mail system, an electronic dictionary, a thesaurus, a book of quotations, and the complete works of Shakespeare.

Companies such as Ashton-Tate (dBase III), Lotus, Adobe Systems (Display Postscript), and Franz Allegro (Common Lisp) have developed versions of their software for the NeXT machine. Dozens of other software vendors are involved in developing software for The Cube.

The NeXT machine was originally intended to sell only to the college market. In a move to bring the machine into the computer mainstream, The Cube will be sold to businesses through Businessland computer stores. The basic system will sell on campuses for $6500, which reflects traditional vendor discounts to colleges and universities. Students and faculty are excited about both the machine's potential and its relatively modest price. The Cube will retail to businesses for approximately $10,000, which makes it highly competitive. If the NeXT machine is to be a success, however, its performance and usefulness will have to live up to its promise.

*Sources:* T. Thompson and N. Baran, "The NeXT Computer," *Byte,* Nov., 1988, pp. 158–175; K. M. Nash, "The Soul of the Next Machine," *Time,* Oct. 24, 1988, pp. 80–81. M. Irsfield, "NeXT Box Goes Retail," *UNIX Today,* April 3, 1989, pp. 4, 48.

While people can deal with information in the form of zeros and ones, we are far more comfortable manipulating information in the form of *characters* found in natural languages such as English. There are three types of characters:

1.  Alphabetic: A, B, C, D... a, b, c, d...

2.  Numeric: 0, 1, 2, 3, 4, 5, 6, 7, 8, 9

3.  Special: +, =, –, /, >, <, $, *, etc.

Over the years, a number of coding schemes have been developed to translate characters into a series of bits. Taken together these bits form a byte, so one character is stored as a single byte of memory.

The two most popular coding schemes are the **Extended Binary Coded Decimal Interchange Code**, or **EBCDIC** (pronounced *EB-see-dick)*, and the **American Standard Code for Information Interchange**, or **ASCII** (pronounced *AS-key)*. Figure 3.3 gives examples of these two codes.

## EBCDIC

EBCDIC was developed by IBM to code information on its mainframes. Using 8-bits, which allows for 256 unique combinations, each character is coded into binary. In addition to ordering the coded numbers, so that 1 (1111 0001) is less than 2 (1111 0010), the letters are also ordered so that comparisons can be made. *D* for example, is less than *E* when their binary equivalents are compared.

```
1 < 2      since      11110001  <  11110010
           and
D < E      because    11000100  <  11000101
```

## ASCII

ASCII was developed as a combined effort by a group of computer manufacturers who hoped it would become the standard for all machines. While it has become the standard for microcomputers, including IBM, and is extensively used by minicomputer manufacturers and many mainframes, IBM continues to use EBCDIC on its mainframes. Like EBCDIC, ASCII codes each character into a series of bits. However, this scheme uses a 7-bit code rather than 8, while maintaining the natural ordering within letters and numbers.

---

**Figure 3.3**        ASCII and EBCDIC codes. Many computer users prefer ASCII to EBCDIC, feeling it uses a more rational bit pattern.

| EBCDIC (8-bits) | character | ASCII (7-bits) |
|---|:---:|---|
| 1100 0001 | A | 100 0001 |
| 1100 0010 | B | 100 0010 |
| 1100 0011 | C | 100 0011 |
| 1100 0100 | D | 100 0100 |
| 1100 0101 | E | 100 0101 |
| 1100 0110 | F | 100 0110 |
| 1100 0111 | G | 100 0111 |
| 1100 1000 | H | 100 1000 |
| 1100 1001 | I | 100 1001 |
| 1101 0001 | J | 100 1010 |
| 1101 0010 | K | 100 1011 |
| 1101 0011 | L | 100 1100 |
| 1101 0100 | M | 100 1101 |
| 1101 0101 | N | 100 1110 |
| 1101 0110 | O | 100 1111 |
| 1101 0111 | P | 101 0000 |
| 1101 1000 | Q | 101 0001 |
| 1101 1001 | R | 101 0010 |
| 1110 0010 | S | 101 0011 |
| 1110 0011 | T | 101 0100 |
| 1110 0100 | U | 101 0101 |
| 1110 0101 | V | 101 0110 |
| 1110 0110 | W | 101 0111 |
| 1110 0111 | X | 101 1000 |
| 1110 1000 | Y | 101 1001 |
| 1110 1001 | Z | 101 1010 |
| | | |
| 1111 0000 | 0 | 011 0000 |
| 1111 0001 | 1 | 011 0001 |
| 1111 0010 | 2 | 011 0010 |
| 1111 0011 | 3 | 011 0011 |
| 1111 0100 | 4 | 011 0100 |
| 1111 0101 | 5 | 011 0101 |
| 1111 0110 | 6 | 011 0110 |
| 1111 0111 | 7 | 011 0111 |
| 1111 1000 | 8 | 011 1000 |
| 1111 1001 | 9 | 011 1001 |

## Parity

With information constantly being transmitted both within the computer and between machines, it is essential to guarantee that information is accurately transferred. Each coded character, whether EBCDIC or ASCII, has a bit added to it prior to transmission. The added bit is called the **parity**, or **check bit**, In the circuitry used to test for odd parity, the digits of the transmitted byte, including the parity bit, are added together. If the result is an odd number (an odd number of 1-bits), it is assumed that the byte was transmitted correctly. Even-parity circuitry tests for an even number of 1-bits.

**Odd and Even Parity**   *Coding the Byte.*   To demonstrate the use of parity bits, let us start with an initial character, code it into EBCDIC and ASCII and then add the appropriate bit used in an *even-parity* system.

In both cases, all the bits in the string were added. In the EBCDIC system, the result was 3, which is an odd number. To produce even parity, prior to transmission an additional one is added, making the sum even. In ASCII, the sum was 2, which is even, so a zero is added. In binary, summing a string of digits produces the same result as counting the number of ones in the string. In EBCDIC the parity bit is the right-most bit, while in ASCII the parity bit is the left-most bit.

*Testing for Accurate Transmission.*   In transmitting the word *HELLO* between two machines using the ASCII code and an even-parity system, an error occurred. The following example demonstrates how the error is detected:

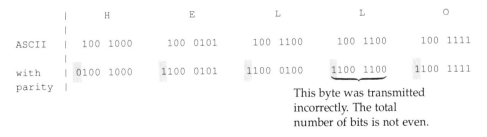

The computer, being unable to determine which bit within the byte was transmitted incorrectly, only knows that an error has occurred. To correct the error, the entire byte is retransmitted.

If a 1-bit was lost or changed during transmission, the parity of the byte would change, indicating a transmission error. While this is not an infallible system, it is possible to lose or incorrectly transmit more than a single bit. The chances of transmitting two bits incorrectly in a single byte are very small.

## ADDRESSES: LOCATING INFORMATION

Primary memory contains thousands of electronic circuits designed to store a single number as a series of zeros and ones (binary digits). As von Neumann suggested, instructions are also coded by the machine as binary digits. For the computer to process instructions and data it must be able to locate the required information. Each memory location has a unique **address**. Just as your home address uniquely identifies where you live, so an address in memory uniquely identifies its location.

A memory location is similar to a mailbox (see Figure 3.4). A mailbox is uniquely identified on the outside by an address and the last names of those living at that address. The address on the mailbox remains the same regardless of the contents of the box, which might change every day. Some days it might contain letters, other days a magazine or a package. Memory works in much the same way. Each location has a unique numeric address that identifies it. While the address of each location is fixed, the contents or *value* of memory can change. Each location can contain data or instructions. Contemporary English-like programming languages do not use numeric addresses when referring to memory. They use symbolic addresses, English-like words that more clearly describe the contents of memory. Such programs refer to memory by using names such as PayRate, Total, InitialValue, or StoreNumber. A symbolic address is similar to the name on the outside of a mailbox. The name on the outside of the mailbox identifies whose mail is inside. The computer associates a unique numeric address with each of these symbolic addresses.

A memory location can store only one item at a time. When new information is stored, the old contents are destroyed. This would be comparable to a mailbox that could hold only a single letter or a single issue of a magazine. If a second letter is pushed into the mailbox, the first falls out the back and is lost. When retrieving information, the mailbox analogy breaks down. When mail is retrieved from a mailbox, the mailbox is empty. When information is retrieved from memory, a copy of the contents is made and this copy is used. The stored information remains intact. Such unique addressing enables the CPU to retrieve information very rapidly.

**Figure 3.4**    Addresses: Each memory location has an identifying address.

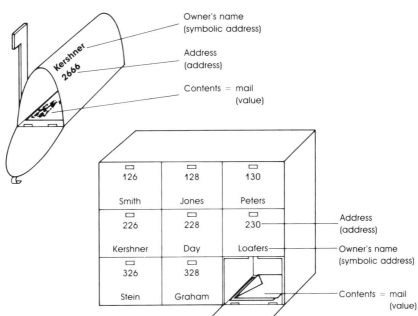

---

## EXECUTING INSTRUCTIONS

For a computer to process, or *execute,* a program, the control unit must move instructions and data from primary memory to the CPU's registers and then return the results to memory. Most modern computers can perform only a single calculation or comparison at once. Programs are executed one instruction at a time. For each instruction, the following steps are followed:

1. *Copy.* The control unit copies, or *fetches,* an instruction from primary memory and stores it in one of its registers.

2. *Decode.* The instruction is decoded by the control unit. If data is required it is fetched from memory. The decoded instruction and any required data are sent to the ALU.

3. *Calculate or compare.* The ALU performs the required calculation or comparison, storing the result in a register.

4. *Store.* The control unit stores the results of the ALU's operation in primary memory or, if the result is to be used immediately, in another register.

This procedure is followed over and over again until all instructions have been executed. Steps 1 and 2 together are referred to as **I-time**, or **instruction time**, which is the time required to interpret an instruction. Steps 3 and 4 make up **E-time**, or **execution time**, the time required to execute an instruction. All four steps require only a small fraction of a second to complete.

## PRIMARY MEMORY

To be effectively used by the CPU, main memory must offer fast, easy access to data. Unfortunately, the faster a memory technology, the more expensive. Information that is not needed for processing is stored on less-expensive secondary storage devices. Primary memory provides direct access to all information. Since each memory location has a unique address, all information can be located in the same amount of time. It is left to the computer to "remember" exactly where each item of data is stored so it can be retrieved.

### Magnetic Core Memory

The primary memory technology of second- and third-generation computers was **magnetic core memory**, often referred to simply as **core**. Core consisted of tiny (1/100 inch) iron oxide (ferrite) rings with several wires threaded through each ring (see Figure 3.5). If enough current passed through the wires, the rings were magnetized in either a clockwise (representing 1) or counter-clockwise (representing 0) direction. Since core remained magnetized when the electric current was no longer present it was called *non-volatile*. Core memory was very reliable and reasonably fast. However, when compared to more recent technologies it was rather bulky, required a significant amount of power to create the directional charges, and was expensive to assemble.

### Semiconductor Memory

**Semiconductor memory** is the common memory technology of current machines. Its size and design make it faster and less expensive than core memory. Semiconductor memory consists of thousands of microscopic integrated circuits etched onto chips of silicon (see Figure 3.6). These circuits either allow electric current to pass over a given path or they stop the current. The presence of current is represented by a 1, while the absence of current is represented by a 0. Semiconductor memory is very compact, making it very fast. It is reliable, uses low power, and is relatively inexpensive.

However, unlike magnetic core, semiconductor memory is *volatile*. Continuous electric current is required to store data. If the current is interrupted, even briefly, all stored information is irretrievably lost. For this reason, today's com-

**Figure 3.5**     Magnetic Cores: (a) A magnetic core memory and (b) a closeup of a magnetic core memory.

(a)

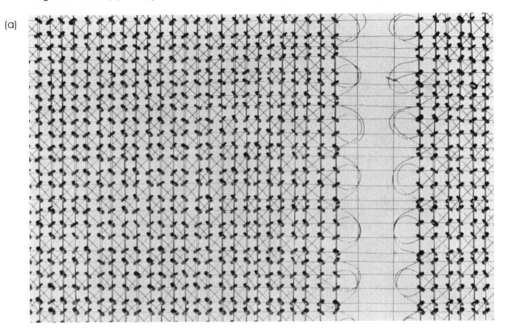

(b)

**Figure 3.6**    Semiconductor Memory: Today's computer makes use of microscopic, integrated circuits etched onto silicon chips.

puter users are advised to regularly save, or copy, the information they have stored in primary memory into secondary storage. In this way, if a power failure does occur, only a small amount of very recent information is lost.

### RAM and ROM

Semiconductor memory comes in two forms: random access memory (RAM) and read only memory (ROM). **Random access memory (RAM)** is general-purpose memory. It is used to store program instructions, initial data, and intermediate and final results from programs. RAM is easily and directly accessed by the CPU, acting as the machine's work space or scratch pad. It is user-programmable memory. A user can store information in RAM, read what is there, or erase the information as desired. RAM is volatile, so information is stored there temporarily. The information is only available when electrical current is present or the user is connected with a larger machine.

The capacity of a computer, especially a microcomputer, is often determined by the amount of RAM it has available. The more RAM, the larger the programs and data that can be stored and processed. Early microcomputers contained between 4K and 16K of RAM. Many of today's micros come standard with 512K to 1 megabyte (1000K) of RAM.

If all the primary memory associated with the CPU were RAM, every time the machine was turned off or the power was interrupted the instructions required by the machine for its operation would be lost. As a result, a portion of primary memory containing vital operating instructions is protected on special chips. This portion of the primary memory is called **read only memory (ROM)** and is pre-programmed or manufacturer defined. The user can read or gain access to the information stored in ROM but cannot change it. ROM is often called *firmware*, because programs are held firm in memory and cannot be altered by the computer user. ROM chips are non-volatile, require fewer circuits, and are faster and less expensive than RAM. In addition to governing start-up procedures, many microcomputers include ROM chips that contain the BASIC programming language.

Some computer engineers and programmers need to store special user-written programs in ROM. **Programmable read only memory**, or **PROM**, chips are designed for this purpose. PROM chips can only be programmed once. Once programmed, they act like standard ROM chips in that their information cannot be changed. If the program placed on a PROM chip contains an error, the error cannot be corrected without replacing the chip. To overcome this problem, some erasable PROM chips have been developed. **Erasable and programmable read only memory (EPROM)** chips must be removed from the computer and specially treated to remove the embedded instructions. Some EPROM chips are treated with ultraviolet light, while others are electronically erased. When these chips are inside a computer they are non-volatile and act like other ROM chips.

## NEW AND CHANGING TECHNOLOGIES

Scientists are constantly experimenting with ways of improving primary memory. Despite the low cost and compact size of semiconductor memory, other technologies are examined and reexamined.

### Bubble Memory

**Bubble memory** was developed at Bell Labs in 1966 in an effort to design a non-volatile, fast, and compact memory. The chips are made of garnet rather than silicon and are coated with a magnetic film. The bubbles are cylinders of magnetic material resting within the magnetic film. Tiny electromagnets produce a magnetic field, causing the cylinders to move or "float" along the circuit path in the chip. These microscopic bubbles and the gaps between them are used to store data. The presence of a bubble represents a one, while the absence of a bubble represents a zero. Bubble memory can be designed as a large-capacity storage device. Furthermore, once the bubbles are produced they do not require continuous current to retain their charge. This is a non-volatile form of memory and could prove invaluable to systems where power failures would cause critical damage. Bubble memory currently is expensive and has not dropped in price along with semiconductor memory. Due to the significant difference in cost, most manufacturers have chosen the cheaper semiconductor memory for their machines.

### Biological Chips

Researchers from a variety of scientific disciplines are investigating the possibility of designing molecular chips using organic (living) and inorganic molecules. Molecular circuits would be significantly smaller (perhaps 1000 times smaller) than solid-state electronic circuits.

Building molecular chips would involve a considerable extension of current genetic engineering. Current research in the area has developed a molecular switch made of an inorganic substance that can change its electrical and optical properties when shot (irradiated) with a laser. This molecular switch would act like an electronic switch and store a single bit of data.

It is somewhat fanciful to imagine a time when enough is known about the structure of genes and the development of molecules that a self-assembling, possibly self-reproducing biological chip could be developed. While such research makes us wonder about the future, it is a very long way from changing the face of modern computers.

### Parallel Processing

Most modern computers following the von Neumann design contain a single ALU and can perform only a single calculation or comparison at one time. Because the ALU performs its function with incredible speed, this is generally not a problem. However, very large and complex problems ranging from weather prediction to weapons research, which require vast numbers of computations and comparisons, find this hinders problem solving. Executing one instruction at a time is called the von Neumann bottleneck.

Computers containing more than one CPU, each with its own primary memory, can execute multiple instructions simultaneously. Such a computer requires a very complex control unit to keep track of its operations. Considerable research is going on in this field, which is called **parallel computing**. A number of companies, including Intel, Sequent, and Encore, are marketing parallel machines. Each company's machines approach the idea of simultaneous processing (parallelism) differently. It is not yet clear whether one design will prove better than the others or whether the different designs will each be used to solve different types of problems. However, parallel computing will directly influence the computers of the future.

## SUMMARY

The processor of a computer is made up of the central processing unit (CPU) and primary memory. The CPU consists of an arithmetic and logic unit (ALU) and a control unit.

The ALU performs the basic arithmetic functions of addition, subtraction, multiplication, and division. It is here that logical decisions using the mathematical operations of less than (<), greater than (>), and equal to (=) are performed. The control unit coordinates the internal activities of the computer.

Registers are very fast, mini-memory devices directly embedded in the CPU. They are used by the control unit and the ALU for temporary storage during the execution of instructions. There are four kinds of registers: accumulators, storage registers, address registers, and general-purpose registers

Primary memory is associated with the CPU and stores instructions and data while a file or program is being processed. Secondary memory is outside the processor and is used for longer-term storage.

All characters must be coded in binary form before they can be used by the computer. The two most popular coding schemes are ASCII (American Standard Code for Information Interchange) and EBCDIC (Extended Binary Coded Decimal Interchange Code). ASCII is a 7-bit code and is the standard for most minicomputers and all microcomputers. EBCDIC is an 8-bit code used on IBM mainframes. To ensure accurate transmission of data, a parity or check bit is added to ASCII and EBCDIC codes.

Each storage location in memory has a unique address that identifies its location. The contents or value of memory is the data stored at a particular address. Each memory location can store only a single item of data or a single instruction.

Programs are executed one instruction at a time. Four steps are required to execute each instruction: (1) The instruction is fetched from memory, (2) It is decoded, (3) The ALU performs the required operation, and (4) The results are stored in a memory device. The time required to perform steps 1 and 2 is I-time, or instruction time, while steps 3 and 4 comprise E-time, or execution time.

Early primary memory consisted of magnetic core. While it was a non-volatile storage medium, it was bulky and expensive to assemble. Current primary memory uses semiconductor memory (RAM) and consists of thousands of microscopic integrated circuits etched on a silicon chip. It is volatile, requiring continuous current to retain stored information. A portion of primary memory called ROM is composed of special non-volatile chips containing vital operational instructions for the computer.

Computer technology is constantly changing. Bubble memory and biological chips may alter the nature of primary memory. Parallel computing, which enables multiple instructions to be processed simultaneously, is altering the way instructions are processed.

## Key Words

As an extra review of the chapter, try defining the following terms. If you have trouble with any of them, refer to the page number listed.

address *(78)*
American Standard Code for Information Interchange (ASCII) *(75)*
arithmetic and logic unit (ALU) *(71)*
bubble memory *(85)*
control unit *(74)*
E-time (execution time) *(80)*
erasable and programmable read only memory (EPROM) *(83)*
Extended Binary Coded Decimal Interchange Code (EBCDIC) *(75)*

I-time (instruction time) *(80)*
magnetic core memory (core) *(80)*
parallel computing *(84)*
programmable read only memory (PROM) *(83)*
random access memory (RAM) *(82)*
read only memory (ROM) *(83)*
registers *(72)*
parity (check bit) *(75)*
semiconductor memory *(80)*

## Test Your Knowledge

1.  Name the four basic components of all computer systems.

2.  What do the letters CPU stand for?

3.  What is the function of the control unit?

4.  List the four logical operations performed by the arithmetic and logic unit (ALU).

5.  In addition to comparisons, what other operations does the ALU perform?

6.  List three alternative names for primary memory.

7.  List two of the names given to the memory not associated with the CPU.

8.  How are registers different from primary memory?

9.  How is a memory location like a mailbox? How does it differ?

10.  Briefly describe the four steps involved in processing every computer instruction.

11.  What are I-time and E-time?

12.  Why were EBCDIC and ASCII developed?

13.  Explain how a computer uses the parity bit to check for accurate data transmissions.

14. Using ASCII in an odd-parity system, code the letter *H* for transmission.

15. Using EBCDIC in an even-parity system, code the letter *I* for transmission.

16. Describe magnetic core memory.

17. Why is semiconductor memory volatile?

18. What is RAM? What is ROM?

19. Explain how PROM and EPROM chips differ from ROM chips.

20. How does parallel computing differ from more traditional computing?

---

## Expand Your Knowledge

1. Research the ASCII system and determine the codes for all 128 characters. List each character and its corresponding code.
   (a) How many non-printing symbols are coded?
   (b) Are uppercase characters less than or greater than lowercase characters?
   (c) How many printable, special characters are coded? What are they?

2. An early computer coding system was called Binary Coded Decimal (BCD) and it used a 4-bit code.
   (a) What was the system able to code? List the characters and the corresponding code.
   (b) Why do you think it was necessary to increase the number of bits from 4, to 7 or 8?
   (c) Is there a relationship between BCD and EBCDIC? If so what is it?

3. In the early 1980s, a number of toxic-waste sites were discovered in Silicon Valley. Write a short paper describing how Silicon Valley became polluted and what has been done to clean up the sites.

4. Write a short paper on the development of the superchip using wafer-scale integration.

5. Write a short paper on parallel computing. Focus on how this new architecture varies from the traditional von Neumann machine.

# 4

# External Memory

**Chapter Outline**

Organizing Information
    Sequential File Organization • Direct Access File Organization •
    Indexed File Organization

Paper Media

Magnetic Tape
    Data Organization

Magnetic Disks
    Data Organization (The Sector Method; The Cylinder Method)

Floppy Disks

Winchester Disks

The Bernoulli Box

Backup

Future Technologies
    Optical Memory • Perpendicular Recording • Superconductors

Most computers today contain both primary and secondary memory. You will recall from Chapter 3 that primary memory is linked directly to the CPU. It provides extremely fast access to information and very compact storage, but the expense of these two factors limits its usefulness. Computer manufacturers today must balance hardware costs against storage capability. As a result, primary memory is normally restricted to temporary storage of information.

External memory, or mass storage, is less expensive and provides slower access to information than primary memory. There is another difference as well. External memory is designed to store vast amounts of information for much longer periods of time. Capacity is critically important in external memory. This chapter will examine external memory in detail.

After studying this chapter, you will be able to:

- Understand how computer files are organized.

- Be familiar with punched media.

- Identify the types of magnetic tape.

- Understand how data is stored and organized on magnetic media.

- Distinguish the different types of magnetic disks.

- Understand the importance of backup on computer systems.

- Discuss some future storage technologies.

## ORGANIZING INFORMATION

We are all familiar with storing information in a file cabinet. A file cabinet is filled with folders, each containing papers, records, or other kinds of related information. Each folder is labeled on the outside with a brief description of the folder's contents. The folders are organized in some way so they can be located. They may be organized alphabetically based on the folder's label or they may be stored by some key, such as the date on which the folder was created.

Information stored in a computer must also be organized so it can be located when needed. A *data item* is a combination of characters, such as names, numbers, addresses, and dollar amounts, that, taken together, have meaning for people. Data items, often called **fields**, are combined to form larger units of meaningful information called **records**, such as mailing addresses or a student's grade report for a given semester. Records combine to form **files**, which are frequently read and processed as a single unit. Files on a computer, just like files in a filing cabinet, are large units of information grouped together on the basis of similar characteristics. Examples of files are all student grades for a given semester, all cake recipes, or all tax information about a given corporation.

Just as there are different ways to organize file folders in a file cabinet, there are different methods of organizing files on a computer. The three most popular methods are sequential file organization, direct access file organization, and indexed file organization.

## Sequential File Organization

This method stores information in some order. Records can be ordered by a key, such as a social security number or an ID number, or information can be stored as it becomes available. To find a given record, the entire file must be searched in order or sequence from the beginning. Each stored item must be checked until the requested record is located. Magnetic tape is the most popular medium for sequential storage, although magnetic disks can be used. This technique is very efficient for files that are processed at regular intervals or where most of the stored information can be processed at once. Examples include payroll processing in which every employee is issued a pay check every week and student billing, in which bills are issued to most students each semester.

## Direct Access File Organization

Using this method, information can be stored in any order, including sequentially. Each record has a unique address, enabling the computer to locate all records in the same amount of time. Information can be located directly without having to examine other records. Magnetic disks are the common medium used for storing such files. Direct access file organization is critical when instant access to information is important. For example, airline reservation systems require quick access to stored information, as do on-line course registration programs and programs that let customers check their current bank balances.

## Indexed File Organization

Indexed file organization is a combination of both sequential and direct access storage techniques. Information is stored sequentially, and each record has a key or index associated with it. Each key is linked with an address that can be used to locate the record directly. Using this method, files can either be processed sequentially or directly. For example, insurance companies use sequential files to process customer bills at regular intervals. To properly handle customer inquiries, the stored information needs to be directly accessible. Magnetic disks are used with this type of organization so that records can be located directly.

## PAPER MEDIA

The oldest form of mass storage is the **computer (punched) card** shown in Figure 4.1. Sometimes called IBM cards or Hollerith cards, their use as a data stor-

**Figure 4.1**    The Computer Card: This data storage device remained in popular use until the late 1970s.

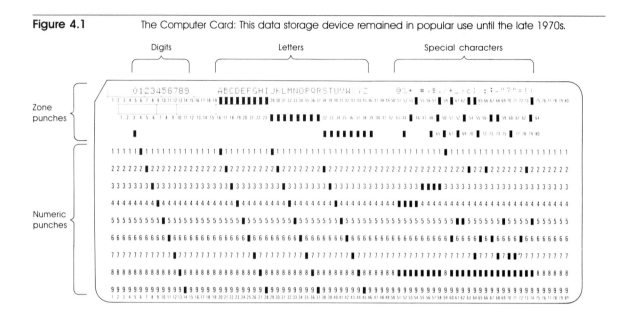

age device is attributed to Herman Hollerith, who created a punched card tabulating machine (see Chapter 2). These cards continued in popular use until the late 1970s.

Each card is 80 columns long, and each column can record a single character. Digits and uppercase letters are represented by one or more holes punched in each column. Characters punched in a given column can be printed in the space above the column so people, as well as computers, can read the information. Many second- and third-generation programming languages such as FORTRAN and BASIC restricted their statements to 80 columns or less, reflecting their card-oriented origins. When cards were popular, they were relatively inexpensive and provided virtually unlimited storage capacity, but they were very slow to read or punch and were bulky and easily damaged.

Another kind of paper medium, **punched paper tape**, was used in the 1940s and even later with teletype machines. Tape was experimented with as an input, output, and storage device for computers in the 1960s and early 1970s. The tape was a one-inch wide continuous strip of paper on which information could be stored as a unique pattern of holes punched across the tape's width. Paper tape did not restrict information to a fixed number of characters and could be viewed as an infinitely long punched card. While paper tape was inexpensive, it was not as durable as cards and correcting errors was very difficult.

The primary drawback of all punched media was their very slow input/output (I/O) speed when compared to the internal speed of the machine. In addition, the punched medium was easily damaged, cumbersome, and not reusable.

## MAGNETIC TAPE

**Magnetic tape** is used to store data in much the same way that audio tape records sound. Magnetic data tapes vary from ½ to ⅛ inch in width and come in three varieties, two of which are shown in Figure 4.2.

1. *Reel-to-reel tape.* This tape is usually ½ inch in width, is used predominantly on mainframes, and typically stores 1600 characters per inch.

2. *Cartridge tape.* This tape is usually ¼ inch in width, is used mostly on mini-computers, and stores approximately 400 characters per inch.

3. *Cassette tape.* This tape is identical to cassette audio tape, is usually ⅛ inch in width, is used on some microcomputers, and stores 200 characters per inch.

Magnetic tape is made of a strong plastic tape (Mylar) coated on one side with an iron oxide, which can be magnetized. Data is stored as microscopic magnetized dots that are created, read, or erased by a magnetic tape unit, or recorder. Advances in magnetic tape technology have produced a ½-inch tape capable of storing as many as 20,000 characters per inch.

### Data Organization

Magnetic tape is divided along its length into parallel *tracks,* or *channels,* and across its width into *frames,* as Figure 4.3 shows.

Each frame stores a single character (or byte) using one of the standard coding schemes such as EBCDIC or ASCII (see Chapter 3). Combinations of characters form fields, while related fields combine to form **logical records**. A logical record, for example, could contain information about a particular student: name, social security number, local address, and student ID number. Records can vary in size, reflecting the nature of the information stored. A piece of blank tape called an **interrecord gap (IRG)** is used to separate logical records for processing. However, this technique results in a great deal of unused tape and considerably increases processing time. Whenever an IRG is encountered, reading stops so that the record can be processed.

To increase data storage and decrease processing time, a number of logical records are usually combined to form a **physical record**, or **block**. A block is a group of logical records that are read and processed at once. Once read in, software divides the blocks into logical records. Each block is separated by a section of blank tape called an **interblock gap (IBG)** as shown in Figure 4.4.

**Figure 4.2**     Two Varieties of Magnetic Tape: (a) reel-to-reel tape and (b) cartridge tape.

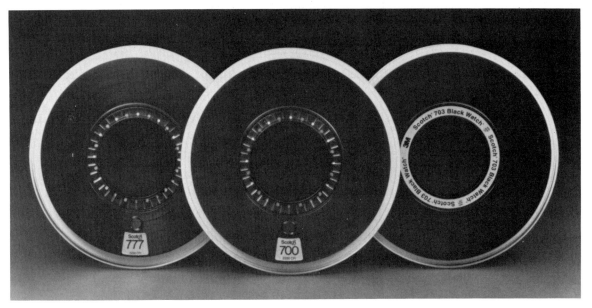

(a)

(b)

**Figure 4.3**    Magnetic Tape: Data are stored on magnetic tape in tracks and frames. Here, arrows pointing up represent binary ones, arrows pointing down represent zeros.

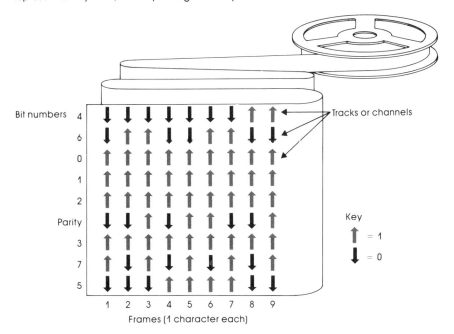

Magnetic tape is a compact storage medium that is highly portable and relatively inexpensive. It can easily be erased and reused. However, it is subject to damage by frequent handling and must be processed sequentially.

## MAGNETIC DISKS

The most widespread form of mass storage is the **magnetic disk** or **hard disk**, which is a direct access storage device. It was first marketed by IBM in 1956 but did not come into common use until the mid 1960s. Its popularity stems from its large storage capacity and the computer's ability to get information to and from the disk very rapidly. Information can be retrieved from disk in less than 0.001 second. A magnetic disk is a flat plate made of plastic or metal that looks somewhat like a phonograph record. Hard disks range in size from 14 inches down to 3 ½ inches in diameter. A **disk pack** is a number of disks stacked together on a single spindle, similar to phonograph records. The number of disks in a disk pack varies from 2 to 12.

Both sides (surfaces) of the disk are coated with a magnetizable compound on which, like magnetic tape, data is stored as magnetized dots. Disk drives

**Figure 4.4**   Records and Blocks: Logical records must be separated by interrecord gaps (IRGs) or interblock gaps (IBGs) on magnetic tape to be individually accessible.

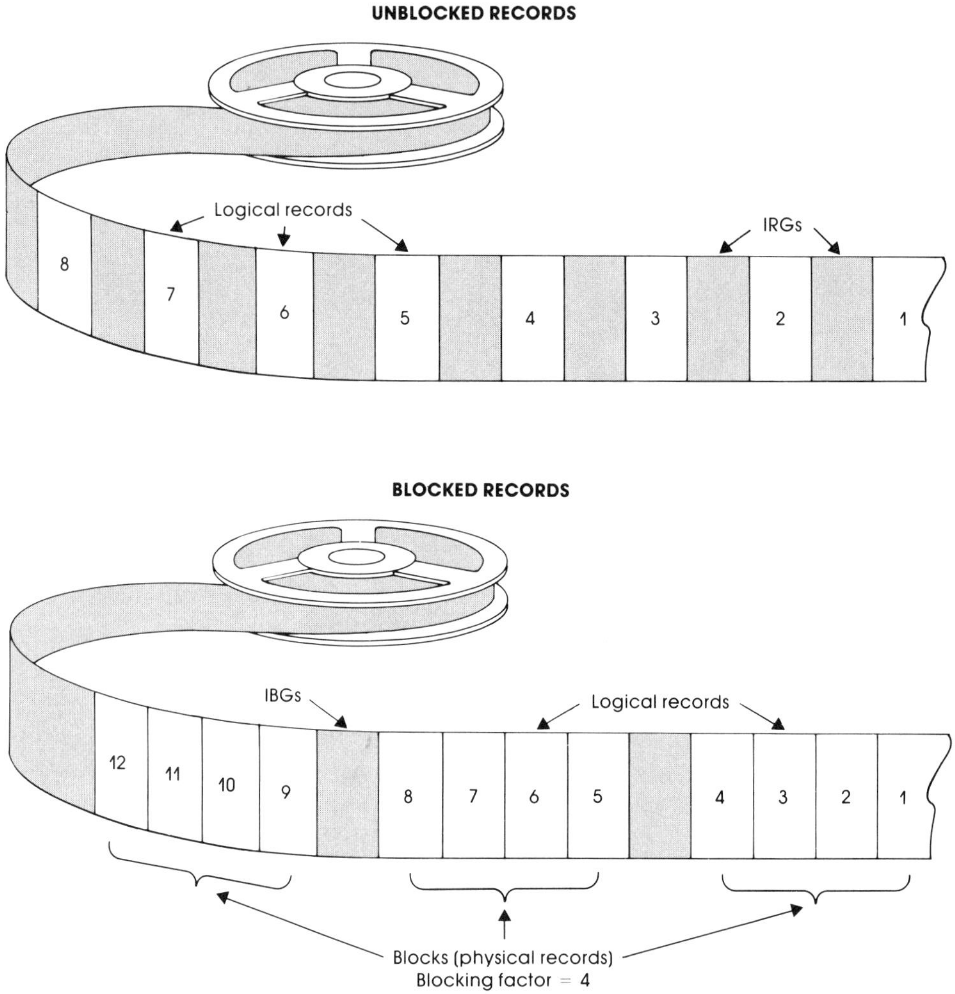

**UNBLOCKED RECORDS**

Logical records

IRGs

8    7    6    5    4    3    2    1

**BLOCKED RECORDS**

IBGs                Logical records

12   11   10   9        8    7    6    5        4    3    2    1

Blocks (physical records)
Blocking factor = 4

have movable **access arms**, which read information from the disks. These arms are similar to the playing arm of a phonograph, which holds the needle. Disk packs have multiple access arms that extend between the disks. Each access arm has a separate read/write head for each recording surface. A **read/write head** is a tiny electromagnet that can create, read, or erase the magnetic dots that store information on the surface of a disk. The topmost and bottommost surfaces of

**Figure 4.5**    Read/Write Heads and Access Arms.

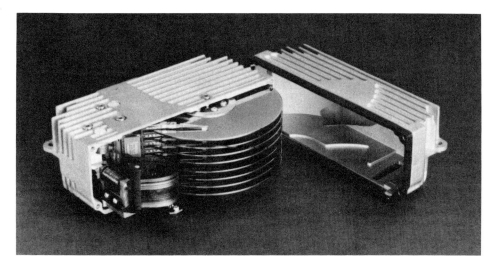

the stacked disks are often unused when recording information because they are easily damaged (see Figure 4.5).

## Data Organization

Each disk surface is divided into tracks similar to a phonograph record. However, a phonograph record has one continuous track running from the outer edge to the center. Magnetic disks are divided into a series of concentric circles (one inside the other), each of which is a separate track. The magnetized dots representing ones and zeros are stored along the tracks. Standard coding schemes such as ASCII or EBCDIC are used to code characters. Data stored on magnetic disks is **addressable**, which means that each record has its own unique address, similar to a street address. For example, a family living at 23 Main Street, Clearfield, has an address that describes the location of their residence. They reside in the community of Clearfield and at the house numbered 23 on Main Street. In much the same way, a disk address uniquely describes the location of a record. The two common disk addressing methods are the sector method and the cylinder method.

**The Sector Method**    The most common sector technique divides each track into an equal number of pieces or *sectors,* much like slices of a pie.

Each sector holds an equal number of characters. Since the tracks closest to the center are smaller than those near the outer edge, the number of characters in each sector is limited by the centermost sectors. This technique wastes valu-

**Figure 4.6**    The Sector Method of Disk Addressing.

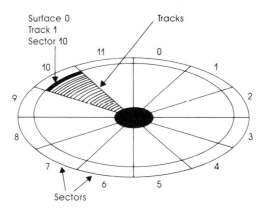

able storage space. An alternative technique uses equal-sized sectors, with different tracks having different numbers of sectors.

The sector method makes storing and retrieving information very straightforward. An address is defined by a surface number, track number, and sector number. This method is used on single disks, floppies, and some disk packs (see Figure 4.6).

**Figure 4.7**    The Cylinder Method of Disk Accessing.

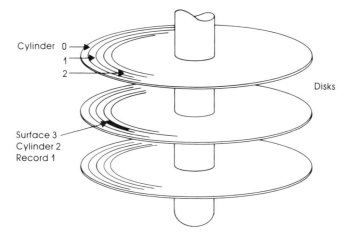

**The Cylinder Method**   The cylinder method was developed to reduce **seek time**, the time it takes to find information on a disk, using the sector method. On all disk packs, all the disks revolve around the spindle at the same rate, all the tracks are aligned so that track 101 on surface 4 is directly above track 101 on surface 6, and all the access arms move in unison. Rather than recording information track-by-track on one surface before moving on to the next surface, information is stored on a track on one disk surface, then on the same track on the next surface, and so on until every disk surface has the same track filled. Only then does the access arm move on to fill the next track out (see Figure 4.7).

The effect is to create a cylinder of stored information. Because of the positioning of all the read/write heads, a single movement of the access arms makes significantly more information available. Thus, seek time is reduced. Using the cylinder method, information can be retrieved without the constant, time-consuming motion of the access arms. An address is defined in the cylinder method by a cylinder number, a surface number, and a record number. This method is used on most hard disk systems.

## FLOPPY DISKS

A second direct access storage device is the **floppy disk**, or **diskette**, a small, single disk used mostly with microcomputers. It was first released in the early 1970s and was 8 inches in diameter. Today floppy disks are commonly available in 5 ¼-inch diameter for machines such as the Apple IIE and IBM PC and compatible models, and in 3 ½-inch diameter for machines such as the Apple Macintosh, IBM Personal System/2, and Commodore Amiga. The 5 ½-inch variety looks like a 45 RPM audio record encased in a flexible plastic envelope (see Figure 4.8). If a held by a corner and shaken slightly, it flops or bends without damaging the disk. This is how the diskettes got their name. The 3 ¼-inch disks, which store more information than larger diskettes, are in a hard plastic case and do not flop. Floppy disks are popular because they are reliable and inexpensive, costing less than half a dollar each if purchased in bulk.

## WINCHESTER DISKS

The **Winchester disk** was invented by IBM in the 1970s and is said to be named for the famed Winchester rifle. In Winchester technology, the disks, access arms, and read/write heads are sealed in an airtight container. This keeps the components free from dust, moisture, and other airborne contaminants and increases the disks' reliability. Since Winchester technology is more precise than other disk technology, storage and retrieval speeds and storage capacity are increased. Win-

**Figure 4.8**    Floppy Disks: (a) Floppy disks are mass storage devices that come in different sizes and (b) have various parts.

(a)

(b)

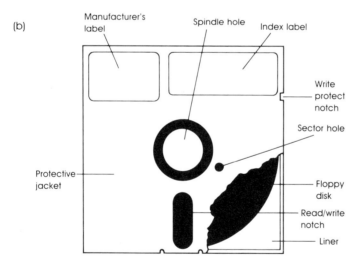

chester disks are usually fixed, which means they cannot be removed from their drives. Recent advances have developed cartridge-like Winchester disks that can be removed along with the access arms. Removable Winchester disks are very expensive, however. Winchester disks are direct access storage devices originally designed to be used with minicomputers and mainframes (14-inch disks). They have gained popularity with microcomputer users, however. Manufacturers have developed large capacity 5 1/4- and 3 1/2-inch varieties (see Figure 4.9).

**Figure 4.9**    Winchester Disks: A direct access mass storage device. Winchester disks have gained popularity with microcomputer users.

Until the early 1980s, most disk systems used removable disk packs with retractable access arms. Winchester disks had replaced most other hard disk technologies by 1987, largely because they are more reliable and less expensive to manufacture and sell.

## THE BERNOULLI BOX

A **Bernoulli Box** is an alternative to the Winchester disk drive system used on microcomputers. Released in the mid-1980s, this direct access storage medium relies on a removable hard disk technology. Each disk is enclosed in a plastic case that forms a cartridge to protect the disk from contamination. Individual Bernoulli cartridges do not have the capacity of microcomputer Winchester disks, but when a cartridge is full it can be replaced. This provides essentially unlimited disk storage. Such devices are popular in businesses where microcomputers are shared by multiple users with different software needs. In this situation, each user has a different cartridge. In addition, Bernoulli Boxes provide easy disk protection where security is important. Because of the price of removable Winchester disks, most Winchester disks in use are not removable. All the information stored on the disk is available to anyone able to turn on the machine. Bernoulli Boxes can be removed for safekeeping. Bernoulli Boxes do have drawbacks. The technology is currently much more expensive than fixed Winchester technology for microcomputers. In addition, Bernoulli Boxes are slower and store less information per disk than Winchester disks. However, each Bernoulli disk stores considerably more data than standard floppy disks.

## BACKUP

Computers break down, lose power, or their software fails to operate as expected, resulting in lost data. To reduce the risk of losing large amounts of information, **backup** or duplicate copies of the information stored in memory are periodically made. Backup is a safety measure. The more critical the information stored on a computer, the more frequently backup copies need to be made. A **full backup** is a complete copy of all the data stored in memory at a given time. A **partial backup** is a copy of those data items that have changed over a given period of time. If the computer does **crash**, or break down, the information that was stored in memory prior to the crash can be reproduced by using the backup files. Some data may be lost because backup copies are not always current, but the last and the most recent items entered are generally the easiest to recreate.

The most popular medium for backup is magnetic tape. Here its sequential nature is not a disadvantage, since everything stored on the backup tape will be needed to restore the lost information to memory. Easy storage, low cost, and reusability are added advantages.

Information stored on microcomputer disks is just as easily if not more easily lost than the mass storage devices on larger systems. Making duplicates of floppy disks and using tape or floppy disks to back up hard disks are essential if microcomputer programs and data are to be protected from unexpected losses.

## FUTURE TECHNOLOGIES

Despite the incredible speeds and storage capacities of today's computers, current hardware research is seeking to significantly increase both the storage capacity and operating speeds of computers.

### Optical Memory

Since the arrival of the home video disk in the late 1970s, significant research has gone into developing a similar technology for use with computers. A number of American, Japanese, and European companies have developed *write once* and then *read only* optical computer disks using a number of different recording techniques. One of the techniques uses lasers to create bubbles or pits on a reflecting surface that is encased in clear glass or plastic for protection. Another technique uses a laser to microscopically alter the reflectivity of the disk's surface. In all cases, the laser beam is deflected differently when pits, bubbles, or other surface changes are encountered while reading back the recorded data.

Optical computer disks are a very compact form of storage (see Figure 4.10). The entire *Encyclopedia Britannica*, for example, can be stored on a single optical disk. The storage capacity of optical computer disks is currently 100 times that of magnetic disks. Billions of characters can be stored on each recording surface. Because these disks are not reusable, their use is limited to storage of unchanging information such as data archives and some large data bases.

Clearly, reusable optical computer disks could have widespread applications. Matsushita Electric in Japan, 3M Corp. in the United States, as well as other firms have developed erasable disks. This technology is expensive, so users favor the much less expensive magnetic medium. However, a removable optical disk is included with the computer recently released by NeXT Corp. Optical technology holds the promise of revolutionizing mass storage in much the way it has revolutionized the record industry.

## Perpendicular Recording

Current disk technology stores information as magnetic dots along tracks on the surface of the disk. These magnetic dots (microscopic magnets) are oblong in

**Figure 4.10**    Optical Disks: Inexpensive optical disks such as this from Sony can hold 250,000 pages of data.

shape and are stored end to end in a straight line. Many Japanese electronics firms and some American researchers are investigating reorienting the tiny magnets so that they lie perpendicular to the recording surface (see Figure 4.11).

By turning the magnetized dots 90 degrees, 100 times more information can be stored. Finding magnetic materials that will allow data to be recorded in this form has been difficult and expensive. While current production costs are high, this variation on disk technology holds the promise of smaller, more compact magnetic disks.

## Superconductors[*]

Tomorrow's computers are likely to look quite different from the computers of today. But however they look on the outside, their internal components will be smaller and more powerful than those used today.

As circuitry becomes smaller, it becomes more and more difficult to produce. Research and development of new production techniques is ongoing. As designers pack more and more circuits onto chips in an effort to produce faster and smaller computers, they have been hindered by the nature of the circuits themselves. The heat generated by electricity passing through tiny circuits that are

**Figure 4.11**   Magnetic Storage: (a) In traditional magnetic storage, oblong dots are stored end to end. (b) In perpendicular magnetic storage, dots lie perpendicular to the recording surface, and 100 times more information can be stored.

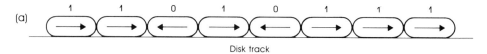

(a)

Disk track

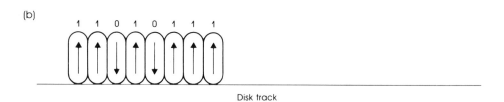

(b)

Disk track

[*] *Source:* Michael Lemonick "Superconductors," *Time,* Vol. 129, Number 19, May 11, 1987, pp. 64–75.

## *On Line*

# SUPERCONDUCTOR BREAKTHROUGHS

Researchers experimenting with superconductors have announced two breakthroughs that could revolutionize data tranmission.

Scientists from Cornell University and the University of Rochester have discovered that a thin film of high-temperature superconducting material could transmit electronic information approximately 100 times faster than today's fiber optic systems.

A high-temperature superconductor is almost a contradiction in terms. The "high" temperatures in question hover around –290 degrees Fahrenheit. But compared to traditional superconducting materials—with temperatures around –460 degrees Fahrenheit—they are "high" indeed. Using ceramic materials, high-temperature superconductors transmit electricity without resistance. Conventional electrical transmissions lose 20 percent of their energy to heat.

The Cornell/Rochester team used a thin film of superconducting material to transmit pulses as short as 10 trillionths of a second, which were accurately received. The results imply that vast amounts of computer, video, and audio information could be transmitted from one location to another in moments using this material.

This could have a major impact on television, telephone, and computer transmission.

A second important breakthrough, which could revolutionize the development of superconducting computer chips, was announced by Toshiba Corp. Toshiba researchers created a lead and yttrium-based superconducting material that had on-off switching capabilities. This reportedly had never been achieved in a superconductor.

The superconductors were used to form a tunnel junction, which is a crucial part of the manufacture of Josephson Junctions.

*Sources:* Michael D. Lemonick, "Superconductors!," *Time*, May 11, 1987, pp. 65–67. Kim McDonald, "New Transmission Properties for Superconductors Discovered," *The Chronicle of Higher Education*, Oct. 14, 1987, p. A5. "Breakthrough Could Create Ultra-Fast Chips," *High Technology Business*, Oct., 1988, p. 49.

packed too closely together can damage the microscopic components and melt circuits.

In the early 1980s, researchers at IBM began investigating building fast, compact memory using an electronic "switch" invented by British Nobel Prize winner Brian Josephson. Josephson's electronic switch, called the **Josephson Junction**, changes states from 0 to 1 at speeds at least 10 times faster than currently used devices. Until the 1980s, these speeds could only be achieved if the circuits were cooled to temperatures approaching absolute zero (–459 degrees Farenheit). At this temperature **superconduction** occurs, in which the resistance and therefore the heat usually associated with the flow of electricity are virtually eliminated. To produce these low temperatures for superconductivity, the junction must be supercooled by surrounding it with liquid helium.

In 1987, scientists experimenting with ceramic compounds rather than metallic alloys found that superconduction could be produced at higher and higher temperatures (98 degrees Kelvin or –283 degrees Farenheit or higher). At these temperatures, superconductive devices become feasible because liquid nitrogen can replace liquid helium. Liquid nitrogen is very inexpensive and long lasting. Superconductivity-related effects that may apply to computers have been reported at temperatures as high as 240 degrees Kelvin or the relatively warm –27 degrees Farenheit.

While IBM discontinued its Josephson Junction project in 1983, a number of its key physicists have left IBM to form an independent company developing and marketing Josephson Junction products.

Superconducting switches have great potential for computers. Using such technology, chip density would no longer be limited by self-generated heat, and speed would increase dramatically. Other memory devices are also possible. Despite recent advances in superconductivity research, computers using this technology are not part of the foreseeable future.

## SUMMARY

Information is stored in the computer's memory in the form of files. Locating information in a sequentially organized file requires that the entire file be searched from the beginning until the information is found. Direct access file organization uniquely addresses information so that it can be easily located without having to examine other data. Indexed file organization uses features from both sequential and direct access organization. Files are sequentially stored and information is addressed for easy access.

The oldest form of mass storage is the computer card, on which characters are stored in the form of holes punched in paper cards. Paper tape stores characters as holes punched in a continuous one-inch strip of paper.

Magnetic tape stores information as magnetized dots along the surface of the tape. Coded information forms logical records that are processed as a unit. To increase the storage capacity of the tape, logical records are combined into blocks or physical records. Magnetic tape is highly portable, inexpensive, and reusable but must be processed sequentially.

A magnetic disk is a flat platter with magnetized dots storing information on tracks. Records are individually addressed for easy access. Addresses can be defined using sectors or cylinders. Floppy disks are used predominantly on microcomputers. A Winchester disk is a device containing disks and access hardware sealed in a container to protect the contents from damage by airborne contaminants. A Bernoulli Box is a replaceable hard disk device used on microcomputers.

Backup is a safety technique whereby stored data is duplicated either on magnetic tapes or floppy disks.

Current research on memory devices is focusing on increased processing speeds and storage capacity. Optical computer memory uses laser optics to store and retrieve information. Perpendicular recording realigns the magnetized dots of stored information on disks. Superconductor research hopes to design memory devices that are more compact and process at faster speeds using the nonresistance properties of superconducting materials.

## Key Words

As an extra review of the chapter, try defining the following terms. If you have trouble with any of them, refer to the page number listed.

access arms  *(96)*
addressable  *(97)*
backup  *(102)*
Bernoulli Box  *(101)*
computer (punched) card  *(91)*
crash  *(102)*
disk pack  *(95)*
fields  *(90)*
files  *(90)*
floppy disk (diskette)  *(99)*
full backup  *(102)*
interblock gap (IBG)  *(95)*
interrecord gap (IRG)  *(93)*

Josephson Junction  *(105)*
logical records  *(93)*
magnetic (hard) disk  *(95)*
magnetic tape  *(93)*
partial backup  *(102)*
physical record (block)  *(93)*
punched paper tape  *(92)*
read/write head  *(96)*
records  *(90)*
seek time  *(99)*
superconduction  *(105)*
Winchester disk  *(99)*

## Test Your Knowledge

1. What is a computer file?

2. Briefly identify the differences between sequential, direct access, and indexed file organization.

3. How was information stored on punched cards?

4. List the three types of magnetic tape.

5. What is the difference between logical and physical records on magnetic tape?

6. Briefly explain how data is stored on magnetic tape.

7. Why is it often necessary to block data on magnetic tape?

8. What is a disk pack?

9. Briefly explain how data is stored on magnetic disks.

10. Define *addressable*.

11. How is an address defined using the sector method of disk addressing?

12. How is an address defined using the cylinder method of disk addressing?

13. How does a floppy disk differ from a hard disk?

14. What are the advantages of Winchester disks over disk packs with retractable access arms?

15. What is a Bernoulli Box? How does this system provide virtually unlimited storage?

16. Why is backup necessary on computer systems?

17. What is the difference between a full and a partial backup?

18. What are the advantages of laser disk technology over magnetic disks?

19. How does perpendicular storage of data on magnetic disks differ from the standard storage techniques?

20. Why are superconductors of interest to computer memory designers?

---

## Expand Your Knowledge

1. Identify 15 applications areas (excluding those listed in the text) where sequential, direct access, and indexed file organization would be appropriate (five for each). For example, direct access files are used for airline reservations.

2. Computers such as the Apple Macintosh and the IBM Personal System/2 use 3 ½-inch floppy disks. Why do you think these two companies switched from the very popular 5 ¼ variety? What are the advantages and disadvantages, if any, of 3 ½-inch floppies over the larger variety?

3. Go to your local computer store and compare the prices and capacities of Winchester disks for microcomputers with Bernoulli Box technology. If you could purchase either one, which would you buy? Why?

4. Write a brief paper on backing up a hard disk on a microcomputer. Include why such backups are necessary, how they are performed, and information about the different media that can be used for such backups.

5. Write a brief paper on one application of superconductivity to areas outside of computing.

6. What is cellular mass storage? How does it differ from other forms of magnetic storage? What are its advantages and its disadvantages?

# 5

# Input and Output

## Chapter Outline

Dedicated Input Devices
Keyboards • Input Alternatives (Joystick; Mouse; Light Pen; Digitizer; Touch Screen; Touch Tablet)

Dedicated Output Devices
Soft Copy: Monitors • Hard Copy: Printers and Plotters (Impact Printers; Non-Impact Printers; Plotters)

The Terminal: An Input/Output Device

Specialized Technologies
The Voice as Input • Voice Synthesis as Output • Print Recognition Technology (Optical Mark Reading; Magnetic Ink Character Recognition; Optical Character Recognition)

Combination Systems
The Automated Cash Register • Automated Teller Machines • The Automated Post Office

Computers are all around us. We use them so often in our daily lives that we may take them for granted. The way we purchase our groceries and do our banking is heavily influenced by computers. Even our mail is increasingly processed by machine. However, we often confuse the computer with the devices we've created to communicate with it. These devices are designed to make working with computers more natural and comfortable. Input and output devices often are responsible for much of the computer's mystique.

The hardware devices attached to a computer are usually referred to as **peripherals** or **peripheral devices**. This connected but external equipment includes input, output, and mass storage devices. Mass storage devices were discussed in detail in Chapter 4, so we will focus here on the other devices we attach to computers. Many peripherals are dedicated to one function or another. However, modern peripherals are often combination devices that may contain input, output, and often memory components at the same time (see Figure 5.1).

After studying this chapter, you will be able to:

- Understand what peripherals are.
- Identify dedicated input or output devices.
- Discuss various keyboard alternatives.
- Understand the major types and uses of computer monitors.
- Distingush impact printers from non-impact printers.
- Describe different types of terminals.
- Understand voice technology and print recognition devices.
- Appreciate the role of input and output devices in assisting the handicapped.
- Discuss common combination systems used by stores, banks, and the Postal Service.

## DEDICATED INPUT DEVICES

In Chapter 1, we defined *input* as the data entered into the computer for processing. This can be either the intial, raw data gathered or it can be the result of previous processing. *Output* was defined as the information, or result of computer processing. An **input device** is computer hardware that transmits data to the computer. An **output device** is computer hardware that communicates the results of computer operations. A *dedicated* device can be used for only one purpose. People use both input and output devices to communicate with computers.

**Figure 5.1**     Computer Peripherals: Modern peripherals often combine input, output, and memory components.

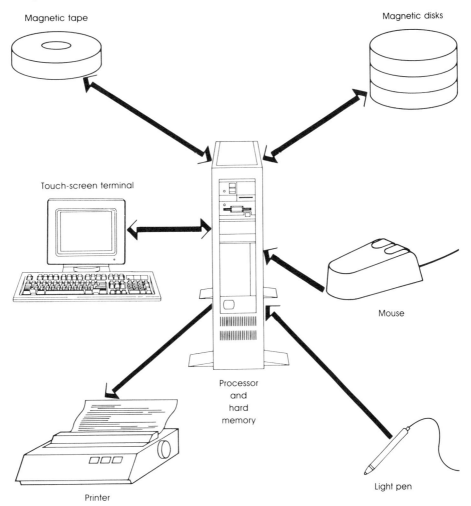

Magnetic tape

Magnetic disks

Touch-screen terminal

Mouse

Processor
and
hard
memory

Light pen

Printer

## Keyboards

Modern keyboards are designed to suit the changing needs of users. Despite an increasing array of alternative input devices, the **keyboard** continues to be the most commonly used means of entering data and instructions into a computer system.

While keyboard layouts differ somewhat from manufacturer to manufacturer, they all have the same basic features (see Figure 5.2). Most keyboards contain:

**Figure 5.2**

Modern Keyboards: Although differing somewhat from one manufacturer to another, modern keyboards such as the (a) IBM PC/enhanced keyboard, the (b) Digital VT240, and the (c) Macintosh Plus all have the same basic features.

(a)

(b)

(c)

1. *The standard typewriter keys.* These keys include a number line at the top and the necessary shift keys for uppercase and lowercase letters.

2. *A numeric keypad.* This resembles the number layout on a hand calculator. Number pads make entering large amounts of numeric data fast and easy.

3. *Special keys.* These keys include CTRL, ESC, BREAK, and others, which are required to communicate with the computer. Keyboards on intelligent terminals, personal computers, and workstations have additional keys, called **function keys**, that can be programmed through the built-in microprocessor to perform specific tasks independent of the main computer.

4. *Arrow keys.* These keys control the cursor. On a typewriter, the typehead moves across each line as we type. A marker indicates the position of the next character to be typed. A cursor on a computer screen functions in the same way. The **cursor** is usually a flashing light, most often in the shape of a rectangle, underscore, or an arrow, that indicates on the screen where the next character will appear.

The keyboard is a wonderfully flexible device for entering data, doing word processing, writing programs, and performing an incredibly long list of other tasks. However, the use of a keyboard as an input device calls for several assumptions about the person who will use the computer. First, a keyboard is used most effectively by a person who is a good typist. The hunt and peck system of typing ("I know the key is out there—I just have to find it!") is frustrating and tedious. In recognition of this, typing-tutor software is available on most personal computers. Second, a keyboard can be used only by someone who is *willing* to type. Recent surveys have shown that many executives resist using a computer. Unfortunately, lack of keyboard skills is only part of the problem. Many executives are uncomfortable typing information into a computer. They consider this a clerical task. As scheduling and decision-aiding programs have become available, this has been changing. Managers are becoming convinced by the considerable evidence available that efficiency and productivity will improve through their use of these machines.

## Input Alternatives

In an effort to make computers easier for everyone to use, a number of keyboard alternatives and enhancements have been developed. Some, such as the light pen and graphics tablet, have been available for specialized use for some time. Yet even these devices have found new uses. Let's turn to some common input alternatives, some of which will be discussed again in Chapter 13 (Computer Graphics).

**Joystick**   The most common keyboard alternative, the **joystick**, is used almost exclusively with home computers and is an integral part of many computer games. A joystick consists of a verticle rod set into a base. The rod, or stick, can easily be moved from side to side and up and down (see Figure 5.3). The cursor or some image replacing the cursor duplicates the rod's motion on the screen. While the joystick is usually used to manipulate the cursor, it can be used to initiate simple requests by pressing the *fire* button.

**Mouse**    In some ways the **mouse** is a joystick's more sophisticated cousin. A mouse is a palm-sized pointing device. It is joined to the computer by a thin, usually coiled cable (see Figure 5.4).

Its underside usually contains a ball designed to roll easily over a smooth, flat surface. The movement of the mouse on a desktop is reflected in the movement of the cursor on the computer screen. On the top of the mouse are one or more buttons. By using the mouse to move the cursor to a specific position and then depressing a button, the user can issue simple commands and make selections among options displayed on the screen.

The mouse was invented as part of a Stanford University research project and was created by Xerox. It became popular with the development of the Apple Macintosh. Looking at this small fast-moving object with a curly tail, it's easy to see how this device got its name.

**Figure 5.3**    The Joystick: Used primarily with home computers, the joystick is the most common keyboard alternative.

**Figure 5.4**    The Mouse: (a) The Macintosh mouse and (b) Microsoft's mouse, which is used with the IBM PC and IBM Personal System 2, are used to issue simple commands and select options.

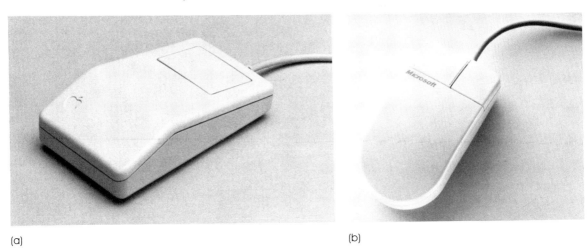

(a)                                                                                    (b)

**Light Pen**    Another very convenient way to interact with a computer is to write or draw directly onto the screen. A **light pen** is a hand-held, pen-like instrument with a light-sensitive point. Like the mouse, it is connected to the computer by a narrow cable. Since the tip of the light pen is much smaller than a finger, it can be used to draw fine lines directly on specially designed monitors (see Figure 5.5). Light pens have been used for some time in computer-aided design and manufacturing (CAD/CAM). Light pens can also be used with a special keypad that allows the designer to change the color and thickness of sketched lines. Lines can be erased and diagrams can be reduced or enlarged in size. Associated software can transform irregular hand-drawn lines into straight lines, alter the angle formed by two lines, and assist the designer in a variety of other ways.

**Digitizer**    Another type of electronic drawing makes use of a **digitizer**, often called a **graphics tablet**. The tablet's surface contains very thin wires etched in a grid pattern. The tablet is connected to the computer by a cable, and a special pen is attached to the tablet (see Figure 5.6). Paper is placed on top of the tablet. As the pen moves across the paper, the sketch is immediately translated into electronic signals and simultaneously appears on the monitor screen. Software then can be used to adjust and manipulate the sketch. Erasures and changes can be made quickly and precisely.

Until the early 1980s, light pens and their associated technology were very expensive, which restricted their use to industrial design. Now, however, some light pens and the software to run them can be purchased for about $100 or even less. They are available for many home and personal computers, including

**Figure 5.5**    Light Pens: Hand-held drawing devices, light pens are commonly used in computer-aided design.

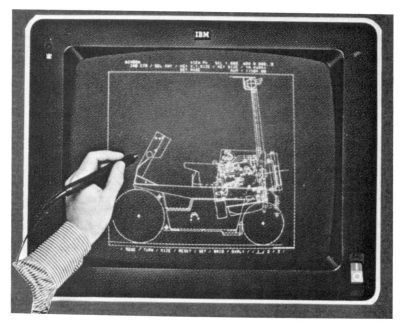

**Figure 5.6**    Digitizer: An electronic drawing device such as this one from Applicon, the digitizer transfers free-form drawings onto the computer screen.

IBM, Apple, Commodore, and Atari. Anyone who can hold a pen and wants to draw can now do so on a microcomputer.

**Touch Screen**    If pointing with a mouse makes computers easier to use, what could be more natural than pointing with your finger? This idea has been incorporated directly into a computer screen in the form of a **touch screen**. A touch screen allows a person to make choices or activate commands simply by putting a finger or stylus on an item displayed on the screen (see Figure 5.7).

---

**Figure 5.7**    The Touch Screen: Touch screens can be used in (a) business applications and (b) by children.

(a)

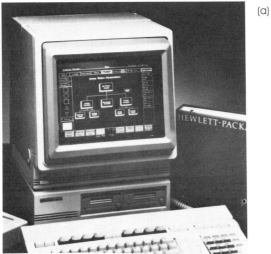

(b)

There are a number of technologies that make touch screens possible. The most common is based on crisscrossing beams of infrared light. When the screen is touched, the infrared light beams are interrupted. The place on the screen where the interruption occurred is registered by light-sensitive receptors and transmitted to the CPU. This is the same principle as the photo-electric eye widely used in security systems and on automatic door-opening mechanisms in stores and airports.

Another common touch-screen design uses a grid of pressure-sensitive electrodes etched into a thin plastic sheet coating the surface of a computer monitor. The electrodes register the position being touched and transmit the information to the CPU. This is similar to the buttons used in many elevators.

Regardless of the technology used, all the devices enable the user to issue computer commands by touching the screen with a finger. Major software packages, including WordStar, have been rewritten to take advantage of touch screens.

Touch screens are well adapted to industries where data are collected so quickly that there is no time to type in information (see Figure 5.8). For example,

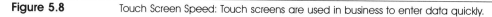

**Figure 5.8**    Touch Screen Speed: Touch screens are used in business to enter data quickly.

traders on the American Stock Exchange in New York can use touch-sensitive terminals to make transactions. Similarly, Chemical Bank's foreign currency traders use touch screens to trade the world's currencies.

Touch screens have also become a popular means of providing information to tourists. In Walt Disney's EPCOT Center in Florida, information directories use terminals with color-graphic touch screens. Visitors can find out about events, check restaurant menus, and even ask directions by touching appropriate entries on information screens scattered around the park. Similar touch screen directories of events and services are being used by large hotel chains and some Manhattan office buildings. The city of Toronto, Canada, has placed such touch-sensitive directories throughout the city to provide visitors with information.

**Touch Tablet**    Koala Technologies Corp. has developed a **touch tablet** called the KoalaPad, which can be used with most home and personal computers. This device features a square surface or pad that is 4 ½ inches on a side connected to the computer by a cable (see Figure 5.9). Like a mouse, it has buttons and can be

**Figure 5.9**        Touch Pads: The KoalaPad acts as a mouse, a touch device, or a graphics tablet.

used as a pointing device. The pad or screen can also act as a touch device, on which a finger can select software instructions, or as a graphics tablet that accepts freehand color drawings and drawings based on predefined objects such as lines, squares, and circles. The KoalaPad has made computers accessible to handicapped people with limited movement. The cable attaching it to the computer makes it possible to move the KoalaPad to the handicapped user. Its large size, compared to that of a mouse, and its touch technology make it easy to manipulate for those with restricted physical mobility.

## DEDICATED OUTPUT DEVICES

Computer output comes in many forms. The results of computer processing can be stored in memory in machine-readable form. When needed, they can be displayed as words, graphs, or pictures on a computer screen. They can be spoken with an increasingly human-sounding computer voice or they can be printed on paper. A copy of a letter on a video screen is temporary. You can read it but it can disappear in a flash. Output in temporary form is often called **soft copy**. Computer output that is printed on paper is often called **hard copy**.

### Soft Copy: Monitors

The screen or monitor connected to a computer is sometimes called a **CRT**. This stands for **cathode ray tube**, which is a television-like screen. CRTs most commonly are *monocromatic*; that is, they display a single color against a darker background. The least-expensive models display white characters on a gray background or green characters against a black or dark gray background. Amber monitors, while more expensive than the standard styles, are increasingly popular. Many users find that these yellow/orange characters on a dark gray background cause less eyestrain and fatigue. Monochromatic monitors are best suited for displaying text and very simple graphs.

CRTs can also display color. *Color graphics* (more correctly *multi-color*) monitors are best suited for the display of graphic elements such as graphs and drawings. Today, color monitors cost only a few hundred dollars more than monochromatic monitors. People see in color, and color graphics monitors make communicating with computers seem more natural. Colored diagrams, charts, and games are far more popular and attention getting than similar displays containing only two colors. As the cost of color monitors has decreased, their popularity in business, education, and the home has risen dramatically.

Until the early 1980s, color graphics monitors were used almost exclusively by engineers and architects to create and display plans and drawings. Today's color graphics monitors and associated software are used in computer-aided design (CAD) and computer-aided manufacturing (CAM). These systems, which will be discussed in Chapter 13, can display a drawing or three-dimensional model and can rotate the model to show different perspectives of the design. The model can also be sliced so that cross sections of the original image can be presented for further examination.

Such advanced graphics systems have other uses as well. By combining color graphics monitors with X-ray (CAT scans) and Magnetic Resonance Imaging (MRI) scanners, doctors can graphically display parts of a patient's body, including the brain and spinal cord, in three-dimensional, computer-enhanced images (see Figure 5.10). These scanners can take pictures at different angles and rotate them on the screen for more careful examination from different angles and perspectives. Using these systems helps doctors make accurate diagnoses without difficult and dangerous exploratory surgery.

Today, computer-generated color graphics are not limited to use by specialists. The cost of both computer hardware and software has decreased dramatically in the last 10 years. Although color graphics monitors are more expensive than monochromatic monitors and require additional special electronics, today they are low enough in price that individuals, small businesses, and organizations can afford them. Color graphics are commonly used in business and in computer games.

Programs such as Lotus 1-2-3, Symphony, MacGraph, and Chart-Master are used in business to design color graphs, maps, and pictures. These graphics features are frequently used along with spoken or printed words. In this way, trends can often be spotted and data can be compared very rapidly. This improves both the accuracy and the speed of decision making.

Video arcade-style and learning games are among the most popular form of computerized entertainment. Color and black-and-white television sets are often used as monitors for home computers, but increasing numbers of inexpensive color graphics monitors are being purchased for use with computer games. The color graphics monitors designed for use with home and personal computers give a clearer picture from a computer program than does a television set doing double duty. In addition, with the purchase of a separate monitor, the television can be returned to the family room or living room and used as it was intended while other family members play computer games.

## Hard Copy: Printers and Plotters

You can read printed information as it comes out of the computer system the next day and several weeks, months, or years later without being connected to a computer. The printed word holds a unique place in our world. It enables us to keep a permanent record of our thoughts, ideas, and history. It is not transient, it has staying power.

Printers, which will be discussed again in Chapter 13, are important output devices in most computer systems. There are two types of printers: impact and non-impact.

**Figure 5.10**    Use of Color Monitors: Today, color monitors are often used in (a) computer-aided design and manufacturing and (b) magnetic resource imaging, which graphically displays parts of a patient's body.

(a)

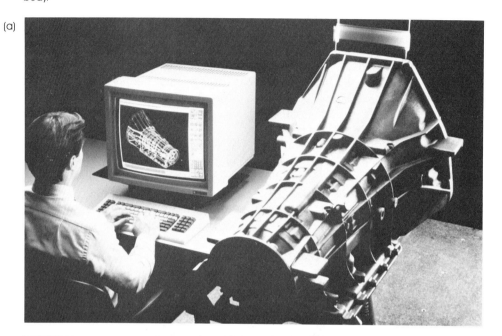

(b)

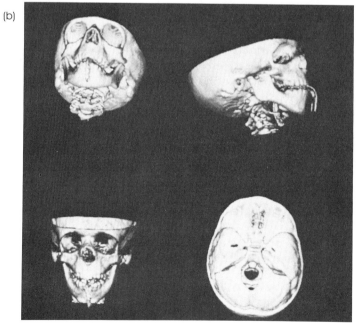

**Impact Printers**   All **impact printers** work the same way. Characters are formed on paper by tiny hammers striking against an inked ribbon to create an inked impression on the paper. Impact printer technology is molded on the familiar print methods of the typewriter.

A **letter-quality printer** is modeled directly after a typewriter. Each strike of a hammer prints a completely formed character on paper. Letter-quality characters are indistinguishable from those formed by an electric typewriter. Just as with typewriters, a variety of striking mechanisms exist in letter-quality printers, among them print balls, thimbles, and daisy wheels. Daisy wheel printers are among the most common (see Figure 5.11). A **daisy wheel** resembles closely spaced spokes on a bicycle tire. On the outer edge of each spoke (sometimes called a petal; hence, daisy) is a single character. All the spokes taken together form a circle or wheel. As the hammer strikes each spoke against the inked ribbon, an entire character is transferred through the ribbon to the paper behind it.

---

**Figure 5.11**      Daisy Wheel Printers: Consisting of a rotating wheel with a set of spokes, daisy wheel printers such as this Panasonic KX-P3131 work by striking an inked ribbon.

The characters typed may be of many kinds. They are not limited to the English alphabet. Various languages and type designes are available. There are also Braille printers, which print the raised dots of Braille in place of the inked impact characters used on other impact printers. By this simple change, hard copy output is readable by the visually handicapped.

Letter-quality printers, like the typewriters they mimic, print clearly but slowly. The fastest can produce no more than 60 characters per second. Although this is slower than other printers, it is faster than what all but the most exceptional typists can produce.

The most popular impact printers are **dot matrix printers**. Their popularity over letter-quality printers stems from their lower cost, faster speed, and versatility. Dot matrix printers are used to produce not only characters, but graphs, charts, and even pictures. Each character typed consists of a pattern of dots. Characters are stored in the computer's memory as a pattern of dots.

The printhead (similar to the hammer in letter-quality printers) contains several rows of tiny pins. As instructions for each character pattern are sent from memory to the printer, the appropriate pins strike an inked ribbon. The pins push the ribbon against the paper to form the dots that make up the character, as Figure 5.12 indicates. Since there are few moving parts, dot matrix printers can type very quickly. The fastest approaches 1000 characters per second. Since each character is formed in memory, a wide range of print sizes, shapes, and fonts can be easily created by programming the computer. Letter-quality printers, on the other hand, are restricted to the characters that can fit on one daisy wheel, print ball, or thimble (a print element). To change type sizes and styles, it is usually necessary to change to a different print element.

Many dot matrix printers are used to print computer graphics as well as standard characters (see Figure 5.13). Essentially, a pattern formed on a video screen is converted into a pattern of dots that is transferred piece by piece to the printer. With the use of multicolored ribbons, graphics can be printed in color by some printers.

---

**Figure 5.12**    Producing a Dot Matrix Character: A series of pins in the printhead strike the paper from left to right to form a character.

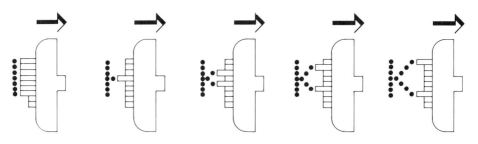

**Figure 5.13**    Dot Matrix Printer: Versatile and fast, dot matrix printers such as this Epson LQ-2550 are the most popular impact printers.

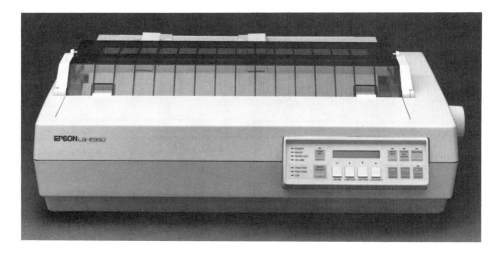

Given the speed and versatility of dot matrix printers, letter-quality printers might seem unnecessary. However, dot matrix type is not as clear as letter-quality type and does not present as professional an image. Dot matrix printers are often used for preliminary drafts of reports and papers, while letter-quality printers are used for final copies or whenever a "finished" look is required.

Unlike other impact printers, **line printers** appear to type an entire line of output at once (see Figure 5.14). Duplicate character sets and multiple hammers are used to strike the paper and ribbon. While fast, line printers are very noisy, often requiring sound-proofing. In addition the print may lack clarity. Although high-speed, impact line printers are still a fixture in many organizations, they are likely to be replaced by high-speed non-impact printers.

**Non-Impact Printers**    A number of alternative printer technologies have been developed that print with a minimum of noise. All **non-impact printers** use a dot matrix technology whereby the characters are sent from memory as a set of dots. No hammers strike the paper, however. Non-impact printers are quiet for this reason.

**Thermal printers** transfer their character dot patterns to special heat-sensitive paper. When character patterns are sent from memory to the printhead, tiny wires are heated. These wires react chemically with special paper, causing the dot pattern for the character to appear. Chemically based **electrostatic printers** work essentially the same way. An electric charge rather than heat activates chemically treated paper. Thermal and electrostatic printers are slow and charac-

**Figure 5.14**    Line Printers: Line printers such as this IBM 4245 type an entire line at a time, but they are noisy and may lack clarity.

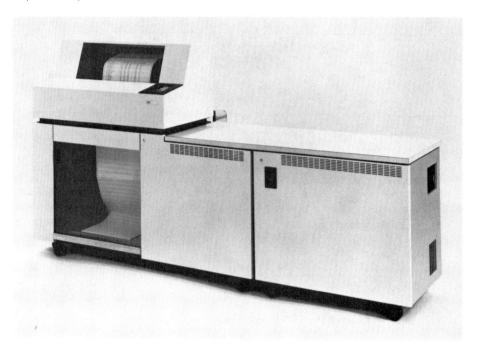

ters lack clarity. While such printers are inexpensive to purchase, the special paper they require is quite expensive. In their defense, they are very light, often portable, and very quiet.

Like thermal printers, **inkjet printers** are quiet. However, their print is clearer than that of thermal printers and they are much faster. In these printers, character patterns are sent from memory and tiny dots of ink are squirted on the surface of the paper to form each character. Inkjet characters contain more dots than other dot matrix characters, making them clearer and easier to read. Inkjet technology is most useful for reproducing color graphics. Printheads containing multiple jets with different color inks produce clear, colorful pages (see Figure 5.15).

**Laser printers** are the fastest printers currently available. They combine lasers with the ink-transfer technology used in many photocopy machines. As with other printers that use dot matrix technology, the characters are transferred from memory. However, the dot density of a laser printer is more than 300 dots per inch, which produces a print indistinguishable from letter quality to the naked eye (see Figure 5.16). In the laser printer, the character pattern sent from

**Figure 5.15**    Inkjet Printers: Clear and quiet, inkjet printers such as this Hewlett-Packard Paintjet form characters by squirting tiny dots of ink onto paper.

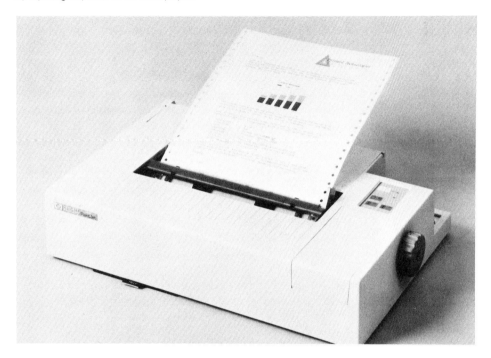

**Figure 5.16**    The Dot Matrix Versus the Laser Printer.

Impact dot matrix output

```
                    INTRODUCTION TO VAX/VMS


    1.  OVERVIEW


    The VAXcluster computers provide an interactive, user-friendly
    environment for creating and editing files, executing programs,
    and managing data.  An extensive help facility is available to
    users; this facility can be accessed by typing the word HELP.
```

Laser output

```
                    INTRODUCTION TO VAX/VMS


    1.  OVERVIEW


    The  VAXcluster computers provide an  interactive,  user-friendly
    environment  for creating and editing files, executing  programs,
    and  managing data.  An extensive help facility is  available  to
    users; this facility can be accessed by typing the word HELP.
```

memory controls the laser, a special type of light beam. The pulsing laser, reflecting the character pattern, passes over an electrically charged drum. The laser neutralizes the drum's charge wherever it touches. When an entire page of information has been transferred to the drum, the drum is coated with a special dry ink that sticks only to the charged spots. Then the drum rolls the full page image onto the paper. Laser printers are quiet and have the ability to print characters of varying sizes and shapes. Since they print entire pages at once, they are very fast. Until recently, laser printers were very expensive. This restricted their use. However, some manufacturers have adapted the replaceable plastic drum, now common on most photocopiers. This advance has dramatically reduced prices and made laser printers easier to keep in good working order. For example, Hewlett-Packard's HP-Laser Jet printer, the size of a desktop copier, can be purchased for less than $2000. Apple's LaserWriter printer, which sells for approximately $2500, can replicate the screen graphics and character shapes produced by the Macintosh.

While laser printers are still more costly than impact printers, their use in industry is increasing rapidly where high-quality graphics and speed are considerations (see Figure 5.17).

**Plotters** Hard-copy output is not limited to words and characters. A **plotter** is an output device specifically designed to reproduce computer graphics. Plotters

**Figure 5.17**    Laser Printers: High-quality graphics can be produced by laser printers such as this Hewlett-Packard Laserjet Series II, which makes use of lasers and electronically charged drums.

have produced high-quality graphs, charts, maps, and blueprints for almost 25 years (see Chapter 13). Using shading and three-dimensional drawing techniques, they can duplicate the most detailed CAD/CAM drawings.

On a plotter, ink-filled pens move across paper to create the graph, chart, or illustration stored in the computer's memory. To produce multicolor drawings, plotters use multiple pens, each containing a different color ink. Most plotters are designed for use with paper of varying dimensions, allowing them to produce drawings of different sizes. The hard-copy output of many plotters is not limited to paper. Drawings can be made directly on transparencies and other materials (see Figure 5.18).

**Figure 5.18**     Plotters: Specifically designed to produce graphics, plotters such as Hewlett-Packard's DraftPro move pens across paper or other materials to produce high-quality graphs, charts, maps, and blueprints.

While dot matrix impact printers can be used to reproduce such drawings, the results lack clarity. Laser-printed graphic output, while clear, is limited to standard letter or legal size paper and black-on-white output.

## THE TERMINAL: AN INPUT/OUTPUT DEVICE

Not too long ago, there seemed to be a clear distinction between input and output. Input consisted of stacks of computer cards, while output was reams of paper. But this distinction is no longer valid. With a few exceptions, both input and output can be accomplished through the same medium. Even the traditional punched cards could be produced as output if the results of one program were then to be used as raw data for another program. Magnetic tape and disks can contain raw data, programs, and results.

As another example, a keyboard and the screen associated with it can mistakenly be considered an input device. We use them to enter data or a program, or to start a game. However, when we run our game or program, the results are often directed back to the screen. As we work at a terminal, it acts as both an input and output device at different stages of the process. In all stages however, the terminal serves as a medium of communication between people and the computer.

The most common means of communicating with a computer is with a **video display terminal**, or **VDT**. In its most standard form, a video display terminal consists of a keyboard attached to a screen or monitor, as Figure 5.19 shows. A person using a terminal is in two-way communication with the computer. Data or a program are entered at the terminal keyboard, and some kind of information is returned on the terminal monitor.

Some terminals are classified as "dumb," while others are said to be "intelligent." A **dumb terminal** is not a terminal used by an inexperienced user. It is a terminal that can be used only for entering data or viewing output. It contains no memory of its own. A dumb terminal must always be connected to a large computer. For example, terminals used to make airline reservations at airports or in travel agencies are dumb terminals. If the computer to which a terminal is connected is not operating, the terminal cannot be used. If data are entered incorrectly at the dumb terminal, they will be transmitted incorrectly. The dumb terminal is a direct communication link with the computer.

An **intelligent terminal** contains its own built-in microprocessor. As a result, it is capable of performing limited processing tasks independent of the computer to which it is attached. Intelligent terminals often have expanded editing capabilities, so the user can manipulate and double check the data before they are sent to the computer (see Figure 5.20).

Increasingly, desktop machines such as personal computers and workstations, which were discussed in Chapter 1, are being used as intelligent termi-

**Figure 5.19**    The Video Display Terminal: Most commonly, a video display terminal consists of a keyboard attached to a screen or monitor. This is a Burroughs model.

**Figure 5.20**    Intelligent Terminals: This Sun workstation can work independently and has expanded capabilities.

nals in offices. These desktop computers are connected or networked to larger computers. They can function as independent machines where data and programs can be edited, organized, and prepared directly. By using special communications software, they can also transfer and receive information, programs, and instructions from a central or larger computer (often called the *main computer*). Files that are transmitted as a unit to a main computer are **uploaded**. Files also can be **downloaded**, or transmitted from the main computer to the desktop machine. Of course, a personal computer or workstation connected to a larger computer can act as a dumb terminal as well, allowing for simple two-way communication without any processing. Using desktop computers to replace terminals has a number of advantages:

- Expanded editing and checking capabilities are available.
- Some processing can be done on the data before they are transmitted to the main computer.
- Data and programs can be entered into the desktop computer for later transmission to the central or main computer.
- Graphics and color become affordable and available, improving tools for analysis and reflecting the fact that people see the world in color.

Using desktop computers, large amounts of data can be assembled and organized over a period of time and transmitted to the main computer all at once. Or data and programs can be entered into the personal computer or workstation even when the main computer is unavailable.

Of course, there are disadvantages as well. Desktop computers are more expensive than most terminals. If the stand-alone processing properties of these machines are not required, then a traditional terminal is a more economical medium for human-to-computer communication.

The capabilities of terminals and desktop machines are continually being improved by manufacturers in an attempt to meet the changing needs of users. Some of these impovements include the use of color monitors, while others involve keyboards designed for easy, comfortable use.

## SPECIALIZED TECHNOLOGIES

Most human communication is oral. We teach our language, our history, even our values and morals by talking to one another. While the vast stores of printed information found in libraries and computer data bases are designed to help us to remember and record our world for the future, we communicate almost entirely through speech. The future will place at least as much value as the past on the spoken word, perhaps more.

# On Line

## ARE VDTS A HEALTH THREAT?

Over the last several years, computers have caused tremendous change in our offices. This change has come with a human cost, however.

Office workers regularly complain that video display terminals (VDTs), including microcomputer screens, cause problems ranging from eyestrain, to finger, arm, and shoulder pain, to chronic backaches. Some insist that VDTs cause cataracts and miscarriages. Over the last few years, researchers have been investigating the health effects of VDTs. Studies have been inconclusive, however. Eyestrain, general body aches, and back strain have been documented, but research indicates that poorly designed physical work environments, including incorrect desk height, poor chair design, poor lighting, and glare are the culprits, not VDTs.

Many workers spend large portions of the day sitting in front of a VDT in the same hunched position. Electronic mail and data bases have eliminated the need to move around. This and the lack of social interaction contributes to stress. To make matters worse, some VDT workers are electronically monitored. Every keystroke entered can be counted by the computer and used as a measure of productivity. One study discovered that some VDT operators experienced higher stress levels than air-traffic controllers because of this.

Properly designed offices and humane managers can eliminate these short-term effects. The long-term health effects of VDTs, if any, are unknown. Since 1983, the National Institute for Occupational Safety and Health (NIOSH) has been investigating reports of "cluster-miscarriages"

among groups of women who are heavy VDT users. Researchers seeking to clarify the situation have produced confusing results. A highly respected California study performed on 1,583 women by Kaiser Permanent Medical Care Program of Oakland, California, found that pregnant *managers* who spend half their week using VDTs were 70 percent *less* likely to have a miscarriage than their peer control group. On the other hand, Kaiser also found that *clerical* workers who spend 20 hours or more per week using VDTs had a 140 percent *higher* risk of miscarriage. These results clearly indicate that something is happening. Unfortunately, no one knows what.

Some workers fear that the radiation emitted from VDTs is harmful. However, higher levels of the same type of radiation are emitted from most household appliances, including irons, hair dryers, and televisions. This radiation is different from X-rays. In response to radiation fears, a Massachusetts firm has developed a radiation-free video monitor. While researchers have found no link between VDT radiation and reported health problems, concerns and health problems among workers using VDTs persist.

*Sources*: David Kirkpatrick, "How Safe Are Video Terminals?," *Fortune*, August 29, 1988, pp. 66–69. Mark A. Pinsky, "VDT Radiation," *The Nation*, January 9/16, 1989, p. 41. John Wilke, "Needham Firm Claims to Build Radiation-Free Computer Screen," *Boston Globe*, March 29, 1989, pp. 61–62.

All of the devices we have been discussing so far have been designed to make it easier for people to communicate with computers. We have gone from typing words, to pointing to printed words and symbols, to actually touching the computer screen. Increasingly, our communications with the computer have become more and more natural. The next step is to make these communications even more human.

### The Voice as Input

For many years, research has been devoted to finding ways for us to talk directly to our computers and for them to talk back to us. The ability of a computer to understand spoken information and instructions is known as **speech recognition**. Speech recognition devices are of two kinds: (1) devices that understand only specific voices and (2) devices that understand natural language as spoken by anyone (see Figure 5.21).

Research and development of devices in the first category have been fruitful. A human  voice, like a fingerprint, is unique to each individual. A word or phrase spoken by one person cannot be exactly duplicated by anyone else.  Our individual speech and sound patterns are unique, as Figure 5.22 indicates. As a result, the electronic signals produced by a person speaking into a microphone are unique. Voice recognition systems based on the voices of specific individuals use this principle.

A limited dictionary of verbal commands consisting of words or phrases are spoken into a microphone and stored in the computer's memory (usually on disk) as electronic signals. In this way, the computer is "taught" a specific vocabulary as spoken by a particular individual. When this person then talks to the computer, issuing verbal commands from this limited vocabulary, the computer compares the spoken words with those in its vocabulary. If a match is found, the appropriate action is taken. Otherwise, nothing happens.

Systems such as this have enormous potential. Large-scale versions of voice recognition systems are used on some Ford automobile loading docks and Lockheed Aircraft assembly lines. They are frequently found in security and military systems. Doors for example, will not be unlocked unless the speaker's voice is recognized.

Recent advances have made voice recognition systems available and affordable for personal computers. The Texas Instruments Professional Computer has a voice recognition system that allows a person to give spoken commands to any existing software package that runs on this machine. Similar but more limited systems are available for Apple computers and IBM PCs.

Such systems are being used to give computer power to severely disabled people who are unable to type or even point accurately at a touch screen. Word processing and spreadsheet software can be redesigned to accept spoken commands, but the use of voice input systems extends beyond traditional software.

**Figure 5.21**    Speech Recognition: Devices that recognize specific voices and spoken language in general enable people and computers to communicate.

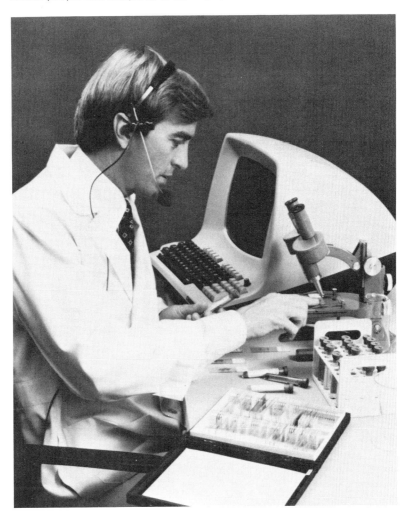

Such systems can be used to operate wheelchairs, elevators, and other mechanical devices, giving greater independence and mobility to handicapped people.

Research and development of devices for *natural language recognition* has been slower. Work that may lead to computers that understand spoken human language and equipment that can understand anyone's speech continues at many universities and corporations. There is as yet no general voice-processing system. Researchers are focusing on several problem areas:

**Figure 5.22**  The Human Voice: Because each person's voice is unique, it produces unique signals that can be graphed. Shown is a spectrogram with three pronunciations of the word *baby*.

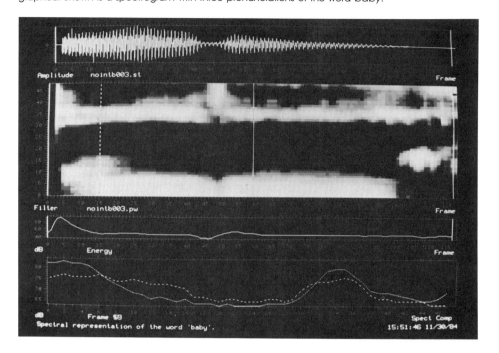

- *Context.* Computers must recognize that words take on different meanings depending upon the context in which they are used.

- *Idioms.* Languages are idiomatic and words do not always have their literal meaning. The computer must understand that "My car broke down on me" does not mean that the automobile came apart on top of my body.

- *Pronunciation.* A given word must be recognized consistently despite variations in its pronunciation. Words spoken with a dialect or an accent would still have to be understood.

- *Noise.* Computers must be able to distinguish the speaker from background noise.

- *Emphasis.* Computers must be able to correctly interpret the speaker's word emphasis and adjust the word's meaning accordingly.

## Voice Synthesis as Output

There are also two types of systems for computerized voice output, or **voice synthesis**. In the simpler systems, frequently used words and phrases are prerecorded and stored in the computer's memory. These sentence components can then be retrieved in any desired order. The number of words that can be used in such systems is limited. Of course, fairly complex thoughts can be expressed even with a limited vocabulary.

The second approach is based on the finite number of sounds that make up natural language. All our spoken words and phrases are combinations of these distinct sounds, or *phonemes*. In this type of voice output system, phonemes, not complete words, are recorded into the computer's memory. The computer is then programmed to synthesize words from these basic building blocks. Theoretically, this method should enable the computer to reproduce all spoken English words. Other languages have a different set of phonemes, but a voice output system can be designed in the same way for them.

The most common use of computerized voice output is for the telephone. Computer-generated telephone messages such as "The number you have reached, 6-3-2-4-1-1-2, has been changed..." are composed of a prerecorded voice saying the first and last parts of the sentence combined with a computer synthesized phone number built out of individually prerecorded numbers.

Like telephone messages, most of the other voice output devices now available form sentences from prerecorded words or phrases. Examples include talking cash registers, children's toys such as Texas Instruments' "Touch and Tell," talking Coke machines, and even talking dashboards in cars, which remind you to "Buckle Up!" Teddy Ruxpin, the talking bear, is another example shown in Figure 5.23.

Synthetic voice output can also be an outstanding aid for the disabled. One use is to give voices to people with extremely limited motor skills who are unable to speak intelligibly. Voice output systems can be combined with other devices such as special keyboards or joysticks. The disabled person manipulates the input device with any part of the body (head, foot, hand) that he or she can use to type out or point to words or phrases, and the speech synthesizer will voice the person's thoughts. Voice synthesis is also used to help handicapped children learn to speak by reinforcing the relationship between the spoken name of an object and its picture pointed to on a touch screen. Children with reading and writing difficulties can improve their skills by associating the spoken word with its printed equivalent.

Speech recognition and synthesis devices have not yet become commonplace, except in science fiction. Yet, as the closest computer equivalent to normal communication, this technology holds enormous potential for creating truly easy-to-use computer systems.

**Figure 5.23**     Voice Synthesizers: Toy manufacturers, such as the company that produces the Teddy Ruxpin talking bear, the telephone company, and car manufacturers are using computerized voice output.

## Print Recognition Technology

All of the devices we've looked at so far have involved the interaction of people with computers. Anything that eases this interaction is said to be **user-friendly**. Voice input and touch screens are considered more user-friendly than keyboards. However, the speed of entering information with any of these devices is limited by the abilities of their human users.

Although speech is the most common and comfortable form of human communication, most of our important communications take place on the printed page. Our businesses, industries, and schools produce mountains of printed material daily. Since computers can interpret all characters and symbols only after they have been translated into machine-readable form, considerable attention has been paid to designing equipment that can directly process printed information.

Techniques used for direct input of printed material fall into three categories: (1) optical mark reading (OMR), (2) magnetic ink character recognition (MICR), and (3) optical character recognition (OCR).

**Optical Mark Reading**    **Optical mark readers (OMR)** are designed to read handwritten pencil marks on specially designed forms. OMR devices are most commonly used for analyzing answers on multiple-choice tests and survey questions. Properly designed forms using this technology can be used for a variety of business applications as well. In an OMR device, a light beam passes over the coded form. The presence of a mark creates an electronic signal that is then entered into the computer and processed (see Figure 5.24).

**Magnetic Ink Character Recognition**    In the late 1950s, a system known as **magnetic ink character recognition (MICR)** was developed and adopted by the American Banking Association (ABA). The ABA sought to automate the processing of the millions of checks Americans issue daily. Automatic processing would speed up transactions at a time when the use of checks was increasing sharply. Under MICR, the numbers on the bottom of checks are printed in a shape designed for easy reading by both people and computers (see Figure 5.25). The ink in which the numbers are printed contains particles of iron oxide. The checks are read as they pass through a machine that senses the magnetic iron oxide in the

---

**Figure 5.24**    Optical Mark Readers: Light beams read hand-written pencil marks on special forms and then pass on the signals to the computer.

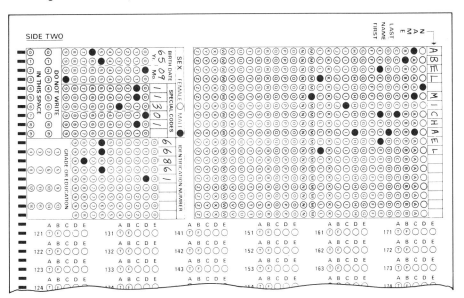

**Figure 5.25**    Magnetic-Ink Characters: Magnetic-ink characters at the bottom of checks are read by processing machines that sense the iron oxide in their ink.

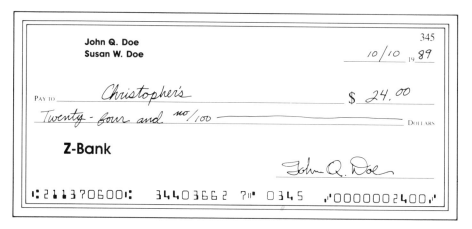

ink. The magnetic numbers are understood by the machine and entered so they can then be processed directly. The design of MICR devices is similar in principle to that of other magnetic devices of the second computer generation, such as magnetic tape. Its continued use reflects its ease and efficiency. Current enhancements combine MICR with computer copying devices. Checks or bills can be processed by MICR readers and simultaneously copied and prepared for electronic transmission.

**Optical Character Recognition**    Optical character recognition (OCR) works by comparing the shape of printed material with similar shapes stored in memory. A photoelectric light beam scans the printed material, transforming it into a unique pattern of light and dark spots. This pattern is then compared with patterns stored in memory. If a match is found, the printed material is entered and processed. In some optical scanners, including those found in supermarket checkout counters, the print information passes over a fixed light source such as a laser beam. Print-recognizable material can also be read by a light source contained in a hand-held wand. This device looks somewhat like a light pen. As a person moves the wand directly over the printed material, the print information is read and entered into the computer for processing. These hand-held readers are increasingly popular in libraries, department stores, hospitals, and factories (see Figure 5.26).

Two forms of print material are suited to optical character recognition: bar codes and direct optical recognition of characters. **Bar codes** are the familiar

**Figure 5.26**   Optical Characters: Photoelectric light beams scan optical characters, match patterns with patterns in the computer's memory, and process the information. The OCR WAND reader is shown.

groups of black bars of varying thickness, such as those found on supermarket products (see Figure 5.27). The most common code is the **Universal Product Code (UPC)**, adopted by the grocery industry in 1973 in anticipation of the widespread use of optical scanners. UPC bars contain information identifying each grocery item with a unique product description, including its manufacturer. For example, a half-gallon of Sealtest 2% milk will have a different code from that found on a quart of 2% milk or milk produced by another dairy. Recently, the U.S. Postal Service began using character and bar code readers to assist in the routing of mail.

**Direct optical character recognition (direct OCR)** has potentially more far-reaching applications than either bar codes or MICR. Printed characters can be read directly by the computer without using special ink. Any printed character, including carefully handwritten characters, can be processed. However, in this technology, the computer is generally programmed to expect characters from particular typewritten fonts (characters with distinct shapes and sizes). Direct OCR devices are designed to suit the user's needs. Individual characters can be read using a hand-held wand, which is common in factories or department stores, or entire pages can be read directly.

**Figure 5.27**     Bar Codes: Black bars of varying thickness found on supermarket products contain information that is read by optical character recognition devices.

Increasingly, when we pay a bill, the portion we return with our payment to the department store, utility company, or credit card company is scanned by a direct OCR device for quick processing.

OCR can be taken a step further. The Kurzweil reading machine was invented to scan machine-printed text and, using voice synthesis, read material to visually handicapped people (see Figure 5.28). A variation on this device reads machine-printed material and directly translates it into machine-usable form ready for computer processing. This is starting to have an inpact in the print and publishing industries.

## COMBINATION SYSTEMS

We do not need to look to the home or office of the future to see how complex computer systems are used. Let us look at three common systems that incorporate a variety of input and output devices.

**Figure 5.28**   The Kurzweil Reading Machine: Invented to scan machine-printed text, the Kurzweil reading machine reads material to visually handicapped people.

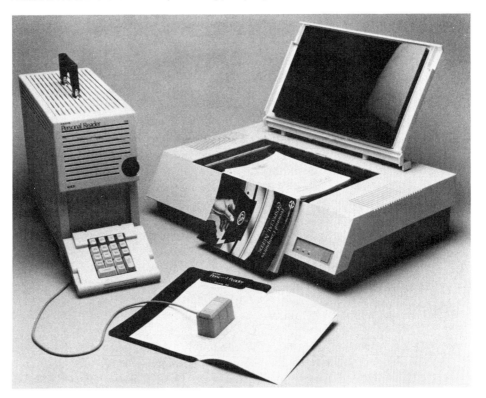

## The Automated Cash Register

Automated cash registers are found in supermarkets, department stores, and restaurants. They process business transactions at the location, or point, where the sale occurs. They are often called **point-of-sale (POS) systems**.

The automated cash register actually contains multiple input and output devices, all housed in a single package. Let us focus on a supermarket system. These cash registers usually have the following input devices:

    an optical bar code scanner
    a numeric keyboard
    an electronic scale (an analog device)

They also have at least some of the following output devices:

    a monitor screen listing item and price
    a printer
    a voice synthesizer

How do these cash registers work? As the clerk passes each item over a window in the countertop, the optical scanner reads the bar code on it. If the scanner cannot read the code or if there is none, as on fresh produce, the clerk types the code on the keyboard. The computer looks up the code on a list, stored in memory, of all the items stocked in the store. When a match is found, the current price is returned and appears on the monitor, and the English name of the item as well as the price are printed on the sales receipt. The amount may be spoken by a voice synthesizer as well. Taxes and any discounts are automatically calculated by the computer after the clerk hits appropriate keys, and the store's inventory records are automatically adjusted to reflect the sale.

How does the customer benefit? Transactions are performed rapidly, so time spent in line at the register is reduced. Fewer errors are made by cashiers, and receipts with the items and their costs are printed in English. Inventory figures are continually updated, providing appropriate sales analysis. This helps the store personnel provide better service by reordering promptly and stocking appropriate quantities of the items customers want. These advantages serve the supermarket as well. Rapid transactions enable fewer registers to serve more customers. Accurate transactions directly save money, and up-to-date inventories prevent stock outages on items that sell well.

Department store systems are similar to those found in supermarkets. Wand readers replace the fixed bar code scanners, reading price tags with distinctly shaped characters that can be understood by both computers and people. Inventory is automatically updated and itemized receipts are produced. In addition, charge cards can be immediately verified. An immediate credit check is run, and if the card is valid, the customer's account is automatically updated for billing. If the card has been reported lost or stolen or the account requires attention, a message is sent to the cashier and the transaction is interrupted. This protects both the card holder and the store.

The automated gas station, a variation on the department store system, is being tested in a number of locations. The customer inserts a plastic card into a special gas pump. An identifying number is then typed into the computerized pump on a small keyboard. If the card is valid, the customer purchases the desired amount of gas and is automatically given a receipt. The customer's account is then automatically updated for later billing (see Figure 5.29).

Restaurant systems are simpler than either supermarket or department store systems. Information is entered at a keyboard that in many cases has the name of the food or beverage item printed directly on the key. When the key is pressed, the item's price is looked up in the computer's memory. As with the other systems, cashier errors are reduced. In hotel and restaurant chains, inventory and ordering can be automatically maintained (see Figure 5.30).

Automated cash registers speed the checkout process, keep accurate records, reduce errors, and enable businesses to provide the products their customers want, whether they are restaurant dishes or the latest fashions. Supermarkets,

**Figure 5.29**    The Automated Gas Station: Completely automating gasoline purchases, this type of station saves time for both the customer and the company.

department stores, and restaurants are in the business of service. The better they serve their customers, the better their business.

### Automated Teller Machines

Just as supermarkets have automated their checkout operations, banks have increasingly automated their services. Whether the customer uses a human teller or an electronic one, most bank transactions immediately update the customer's account.

The banking industry is increasingly moving toward the use of **automated teller machines**, or **ATMs**, for basic banking transactions. ATMs are accessible 24-hours a day and can be found outside banks, in supermarkets, airports, malls, on college campuses, and in many other locations. Banks find they reduce paperwork, since all transactions are entered directly into the computer. They also reduce labor costs, since ATMs can perform many of the basic transactions previously requiring a human teller (see Figure 5.31).

To use an ATM, the customer needs a plastic card that is associated with one or more of the customer's accounts. The customer chooses a unique personal identification number (PIN) that acts as a password. The PIN typically consists

**Figure 5.30**     Restaurants: Automated cash registers speed the checkout process and keep accurate records in the restaurant industry.

of a sequence of four numerals known only to the customer. When a customer inserts the card into the ATM, the magnetic strip  on the back of the card is read by the machine and links the user with the bank's computer. Then the customer confirms his or her identity by pushing keys on a simple keyboard and following simple, straightforward instructions that appear on a monitor. These instructions guide the customer in common transactions such as cash withdrawals, deposits, and transfers of funds between accounts. The banking industry has found that automatic teller machines make operations more efficient.

ATMs, however, are not without their failings. Customers are often frustrated by machines that are not operating (down), that run out of cash, or that don't respond as expected. Although we feel a bit childish, we all count the cash re-

**Figure 5.31**    Automated Teller Machines: The banking industry has found that automatic teller machines make operations more efficient.

ceived at an ATM even though there is often no person to complain to if the transaction was incorrect. Many people feel that ATMs are removing a significant component of human interaction from our lives. One common complaint is that banks are no longer in the business of serving customers, but are only interested in making money. Some banks, such as Goldome, encourage customers to use ATMs by charging for transactions performed by human tellers. While this move may have economic justification, it also increases our reliance on machines while reducing our contacts with other people.

Banks also have negative ATM experiences. They lose hundreds of thousands of dollars annually due to lost, stolen, or misused cards. Despite the negative aspects of ATMs, they have radically changed the way most people use banks.

### The Automated Post Office

While automated cash registers and teller machines have been changing the way we shop and bank, a quiet revolution has been occurring in post offices around the country.

If you look at the bottom of business envelopes you receive, you may find bar codes printed on them (see Figure 5.32). Almost 80 percent of all mail processed daily (except in holiday periods) by the U.S. Postal Service is first-class business mail. This mail is usually machine printed or typed. In an effort to process the mail more quickly and economically, the Postal Service is using special equipment that can optically scan an envelope, find and interpret the address, and sort the envelope appropriately.

While reading an address on an envelope may seem a simple task, it is really quite complex. Researchers at the State University of New York at Buffalo are assisting in the design of an expert system that can (1) distinguish the mailing address from other material printed on the envelope no matter where the address is typed, (2) analyze any character shape, and (3) use a complex dictionary of addresses to print the zip code in bar code form for further processing.

The address on an envelope is read by a sophisticated optical character reader as it comes into the regional post office near the sending point. The computer finds and interprets the address in an effort to either confirm the zip code if it is present or generate the zip code if it is absent. The computer then prints the bar code equivalent of the zip code on the envelope. The envelope is then routed to the regional post office nearest its destination. The bar code is read by a simpler optical bar-code reading machine and routed to the local post office for distribution. At present, businesses are using only the five-digit zip code, so final sorting is still done by hand. When the nine-digit zip code becomes com-

---

**Figure 5.32**     The Automated Post Office: Bar codes at the bottom of business correspondence speed postal processing.

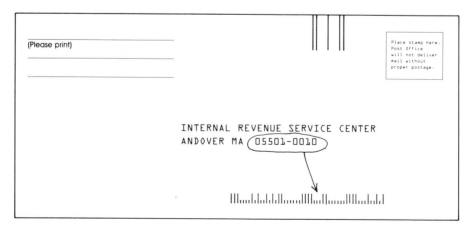

mon on business mail, mechanical bar code sorters will be able to sort mail based on the nine-digit zip by individual block or office building. The mail for a single destination will be automatically placed in a bag. At present, only about 50 percent of all business mail can be read and processed automatically.

Computers and peripherals are changing our world, from supermarkets, to post offices, to our homes. Change often has both positive and negative effects. To enhance the positive effects, we must be aware of changes brought by computers. We must understand how these devices work and demand that businesses and manufacturers balance cost-cutting measures with the very real need of people to interact with one another.

## SUMMARY

A computer is useless unless it can communicate with people. Input and output devices are designed to make communication between people and computers possible. Increasingly, peripheral devices are becoming more user-friendly.

While the keyboard is still the primary input device, devices such as the mouse, joystick, and touch screen are common. Such easy-to-use devices enable users to rapidly point to and select information found on a computer screen. Specialized input alternatives, such as touch tablets, light pens, and graphics tablets, have brought computer graphics into our homes, schools, and businesses.

Output devices produce information in a variety of forms. Images can be produced on monitors or printed directly on paper. The availability of color is making computer use more natural. Printers and plotters provide hard copies of graphs as well as the printed word. Impact printers include both dot matrix and daisy wheel printers. Non-impact printers include thermal, inkjet, and laser printers.

Increasingly, peripherals serve as both input and output devices. Terminals provide visual confirmation of information going into our computers and also display the results of our work. Mice, touch tablets, and light pens enable us to directly interact with images on our monitors, making computer use easier. Touch screens find popular use on information terminals located in stores, malls, and amusement parks.

Specialized technologies are being developed that will enable us to talk to our computers and have them respond to us in the same way. Computerized voice output is called voice synthesis, while the ability of a computer to understand the spoken word is called speech recognition.

Computers can read printed information. Grocery and retail purchases can be automatically processed by computers using optical scanners. Many restaurants and retail stores make use of computerized cash registers called point-of-sale (POS) systems that not only calculate change but check credit and keep track of inventory. Even the post office is automating the process of sorting the mail.

Peripheral devices have become so heavily used in the everyday world that we often do not recognize them as input and output devices for computers.

## Key Words

As an extra review of the chapter, try defining the following terms. If you have trouble with any of them, refer to the page number listed.

automated teller machine (ATM) *(147)*
bar codes *(142)*
cathode ray tube (CRT) *(122)*
cursor *(115)*
daisy wheel *(125)*
digitizer (graphics tablet) *(117)*
direct optical character recognition (direct OCR) *(143)*
dot matrix printer *(126)*
download *(134)*
dumb terminal *(132)*
electrostatic printers *(128)*
function keys *(115)*
hard copy *(122)*
impact printers *(125)*
inkjet printers *(128)*
input device *(112)*
intelligent terminal *(132)*
joystick *(115)*
keyboard *(113)*
laser printers *(128)*
letter-quality printers *(125)*

light pen *(117)*
line printers *(127)*
magnetic ink character recognition (MICR) *(141)*
mouse *(116)*
non-impact printers *(127)*
optical character recognition (OCR) *(142)*
optical mark readers (OMR) *(141)*
output device *(112)*
peripherals (peripheral devices) *(112)*
plotter *(130)*
point-of-sale (POS) system *(145)*
soft copy *(122)*
speech recognition *(136)*
thermal printers *(127)*
touch screen *(119)*
touch tablet *(121)*
Universal Product Code (UPC) *(143)*
upload *(134)*
user-friendly *(140)*
video display terminal (VDT) *(132)*
voice synthesis *(139)*

## Test Your Knowledge

1. What is a peripheral device?

2. List four types of keys found on computer keyboards.

3. List and describe four keyboard alternatives.

4. What does CRT stand for?

5. What does VDT stand for?

6. Define hard copy.

7. Hard copy and soft copy both describe computer output. How are they different?

8. Describe how an impact printer creates characters.

9. Identify three types of non-impact printers. How are they alike? How do they differ?

10. How do impact and non-impact printers differ?

11. List three types of dot matrix printers.

12. Does a laser printer use dot matrix technology? Support your answer.

13. What is a plotter?

14. What is an intelligent terminal? How is it different from a dumb terminal? How is it different from a personal computer?

15. Peripherals are becoming more user-friendly. Explain why this statement is true or false.

16. OCR devices, which read typed characters, and MICR are similar since they both process data that humans can read directly. How are they different?

17. What is voice synthesis? Explain the two techniques used to create voice output.

18. List those peripherals that can be used to assist the handicapped.

19. List the advantages of automated teller machines. What are the disadvantages?

20. How does the U.S. Postal Service use optical character recognition to process the mail?

---

## Expand Your Knowledge

Write a brief paper on each of the following questions.

1. Line printers *appear* to type entire lines at once. However, they do not actually do so. How does a line printer work? Is there more than one kind? If so, explain how they differ.

2. Why have some supermarkets chosen to attach voice synthesis devices to their cash registers? What are the benefits to customers? Why are other supermarkets not using these devices?

3. Nan Davis and Professor Jerry Petrofsky made medical history. What did they do? How were computers involved? Why is this kind of research important?

4. What are the positive and negative consequences of the falling cost of peripheral devices?

5. Examine the output from a laser printer under a magnifying glass. Explain why the eye sees this output as solid lines rather than dots.

6. Visit your local supermarket. Interview customers and store personel, getting their reaction to using automated cash registers. Analyze your results, focusing on the following:

   (a) Do customers view the systems favorably?
   (b) Are customers comfortable using such systems?
   (c) Do store personel find them as useful as they expected?
   (d) What in-store problems have these automated systems caused?
   (e) Did the stores experience any unexpected benefits?

7. Visit a local retail store such as J.C. Penney or K mart and analyze their POS system using the guidelines detailed in question 6.

# 6

# Designing Algorithms

**Chapter Outline**

Problem Solving
    What Is an Algorithm? • Why Program?

Flowchart Versus Outline

Choosing a Plan

Top-Down Analysis

Problem-Solving Steps
    Define the Problem • Define the Output • Define the Input • Define the
    Initial Algorithm • Refine the Algorithm • Define the Program

Sample Problems and Solutions
    Example One • Example Two

Problem solving is a continuous human endeavor. All working and learning is problem solving. From struggling with our first steps, to learning to talk, to making our way in the world, our days consist of solving problems. This makes it sound as if our lives are a continuous struggle, an uphill battle against insurmountable odds. Clearly, for most of us that is not the case. The trouble with the phrase *problem solving* is that we instantly imagine major problems such as world hunger or the possibility of nuclear war. However, if we redefine *problem* as a task that needs to be completed, we easily see that we are solving problems—completing tasks—all day long. Most of us are not even conscious that the process is ongoing. We make decisions and choose among alternatives without realizing we are doing so. This chapter explores the steps in problem solving and introduces you to computer programming.

After studying this chapter, you will be able to:

- Explain why learning to program is valuable.
- Illustrate how flowcharts and pseudocode are used.
- Understand top-down analysis.
- Trace the steps in problem solving.
- Identify and demonstrate the six steps in writing a program.

## PROBLEM SOLVING

Let us look at a problem we solve essentially unconsciously every day. The problem is eating lunch. You may think that this is not a problem because it doesn't require making decisions. Let's examine the process involved in eating lunch.

Figure 6.1 indicates the step-by-step set of instructions, in pictorial form, for solving the problem of eating lunch. Notice that the diamond-shaped boxes indicate the decisions and alternatives used in solving this particular problem. Clearly, eating lunch involves making many decisions. If we are hungry at lunchtime, it does not necessarily follow that we will be eating lunch. We may have decided to diet today or we may have a class from noon to one requiring that we eat later. Where to eat requires decisions as well. Do we eat on campus or off? If we choose to eat on campus we need to find an appropriate eating place. Once we find an eating place, the decisions really begin. What to eat and how to pay for it must be considered.

Obviously, everyday solutions are seldom documented in such detail. If we did, it is clear that nothing would ever get done. But what if we wanted to train our household robot to do a task for us? Would this detail be appropriate given the entity that would be carrying out the task? The amount of directions needed to complete a task is related to the difficulty of the task and the intelligence level of the person or thing carrying out the task.

**Figure 6.1** "Eating Lunch" Flowchart.

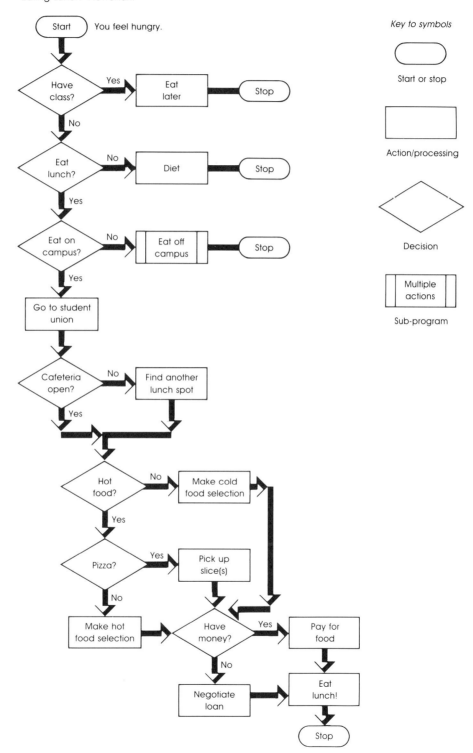

### What Is an Algorithm?

A procedure for solving a problem is called an **algorithm**. It is a step-by-step set of instructions or directions that, if carried out exactly, solves the problem. An algorithm sounds complex, yet it need not be. A recipe is an algorithm. To solve the problem of baking a cake, you need simply follow the recipe on the back of a cake mix box. If the directions are followed exactly, meaning that the cake mix is combined with the correct amount of water and eggs and baked for the specified amount of time, the solution to our problem, a cake, will be created.

While a computer is a machine that follows specific instructions very rapidly, it does only and exactly what it is told. As a result, algorithms are needed to design these specific instructions. Computers will always follow your instructions, assuming, of course, that the instructions are given in a way the computer can understand. An algorithm written so that it can be carried out by a computer is called a **program**. To be understood by a computer, the program must be written in a programming language.

### Why Program?

As we have seen in earlier chapters, thousands of computer programs are already available. Unless we plan on becoming a programmer, why should learning to design algorithms or write programs be necessary? In the first place, problem solving is not limited to working with computers. Our unconscious techniques may be adequate for eating lunch, but they are unlikely to provide success for solving the increasingly difficult problems of our complex world. The process of carefully designing an algorithm for a computer is a critical thinking technique that can be applied to any problem. We cannot solve the problems of world hunger, find a cure for cancer, or even plan for a successful career unless we learn to think critically and approach problems in a rational way. Learning to design algorithms is not just a computer skill; it is a life skill.

Second, no matter how many programs are already written, situations will arise in which existing programs are inadequate. For example, while many accounting programs exist, they are often too general or too specific to meet the needs of a particular business. A business can either alter its accounting procedures to fit the available software, which rarely is satisfactory, or write a program that exactly suits its needs. Since our problems are individual, we prefer our solutions (programs) to be individual as well.

Last of all, many of the software packages currently available encourage the user to develop additional instructions to tailor the package to individual needs. Some programs, such as dBASE III Plus, Excel, and Lotus 1-2-3, guide the user in creating commonly used sets of instructions. The techniques necessary for creating these additional instructions are identical to those necessary for designing a program.

Problem-solving skills, whether used to write programs, use prewritten software, or find a cure for cancer, enable us to deal effectively with the world.

## FLOWCHART VERSUS OUTLINE

Over the last few years, a considerable debate has occurred over what is the best way for programmers to design their algorithms before they begin to program. Two popular techniques exist and both have their proponents. A pictorial method of depicting an algorithm in which the focus is on the program's logical flow, such as in Figure 6.1, is called a **flowchart**. Flowcharts are particularly useful as a diagram of the final algorithm. However, flowcharts are difficult to modify and reflect programming languages designed in the second and third generation of computers.

Flowcharts focus on the program's logical flow or the order in which statements will be acted upon by the computer. There is an alternative technique for displaying an algorithm that focuses on the development of detailed and easy-to-follow instructions. **Pseudocode** is a written method using English phrases in outline form to indicate the step-by-step instructions necessary for solving a problem. Each statement or formula represents a single task in pseudocode. It has the appearance of a computer program, yet all the statements are in English; hence the name *pseudocode*. It looks like computer code but it's still English. While it is possible to write pseudocode in any spoken language, English most closely matches many programming languages. One advantage of pseudocode is that it is easy to modify or expand. For example, a complex statement can be broken down into a series of simpler statements. These simpler English statements can then be directly translated into program statements written in a computer language.

Both techniques have their place in programming. However, the use of pseudocode more closely matches the way people solve problems. We will use pseudocode outlines to display algorithms throughout this chapter.

## CHOOSING A PLAN

Let us look at our natural, although often unconscious technique for solving problems. The same method is used whether we are writing a 20-page research paper or planning a party. When we are planning a party, what is the first step? As soon as the idea strikes us, we start making a list. Our list might look something like this:

food
possible location
music
guests

Notice what we have done. The problem of planning a party has been broken down into parts. Each of the four items listed is essential to the success of a party. The next planning step would be to take each of the topics listed and break them down into smaller and smaller steps until each small task is manageable. For example, *food* might become: beverages, junk food, hot snacks.

If we put all our scraps of paper together, our party's outline might take the following form:

Food
    Beverages
      Wine
      Soft drinks
    Junk food
    Hot snacks
Possible locations
    My house
    On campus
    Friend's house
Music
    Records
    Tapes
    Video
    Live band
Guests
    Who to invite
      Self
      Penny A. Day
      Frank N. Stein
      Phil Errup
      ————
      ————

    How to invite
      Send invitations
      Call on phone

## TOP-DOWN ANALYSIS

A large, complex task is clearly unmanageable if attacked directly. The problem must be broken down into its basic parts, into a series of subproblems. Each of these smaller problems in turn can be divided into separate, smaller tasks. The goal is to identify the subproblems that can be solved directly.

This method of making a problem manageable is called **top-down analysis**. Top-down analysis is not limited to use with computers. It is the standard problem-solving technique in all fields from business and medical research to life's daily problems.

## PROBLEM-SOLVING STEPS

Before we can begin to program, we must break down the problem into manageable parts. The most difficult part of the process is defining the algorithm in sufficiently detailed steps so that the computer can follow its instructions. People naturally think at a level of abstraction far too complex for even the most advanced and futuristic computer. When people solve problems, they make all kinds of assumptions about how the world works. In a sense, when defining problems for computers, we need to think simply. The assumptions we make need to be identified and included in our instructions. For the present, the world of the computer is very detailed, requiring simple instructions. There are six steps in focusing attention on the details needed to successfully write programs. We need to (1) define the problem, (2) define the output, (3) define the input, (4) define the initial algorithm, (5) refine the algorithm, and (6) define the program.

### Define the Problem

Before attempting to solve any problem or design any program, it is necessary to have a clear understanding of the goal. While this may seem obvious, it is a critical step. When designing a program, the first step is to write a clear but general statement of the problem. In this way, the problem is looked at with a critical eye. A problem that seemed clear in our minds can be very difficult to write down on paper. The action of writing a problem statement focuses attention on the assumptions we make. For example:

Problem:    Calculate the miles per gallon your car gets.

Since this is a frequently performed task, its solution may seem obvious. As the problem is defined it cannot easily be solved by a computer. In fact, it could not be solved by a person who is not familiar with cars. Too many assumptions have been made. The following is a better problem definition:

Problem:    Using two consecutive odometer readings, calculate the
            miles per gallon your car obtained between gasoline fill ups.

The key difference between these statements is that the second problem statement specifies many of the assumptions, such as using two odometer readings obtained between fill ups, absent in the original definition.

### Define the Output

It may seem a bit backwards to define the results at the outset. However, we must know where we are going in order to figure out how to get there. To write a program or solve any problem, the expected results need to be identified. Decisions are made at this stage. For example, what elements would we want included in the output of a program to print out a list of a student's grades? Is the student's name alone sufficient? What would happen if there were two John Smith's in the class? Adding the social security number might help. What about using *only* the social security number? If that is done, will the instructor be able to locate student grades easily? By asking questions such as these about the end product, attention is focused on the specifics of the problem. Our field of view is narrowed and those items that are really important in the output are identified. In the miles-per-gallon problem just specified, the only output required is the miles per gallon.

Output:   miles per gallon

## Define the Input

Once we know where we are going, we can look critically at the information needed to get there. Our attention can focus on the information (input) needed by the computer to produce the desired result. For example, to produce a student grade list, what information is needed? Should student addresses or year in school be part of the input? These questions should not be offhandedly dismissed. Will they be needed to produce the required output? An instructor might want to send notices to students doing poorly at the midterm or gather statistics on how well students in a given grade perform.

Just as with output, the decisions made when identifying the necessary input will have a direct effect on the results of the program. It is often the case that much of the input appears as output without being changed. Let us look at the input required by our miles-per-gallon problem.

Input:   old odometer reading
new odometer reading
gallons used

In order to calculate miles per gallon, all three of these values must be known.

## Define the Initial Algorithm

By this stage, our attention is clearly on the problem. A clear and concise statement of the problem has been written, and initial information (input) as well as the anticipated results (output) have been identified. To identify the steps needed to solve the problem, it is often helpful to work through the problem step by step using specific sample data. If the problem cannot be solved with pencil and paper using sample data, it will be impossible to write a program to solve it. As we work through the problem with sample data, we must clearly identify each of the steps used in solving the problem. More than one set of sample data may be needed before all the specific steps have been identified. By writing down the steps followed in solving the problem, we are developing an initial algorithm. The algorithm identified this way will be a sequence of instructions. These instructions should be so clear and straightforward that anyone or anything could follow them. The initial algorithm for our miles-per-gallon problem could look like this:

Initial algorithm:    Get old odometer reading
Get current odometer reading
Get gallons used
Calculate miles per gallon
Write out miles per gallon

## Refine the Algorithm

Our initial algorithm needs to be examined with a critical eye. Assumptions have been made and steps have been left out of our solution. Each step in our algorithm is not simple enough for our detail-minded computer. It is unlikely that an initial algorithm will work perfectly. We can expect to refine the steps many times before all the details are specified. Only then will the algorithm indeed solve the problem.

Let us look at our miles-per-gallon algorithm. If we apply sample data, we immediately find that the algorithm cannot be used to solve the problem. The phrase "calculate miles per gallon" does not provide sufficient detail to solve the problem and must be further clarified.

Refined algorithm:    Get old odometer reading
Get current odometer reading
Get gallons used
Calculate miles traveled
Calculate miles per gallon using miles
   traveled and gallons
Write out miles per gallon

This algorithm can now be translated into pseudocode, which combines English-like phrases and mathematical symbols. The symbol $\leftarrow$ represents the words *is defined by*.

Pseudocode:    Get old odometer reading
Get current odometer reading
Get gallons used
Miles traveled $\leftarrow$ current odometer – old odometer
Miles-per-gallon $\leftarrow$ miles traveled / gallons used
Write out miles per gallon

At this stage, if we apply sample data to our algorithm we get the expected results.

## Define the Program

In all of the five preceding steps, no mention was made of a specific programming language. The algorithm, written in the English-like sentences of pseudocode, does not depend on any particular computer language. The step-by-step set of instructions specified in the algorithm is a method for solving the problem. Translating these instructions into Greek, Pascal, or BASIC has no bearing on the solution.

The algorithm must be prepared for use by a computer by translating it into a programming language. Figure 6.2 is the translation of the miles-per-gallon algorithm into BASIC and Pascal.

Remember, computers do not "speak" English or any other natural language. They do not even speak pseudocode. If they did, Step 6 would not be necessary. The choice of computer language depends both on the problem and the availability of languages. We will take a closer look at the various programming languages in Chapter 8.

---

## SAMPLE PROBLEMS AND SOLUTIONS

Now let us look at a number of common problems. Most people, at some time or other, work for an hourly wage. We are all familiar with the method used for calculating such wages. Using this as an example, we can pay attention to the process of designing the algorithm rather than struggling with formulas. The first example calculates the wages of an hourly employee using the steps just discussed.

### Example One

*STEP 1: Define the Problem.* In this example, the following statement explains what we want to know:

> Calculate the gross wages (total, before taxes, and other deductions) of an hourly employee. You know the number of hours worked and the employee's pay rate.

This statement is clear and concise. We will see in Step 5, though, that it will still be necessary to make sure we know what is being asked. There is nothing obvious about the statement "calculate the gross wages of an hourly employee" unless it is assumed that everyone either knows the appropriate formula or can easily find it out. When working with computers, it is best to make no assumptions and to specify everything in detail. In this way, the machine's need for specifics will not be a surprise.

*STEPS 2 & 3: Define the Output and Input.*

OUTPUT              ←              INPUT

wages of employee  ←  $\left\{ \begin{array}{l} \text{hours worked by employee} \\ \text{pay rate of employee} \end{array} \right.$

**Figure 6.2**          Miles-per-Gallon Algorithm in BASIC/Pascal.

## BASIC

```
100   REM  -- USING ODOMETER READINGS AND GALLONS, --
105   REM  --      CALCULATE MILES-PER-GALLON. --
110   PRINT "ENTER OLD ODOMETER READING: "
120   INPUT O
130   PRINT "ENTER CURRENT ODOMETER READING: "
140   INPUT C
150   PRINT "ENTER GALLONS USED: "
160   INPUT G
165   PRINT
170   LET   T = C - O
180   LET   M = T / G
190   PRINT " MILES-PER-GALLON =", USING "###.##",M
200   END
```

### Algorithm

Get old odometer reading

Get current odometer reading

Get gallons used

Calculate miles traveled
   Miles traveled ← Current
   odometer – Old odometer

Calculate miles per gallon
   Miles per gallon ← miles
   traveled / gallons used

Write out miles per gallon

Note: While standard BASIC restricts variable names to a letter followed
by a number, the BASIC found on most micros allows the use of longer
names such as "GALLONS". However, only the first two characters (GA)
are actually recognized by some systems.

## Pascal

```
program travel(input, output);
   (*  Using odometer readings and gallons,    *)
   (*     Calculate miles-per-gallon.          *)
var
   oldodometer, currentodometer: real;
   gallons, milestraveled: real;
   mpg: real;
begin
   write('Enter old odometer reading:');
   readln(oldodometer);
   write('Enter current odometer reading:');
   readln(currentodometer);
   write('Enter gallons used:');
   readln(gallons);
   writeln;
   milestraveled := currentodometer - oldodometer;
   mpg := milestraveled/gallons;
   writeln;
   writeln('Miles-per-gallon = ',mpg:4:1);
end.
```

### Algorithm

Get old odometer reading

Get current odometer reading

Get gallons used

Calculate miles traveled
   Miles traveled ← Current
   odometer – Old odometer

Calculate miles per gallon
   Miles per gallon ← miles
   traveled / gallons used

Write out miles per gallon

Note: The English-like words such as gallons, oldodometer, and mpg can
be of any length. Names such as oldodometer and mpg were chosen to be
long enough to be clearly understood and short enough to be easily typed.

*STEP 4: Define the initial algorithm.* List the step-by-step instructions for solving the problem:

> Get hours and pay rate
> Calculate wages
> Print wages

*STEP 5: Refine the Algorithm.* Look at each statement in the algorithm carefully. If a statement is clear it requires no further refinement. Remember, the algorithm must specify everything. For the computer to carry out the procedure, each step must specify exactly what is to be done. The statement "calculate wages" may seem clear to us, yet our computer will need more precise instructions in order to do this. This phrase requires further refinement:

> Get hours and pay rate
> Calculate wages
>    wages  ←  hours × pay rate
> Print wages

Our algorithm is composed of English phrases in outline form, or pseudo-code. It has the appearance of a computer program, yet all the statements are in English.

*STEP 6: Define the Program.* If our algorithm has been properly designed, it should be easy for us to translate it into any computer language. For demonstration purposes, we will translate our algorithm into both BASIC and Pascal, as shown in Figure 6.3.

Even if we know neither BASIC nor Pascal, we can see that our algorithm can be translated directly into a computer language with only minor changes.

Let's examine a somewhat more complex problem. As with the first payroll problem, we will follow the same six steps for designing an algorithm. As we move through these steps, we must carefully examine all of our assumptions. Computers have no built-in understanding. We must specify every step if we expect the computer to complete the task.

## Example Two

*STEP 1. Define the Problem.* The following statement defines the problem:

> Calculate the gross wages (before taxes and deductions) of an hourly employee, including overtime. You know the hours worked and the employee's pay rate.

While this problem statement is clear, we must bear in mind that phrases such as *gross wages* and *overtime* are meaningless to a computer. Our algorithm must define every term by expressing it as a formula. Only then will the computer be able to follow our instructions.

**Figure 6.3**          Gross Wages Algorithm in BASIC/Pascal.

**BASIC**

```
10    REM -- Using hours and payrate --
15    REM -- calculate wages.         --
20    PRINT "ENTER HOURS AND PAYRATE: "
30    INPUT H, R
40    LET  W = H * R
50    PRINT USING "WAGES = ##.## ";W
60    END
```

**Refined Algorithm**

Get hours and pay rate
Calculate wages
 wages ← hours × pay rate
Print wages

Note: While standard BASIC restricts variable names to a letter followed by a number, the BASIC found on most micros allows the use of longer names such as "WAGES". However, only the first two characters (WA) are actually recognized by some systems.

**Pascal**

```
Program PayrollA (input, output);
(*   Using hours and payrate      *)
(*   calculate wages.             *)
var
  hours, payrate, wages : real;
begin
  write('Enter hours and payrate: ')
  readln(hours, payrate);
  wages := hours * payrate;
  writeln('wages = ',wages:5:2)
end.
```

**Refined Algorithm**

Get hours and pay rate
Calculate wages
 wages ← hours × pay rate
Print wages

*STEPS 2 & 3. Define the Output and Input.* Note that the output and input for this problem are the same as those in the preceding problem.

OUTPUT          ←          INPUT

wages of employee  ←  $\begin{cases} \text{hours worked by employee} \\ \text{pay rate of employee} \end{cases}$

*STEP 4. Define the Initial Algorithm.* List the step-by-step instructions for solving the problem:

> Get hours and pay rate
> Calculate wages using formula
> Print hours, pay rate, and wages

Not surprisingly, this initial algorithm is nearly identical to the one devised in the previous problem. In the most general way, the same problem is being solved. In both examples we are trying to determine the wages of an employee given the total number of hours worked and the employee's rate of pay. The differences occur when the phrase "calculate wages using formula" is examined.

*STEP 5. Refine the Algorithm.* The phrase "calculate wages using formula" should bring to mind a number of questions. They include: What is the formula? How is overtime determined? What is meant by overtime? If questions arise, then our algorithm is incomplete. Our algorithm needs to be refined until our literal-minded computer can successfully follow the algorithm to its logical conclusion. The algorithm must be generalized enough to be able to calculate the wages of *any* employee. However, it is easier to recognize the steps needed by looking at a specific problem. Let us assume our employee worked for 46 hours at a regular rate of $5 per hour, and that overtime begins after 40 hours of work and is paid at time and a half.

Forty-six hours consists of 40 hours at the regular rate and 6 hours at time and a half. Therefore:

$$
\begin{array}{llll}
& \text{overtime} & \text{pay} & \\
& \text{rate} & \text{rate} & \\
\text{weekly} & \downarrow & \downarrow & \text{weekly} \\
\text{hours} \to 40 \times & & \$5.00 = 200.00 \leftarrow & \text{wages} \\
\text{overtime} & & & \text{overtime} \\
\text{hours} \to 6 \times & 1.5 = 9 \times & \$5.00 = \underline{45.00} \leftarrow & \text{wages} \\
& & \$245.00 \leftarrow & \text{total wages}
\end{array}
$$

With this example as a model, it is clear that first we determined the number of overtime hours the employee worked. Next, overtime wages were calculated. Then overtime wages were added to regular weekly wages to find gross wages. The *refined algorithm* might look like this:

> Get hours and pay rate
> Calculate wages
>    calculate overtime hours worked
>    calculate regular weekly wages
>    calculate overtime wages
>    gross wages ← regular weekly wages + overtime wages
> Print hours, pay rate, gross wages

Using this technique, it was easy for us to write a refined algorithm. However, a critical look at the algorithm finds that it is still incomplete. This algorithm applies only when an employee has worked overtime. What happens if that's not the case? Since this algorithm will not work for all situations, it requires more revision.

Let us try to refine our algorithm further so it can be used to calculate the wages of various employees. Using another set of sample data, let's revise our algorithm again. If another employee worked 35 hours for $5 per hour, what would be the gross wages?

Now, 35 hours consists of 35 hours at the regular rate, and no hours at the overtime rate. Therefore:

$$
\begin{array}{ccc}
\text{weekly} & \text{pay} & \text{weekly} \\
\text{hours} & \text{rate} & \text{wages} \\
\downarrow & \downarrow & \downarrow
\end{array}
$$

$$35 \ \times \ \$5.00 \ = \ \$175.00$$

This example shows that early in our calculation we must decide, based on the number of hours worked, whether the employee is entitled to overtime benefits. The answer to that question will determine which wage formula to use. Now we can further refine our algorithm as follows:

> Get hours and pay rate
> If hours > 40
>     calculate overtime hours
>     calculate regular weekly wages
>     calculate overtime wages
>     gross wages ← regular weekly wages + overtime wages
> Otherwise
>     gross wages ← hours × pay rate
> Print hours, pay rate, gross wages

If we look closely at our sample solution, we realize we made some significant assumptions that are not necessarily true. We assumed, for example, that overtime is defined as any number of hours greater than 40 and that the overtime rate is time and a half. While these assumptions are based on practices that are often true, we do not know that they are true for this particular company. This company might not pay overtime unless more than 50 hours are worked, and the overtime rate might be double time. Assumptions are not necessarily wrong, but they must be verified before they are used in a program. In this example, overtime is granted for all hours that are more than 40, and the overtime pay rate is time and a half.

The final step in defining our algorithm is to provide all of the formulas that are needed. Here is the *refined algorithm:*

Get hours and pay rate
If hours > 40
  calculate overtime hours
    overtime hours  ←  hours − 40
  calculate regular weekly wages
    regular weekly wages  ←  40 × pay rate
  calculate overtime wages
    overtime wages  ←  overtime hours × 1.5 × pay rate
  gross wages  ←  regular weekly wages + overtime wages
Otherwise
  gross wages  ←  hours × pay rate
Print hours, pay rate, gross wages

All of the phrases used in our algorithm are in English, although a bit mathematical in style. This again is pseudocode.

*STEP 6. Translate the Algorithm into a Computer Language.* Since this algorithm is more complex than that in the first example, the translations for the computer will also be more complex. However, the special relationship between the algorithm and the completed program is still obvious, as Figure 6.4 shows.

Our algorithm clearly solves the stated problem, and the translation from pseudocode to a programming language is fairly straightforward. Some experts might argue correctly that our algorithm is not completely general. The algorithm is only valid for the special case where overtime is granted for all hours greater than 40 and the overtime rate is time and a half.

We could further refine our algorithm, making it still more general:

Get company's regular hours and overtime rate
Get employee's hours and pay rate
If hours worked > regular hours
  calculate overtime hours
    overtime hours  ←  hours worked − regular hours
  calculate regular weekly wages
    regular weekly wages  ←  regular hours × pay rate
  calculate overtime wages
    overtime wages  ←  overtime hours × overtime rate × pay rate
  gross wages  ←  regular weekly wages + overtime wages
Otherwise
  gross wages  ←  hours × pay rate

Figure 6.5 shows the algorithm as it translates into BASIC and Pascal.

Designing a program requires careful thought. Our unconscious problem-solving technique must be made conscious. We must always remember that computers are not thinking machines.

Therefore, our algorithms must lead the computer step by step through the solution of the problem. Our algorithms will naturally reflect the way each of us

**Figure 6.4**     Gross Wages Refined Algorithm in BASIC/Pascal.

## BASIC

```
100    PRINT "ENTER HOURS AND PAYRATE:"
110    INPUT H, R
115    REM -- DEPENDING ON HOURS WORKED DOES --
116    REM -- EMPLOYEE GET OVERTIME PAY. --
120    IF H > 40 THEN 150 ELSE 200
150       O = H - 40
160       R = 40 * R
170       O1 = O * 1.5 * R
180       W = R + O1
190    GOTO 300
195    REM -- CALCULATE WAGES WITHOUT --
196    REM -- OVERTIME PAY. --
200       W = H * R
300    PRINT "  HOURS    RATE    WAGES"
310    PRINT USING "    ##      #.##   ###.##";H,R,W
999    END
```

## Algorithm

Get hours and pay rate
If hours > 40
   calculate overtime hours
      overtime hours ← hours − 40
   calculate regular weekly wages
      regular weekly wages ← 40 × pay rate
   calculate overtime wages
      overtime wages ← overtime hours ×
      1.5 × pay rate
   gross wages ← regular weekly wages +
   overtime wages
Otherwise
   gross wages ← hours × pay rate
Print hours, pay rate, wages

## Pascal

```pascal
program payrollB (input, output);
var
   hours, payrate, othours, otwages: real;
   regwages, wages : real;
begin
   write('Enter hours and payrate: ');
   readln (hours, payrate);
   (*  Depending on hours worked does  *)
   (*    employee get overtime pay.    *)
   if hours > 40 then
     begin
       regwages := 40 * payrate;
       othours := hours - 40;
       otwages := othours * 1.5 * payrate;
       wages := regwages + otwages;
     end
   else
     (*  Calculate wages without  *)
     (*       overtime pay.       *)
     wages := hours * payrate
   writeln(' HOURS   RATE   WAGES');
   writeln(hours:5, rate:8:2, wages:9:2);
end.
```

## Algorithm

Get hours and pay rate
If hours > 40
   calculate overtime hours
      overtime hours ← hours − 40
   calculate regular weekly wages
      regular weekly wages ← 40 × pay rate
   calculate overtime wages
      overtime wages ← overtime hours ×
      1.5 × pay rate
   gross wages ← regular weekly wages +
   overtime wages
Otherwise
   gross wages ← hours × pay rate
Print hours, pay rate, wages

Note: The English-like words such as hours, wages, and otwages can be of any length. Names such as othours were chosen to be long enough to be clearly understood and short enough to be easily typed.

**Figure 6.5**        More General Gross Wages Algorithm in BASIC/Pascal.

**BASIC**

```
 95    PRINT "ENTER REGULAR HOURS AND OVERTIME RATE: "
100    INPUT T, P
105    PRINT "ENTER HOURS AND PAYRATE:"
110    INPUT H, R
115    REM -- DEPENDING ON HOURS WORKED DOES --
116    REM -- EMPLOYEE GET OVERTIME PAY. --
120    IF H > T THEN 150  ELSE 200
150       O = H - T
160       R1 = T * R
170       O1 = O * P * R
180       W = R + O1
190    GOTO 300
195    REM -- CALCULATE WAGES WITHOUT --
196    REM -- OVERTIME PAY. --
200       W = H * R
300    PRINT " HOURS   RATE    WAGES"
310    PRINT USING "   ##     #.##   ###.##";H,R,W
999    END
```

**Pascal**

```
program payroll2 (input, output);
var
  hours, payrate, othours, otwages: real;
  regwages, wages, reghours, otrate : real;
begin
  write('Enter regular hours and overtime rate: ');
  readln (reghours, otrate);
    (*  Depending on hours worked does  *)
    (*   employee get overtime pay.     *)
  write('Enter hours and payrate: ');
  readln (hours, payrate);
  if hours > reghours then
    begin
      regwages := reghours * payrate;
      othours := hours - reghours;
      otwages := othours * otrate * payrate;
      wages := regwages + otwages;
    end
  else
    (*  Calculate wages without  *)
    (*      overtime pay.        *)
    wages := hours * payrate;
  writeln(' HOURS   RATE   WAGES');
  writeln(hours:5, rate:8:2, wages:9:2)
end.
```

**Algorithm**

Get regular hours and overtime rate
Get hours and pay rate
If hours > regular hours
  calculate overtime hours
      overtime hours ←
      hours – regular hours
  calculate regular weekly
  wages
      regular weekly wages
      ← regular hours × pay
      rate
  calculate overtime wages
      overtime wages ←
      overtime hours × over-
      time rate × pay rate
  gross wages ← regular
  weekly wages + overtime
  wages
Otherwise
  gross wages ← hours ×
  pay rate
Print hours, pay rate, wages

Note: The English-like
words such as hours,
wages, and otwages can be
of any length. Names such
as othours were chosen to
be long enough to be
clearly understood and
short enough to be easily
typed.

deals with the world. However, they must be detailed enough so that our machines can follow them.

Research in the artificial intelligence area of natural language processing is attempting to teach computers to speak and understand human languages such as English. Should such natural-language processing become commonplace, we would have no need for computer languages. However, we would still need to develop algorithms. Regardless of what language computers speak, they will still be machines requiring very detailed instructions.

## SUMMARY

We solve problems every day. For a computer to solve a problem, not only must the solution be very detailed, it must be written in a form the computer can understand. An algorithm is a procedure for solving a problem. It is a step-by-step set of instructions that, if carried out, exactly solves the problem. While a computer follows instructions very rapidly, it does only and exactly what it is told. Algorithms are used to design these very specific instructions.

A program is an algorithm written in a programming language so that the algorithm can be carried out by a computer.

Learning to design algorithms and write programs is important for a number of reasons. First, the process of carefully designing an algorithm for a computer is a critical thinking technique that can be applied to any problem. Learning to design algorithms is not just a computer skill; it is a life skill. Second, no matter how many programs have been written, more are required to meet the needs of a changing world. Third, to make effective use of many of the most popular software packages, the user needs to develop a series of instructions to tailor the package to individual needs. Knowing how to design algorithms makes this process very straightforward.

Two different techniques are commonly used for designing algorithms. A flowchart is a pictorial method of depicting an algorithm in which the focus is on the program's logical flow. Pseudocode, on the other hand, is a written method using English phrases and formulas in outline form to indicate the step-by-step instructions necessary for solving a problem.

Large, complex tasks are unmanageable if attacked directly. Top-down analysis is a technique for breaking down problems into subtasks. These subtasks can be further divided, if necessary, until each subtask can be solved directly.

There are six steps needed to effectively design programs. They are: (1) Define the problem, (2) Define the output, (3) Define the input, (4) Define the initial algorithm, (5) Refine the algorithm, and (6) Define the program. The first five of these steps can be used to solve any problem in any field and are unrelated to computers.

## Key Words

As an extra review of the chapter, try defining the following terms. If you have trouble with any of them, refer to the page number listed.

algorithm *(158)*  
flowchart *(159)*  
program *(158)*  

pseudocode *(159)*  
top-down analysis *(160)*  

## Test Your Knowledge

1. Explain the difference between an algorithm and a program.

2. Why is a detailed algorithm necessary prior to writing a program?

3. Is a recipe a program? Explain your answer.

4. Give two reasons why learning to program is a valuable skill.

5. Name the two common techniques used when describing algorithms.

6. What is a flowchart?

7. How is a flowchart different from pseudocode?

8. How does pseudocode differ from a program?

9. Explain top-down analysis.

10. List the six steps involved in writing programs.

11. How is using sample data helpful in designing an algorithm?

12. Why do algorithms need to be refined?

13. Algorithms are designed to be computer-language independent. What does this mean?

14. Could the miles-per-gallon program be used to calculate the average miles per gallon used on a long trip during which more than two gasoline fill ups were required? Explain your answer.

15. Rewrite the gross wages algorithm given on the top of page 170 to reflect overtime given only after 50 hours with an overtime rate of twice the standard rate (2.0).

## Expand Your Knowledge

1. Write an algorithm to convert from fahrenheit degrees to centigrade.

2. Write an algorithm to calculate the grade-point average achieved by a student in your school in a given semester.

3. An instructor has given an exam to a class. Write an algorithm for calculating the mean (average), median (middle grade), and mode (most common grade) for the class.

4. Write an algorithm to solve the following problem: An instructor in a pass/fail course wants to write a program to determine if students are passing the course. Two exams are given in the course, a midterm and a final. Each exam contains 100 points. The midterm is worth 40 percent of the final grade and the final is worth 60 percent of the final grade. A course average of 50 points is required to pass.

5. Write an algorithm to solve the following problem: You plan to travel to Europe during Spring Break on the newest of the low-cost airlines. The price of a one-way ticket is $99. To keep ticket prices low, the airline charges a baggage fee for all checked baggage. The baggage charge for a one-way trip is $3.00 plus 12 cents per pound. If you know the weight of your luggage, how much will the one-way trip to Europe cost?

# 7

# Processing a Program

**Chapter Outline**

Files

Translating Programs

Executing Programs

Debugging
   Hand Simulation • Intermediate Results

Testing

As we have seen, computers help people by solving problems. To solve problems, computers must use appropriate programs. A program is a step-by-step set of problem-solving instructions written in a programming language so that the instructions can be carried out by a computer. These step-by-step instructions (or algorithms) are often called the logic of the program. In the previous chapter, we examined the steps involved in developing an algorithm and converting it into a computer program. Designing the program does not itself solve the problem, but it is an essential first step in that direction. The program is the blueprint the computer will follow when solving a problem.

Once an algorithm has been developed on paper it must be written in a programming language so it can be understood by the computer. Then it is entered into the computer and, using the appropriate data, it is processed in the CPU.

After studying this chapter, you will be able to:

- Understand the use of computer files.

- Explain the difference between an interpreter and a compiler.

- Distinguish between a source program and an object program.

- List and define the different types of program errors.

- Understand how to correct program errors (debugging).

## FILES

Every program run on a computer requires the use of computer files. This is true whether the program is a prewritten application package, such as a word processor, or a user-designed program written in a computer language such as Pascal or BASIC. In addition, all the data required by software are stored in a computer in the form of files. We explained in Chapter 4 that a computer file, like paper files stored in a file cabinet, is a collection of related information. For example, a computer file can contain a letter entered into a word processor, lists of information such as student names and grades in a course, or the data required by a given program.

Paper files in a file cabinet are identified by a word or phrase written on the tab of the file folder. This label names and describes the contents of the folder. For example, paper folders might be labeled *Tax Info. 1990* or *CS 101 Class Notes*. In much the same way, all computer files have names. Each file name must be unique. Computers can distinguish one file from one another because they have different names. For example, the computer would have no difficulty distinguishing between these two files: *taxinfo.90* and *taxinfo.91*. The file names themselves mean nothing to the computer. To the machine, any unique set of random characters (letters and digits) would be as useful a file name as characters that form words. However, human beings as well as computers must be able to read computer file names. It is important to choose file names that are meaningful. File names should suggest the contents of the file. While names such as *apple, stuff,* or *xyz123* might be valid file names, they are not likely to identify the contents of the file. Useful file names are critical for finding information. Meaningful file names include *resume,* describing a file containing a resume; *gradeinfo,* containing grade information; or *taxcalc,* a program to calculate federal tax returns.

## TRANSLATING PROGRAMS

Once a program is entered into a file, it must be processed in order to get results. Today, most user-designed programs are written in high-level, English-like computer languages such as Pascal, COBOL, BASIC, or C. However, computers *do not* understand these high-level computer languages. These languages are designed for human use, to make the task of programming easier. Computers understand only bits—the 1's and 0's of machine language. As a result, a program written in a high-level language must be translated into machine-readable form or it will be meaningless to the computer.

A **compiler** is a program that takes as input the program written in a high-level language and translates it, producing a machine-readable version of the program as output. The high-level language version of the program is called the **source program** or **source code** (the words *program* and *code* are interchangeable).

The translated machine-language version is called the **object program** or **object code**. The source program is the input, the object program is the output. A compiler translates the entire source program in a single operation. The translated program is incomplete. To be processed and produce output, it must be combined with other programs that reside in memory. These programs, which control input, output, and critical processing tasks such as disk access, are called **utility programs**. In addition, the object program may require prewritten mathematical routines, such as square root, that are combined at this stage. This linking of programs is automatically performed by a **linkage editor** or **link/load** program. The resulting loader program is ready to be processed. An object program can be loaded and run, or *executed*, as often as the user wishes to skip the translation phase.

For some computer languages, most notably BASIC, there is an alternative to translating an entire program before it is executed. An **interpreter** translates and executes a program one statement at a time. In other words, each program statement is translated and then executed before another statement is translated.

There are advantages and disadvantages to both procedures. Despite the careful efforts of the programmer, programs rarely translate perfectly the first time. Something in a statement or a series of statements may be inaccurate, missing, or typed incorrectly. Statements with such problems cannot be translated by the computer. Errors made in the use and structure of the programming language are called **syntax errors**. Syntax errors can occur in spoken languages, such as English, as well as computer languages. They are errors in grammar, spelling, and punctuation. Any error in a computer program is called a **bug**. Finding and correcting errors is called **debugging**.

Since an interpreter can translate and execute a statement as soon as it is typed in, errors are identified immediately. This makes it possible to correct mistakes immediately rather than waiting for the entire program to be keyed in and then translated by a compiler. Beginning programmers often find such immediate reinforcement supportive. On the other hand, every time such a program is used, each statement must be translated again. This is very time-consuming. Figure 7.1 shows how an interpreter works.

**Figure 7.1**    How an Interpreter Works.

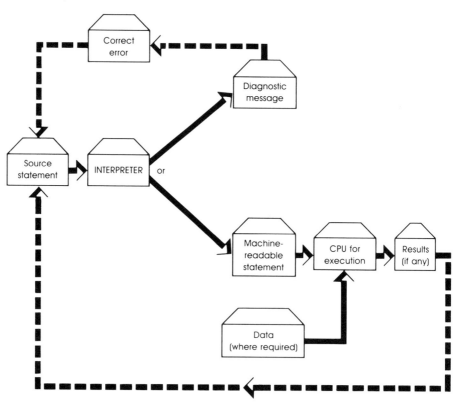

# On Line

## THE HISTORY OF THE BUG

In common English, a bug is an insect. The word *bug* in computer jargon means a programming error, but it has ties to these humble creatures.

During the development of the Harvard Mark I, the system abruptly stopped working one hot summer day. The Harvard Mark I's program was directly wired into its circuitry, so anything that interfered with the system's circuits would interrupt its processing. Researchers began a careful search of all the circuits and relays. Beneath an electromagnetic relay, they discovered a smashed moth. The moth was carefully removed with tweezers so the relay would not be damaged. The Harvard Mark I returned to operation, and the smashed moth was taped to a log book as evidence.

Whenever Harvard Mark I researchers encountered errors after the incident, they jokingly said they were searching for "bugs" as they examined the circuitry. Over the years, system and programming errors became known as bugs.

*Source:* M. Zientara, "Capt. Grace M. Hopper and the Genesis of Programming Languages," *Computerworld*, Nov. 16, 1981, p. 50.

A compiler, on the other hand, translates an entire source program at once. Correcting errors is more difficult, since a single error may affect many statements but may not be detected until the entire program has been entered. However, once the source program has been compiled properly, the resulting object program can be run repeatedly. Figure 7.2 shows how a compiler works.

When a program is translated by an interpreter or a compiler, two results are possible as each statement is converted into machine code. Either the statement translates and the process continues, or an error message is produced that attempts to diagnose the problem. Such **diagnostic messages** attempt to locate the syntax errors that made the statement impossible to translate. Corrections must be made to the source program. The corrected source program statement is then translated. This process is repeated until no syntax errors appear. Only when all syntax errors are corrected and a valid translation is made can a program produce the desired results.

Using the miles-per-gallon example in Chapter 6, the programs in Figure 7.3 have statements that contain syntax errors and cannot be translated. Whenever a compiler or interpreter encounters such statements, the incorrect statement is identified and a diagnostic message is produced to assist the programmer in the statement's correction.

**Figure 7.2**        How a Compiler Works.

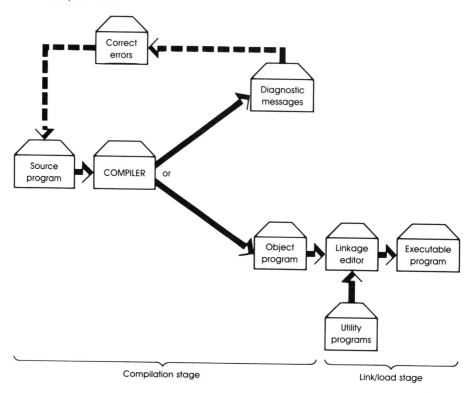

Compilation stage                    Link/load stage

Figure 7.4a contains the BASIC program along with the associated diagnostic messages. Lines 130 and 170 contain errors. In line 130 the word PRINT is missing, and in line 170 the formula has been written backwards:

```
170   LET   C - O = T      should appear as
170   LET   T = C - O
```

As you can see, when these statements are corrected, the program translates and can be executed.

In a similar fashion, the Pascal program in Figure 7.3b contains three syntax errors. When compiled (Figure 7.4b) these errors are identified and suggestions are provided for their correction. Diagnostic messages indicate the location in a program where translation became impossible. The messages try to assist the programmer. However, the messages themselves sometimes require interpretation. For example, look at the first message produced by the program in Figure 7.4b:

```
Error 41: Unknown identifier or syntax error
```

**Figure 7.3**   Programs with Errors: Compilers and interpreters identify incorrect statements and issue diagnostic messages in (a) BASIC and (b) Pascal.

(a) **BASIC**

```
100 REM -- USING ODOMETER READING AND GALLONS, --
105 REM --      CALCULATE MILES-PER-GALLON. --
110 PRINT "ENTER OLD ODOMETER READING: "
120 INPUT O
130 "ENTER CURRENT ODOMETER READING: "
140 INPUT C
150 PRINT "ENTER GALLONS USED: "
160 INPUT G
165 PRINT
170 LET C - O = T
180 LET M = T / G
190 PRINT "MILES-PER-GALLON =", USING "###.##";M
200 END
```

(b) **Pascal**

```
program travel (input,output);
  (* Using odometer readings and gallons  *)
  (*      calculate miles-per-gallon.     *)
var
  oldodometer, currentodometer: real;
  gallons, milestraveled : real;
  mpg : real;
begin
  write('Enter old odometer reading: ');
  readln(oldodometer);
  wrte('Enter current ododmeter reading: ');
  readln(currentodometer)
  write('Enter gallons used: ');
  readln(gallons);
  milestraveled := currentodometer - oldodometer;
  mpg = milestraveled/gallons;
  writeln(' Miles-per-gallon = ',mpg:5:2);
end.
```

**Figure 7.4**     Miles-per-Gallon Program with Diagnostic Messages in (a) BASIC and (b) Pascal.

(a) **BASIC**

```
100 REM -- USING ODOMETER READING AND GALLONS, --
105 REM --          CALCULATE MILES-PER-GALLON. --
110 PRINT "ENTER OLD ODOMETER READING: "
120 INPUT O
130 "ENTER CURRENT ODOMETER READING: "
140 INPUT C
150 PRINT "ENTER GALLONS USED: "
160 INPUT G
165 PRINT
170 LET C - O = T
180 LET M = T / G
190 PRINT "MILES-PER-GALLON =", USING "###.##";M
200 END
Ok
RUN
ENTER OLD ODOMETER READING;
? 1234
Syntax error in 130
Ok
130 "ENTER CURRENT ODOMETER READING: "
130 PRINT "ENTER CURRENT ODOMETER READING: "          (correction)
RUN
ENTER OLD ODOMETER READING:
? 1234
ENTER CURRENT ODOMETER READING:
? 1900
ENTER GALLONS USED:
? 20
Syntax error in 170
Ok
170 LET C - O = T
170 LET T = C - O          (correction)
```

This is trying to tell the programmer that the word *wrte* cannot be translated. It has been misspelled and should have been *write*. The remaining error messages more clearly identify and correct what is wrong with each statement.

---

**Figure 7.4**          Continued

(b) **Pascal**

```
program travel (input,output);
   (* Using odometer readings and gallons   *)
   (*        calculate miles-per-gallon.     *)
var
   oldodometer, currentodometer: real;
   gallons, milestraveled : real;
   mpg : real;
begin
   write('Enter old odometer reading: ');
   readln(oldodometer);
   wrte('Enter current ododmeter reading: ');
      ^
Error 41: Unknown identifier or syntax error.
   readln(currentodometer)^

Error 1: ';' expected.
   write('Enter gallons used: ');
   readln(gallons);
   milestraveled := currentodometer - oldodometer;
   mpg = milestraveled/gallons;
       ^
Error 7: ':=' expected.
   writeln(' Miles-per-gallon = ',mpg:5:2);
end.
```

---

## EXECUTING PROGRAMS

A program's complete translation implies nothing about the results produced by the program. Translation simply converts the program from a high-level language into machine-readable form. The machine-readable instructions, the logic of the program, may very well be faulty. If that is the case, the program results will not provide a useful solution to the problem. It is as though you received an invitation to a party, including directions, in the mail. Unfortunately, you find that the directions are written in a language that you cannot read. After finding someone to translate the directions, you leave for the party. If the translation is accurate, you will arrive at the party only if the directions are also correct. But if the directions are wrong—perhaps calling for a right turn where you should make a left—no matter how carefully you follow them you will never get to the party. The same is true with a computer program. An accurate translation of the program (compiler or interpreter) will only produce the expected results if the instructions, the logic of the program, are correct.

**Figure 7.5**  Executing a Program.

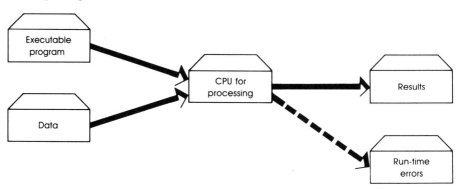

**Figure 7.6**  Properly Executed Programs in (a) BASIC and (b) Pascal.

(a)  **BASIC**

```
100 REM -- USING ODOMETER READING AND GALLONS, --
105 REM --          CALCULATE MILES-PER-GALLON. --
110 PRINT "ENTER OLD ODOMETER READING: "
120 INPUT O
130 PRINT "ENTER CURRENT ODOMETER READING: "
140 INPUT C
150 PRINT "ENTER GALLONS USED: "
160 INPUT G
165 PRINT
170 LET T = C - O
180 LET M = T / G
190 PRINT "MILES-PER-GALLON =", USING "###.##";M
200 END
Ok

RUN
ENTER OLD ODOMETER READING:
? 1234
ENTER CURRENT ODOMETER READING:
? 1900
ENTER GALLONS USED:
? 20
MILES-PER-GALLON =              33.30
```

Translating the program only makes it possible for the computer to follow the instructions. For the computer to produce the desired results, the program has to be run, or executed. When executing a program, each translated statement must be sent to the CPU, where the instructions can be followed. If data are to be processed, the data are read into the machine during the execution phase and results are produced (see Figure 7.5).

When a program is executed, three things can happen: (1) The program can work perfectly, producing the expected results; (2) The program can produce incorrect results; or (3) The program can stop executing or running, with the computer printing an error message (**run-time error**). A program that does not produce the desired results is said to have **aborted** or **bombed**.

Obviously the first result is the most desirable, as shown in Figure 7.6. However, programmers usually expend considerable effort adjusting a program's statements or code before correct results appear.

---

(b)  **Pascal**

```
program travel (input,output);
   (* Using odometer readings and gallons   *)
   (*        calculate miles-per-gallon.     *)
var
   oldodometer, currentodometer: real;
   gallons, milestraveled : real;
   mpg : real;
begin
   write('Enter old odometer reading: ');
   readln(oldodometer);
   write('Enter current ododmeter reading: ');
   readln(currentodometer);
   write('Enter gallons used: ');
   readln(gallons);
   milestraveled := currentodometer - oldodometer;
   mpg := milestraveled/gallons;
   writeln(' Miles-per-gallon = ',mpg:5:2);
end.
Running
Enter old odometer reading: 1234
Enter current odometer reading: 1900
Enter gallons used: 20
  Miles-per-gallon = 33.30
```

Run-time errors are the easiest execution errors to correct. This is because the error message hints at what is wrong. Run-time errors occur when the computer finds it impossible to complete the instruction being executed. For example, a calculation could result in the machine being asked to divide by zero (Figure 7.7), or to read more data than are available. If the correction requires a change in the program rather than the data, the source program must be adjusted. Then the translation process must be completed all over again before the revised program can again be executed.

---

**Figure 7.7**   Run-Time Errors in (a) BASIC and (b) Pascal.

(a) **BASIC**

```
100  REM -- USING ODOMETER READING AND GALLONS, --
105  REM --         CALCULATE MILES-PER-GALLON. --
110  PRINT "ENTER OLD ODOMETER READING: "
120  INPUT O
130  PRINT "ENTER CURRENT ODOMETER READING: "
140  INPUT C
150  PRINT "ENTER GALLONS USED: "
160  INPUT G
165  PRINT
170  LET T = C - O
180  LET M = T / G
190  PRINT "MILES-PER-GALLON =", USING "###.##";M
200  END
Ok
RUN
ENTER OLD ODOMETER READING:
?  1234
ENTER CURRENT ODOMETER READING:
?  1900
ENTER GALLONS USED:
?  0
Division by zero
```

If the program executes completely and there is no output or incorrect output results, there is a **logic error** in the program (Figure 7.8). A logic error occurs when the algorithm or logic of the program is incorrect. A computer will exactly follow the instructions provided. If these instructions are incorrect (garbage in) the expected results will not appear (garbage out). Logic errors are the most difficult to correct. No error messages have been produced to guide the programmer and the programmer must go back and re-analyze the algorithm and adjust it so that it solves the problem.

(b) **Pascal**

```
program travel (input,output);
   (* Using odometer readings and gallons   *)
   (*        calculate miles-per-gallon.      *)
var
   oldodometer, currentodometer: real;
   gallons, milestraveled : real;
   mpg : real;
begin
   write('Enter old odometer reading: ');
   readln(oldodometer);
   write('Enter current ododmeter reading: ');
   readln(currentodometer);
   write('Enter gallons used: ');
   readln(gallons);
   milestraveled := currentodometer - oldodometer;
   mpg := milestraveled/gallons;
   writeln(' Miles-per-gallon = ',mpg:5:2);
end.
Running
Enter old odometer reading: 1234
Enter current odometer reading: 1900
Enter gallons used: 0
Run-time error 02, PC=2E32
Program Aborted
```

**Figure 7.8** Programs with Logic Errors in (a) BASIC and (b) Pascal.

(a) **BASIC**

```
100 REM -- USING ODOMETER READING AND GALLONS, --
105 REM --          CALCULATE MILES-PER-GALLON. --
110 PRINT "ENTER OLD ODOMETER READING: "
120 INPUT O
130 PRINT "ENTER CURRENT ODOMETER READING: "
140 INPUT C
150 PRINT "ENTER GALLONS USED: "
160 INPUT G
165 PRINT
170 LET T = C - O
180 LET M = T - G
190 PRINT "MILES-PER-GALLON =", USING "###.##";M
200 END
Ok

RUN
ENTER OLD ODOMETER READING:
? 1234
ENTER CURRENT ODOMETER READING:
? 1900
ENTER GALLONS USED:
? 20
MILES-PER-GALLON =                    646.00
```

---

## DEBUGGING

As we have seen, any error found in a program is called a bug, and the process of correcting errors is called debugging. There are three kinds of program bugs: (1) syntax errors, (2) run-time errors, and (3) logic errors. It is generally easy to locate and correct syntax and run-time errors, because the computer's error messages indicate the location and nature of the error.

Logic errors, on the other hand, indicate an error in the programmer's solution to the original problem. A logic error will occur when the algorithm is incorrect and does not solve the problem. Logic errors will also occur when an algorithm has been incorrectly programmed; that is, when the program statements do not correctly state the steps to be taken by the computer.

(b) **Pascal**

```
program travel (input,output);
  (* Using odometer readings and gallons  *)
  (*       calculate miles-per-gallon.    *)
var
  oldodometer, currentodometer: real;
  gallons, milestraveled : real;
  mpg : real;
begin
  write('Enter old odometer reading: ');
  readln(oldodometer);
  write('Enter current ododmeter reading: ');
  readln(currentodometer);
  write('Enter gallons used: ');
  readln(gallons);
  milestraveled := currentodometer - oldodometer;
  mpg := milestraveled - gallons;
  writeln(' Miles-per-gallon = ',mpg:5:2);
end.
Running
Enter old odometer reading: 1234
Enter current odometer reading: 1900
Enter gallons used: 20
 Miles-per-gallon = 646.00
```

Correcting logic errors requires attention and persistence. The two most common methods for correcting logic errors are hand simulation, or desk checking, and the printing of intermediate values.

## Hand Simulation

In **hand simulation**, or **desk checking**, the programmer uses pencil and paper to act the part of the computer. Starting with the very first program statement, the programmer follows the instructions set down in the program just as the computer would. By stepping through each instruction and knowing what the expected result should be at each stage, the programmer should be able to identify the step or steps that are producing the error and correct them. This is a time-consuming procedure. The programmer must carefully follow the instructions exactly as they are written, not as they were intended to be.

### Intermediate Results

Every program contains some statements that produce output. In addition, throughout the program, partial or intermediate results have been calculated and stored in memory. These results are not usually printed as output since they are not needed to support the program's conclusions. When an executed program produces results that are incorrect, it is often useful to go back and examine these intermediate results. The programmer should go back to the source program and add output statements to enable all temporary results to be printed as output. When this new version of the program is reviewed, not only will the original results (incorrect as they may be) be produced, but all the intermediate results will be visible as well. By examining these intermediate results and comparing them to the expected results at each stage, the programmer can locate the source of the problem and correct it.

The miles-per-gallon examples found in Figure 7.8 translate without syntax errors. However, as indicated they do not produce the correct results. With an old odometer reading of 1234 miles, a current reading of 1900 miles, and 20 gallons of gasoline used, we can see that the miles per gallon calculated should be 33.3.

|   | |
|---:|---|
| 1,900 | current odometer reading |
| – 1,234 | old odometer reading |
| 666 | total miles traveled |

mpg = total miles traveled / gallons used
mpg = 666 / 20 = 33.3

Unfortunately, the programs in Figure 7.8 do not produce the expected results. In Figure 7.9 additional statements have been added to both the BASIC and Pascal programs to write out the values of total miles traveled and gallons used. An examination of these values and the programs reveals that the formula for calculating miles per gallon in each program is incorrect. A subtraction sign has been used instead of division. Correcting this error produces a program that executes properly. The now-extraneous output statements can be removed.

Programmers often use hand simulation and the printing of intermediate results to analyze and correct errors in an algorithm. Some systems include special software debugging tools to assist programmers in finding and correcting errors.

## TESTING

Once a program appears to work and produces the expected results for a given set of data, it should be tested for accuracy. It is possible that a program will work with one set of data and not with another. Every section of the program's

---

**Figure 7.9**        Incorrect Results: When program results are incorrect, obtaining intermediate results may help the
programmer find the error in (a) BASIC and (b) Pascal.

(a)  **BASIC**

```
100 REM -- USING ODOMETER READING AND GALLONS, --
105 REM --        CALCULATE MILES-PER-GALLON. --
110 PRINT "ENTER OLD ODOMETER READING: "
120 INPUT O
130 PRINT "ENTER CURRENT ODOMETER READING: "
140 INPUT C
150 PRINT "ENTER GALLONS USED: "
160 INPUT G
165 PRINT
170 LET T = C - O
175     PRINT "T =",T
176     PRINT "G =",G
180 LET M = T - G
190 PRINT "MILES-PER-GALLON =", USING "###.##";M
200 END
Ok
```

```
RUN
ENTER OLD ODOMETER READING:
? 1234
ENTER CURRENT ODOMETER READING:
? 1900
ENTER GALLONS USED:
? 20
T =               666
G =                20
MILES-PER-GALLON =                646.00
180 LET M = T / G                                      (correction)
RUN
ENTER OLD ODOMETER READING:
? 1234
ENTER CURRENT ODOMETER READING:
? 1900
ENTER GALLONS USED:
? 20
T =               666
G =                20
MILES-PER-GALLON =                33.30
DELETE 175
Ok
DELETE 176
```

**Figure 7.9**    (b)  **Pascal**

```pascal
program travel (input,output);
  (* Using odometer readings and gallons  *)
  (*       calculate miles-per-gallon.    *)
var
  oldodometer, currentodometer: real;
  gallons, milestraveled : real;
  mpg : real;
begin
  write('Enter old odometer reading: ');
  readln(oldodometer);
  write('Enter current ododmeter reading: ');
  readln(currentodometer);
  write('Enter gallons used: ');
  readln(gallons);
  milestraveled := currentodometer - oldodometer;
  mpg := milestraveled - gallons;
  writeln(' Miles-per-gallon = ',mpg:5:2);
end.
```

```
Running
Enter old odometer reading: 1234
Enter current odometer reading: 1900
Enter gallons used: 20
 Miles-per-gallon = 646.00
```

```pascal
program travel (input,output);
  (* Using odometer readings and gallons  *)
  (*       calculate miles-per-gallon.    *)
var
  oldodometer, currentodometer: real;
  gallons, milestraveled : real;
  mpg : real;
begin
  write('Enter old odometer reading: ');
  readln(oldodometer);
  write('Enter current ododmeter reading: ');
  readln(currentodometer);
  write('Enter gallons used: ');
  readln(gallons);
  milestraveled := currentodometer - oldodometer;
      writeln('milestraveled =', milestraveled:5:2);
      writeln('gallons =',gallons:5:2);
  mpg := milestraveled - gallons;
  writeln(' Miles-per-gallon = ',mpg:5:2);
end.
```

```
Running
Enter old odometer reading: 1234
Enter current odometer reading: 1900
Enter gallons used: 20
milestraveled =666.00
gallons =20.00
 Miles-per-gallon = 646.00

program travel (input,output);
   (* Using odometer readings and gallons   *)
   (*       calculate miles-per-gallon.     *)
var
   oldodometer, currentodometer: real;
   gallons, milestraveled : real;
   mpg : real;
begin
   write('Enter old odometer reading: ');
   readln(oldodometer);
   write('Enter current ododmeter reading: ');
   readln(currentodometer);
   write('Enter gallons used: ');
   readln(gallons);
   milestraveled := currentodometer - oldodometer;
      writeln('milestraveled =', milestraveled:5:2);
      writeln('gallons =',gallons:5:2);
   mpg := milestraveled / gallons;
   writeln(' Miles-per-gallon = ',mpg:5:2);
end.

Running
Enter old odometer reading: 1234
Enter current odometer reading: 1900
Enter gallons used: 20
milestraveled =666.00
gallons =20.00
 Miles-per-gallon = 33.30
```

code must be thoroughly tested. Test data should be chosen to resemble the real-life data that the program would normally deal with. For example, it is common for real-life programs to encounter incorrect or insufficient data. A well-written program should deal with common and even unexpected errors in some reasonable way.

Developing successful programs is 10 percent inspiration and 90 percent concentration. While it is possible to design and debug programs by randomly changing things to see what happens, this technique is very inefficient. It is time-consuming and produces programs that are difficult to adjust and impossible to follow. Careful planning, attention in designing algorithms, and patience in debugging programs ensures their accuracy and produces rewarding results.

## SUMMARY

Computer programs, both prewritten applications packages and user-designed programs, use computer files. A computer file is a collection of related information. Unique file names distinguish one file from another. Well-chosen file names help to identify the contents of the file.

Programs written in high-level languages cannot be directly understood by computers. They must be translated into machine-readable form. The high-level language version of the program is the source program, the machine-language version is the object program.

A compiler translates an entire source program in a single operation. The translated object program is then executed. An interpreter translates and executes a program one statement at a time. During translation, a program's individual statements either translate or produce syntax errors.

Translating a program only makes it possible for the computer to follow the indicated instructions. For the computer to produce results, the program must be executed. An executed program can either (1) work perfectly, (2) produce incorrect results, or (3) stop executing as the result of run-time errors.

Debugging is the process of correcting program errors. Debugging includes desk checking and the listing of intermediate results to verify computations.

Test data should be used to verify that all sections of a program operate properly.

## Key Words

As an extra review of the chapter, try defining the following terms. If you have trouble with any of them, refer to the page number listed.

aborted (bombed)  *(186)*
bug  *(180)*
compiler  *(179)*
debugging  *(180)*
diagnostic messages  *(181)*
hand simulation (desk checking)
   *(191)*
interpreter  *(179)*

linkage editor (link/load program)
   *(179)*
logic error  *(189)*
object program (object code)  *(179)*
run-time error  *(186)*
source program (source code)  *(179)*
syntax errors  *(180)*
utility programs  *(179)*

## Test Your Knowledge

1. How should file names be chosen?

2. Give two examples of well-chosen file names.

3. What is a compiler?

4. How is a source program different from an object program?

5. How does an interpreter differ from a compiler?

6. What role does a linkage editor play in processing a program?

7. What is a syntax error? What causes it?

8. What role do diagnostic messages play in error correction?

9. If a program translates correctly, does that imply that the correct answers will be produced when executed? Defend your position.

10. What occurs when a program is executed?

11. What are the three types of errors frequently encountered in programs?

12. Why are logic errors so difficult to find?

13. What is a bug in a computer program?

14. How is desk checking used to debug a program?

15. How are intermediate results used to debug a program?

## Expand Your Knowledge

1. Go to your school's computing center and find out what language translators are available. What departments are heavy users of these translators? Are they compilers or interpreters?

2. Prewritten software can contain errors. Go to a local computer store and investigate what a user can do if such software contains errors and does not perform properly.

3. Using the hourly salary with overtime example analyzed in Chapter 6, develop a set of test data that could be used to check the program. What kinds of incorrect data might a user type into the program? Include these in your test data.

# 8

# Programming Languages

**Chapter Outline**

Types of Computer Languages
   Machine Language • Assembly Language • High-Level Languages •
   Natural Language Processing

Choosing a Computer Language

Common Languages
   FORTRAN (Uses and Limitations; Organization)
   BASIC (Uses and Limitations; Organization)
   Pascal (Uses and Limitations; Organization)

Other Popular High-Level Languages
   ALGOL • COBOL • LISP • LOGO

Languages Gaining in Popularity
   Ada • C • Modula-2

Computers are machines. They are tools for problem solving that require detailed instructions to perform any task. These instructions, or programs, must be provided in languages that computers can understand. As we have seen, computers do not understand human language. Programming languages have been developed so that people and computers can communicate relatively easily.

It certainly would be easier to talk to a computer in English than it is to write a computer program. Yet English—or any human or natural language for that matter—can be ambiguous. The literal meanings of our words may not fully express our intentions. We often say one thing and mean another or give incomplete directions. Our facial expressions, tone of voice, and body language usually help us to communicate and often change the meaning of our words. Natural language is rich in slang and idiomatic expressions, and our colorful speech may lead to misunderstandings. For example, a student rushes into class late and in a frustrated voice says to a friend who is not a native speaker of English, "My car broke down on me!" The friend responds, "Oh no! Were you badly hurt?" The friend interpreted the statement literally and understood that the car had actually broken on top of the speaker, causing possible physical injury. The idiom, of course, simply implied that the car was not operating properly.

Communicating with computers leaves no room for ambiguity. Computers require very specific instructions. We cannot simply tell the machine to perform addition, we must specify that $A$ is added to $B$ and $C$ in a mathematical expression: $A + B + C$.

A **programming language** is a language that people use to communicate with computers. It has a specific and limited vocabulary and a set of syntax rules for structuring statements. Each word, phrase, and symbol has a very specific meaning and must appear in a particular order to be understood by the computer. These programming languages are the subject of this chaper.

After studying this chapter, you will be able to:

- Describe the categories of computer languages.

- Explain the differences between low-level and high-level languages.

- List the criteria for choosing a programming language.

- Identify the most commonly used programming languages.

- Describe the advantages and disadvantages of three of the most common computer languages.

- Discuss the differences between the newest computer languages and existing languages.

## TYPES OF COMPUTER LANGUAGES

There are hundreds of different computer languages but only a few, such as FORTRAN, BASIC, Pascal, and C, are widely used. A number of attempts have been made to develop a single language that does all things well. Such languages have not caught on, however. These languages are by necessity very complex, difficult to learn, and usually run only on large systems.

Computer languages relate to the computer in different ways. In a sense, not all computer languages are "created equal." Computer languages fall into a number of broad categories. The less complex the language's statements (the lower its sophistication level), the closer its relationship to the machine itself. The higher the sophistication, the easier it is to use the language to write programs. From lowest to highest, the classifications are:

- machine language
- assembly language
- high-level languages
- natural language processing

Early computers, built in the late 1940s and early 1950s, were programmed by adjusting the wires and switches that made up the machine. The resulting circuitry solved a particular problem. To solve another problem, the wires and switches had to be readjusted. This was a very slow and arduous task requiring an intimate knowledge of the machine. Putting a program into the machine often required an entire day.

As we saw in Chapter 2, von Neumann developed the concept of the stored program, in which a lengthy sequence of instructions could be stored in the computer's memory along with data. This became possible when instructions were expressed as a code that corresponded to the circuit path needed to solve a problem. Von Neumann's ideas lead to the development of machine language.

### Machine Language

A **machine language** is a code used to communicate with a particular computer. Instructions are coded as groups of ones and zeros (binary numbers), which represent the electronic pathways necessary for solving a problem. Machine language or machine code is the only language the computer directly understands. It is the computer's "native" language. Since computers manufactured by different companies have unique internal designs, each brand and model of computer has a unique, **machine-dependent** machine language. An IBM mainframe will have a different machine language or code from a Digital Equipment Corp. machine. Similarly, the machine code for the Macintosh is different from that used by the IBM Personal System/2 or Commodore Amiga.

Every statement in machine language contains an instruction and the data or the location of the data that the instruction will use. Compared to rewiring the machine for each problem, machine language was a giant step forward. However, writing long sequences of binary digits is as intricate as plugging in hundreds of wires. It is very easy to make mistakes. Machine language is very difficult to write, incredibly error-prone because it is entered by humans, and requires considerable knowledge of machine hardware since its statements represent circuit paths.

## Assembly Language

Because writing programs in machine language is so tedious and prone to errors, **assembly languages**, or simply **assemblers**, were invented. Instead of statements consisting of long series of zeros and ones, assembly language instructions contain easily remembered abbreviations or mnemonics such as SUB for subtract, CLR for clear, or MOV for move. Data are specified directly as numeric quantities or represented by a name given to the location in computer memory where the required data can be found.

Compared to machine language programs, assembly language programs are much easier for people to write and fairly understandable to read. However, like machine languages before them, assembly languages are machine-dependent. Different computers require different assembly languages, and programs written for one machine will not run on another. Moreover, assembly-language programs cannot be executed (processed) directly by a computer. First they must be translated, or *assembled*, into machine-readable form (machine code) before they can be processed. Despite their considerable improvement over machine language programs, assembly language programs are still very detailed. They are usually quite long and, like machine language, are error-prone. Each assembly language statement translates directly into a single machine language instruction. A thorough knowledge of the computer hardware on the part of the programmer is often required for writing efficient code. Figure 8.1 illustrates the mathematical equivalent of $C = A + B$.

With the development of high-level languages, fewer problems are being solved with assembly languages. However, assembly languages continue to be valuable tools for solving the kinds of problems that call for direct communication with the computer's hardware. Much of the operating system software used to operate computer systems is written in assembly languages. In addition, program sections that "talk" to peripheral devices such as printers, disk drives, and monitors frequently use assembly language. Assembly language programs run very quickly and take up very little space in memory.

---

**Figure 8.1**    Assembly Language Example: This program segment is written in MACRO-11, the assembly language of the VAX-11 family of computers from Digital Equipment Corp. The program picks up two integers stored in memory, adds them, and puts the result back into memory. This is the mathematical equivalent of $C = A + B$.

```
A:    .WORD       123          :reserve a word for A and initialize
B:    .WORD       307          :reserve a word for B and initialize
C:    .BLKL       1            :reserve a long word for C
      .ENTRY      EXAMPLE.0    :define entry point into code
      CLRL        R7           :set 32-bit registers R7 and
      CLRL        R8           : R8 to zero
      MOVW        R7,A         :bring A and B from memory into and
      MOVW        R8, B        : R8 in the CPU, respectively
      ADDL2       R7,R8        :add R7 and R8, result in R8
      MOVL        R8,C         :move R8 to memory in C
      $EXIT-S                  :exit program
      .END        EXAMPLE      :end of code
```

## High-Level Languages

Although assembly languages were an improvement over machine language, programmers still had to concentrate on the machine rather than on the problems they were solving. The development of high-level programming languages allowed programmers to focus on finding procedures to solve problems. In contrast to both machine and assembly languages, they no longer had to concentrate on how the computer would process the program.

High-level languages have a structure more like that of natural languages such as English. Each high-level language is designed around a set of rules that define how words and mathematical expressions can be combined within the language. These rules are known as the *syntax* of the language.

High-level languages are easier for people to understand than assembly or machine languages because they use familiar English terms and follow a limited set of rules. Statements resemble a combination of English sentences and mathematical equations.

Unfortunately, while people find high-level languages somewhat readable, computers do not. High-level languages, like assembly language programs, must be translated into machine-readable form before they can be processed by any computer. One statement in a high-level language may translate into many machine-level instructions. A translator program is required to handle many of the hardware details that would have required the programmer's attention in a lower-level language. As discussed in Chapter 7, translator programs transform statements written in a particular high-level language into the machine language appropriate for the specific computer being used. While high-level languages remain essentially the same from machine to machine, translator programs are keyed to specific computer hardware. As a result, most high-level languages are **machine-independent**, which means they will operate on any computer for which an appropriate translator program exists. High-level languages are **portable**, meaning that programs can be moved from machine to machine with only minor changes required. In this way, programs can solve problems on machines used by many different people.

Programming in a high-level language is easier, less time-consuming, less frustrating, and less error-prone than assembly language programming. For these reasons, high-level languages lend themselves to the solution of more complex problems than their lower-level counterparts.

## Natural Language Processing

As we have seen, computer languages have become more and more "English-like" over the years. The next logical step in the development of computer languages would seem to be systems that understand natural languages, the languages spoken by people. A major research area today within the computer science field of artificial intelligence is natural language processing, or natural language understanding.

Scientists studying natural language and its implications for computers approach the topic from two different directions. Some computer scientists work with colleagues in linguistics and psychology to explain how people learn and understand language. Computer models of natural language are developed to better understand how we use language. The more closely the computer model mimics natural language, the more clearly language and the human learning process is understood. The focus is on understanding language and the human mind.

The other approach, popularized by Japanese research and reflected in some applications software available in the United States, is the development of software that appears to understand natural language. However, such natural language systems may not process language the way people do. The focus here is on the computer and getting the machine to "speak" in human ways. In such systems, a person can give a computer an instruction or information in ordinary sentences and receive appropriate answers from the computer. For example, the user may tell a data base to "List the names of all clients whose permanent residence is Alaska" or ask "How many students received a grade lower than C on the first exam?"

While such systems use queries written in what appears to be natural language, the scope of the questions, the structure of the sentences, and the allowable vocabulary are by necessity very limited. With such limited queries, natural language systems can work effectively. Unfortunately, users may get a false sense of the capabilities of the system and they may lose sight of the system's limitations. Novice users may begin to expect the system to behave much like the computers on Star Trek—able to answer almost any question. When such systems fail to answer questions outside their sphere of knowledge, users can become confused and frustrated.

The development of programs that truly understand the spoken word is not really around the corner. Such systems will require a far greater understanding of human learning and the use of language than currently exists. However, the use of natural language systems for specific purposes will continue to expand as the need for computerized information by unsophisticated users becomes more and more important.

## CHOOSING A COMPUTER LANGUAGE

Today hundreds of computer languages exist. With such variety, how do programmers choose the languages they use? Ideally, programs should be written in the language that is most appropriate to the task. Of course, "most appropriate" will mean different things in different settings. The following criteria can prove helpful when choosing a language:

1. *Familiarity.* In many cases, programmers simply choose from among the languages they know best. While most programmers can learn a new language fairly quickly, a problem that requires an immediate solution allows no lead time for learning.

2. *Availability.* Not all languages are available on all machines. Availability is not limited exclusively by hardware, it is often limited by what an organization can afford. Translator programs can be very expensive and organizations may choose to use what they already own rather than purchase additional software to solve a specific problem.

3. *Suitability.* Some languages are particularly well suited to solving specific types of problems. For example, FORTRAN is an excellent language for solving scientific and engineering problems. COBOL is very effective in generating the voluminous output required by many businesses, and MUMPS was developed for the medical community to assist doctors in diagnosing diseases. For consistency, many organizations require that all programs be written in a specific language or selected from a limited number of languages. In such cases, programmers have no choice but to use what is required. For example, the U.S. Department of Defense intends to require that all programs written for the military use Ada.

4. *Efficiency.* Assembly language programs run faster than those written in high-level languages but they take longer to write and debug. As a result, most applications are written in high-level languages. However, not all translator programs are equally good. Even within a specific language,

many translators are available and some execute programs faster than others. A program written in UCSD Pascal, for example, will run much slower than one written in the more recently released TURBO Pascal.

5. *Longevity.* Computer hardware changes constantly. Such changes need to be considered when choosing a programming language. Languages that are standardized and popular are more likely to survive rapidly changing technology. Some older languages, such as COBOL, seem to live longer than expected simply because of the vast numbers of programs that exist in the language. In many cases, it is less time-consuming and therefore less expensive to update and modify an existing code than to rewrite it in a language that might be more efficient.

6. *Supportability.* A language must be chosen with an eye to the future. A language that is no longer being updated and improved is a poor choice in the changing world of computers. A program will not be overly valuable if it is written in a language that is not available on the new machine an organization purchases. Within organizations, a language able to be used by more than one programmer can be very important. In this way, programmers can help each other debug programs, and modifications can be made by someone other than the original programmer.

## COMMON LANGUAGES

To more clearly understand the differences between languages, we will examine in detail three of the most popular languages. Three programs will be presented that illustrate the algorithm developed in Chapter 6 for calculating the pay due to an individual who works for an hourly wage with overtime. However, one cannot get a true feel for the variety of programming languages with only three examples. As a result, we will briefly examine a number of other commonly used and new up-and-coming languages.

### FORTRAN

FORTRAN is an acronym for FORmula TRANslation. It was created at IBM in 1954 and two years later became the first high-level language to be commercially available. It was designed to process the large amounts of numeric data common in mathematical, scientific, and engineering problems.

**Uses and Limitations**    FORTRAN was the first widely used programming language. It is still in use after more than 30 years, which makes it very, very old in terms of the life span of modern computers. FORTRAN is a concise, compact language whose statements closely resemble mathematical equations. This is its outstanding feature. FORTRAN remains, as its developers intended, one of the best languages for programs involving numeric information and complicated formulas. To ensure that a program written in FORTRAN will run on a variety of computers with little or no modification, there is a standard version. This makes FORTRAN programs highly portable. The FORTRAN standard has been regularly revised and updated.

FORTRAN has some shortcomings. Designed to handle numeric information, it is difficult to process character information (data expressed in letters) using FORTRAN. Despite changes reflected in the recent standard (FORTRAN 77), input and output statements are very formal and inflexible, which makes them difficult to use. FORTRAN does not deal well with information stored in multiple files. These factors make it a poor language for most business applications. In addition, FORTRAN programs are often hard to follow by simply reading them. They require extensive documentation explaining how the program works.

**Organization**    As we can see in Figure 8.2, a program written in FORTRAN consists of a sequence of statements.

Statements appear one to a line in the order in which they are executed. Branching statements, which alter the order in which statements are executed, are included where necessary. The IF-THEN/ELSE/ENDIF block is an example of a branching statement. All statements must start in specific locations on the line and may be no more than 72 characters long. This length reflects the format of punched computer cards that were used as standard input when the language was developed. Statement numbers, such as 10, 40, and 50, appear at the left margin of those statements referenced within the program. Reserved words are used to indicate tasks the computer is to perform, such as READ, WRITE, and FORMAT. Large, complex programs are often divided into parts called **subprograms**. Each subprogram solves a specific part of the problem.

## BASIC

BASIC, which stands for Beginner's All-Purpose Symbolic Instruction Code, was invented in the early 1960s by Thomas Kurtz and John Kemeny to teach programming at Dartmouth College. BASIC was derived in part from FORTRAN and in some ways is a simplified version. It became available for general use in 1965. BASIC was designed to allow users to communicate, or *interact*, with the computer as programs executed. In other words, data is supplied by the user as needed by the program. This produces an environment where programmers are actively involved in the processing of a program. BASIC programs are more user-friendly than those written in FORTRAN.

**Uses and Limitations**    Many people believe that BASIC is easy to learn and use. Beginners can write and run simple programs after only a few hours of

---

**Figure 8.2**  A FORTRAN Program.

```
C       FORTRAN 77 PROGRAM
C       CALCULATE HOURLY· SALARY
C
C       INPUT DATA
        READ(5,10) REGHRS, OTRATE
        READ(5,10) HOURS, RATE
10      FORMAT(F4.1,2X,F5.2)
C
C       CALCULATE GROSS WAGES WITH OVER TIME FORMULA
        IF (HOURS .GT. REGHRS) THEN
            OTHRS = HOURS -REGHRS
            REGPAY = REGHRS * RATE
            OT = OTHRS * OTRATE * RATE
            GROSS = REGPAY + OT
        ELSE
C       CALCULATE GROSS WAGES WITH NO OVERTIME
            GROSS = HOURS * RATE
        ENDIF
C
C       OUTPUT RESULTS
        WRITE(6,40)
40      FORMAT(1X,'  HOURS   RATE   WAGES')
        WRITE(6,50) HOURS, RATE, GROSS
50      FORMAT(3X,F4.1,2X,F5.2,1X,F8.2)
C
        STOP
        END
```

A statement with a "C" in column 1 is a COMMENT. A comment serves as explanation of the code and is not executed.

This FORMAT statement describes the data for the above READ.

The next 5 statements calculate gross salary if overtime is worked.

This statement calculates gross salary if there is NO overtime.

This FORMAT statement describes output.

This FORMAT statement describes output.

study. There are relatively few commands to learn. BASIC handles many programming details for the user and can be used to solve a wide variety of problems. It can process both numbers and characters (letters and symbols) and can be used to solve fairly complex mathematical problems. It is usually an interpreted language, although there are compilers. BASIC interpreters and compilers require little memory and run on even a minimally equipped microcomputer. As a result, BASIC is the most commonly used language for microcomputer programming.

However, because BASIC has so few rules, programs written in this language are hard to follow. BASIC does not foster good programming style. Many consider BASIC a "quick and dirty" language. Its very strength of simplicity for quick learning is its major weakness. It tempts novices to try to solve a problem without first working through the steps needed for the solution. While BASIC was not designed to handle large amounts of data, its availability on microcomputers and ease of learning has led to its use by many small businesses. There is a standardized version of BASIC but it is very limited. Most translator manufacturers produce versions with many modifications and extensions. As a result, there are many different BASICs, and programs may require major changes for use on different machines. Long programs can be very difficult to follow and a person must rely on documentation in order to understand the program.

**Organization**    Figure 8.3 illustrates the BASIC solution to the salary problem whose algorithm was developed in Chapter 6.

BASIC statements are usually entered one per line with each line consecutively numbered. Programs terminate with the END statement. While subprograms exist, they are not as flexible as subprograms in other high-level languages and programs are frequently written as single units.

In BASIC, reserved words such as INPUT, PRINT, and GOTO are used to direct the computer to perform a specific task. Some BASIC translator programs require that variable names be restricted to a single letter, possibly followed by a number for numeric quantities and a letter followed by a dollar sign ($) for characters. Such variable names make undocumented programs rather unreadable.

Despite its availability on microcomputers, the tendency by its users to design hard-to-follow programs has lead the National College Board to choose Pascal rather than BASIC as the language of its Advanced Placement (AP) exam. The AP exam awards college credits for programming skills learned in high school. In an effort to return BASIC to its intended purpose as an easy-to-learn teaching language, Kemeny and Kurtz have developed a structured version of BASIC called TRUE BASIC. TRUE BASIC provides for additional syntax rules and encourages longer, more meaningful variable names, making its programs easier to read.

## Pascal

Pascal was written in 1968 by Niklaus Wirth of Switzerland. It was intended as a general-purpose teaching language emphasizing top-down design. Its syntax structure supports well-designed algorithms. The language is named after the French mathematician Blaise Pascal, who invented an early mechanical calculator (see Chapter 2). The first compiler was made available in 1971. Pascal is a powerful language capable of dealing with numbers as well as characters. Be-

**Figure 8.3**    The BASIC Solution: This is the BASIC solution to the salary problem whose algorithm was developed in Chapter 6.

```
 95    PRINT "ENTER REGULAR HOURS AND OVERTIME RATE: "
100    INPUT T, P
105    PRINT "ENTER HOURS AND PAYRATE: "
110    INPUT H, R
115    REM -- DEPENDING ON HOURS WORKED DOES --
116    REM -- EMPLOYEE GET OVERTIME PAY. --
120    IF H > T THEN 150  ELSE 200
150       LET O = H - T
160       LET R1 = T * R
170       LET O1 = O * P * R
180       LET W = R + O1
190    GOTO 300
195    REM -- CALCULATE WAGES WITHOUT --
196    REM -- OVERTIME PAY. --
200       LET W = H * R
300    PRINT "  HOURS   RATE    WAGES"
310    PRINT USING " ##     #.##  ###.##",H,R,W
999    END
```

Data is entered with an INPUT statement.

REM stands for REMARK and like the comment in FORTRAN explains the code.
All statements are numbered. Statements are executed in numeric order unless an alternative is specified.
ELSE 200 causes a branch to statement 200.
GOTO 300 causes a branch to statement 300.
PRINT statements produce output. # indicates the location of a number.

cause it is easy to learn and imposes good programming style, it is taught as a first programming language in many colleges and universities.

**Uses and Limitations**    Pascal's strength lies in its structure. It can be used to solve a wide range of programming problems. Yet Pascal has relatively few commands, and a novice programmer can learn to write simple programs very quickly. At the same time, it is better suited than many other languages to the development of large, complex programs. Using Pascal's international standard, most Pascal programs are portable. With its limited number of commands, fast compilers requiring very little memory are available on most microcomputers. Pascal is rapidly becoming a real competitor to BASIC as the primary microcomputer language.

Pascal has weaknesses as well. Because it is so powerful, its commands are very brief and concise. Documentation containing full translations helps to clarify the code. Pascal was not intended as a language for business applications and is limited in its ability to handle multiple files. Despite this, many businesses use Pascal for such applications.

**Organization**    As we can see in Figure 8.4, each program starts by stating the program name and specifying the files required by the program.

If only (input, output) are listed, data is expected to be entered from the keyboard with output going to the screen. The statements immediately following the var, identify whether the values used by or calculated within the program will be integers, reals, characters, or true or false. Pascal encourages the use of subprograms.

Statements need not be entered one to a line. Placing more than one statement on a line is possible. Each statement must end with a semicolon. Usually, statements are written in standard outline form indented from the left margin to indicate the relationships between statements. Use of outline style has proven so easy to follow that modifications of this technique are now used with older languages such as BASIC and FORTRAN.

---

**Figure 8.4**        The Start of a Pascal Program.

```
program payroll2 (input, output);
var
   hours, payrate, othours, otwages: real;
   regwages, wages, reghours, otrate : real;
begin
   write('Enter regular hours and overtime rate: ');
   readln (reghours, otrate);
      (*  Depending on hours worked, does    *)
      (*    employee get overtime pay?        *)
   write('Enter hours and payrate: ');
   readln (hours, payrate);
   if hours > reghours then
      begin
        regwages := reghours * payrate;
        othours := hours - reghours;
        otwages := othours * otrate * payrate;
        wages := regwages + otwages;
      end
   else
      (*  Calculate wages without   *)
      (*    overtime pay.           *)
      wages := hours * payrate
   writeln(' HOURS   RATE   WAGES');
   writeln(hours:5, rate:8:2, wages:9:2)
   end.
```

var stands for variable. This section lists all variables used in the program and their type. begin indicates where the code starts.

Calculates wages including overtime.

Calculates wages without overtime.
write contains a description of the output.

## OTHER POPULAR HIGH-LEVEL LANGUAGES

In addition to the languages described, hundreds of other computer languages exist. While programs have been written in all of them, only a few are commonly used and several new languages are gaining acceptance for specific purposes. Let us examine some of these languages.

### ALGOL

Standing for ALGOrithmic Language, ALGOL was developed by a group of international computer scientists in the late 1960s. It was designed for scientific programming and is not suited to operations on multiple files. ALGOL has found more use among European programmers than among those in the United States. Its structure significantly influenced the development of Pascal.

### COBOL

COBOL stands for COmmon Business Oriented Language. It was invented in the late 1950s at a conference organized by the U.S. Defense Department and attended by representatives of government and industry. The purpose of the conference was to develop a standard language for business applications in which programs could easily be moved from one machine to another. To spur the use of COBOL, in the 1960s the federal government required that all the computers it purchased run COBOL and all government software be written in COBOL. Use of any other language required convincing evidence that COBOL was not appropriate. Since the government was the largest consumer of computer products at the time, COBOL spread rapidly.

COBOL uses English verbs such as READ, WRITE, ADD, SUBTRACT, MOVE, and COMPUTE to indicate the operations to be performed. COBOL was designed as an English-like, self-documenting language that a non-programmer could follow. It deals well with large amounts of character data, such as names and addresses. Numeric data, including dollars and cents and numeric codes such as social security numbers are easily processed. The language is not designed to perform complex calculations. In addition, COBOL programs are incredibly wordy, making it is almost impossible to write a short COBOL program.

### LISP

LISP, for LISt Processing, was developed in 1958 at The Massachusetts Institute of Technology (MIT) by John McCarthy as a language for developing artificial intelligence (AI) programs. It is an interactive language designed to manipulate non-numeric information such as characters, symbols, words, phrases, and even shapes. Objects are associated with lists of features. LISP is the most popular AI

**Figure 8.5**        LISP: This illustrates the LISP version of the salary problem discussed in Chapter 6.

```
(defun compute-wages ()                                          Read in data.
 (princ "Enter hours worked > ")                                 Read in hours worked.
 (setq hours (read))
 (princ "Enter pay-rate > ")                                     Read in pay rate.
 (setq payrate (read))
 (princ "Enter number of regular hours > ")                      Read in regular hours.
 (setq regular-hours (read))
 (princ "Enter overtime pay-rate > ")                            Read in overtime payrate.
 (setq overtime-rate (read))
 (wages hours payrate regular-hours overtime-rate))

(defun wages (hours payrate regular-hours overtime-rate)         Calculate wages.
 (cond ((> hours regular-hours) (+ (* regular-hours payrate)
 (* (- hours regular-hours) overtime-rate)))
 (T (* hours payrate))))
```

language and it is used in applications areas such as natural language processing, robotics, developing mathematical proofs, and pattern recognition. Figure 8.5 illustrates the LISP version of the problem discussed in Chapter 6.

## LOGO

Based on LISP, LOGO was developed by Seymour Papert in the early 1960s at MIT. It is an interactive language designed to teach programming to children. It makes use of on-screen graphics to develop and reinforce problem-solving skills. By using a limited set of commands, children can draw complex pictures by moving a cursor called a *turtle* around the screen. Originally this cursor was a triangle, but recent versions include a variety of shapes. Commands are grouped together, allowing the user to create larger and more complex pictures. In this way, new instructions, actually simple subprograms, are developed. LOGO is widely used in grade schools to introduce computers, programming, and problem-solving methods in an entertaining environment.

## LANGUAGES GAINING IN POPULARITY

A number of languages are gaining in popularity, including some that were designed in the 1970s.

### Ada

Ada was introduced in 1980 after considerable study and revision. It is named after Lady Ada Lovelace, the first programmer (see Chapter 2). It was commissioned by the U.S. Department of Defense, the largest purchaser of software in the world. The department's existing software, written in dozens of languages, was becoming increasingly difficult to maintain and update. Officials decided they needed a single language capable of doing every computer-related task. Ada was the result. Ada is an all-purpose computer language that can be used to program everything from business applications to **embedded computers**. Embedded computers are computers built into other devices. They are an integral part of large electromechanical weapons systems such as missiles, submarines, and airplanes as well as non-military devices such as microwave ovens, automobiles, hospital intensive care unit equipment and air traffic control systems.

Like Pascal, Ada is a highly structured language. Unlike Pascal, it is capable of communicating directly with the computer hardware as if it were an assembly language. It is ideal for creating very large software systems in which subsystems are developed independently by different teams of programmers. With Ada, program changes and adaptations are easy to make and require only minimal changes to the larger system.

Ada requires a very large compiler and must be run on computer systems with considerable memory. The Defense Department intends to exert considerable pressure on software developers to encourage the use of Ada. Eventually the Defense Department plans to refuse any programs not written in Ada.

### C

C is a programming language developed at Bell Labs in the early 1970s by Dennis Ritchie. Many computer experts consider C to represent the modern form of the assembly language. C has the syntax structures found in such high-level languages as Pascal along with the ability to communicate directly with the hardware. C is very portable. It is used not only to develop operating systems (for which it was originally designed), but for language compilers, editors, word processors, and many other popular software systems. C is used to develop operating systems on minis and micros, and many microcomputer and workstation compilers are available. Programs written in C require very little memory and are extremely efficient. Unfortunately, C is not user-friendly; it is difficult to learn. Considerable programming skill is needed to write or understand C programs.

### Modula-2

Modula-2 is an improved and updated version of Pascal. It was developed by Niklaus Wirth, who created Pascal, and was released in 1978. Designed to teach programming and computer concepts, Pascal unexpectedly gained wide use in custom-designed software for business and industry. Modifications needed to make Pascal better-suited to these purposes led to the development of Modula-2. In Modula-2, the structured features of Pascal are combined with the ability to control system hardware. Modula-2 is designed to support the writing of large programs through the careful use of subprograms or modules. Additional features enable the programmer to directly manipulate peripheral devices and memory. Modula-2 is increasingly finding use as a teaching language in computer science departments at many universities.

As we have seen, programming requires careful planning and organization. Before writing the code for a given algorithm, the programmer must consider which language would be most appropriate. Few languages do all things equally well, and not all languages are available on all machines. Using a language suited to the application can ease the task of programming.

## SUMMARY

There are four categories of computer languages. From the lowest to highest these are: machine language, assembly language, high-level languages, and natural language processing.

Machine language consists of instructions coded as a series of ones and zeros. It is the only language that the computer directly understands. Each type of computer has its own code. These languages are machine-dependent.

Assembly language instructions contain mnemonics specifying tasks to be performed by the computer. Like machine languages, assembly languages are machine-dependent. Assembly language programs cannot be executed directly by the computer. They must first be translated, or assembled, into machine-readable form.

High-level languages have a structure similar to natural languages. These languages are machine-independent and portable. High-level languages must be translated into machine-readable form to be understood by the computer.

Natural language processing, or natural language understanding, is a research area within artificial intelligence that is looking at the development of computer languages and systems that understand and use natural language.

Hundreds of computer languages exist today. When choosing the most appropriate language for a given task, the following criteria should be considered: familiarity, availability, suitability, efficiency, longevity, and supportability.

A wide variety of high-level languages is available, each with its own strengths and weaknesses.

FORTRAN, which stands for FORmula TRANslation, supports mathematical, scientific, and engineering programming. It is a highly standardized language that has been regularly updated and revised.

# On Line

## SELECTING A PROGRAMMING LANGUAGE THE EASY WAY

With such a large selection of programming languages it can be difficult to choose one for a particular project. However, most people already have a fairly good idea of how various automobiles compare. So to assist those trying to choose a language, this list matches programming languages with automobiles.

Assembler: A Formula I race car. Very fast, but difficult to drive and expensive to maintain.

FORTRAN II: A Model T Ford. Once it was king of the road.

FORTRAN IV: A Model T Ford.

FORTRAN 77: A six-cylinder Ford Fairlane with standard transmission and no seat belts.

COBOL: A delivery van. It's bulky and ugly, but it does the work.

BASIC: A second-hand Rambler with a rebuilt engine and patched upholstery. Your dad bought it for you to learn to drive. You'll ditch the car as soon as you can afford a new one.

C: A black Firebird, the all-macho car. Comes with optional seat belts and an optional fuzz buster ("escape to assembler").

Pascal: A Volkswagen Beetle. It's small but sturdy. Was once popular with intellectuals.

Modula-2: A Volkswagen Rabbit with a trailer hitch added on.

LISP: An electric car. It's simple but slow. Seat belts are not available.

LOGO: A kiddie's replica of a Rolls Royce. Comes with a real engine and a working horn.

Ada: An army-green Mercedes-Benz staff car. Power steering, power brakes, and automatic transmission are all standard. No other colors or options are available. If it's good enough for the generals, it's good enough for you. Manufacturing delays due to difficulties in reading the design specifications are starting to clear up.

*Source:* D. Solomon and D. Rosenblueth, University of Waterloo, Waterloo, Ontario, BITNET, Oct. 1986.

BASIC, which stands for Beginner's All-Purpose Symbolic Instruction Code, was invented as a tool to teach programming. It is an interactive language. BASIC interpreters and compilers require little memory and run on most microcomputers.

Pascal, named after the mathematician Blaise Pascal, is a general-purpose teaching language emphasizing top-down design.

ALGOL, which stands for ALGOrithmic Language, was designed for scientific programming. It is more popular in Europe than in the United States.

COBOL, which stands for COmmon Business Oriented Language, was invented with the support of the U.S. Department of Defense as a standard language for business applications.

LISP, which stands for LISt Processing, is the dominant language for artificial intelligence programming. It is designed to manipulate lists of non-numeric information.

LOGO was developed as an interactive language to teach programming to children. It makes use of on-screen graphics to develop and reinforce problem-solving skills.

Ada, named after Ada Lovelace, the first programmer, was commissioned by the Department of Defense to be an all-purpose computer language capable of doing all computer-related tasks. It is a highly structured language and is capable of communicating directly with computer hardware.

C is often considered a modern form of assembly language. It has syntax structures of a high-level language along with the ability to communicate directly and easily with computer hardware. C is very portable.

Modula-2 is an improved version of Pascal and has the ability to control system hardware. Modula-2 is designed to support the development of large programs through the careful use of subprograms.

## Key Words

As an extra review of the chapter, try defining the following terms. If you have trouble with any of them, refer to the page number listed.

assembly language (assembler) *(202)*      machine language *(201)*
embedded computers *(214)*                 portable *(204)*
machine-dependent *(201)*                  programming language *(200)*
machine-independent *(204)*                subprogram *(207)*

## Test Your Knowledge

1. List the four levels of computer languages.

2. How does assembly language differ from machine language?

3. How do high-level languages differ from assembly languages?

4. Why do high-level languages require translators to be understood by computers?

5. When is a computer language machine-independent?

6. What is natural language processing? Describe the two different research approaches used in this field.

7. List the criteria programmers should use when selecting a computer language.

8. Briefly describe FORTRAN. What are its most important features? What are its limitations?

9. Briefly describe BASIC. What are its most important features? What are its limitations?

10. Briefly describe Pascal. What are its most important features? What are its limitations?

11. Define *portable* as it applies to computer languages.

12. Identify and briefly describe four other commonly used computer languages.

13. What do COBOL and Ada have in common?

14. Describe three languages gaining in popularity.

15. What single feature is most likely to lead to an increase in the use of Ada?

## Expand Your Knowledge

1. Talk with people in your computing center. Write a short report indicating the two most widely used computer languages on campus. Identify the departments that use them and what applications they are used for.

2. Talk to people in your computer science department. Write a short report examining the language used to teach programming to CS majors. Why was this language chosen? Has the department considered changing languages? If so, what languages have been considered and why?

3. Make a list of the languages provided by your computing center. Identify the machines they run on and the department or group that uses each language most.

4. Some people feel that everyone should use the same computer language. Others feel such a move would be unrealistic. Choose one position and defend it.

5. Go to your local bookstore and examine the books available on computer languages. What languages are represented? Judging from the number of books available, which are the most popular languages? Has the store had requests for books on languages such as Ada and Modula-2?

# 9

# Introduction to Applications Software

**Chapter Outline**

Types of Software

Applications Software
   Specialized Applications Software (Science, Engineering, and
   Mathematics; Medicine; Education and Training; Business Use; Home
   Use) • General-Purpose Applications Software (Word Processing;
   Electronic Spreadsheets; Data Base Software; Graphics Software;
   Communication Software)

Expert Systems

Our Changing Libraries

Software Integration
   Integrated Environments • Integrated Packages • Package Integrators •
   Families of Software

In the hands of different individuals, computers become different machines—tools actually—suiting the particular needs of each. For the artist the computer can be a drafting table and paintbrush. For the writer it is organizer, reference library, and typewriter. For the business executive it is a record-keeper and bookkeeper, holding and organizing inventory, employee, and tax information. Applications software is what transforms the machine, making it a tool specific to hundreds of tasks. This chapter examines applications software and how it is used.

After studying this chapter, you will be able to:

- Identify the three categories of computer software.

- Describe the difference between specialized and general-purpose applications software.

- Describe some uses of specialized software in science, education, business, and the home.

- List five types of general-purpose applications software.

- Discuss the uses of each type of general-purpose applications software.

- Discuss expert systems as examples of applications software.

- List the ways that applications software is changing our libraries.

- Define software integration.

- Describe the differences and similarities between integrated packages, package integrators, and families of software.

## TYPES OF SOFTWARE

Software is the driving force of the computer. Programs make the system work, giving it the instructions and the ability to do all the jobs we call on it to perform for us. Computer software is divided into three major types: systems software, development software, and applications software. **Systems software** controls the operation of the machine, the most basic functions the computer performs. The ways in which the computer receives input, produces output, manages and stores data, and carries out or executes the instructions of other programs are all determined and controlled by systems software.

The most important component of systems software is the **operating system**, which coordinates or oversees the tasks performed by the computer. Operating systems integrate the instructions of a specific program with the actual wiring of the computer's hardware. The operating system also provides communication between the user and the programs. It directs the flow of information among the components of the computer system, such as the processor, memory, and peripheral devices. Different computers have different operating systems or environments. The operating system determines the "personality" of the computer.

For example, the Macintosh uses pictures and a mouse to point to functions, while the IBM PC and compatibles use arrow keys and commands entered at the keyboard.

**Development software** programs are used to create, update, and maintain other programs. Such software is used to write operating systems as well as all applications packages. Programming languages are the prime examples of development software.

**Applications software** programs allow the computer to perform particular tasks or solve specific problems. Applications software is required by computers of all sizes, from micros to mainframes, and handles tasks both large and small. Airline reservation systems, spacecraft design, air traffic control systems, payroll operations, arithmetic and language drills, the printing of newsletters, and billing all require applications software. There are programs to help students select colleges and locate sources of financial aid, programs to entertain us, and programs to help fill in our family trees.

From one point of view all software is applications software. Operating systems run computers, computer languages are used to write programs, checkbook programs keep track of checks, and other programs provide games to entertain us. Each program was created with a specific purpose or application in mind. But in general usage, applications software describes specifically those packages written to solve a human problem or satisfy a human need and does not include those programs that make computers work.

Virtually all the applications programs written today are designed to be used by non-programmers. While a significant amount of software is written by business and research organizations to satisfy their needs, considerable software is written by software "houses" or companies to be marketed to the general public. These packages range from sophisticated three-dimensional graphics programs used to design aircraft to straightforward microcomputer spelling or arithmetic drills used by children. Applications software encompasses these and much, much more.

## APPLICATIONS SOFTWARE

Applications software falls into two general groups. Those programs that focus on a very specific task or group of tasks are called **specialized applications software**. These packages include software to teach typing, assist real estate agents and restaurant managers, calculate federal taxes, or perform the bookkeeping tasks of a major corporation. The other group of **general-purpose applications software** includes programs that focus on particular areas but can be adapted to individual needs. For example, a word processing program can be used to create any kind of document from a personal letter to a government report. A spreadsheet can contain the family budget or project the growth in domestic car sales. While such software focuses on a specific task, the program has varied enough capabilities to perform a variety of subtasks. For example, a word processor focuses on the task of preparing documents but, more specifically, can focus on the writing of a history term paper or a letter to grandma.

## Specialized Applications Software

Specialized applications software packages make it possible for us to use computers to solve specific problems or satisfy particular needs. So many of these programs have been developed that it would be impossible to examine them all. We will look at some software that has affected various areas of our lives.

**Science, Engineering, and Mathematics**   Few areas have felt the impact of computers as dramatically as the sciences. Modern laboratories use computers to perform data analysis, such as tabulating the influence of marijuana in controlled-drug experiments, and monitoring and running sophisticated experiments, such as stress-testing new cars. Scientists and engineers use computers to forecast the weather, to assist in predicting earthquakes and volcanic eruptions, and to search for scarce resources such as water, oil, and natural gas (see Figure 9.1). Statistical packages turn mountains of census data, for example, into meaningful information about the American family.

Computer photo enhancement and analysis has advanced our knowledge of space and our planet. Satellite pictures can locate polluting industries and make international weather projections. Analysis of satellite and spacecraft pictures enables us to venture to the stars to plan for the future and study the past. Software has helped people land on the moon and locate the Titanic.

Computer-aided design (CAD) systems use three-dimensional graphics in the development of blueprints and architectural design (see Chapter 13). Architects use CAD systems to design buildings and entire towns, designers to plan aircraft, automobiles, spacecraft, and even computer chips (see Figure 9.2).

Not only can external structures be designed, but the placement of internal parts can be positioned and displayed in color. For example, computer-generated building plans can include such items as air ducts and electrical wiring. CAD pictures can be rotated so the object can be viewed from all angles and directions.

**Medicine**   Running the office of a doctor, dentist, or other health-related professional is a sophisticated business. Specialized software maintains patient records, keeps track of appointments, generates patient bills, and processes insurance claim forms. Medical tests that used to take days to process in a lab now can be done in minutes in the doctor's office by specialized equipment. This equipment contains embedded microprocessors that are, in effect, specialized programs. Programs also exist to tailor diet and exercise routines to individual patients.

**Figure 9.1**     Computers and the Sciences: Computers in the laboratory find use in drug experiments, the stress-testing of new cars, searching for oil and gas, and, here, in weather forecasting.

In hospitals, applications programs run on large mainframes to process patient bills, maintain records, keep track of inventory, assist in meal preparation, and handle the mammoth data-processing tasks associated with running any large organization. In addition, software is available that helps doctors diagnose illness, monitor patient progress, and analyze blood and urine samples. Specialized software systems monitor babies in neonatal intensive care units, alert pharmacists to possible drug interactions, and assist in the analysis of X-rays, CAT scans, and other medical procedures. Specialized software has been at the forefront of advances in modern medicine.

**Education and Training**     Computers are now an academic discipline, used as an educational aid from kindergarten through graduate school. They also help modern schools run more efficiently.

Since their first appearance, computers themselves have become a topic of study and the subject of an increasing number and variety of courses. Courses in computer literacy and programming are becoming basic educational requirements in many states. Students in elementary school learn computer logic through the programming language LOGO while their older brothers and sisters study BASIC and Pascal. An increasing number of schools are making word processing software available to improve students' reading and writing skills.

**Figure 9.2**          Computer-Aided Design: Computers are used in the construction of aircraft and spacecraft.

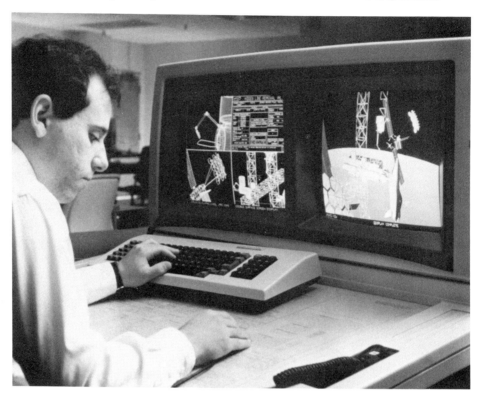

Course offerings in computer science and information systems are among the most popular in many colleges. Computer courses in continuing education programs are very popular as adults try to catch up with the micro-generation. Short courses in the use of spreadsheets, data base software, and word processing are popular all across the country.

In the classroom, educational software uses graphics and sound to motivate students to learn. The most common educational packages reinforce the material taught in the classroom. Drill and practice routines, often in the form of games, support the math and reading curricula of many schools. Some learning games encourage slow learners to learn at their own rate through tutorials, while others provide enrichment for students exploring new areas. Self-paced instructional programs, called **computer-assisted instruction (CAI)**, make use of the ever-patient computer to give students immediate reinforcement when learning or reviewing material. Advanced programs can adjust to individual student needs, skipping unneeded sections and spending more time on areas where the student has difficulty. Some packages can even keep track of the student's progress and identify problem areas.

More exciting are programs that expand the horizons of students. There are programs to assist the handicapped in learning to their fullest potential, to help students choose a college, to study for standardized tests, or to teach colors and numbers to preschoolers. Computer simulations can depict the nervous system, the solar system, or an economic system. Students can reenact historic battles or analyze a rocket's lift-off and path in flight. In a computer simulation, students can see how a change can affect an entire system and they can test the effects of various solutions to a problem. The simulators used by most elementary and secondary schools run on microcomputers, but there are mainframe simulators as well. Medical schools and teaching hospitals use such systems to teach students correct diagnostic techniques. A simulated, unconscious patient with a set of symptoms is presented to the student-doctor and the "game" is to make the patient well. It is as painless a learning technique for the student-doctor as it is for the patient, and mistakes are not fatal. Pilots train in flight simulators that combine mock aircraft with sophisticated computer-simulated visuals and equipment signals, enabling them to practice skills that would be too costly in terms of lives and equipment to test in real aircraft.

Computers are also used in a wide variety of other subjects ranging from math to psychology, English, and music. Laboratory sciences increasingly use computers to maintain, control, and evaluate experiments. Numerous colleges and universities encourage students to purchase their own machines by arranging for their purchase at considerable discounts. Many college bookstores and local computer stores, recognizing a new and growing market, offer computers and software for rent on a semester basis. Some schools, such as Clarkson, Carnegie Mellon, Dartmouth, Boston College, and the three U.S. military academies, require that students purchase machines at the start of their first year. These micros can be used as stand-alone computers or can be connected to the university's mainframe when appropriate. Clearly, computers are changing not only how we learn, but *what* we learn.

Management of schools is similar to management of a business. Both generate reports, maintain records, purchase supplies, pay employees, and so on. Software for data processing is used for these tasks. Computers manage the office paperwork, maintain school budgets, perform accounting tasks, and control the inventory of everything from crayons to computers. Many small districts use microcomputers to calculate and prepare payroll checks. In addition, computers grade papers, keep and update class lists, manage student records, and maintain course information. Applications packages that provide up-to-date information on career guidance and college selection are available in the secondary schools.

**Business Use**    An incredible amount of applications software exists to help run our businesses. Indeed, businesses are the largest consumers of applications software. The modern office makes significant use of such general-purpose packages as word processing programs and data base systems. But specialized software abounds as well. For both large and small systems, software is available to manage inventories, perform standard bookkeeping tasks, prepare payrolls, produce accounting reports, and analyze business finances. Not only can checkbooks be balanced, the actual checks themselves can be printed. Executives use computer simulations to analyze business trends. Software allows for up-to-the-minute reporting, which assists in decision making. There are programs to control industrial robots that perform boring or dangerous tasks in factories (see Figure 9.3). Programs control such industrial processes as combining chemicals to produce mixtures, cleansers, or drugs and maintaining the critical temperatures necessary for processing food and medicines. Computer programs monitor the safety of our power plants, the performance of trains, and the sale of concert tickets.

---

**Figure 9.3**      Software in Manufacturing: An array of software is used in manufacturing, including controlling these industrial robots.

# Computer Hardware

The IBM PC Convertible, a briefcase-sized laptop as powerful as a desktop computer. *(IBM)*

The Mac II uses the Macintosh Operating System. *(Apple Computer, Inc.)*

The IBM PS/2 Model 50Z can run under DOS or OS/2. *(IBM)*

The Sun 386i workstation. *(Sun Micro-systems, Inc.)*

The DEC VAX 8800 microcomputer, sometimes called a supermini. *(Digital Equipment Corp.)*

The IBM 3090/600 mainframe computer can serve hundreds of users at one time. *(IBM)*

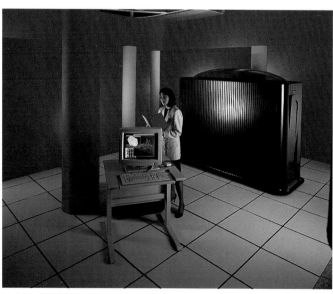

The CDC ETA10 supercomputer can execute billions of instructions per second. *(Control Data)*

(a)

(b)

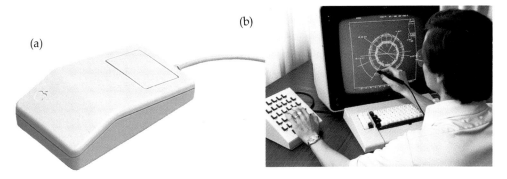

Some graphic input devices are (a) the mouse, used to drag images across the screen *(Apple Computer, Inc.)*; (b) a lightpen, used to draw images directly on the screen *(IBM)*; (c) a digitizer *(IBM)*; and (d) a graphics tablet, used to transfer images from a surface to the screen *(IBM)*.

(c)

(d)

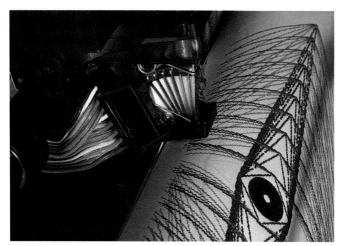

Inkjet plotters spray "jets" of ink onto paper. *(Ken Whitmore/BASF)*

Laser printers are the most advanced type of printing technology. *(Hewlett Packard)*

# Computer Applications

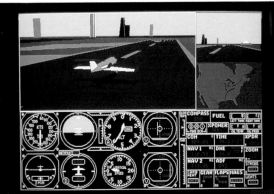

Microsoft's popular computer game, *Flight Simulator.* (*Microsoft*)

A still-life generated by computer. (© *Lucasfilm Ltd. (LFL) 1982. All Rights Reserved.*)

A computerized music system. (*IBM*)

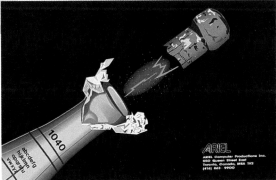

Computer graphics are often used in advertising. (*Dicomed Corporation*)

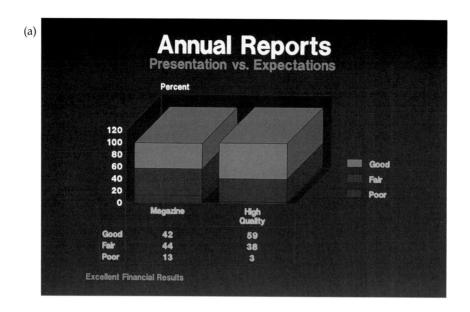

Computer graphics can enhance the appearance of (a) annual reports and (b) sales figures. *(Lotus)*

PCs have fueled the popularity of desktop publishing. *(IBM)*

Architects use computers to show clients exactly what a building will look like. *(Omnibus Computer Graphics)*

An engineer using a CAD/CAM system. *(Ford Motor Co.)*

Computers have become a necessity in industry. *(E.I. du Pont de Nemours & Co.)*

A geological simulation on a PS/2 monitor. *(IBM)*

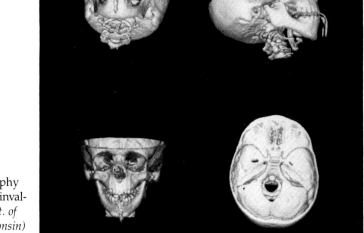

Computerized axial tomography (CAT) scans have become an invaluable tool in medicine. *(Dept. of Neurology, University of Wisconsin)*

In the small business environment, the most popular packages are those that maintain business records and automate accounting procedures. Programs that keep track of the money expected from sales, the cost of equipment and supplies, and the payment of salaries and taxes are also in high demand.

Increasingly, many small business computer owners are subscribing to one or more computer information services such as CompuServe and Dow Jones. These services provide easy access to investment information, help identify market trends, and provide up-to-date national and world news.

**Home Use**    Today, computers are found in many homes and are used there in a wide variety of ways. The most common uses include recreation, word processing, record keeping and money management, education, and, increasingly, home environment control. Home computer usage reflects our work, our play, and our imagination.

Computers may seem like expensive toys, since they are commonly used to relax, amuse, and entertain us. Computer games fascinate adults and children alike, whether they are arcade-style games that emphasize eye-hand coordination or interactive fiction games in which our strategy and problem-solving ability can affect the outcome. Such popular board games as chess, backgammon, and Monopoly have been redesigned for the computer. Computer simulation games that recreate real-life situations are rapidly gaining in popularity. Flight Simulator allows us to try our hand at flying a light plane, and other simulations let us pilot World War II submarines or play the stock market.

We can also become creative in the arts via our home machines. Painting programs allow us to express our creative nature without getting our hands dirty, and music software turns the home into a recording studio.

Other recreational uses aid hobbyists who need to process or store large amounts of information. For example, software is available to keep track of stamp or record collections, trace genealogy, maintain an exercise program, and provide shopping lists and recipes for cooking gourmet dinners.

The most common use of computers in the home is for word processing (see Figure 9.4). Word processing packages turn the home computer, with an associated printer, into a text-manipulating typewriter that can be used for all types of family correspondence as well as for reports and papers needed at school, for volunteer activities, or for office work. With the addition of even simple graphics packages, greeting cards, newsletters, flyers, banners, and calendars can be easily created.

Personal computers can keep track of all kinds of household information, from recipes to tax data. There are programs to manage the family checkbook, keep track of all bank and investment accounts, maintain tax records, and organize any other kind of information that may accumulate. However, with the exception of software to assist with the preparation of federal tax returns, most software for home money management has not been overwhelmingly successful. Most people, including the majority of home computer owners, find it easier to

**Figure 9.4**            Word Processing at Home.

continue to balance their checkbooks the old-fashioned way by using paper, pencil, and a hand calculator. Investment and financial software are popular with people for whom investing is a hobby or who personally manage large investments.

As our educational system puts increased importance on the use of computers in the schools, many families feel that their children need a home computer to keep up with their peers or have an advantage in the changing work place. In the home, educational software entertains preschoolers while teaching reading-readiness skills and provides drills related to what older children are learning in school. Home computer owners who are interested can learn to program in languages such as BASIC, C, Pascal, and Modula-2, using advanced but inexpensive software for these purposes.

Software is also becoming available to replace self-help and do-it-yourself books. It is now possible to learn how to type, speak a foreign language, reduce tension through biofeedback, play a guitar, or keep in shape with computer software.

Microcomputers are able to regulate the physical environment of the home as well. While this is not yet a common application, both the software and the technology exist to make our homes safer and more comfortable while reducing heating and cooling costs. With the addition of special sensing devices, micro-computers can regulate the temperature, control the lights, and monitor the home's fire and security systems. Computers can even answer the telephone and take messages when the family is away. If sensors are activated, advanced systems can even place telephone calls to the fire or police departments.

## General-Purpose Applications Software

The most popular of the numerous types of applications software continues to be packages dedicated to word processing, spreadsheets, data base management, graphics, and communications. These five types are the critical building block programs with which almost any task can be accomplished. Indeed, every user will have at least one of these. We will look briefly at these five types of applications software and see how each of them is a unique tool. A more detailed look at each of these is found in Chapters 10 to 14.

**Word Processing**    Writing with a computer is known as **word processing**. Just about any printed text can be easily created using a word processor. Applica-

---

**Figure 9.5**    Word Processing Screen: Microcomputer word processing programs can be used to write letters.

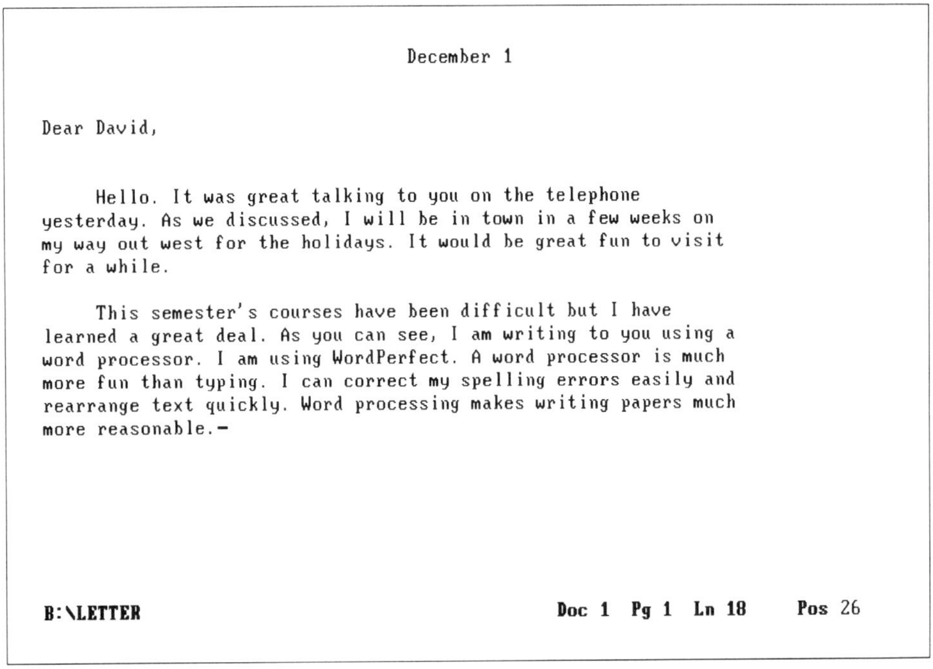

```
                                    December 1


       Dear David,


             Hello. It was great talking to you on the telephone
       yesterday. As we discussed, I will be in town in a few weeks on
       my way out west for the holidays. It would be great fun to visit
       for a while.

             This semester's courses have been difficult but I have
       learned a great deal. As you can see, I am writing to you using a
       word processor. I am using WordPerfect. A word processor is much
       more fun than typing. I can correct my spelling errors easily and
       rearrange text quickly. Word processing makes writing papers much
       more reasonable.-




       B:\LETTER                                    Doc 1  Pg 1  Ln 18      Pos 26
```

tions include reports, memos, term papers, letters, and even mailing labels (see Figure 9.5). Word processing software, whether it is an applications package used on a microcomputer or a dedicated system, is a tool for manipulating words, sentences, and paragraphs before they go on paper. Text can be entered, deleted, corrected, and reorganized quickly and easily. Equally important, text can be formatted or laid out for printing. An error-free document with underlining, boldfaced type, and straight right-hand margins like those in this text, can easily be produced. Advanced word processing packages called desktop publishers, with sophisticated formatting abilities, can even produce printed matter that would otherwise require professional typesetting.

Word processing , which will be discussed more fully in Chapter 10, is by far the most popular application available for microcomputers. Recent surveys by Consumers Union indicated that more than 90 percent of personal computer owners have at least one word processing package and that 25 percent of home computing involves word processing. Even hunt-and-peck typists can produce perfect copy with this software. Revisions can be easily made and the revised document printed out without having to be completely retyped.

Many word processing systems include spelling checkers, which compare each word that is typed with an electronic dictionary. Errors are pointed out and some systems even guess at the correct spelling or suggest words that are similarly spelled. A number of advanced systems include a computerized thesaurus that lists synonyms of specific words on request.

Word processors are being used to improve the writing skills of students from grade school through college. Students appear to be much more willing to revise and reorganize their papers when retyping is not required.

**Electronic Spreadsheets**   When numbers, formulas, and mathematical calculations are involved, an electronic spreadsheet is the software required. A spreadsheet manipulates rows and columns of numbers in much the same way a word processor manipulates words. Spreadsheets are most frequently used to solve business and financial problems but they can be used to balance checkbooks, maintain the family budget, or calculate student grades.

Each spreadsheet location is identified by a specific row (going across) and column (going down). The intersection of a row and column is called a cell.

|   | A | B |
|---|---|---|
| 1 | January | 23.21 |
| 2 | February | 75.16 |

The highlighted box containing 75.16 is the intersection of row 2 and column B. Some cells may contain a word (January) or a formula that describes the properties or qualities of the number that will go there. As with a word processor, the entered information can be easily changed, deleted, or manipulated. New data can be quickly added.

A spreadsheet's most important feature is its ability to use formulas to perform calculations on the data stored within its cells. Formulas can be as simple as the sum of a given column or they can specify a complex relationship between cells. A cell's formula can call for simple arithmetic operations, such as addition and subtraction, or more complex sequences of operations, such as averaging, determining the maximum/minimum, and the solution of trigonometric functions. To calculate the value according to a formula, the software uses the numeric values found in specific cells. The result of the calculation is placed in the cell where the formula resides. For example, if we kept track of how much we spent on telephone and car expenses for a four-month period, we could use a spreadsheet formula to calculate the totals (see Figure 9.6).

The highlighted cell contains the formula: SUM(B3..B6), which sums the numbers 23.21, 75.16, 55.11, and 52.21.

Values calculated by formulas are readjusted every time the values of the appropriate cells change. So, if we realize we'd forgotten a car repair bill in our January totals, resulting in a true figure of $123.45, we would simply change the contents of the affected cell (C3) to that amount. In response to this change, the column sum would change to $268.11. The spreadsheet performs the recalculation automatically.

This ability to have formulas reflect changes in the sheet makes the electronic

---

**Figure 9.6**    The Electronic Spreadsheet: This Lotus 1-2-3 spreadsheet keeps track of telephone and car expenses for the period from January to April.

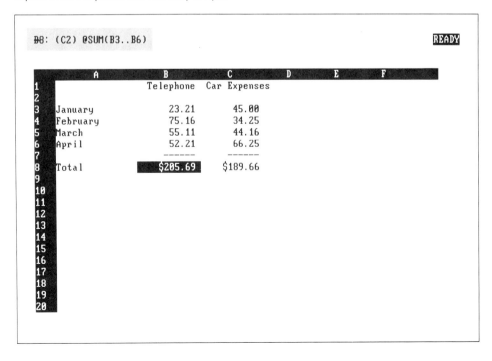

spreadsheet a valuable tool for testing or predicting change. For example, a spreadsheet can examine the effect on the cost of textbooks if all publishers raise prices by 10 percent next year. By adjusting formulas and data we can ask what would happen if prices were raised by 15 percent. How much more would students have to pay? In this way, we are using spreadsheet software to help predict something that has not happened yet. Such prediction is called a *what if*. Such what ifs assist the spreadsheet user in making sound decisions. Spreadsheets will be discussed in greater detail in Chapter 11.

**Data Base Software**    We think of computers as incredibly fast calculating devices. Computers are also incredibly competent devices for storing large quantities of data and locating information for us when we want it. We often call on computers to locate particular pieces of stored information and organize them in some way that is useful to us. A computerized collection of information is known as a **data base**. A data base is organized into files so that information can be easily stored, changed, and retrieved. Such systems are useful whenever large amounts of information are involved, as you will see in Chapter 12.

Two types of data base software are available. The simpler variety organizes information into a single file and is called a **file management system**. These systems are useful for storing information such as mailing lists or an organization's membership data, which will frequently be changed. File managers are used to search through the file for particular data, sort it, and print the results. For example, we may want to mail special information to all New York residents in the data base or determine the number of women who graduated in 1960, 1970, and 1980.

When the information to be stored is more complex, a **data base management system (DBMS)** is used. Large businesses or institutions need this system when the information stored has many uses and is frequently changed. Data base management systems can contain many files. These files may hold different but related items of information. A university system would have files for student billing, grades, and registration information, in addition to employee payroll and benefit records. Such systems contain all the features of file managers and are also able to combine information from the different files. For example, after searching the billing file for the names of all students with overdue accounts, registration information could be withheld from them until their bills are paid.

Data base software makes information easily available to users, enabling them to make more informed decisions.

**Graphics Software**    Affordable, high-quality computer graphics packages are a fairly recent arrival on the software scene. With the addition of special graphics monitors, software has been developed that can duplicate photographs, design and rotate three-dimensional objects, or simply create charts and diagrams that make statistical information easier to understand.

The most popular of the computer graphics packages design graphs and charts for business use. Graphics software also has statistical and scientific applications, such as graphs that summarize the results of an opinion poll or a laboratory experiment. Such software is designed to transform information stored in computer files and present it in diagram form. Graphics allow us to summarize and understand vast amounts of information very quickly. Many spreadsheet and statistical packages include the ability to create some graphs and charts. Figure 9.7 shows a graph created by Lotus 1-2-3.

High-quality graphics are increasingly used to present information quickly in meetings and conferences. Software using multiple colors or gray shades is now available to produce dramatic effects. With graphics software, graphs and diagrams can be adjusted and descriptive text can be added. The graph or chart can be made larger or smaller. New columns or lines can be inserted.

In addition to packages that produce specific types of graphs and charts, *object-oriented graphics* packages can be used to create almost any imaginable image by placing symbols such as circles, lines, and rectangles or entire pictures

**Figure 9.7**    Graphics Software: This Lotus 1-2-3 graph is an example of how software can help summarize information.

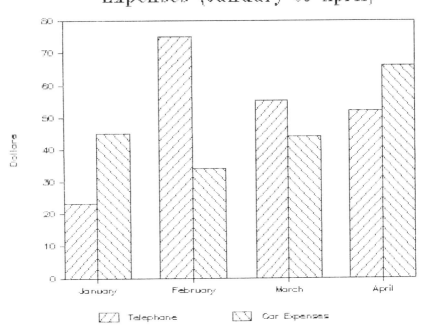

---

**Figure 9.8**        The Computer as Artist: Object-oriented graphics packages can be used to create a vast array of images on the computer screen.

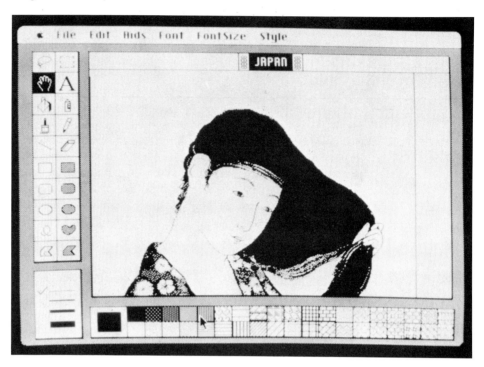

wherever the user wishes on the screen. Figure 9.8 shows one such image. These packages are used for everything from do-it-yourself greeting cards to professional newsletters. A number of packages can create color slides from screen displays. Computer graphics will be discussed in greater detail in Chapter 13.

**Communication Software**    In our increasingly fast-paced society, rapid, reliable access to people and information is critical. The significance of communication software is that it provides access to shared ideas and information. Telephone lines and surface mail can connect us with offices, businesses, homes, and people almost anywhere. But it is not always possible to reach people by phone when we want to, and the mail is slow and sometimes unreliable. Computers are able to act as bridges between people and the information and ideas they require.

With communication software and specialized hardware, users can connect their machines with other computer systems regardless of location, assuming they have permission to do so. Students can use communication packages to dial into their university's mainframe to do course work at home, while re-

# On Line

## ST. SILICON'S HOSPITAL MAKES HOUSE CALLS

Wouldn't it be nice to find a doctor who makes house calls 24 hours a day? Well, doctors associated with St. Silicon's Hospital do just that—using a computer. Anyone with a medical or dental problem can contact St. Silicon's 24-hour medical-information bulletin board. Callers can ask specific questions or read the answers to questions others have asked.

St. Silicon's Doc-in-a-Box for medical questions and Dent-in-a-Box for dental questions were started by Thomas M. Greender of Case Western Reserve University School of Medicine in Cleveland, Ohio, as an internal bulletin board for students and staff in the school's Department of Family Medicine. The system became public when people in the local community discovered the bulletin board's phone number and began leaving questions in hopes that they would be answered. Their hopes were realized. Today the medical school's staff doctors take turns replying to inquiries. The questions and answers are maintained in a data base available to all callers.

In addition to providing a service, the bulletin board offers medical students and residents valuable educational information. The questions most frequently asked of Doc-in-a-Box are those that patients either forgot to ask or were afraid to ask during visits to their physicians. Common questions are asked about sex, sexual dysfunction, and the side effects of medication.

St. Silicon's Doc-in-a-Box and Dent-in-a-Box receive hundreds of questions each week from all over the United States.

*Source:* "St. Silicon's Hospital Offers 'Doc-in-a-Box,'" *The Chronicle of Higher Education,* p. 21.

searchers connect to supercomputers in distant cities. Similarly, a company's employees can connect to the organization's mainframe from home or other remote locations to get or receive messages (electronic mail) or transmit documents.

Researchers, scientists, and administrators have organized long-distance networks of telephone-connected computers through which information can be exchanged and resources can be shared. Papers, reports, and ideas can be transmitted between machines very quickly and programs and equipment can be shared among participants who live and work in distant locations.

Microcomputer as well as mainframe users can connect to computer information services and gain access to everything from recent publications on medical research to airline flight schedules and up-to-the-minute stock quotes. Using electronic bulletin boards, users shop electronically, leave messages for friends, and share user-written software. Chapter 14 goes into more detail about computer communication.

We have just examined the range of software available on today's computers.

The possible applications are limited only by our imagination. Let us look at two uses whereby application software has introduced images of the future—today.

## EXPERT SYSTEMS

**Expert systems** are computer programs that attempt to duplicate the ways in which professionals make decisions. These are the most advanced, most sophisticated types of special-purpose applications. An expert system, sometimes called a **knowledge-based system**, may analyze a range of symptoms in order to diagnose disease, design computer circuits, or write a computer program.

An expert system is a collection of rules used by human experts, an organized set of human knowledge in a narrow discipline. Human experts use rules of thumb, or **heuristics**, that may or may not be written down when they evaluate situations or make decisions. These rules are combinations of formal learning, experience, and common sense. What makes human decision making so difficult to predict is that our rules of thumb are often applied unconsciously; that is, they spring up from our mind. Our logic is often based on imprecise information, intuition, or feeling. The decision-making process often looks something like this:

If the car doesn't start and the lights don't work, then the battery is dead.

Such rules of thumb can be abstracted to the form:

If *A* and *B* and *C* are occurring, then in all likelihood the problem is *X*.

An expert system records these rules of thumb as a series of if/then statements. Rules for combining if/then information also go into the system. This forms a knowledge base or a data base of knowledge questions. To create the data base, human experts are interviewed in detail and tracked as they go about their work so that the rules they have developed by experience can be formally recorded. Each rule (if/then statement) reflects a specific piece of the human expert's knowledge. In addition to the rules that form the knowledge base, a set of programs is developed to manipulate the rules to make judgments or intelligent guesses in a human-like fashion. As the software is being developed, new rules may be added and previous rules modified based on continued observation and testing within the specific area of expertise.

Expert systems are usually designed for use by people with little or no computer experience. Standard English, including the vocabulary of the particular discipline, is used in the if/then statements. In systems designed to assist doctors, medical terms are used. Many systems allow users to ask the system for information about the rules used by the system to make decisions.

Expert systems exist in a wide variety of fields. In medicine they include

CADUCEUS, which diagnoses 500 diseases by cross referencing more than 3000 symptoms; PUFF, which is used to analyze breath samples in the diagnosis of cardiopulmonary disease; and MYCIN, which analyzes blood samples to diagnose blood diseases and recommends drug treatments. Similarly, systems such as PROSPECTOR aid in the discovery and evaluation of mineral deposits, and XCON is used by Digital Equipment Corp. to configure minicomputers for clients. A U.S. Coast Guard system analyzes distress signals sent out by ships in danger and provides assistance in locating them. The U.S. military has included expert systems in its Strategic Defense Initiative (SDI) research.

The decision-making ability of well-designed expert systems is quite high. However, people are often reluctant to use such systems. As with all computer programs, expert systems are tools that can help people make faster, easier, wiser decisions. While expert systems have proven successful, their advantages will not be widespread until people are willing to consult the expert system just as they would a human expert or a textbook.

## OUR CHANGING LIBRARIES

We think of libraries as repositories of the printed word. As such they are the keepers of the culture, writings, and experiences of humanity. Traditionally, libraries have been filled with books, but now they are changing. Although books remain predominant in our libraries, information is available on other media as well. Records, audio and video tapes, games, and, increasingly, software and computers can be consulted and borrowed in libraries. In the Peterborough, New Hampshire, town library, for instance, patrons borrow personal computers in much the same way they borrow books. In many places across the country, card holders can come to the library, use a microcomputer there or borrow software to take home and try out on their own computer.

Libraries, however, are more than book or media exchanges. Libraries are information resources. Card catalogs, reader's guides, and the like are data bases of information organizing the printed word. Increasingly these data bases are being computerized (see Figure 9.9). Computerized catalogs are now found in most of our nation's largest libraries, such as the Library of Congress and the New York Public Library, university libraries such as Carnegie Mellon and Columbia, and a majority of the nation's medical libraries. An increasing number of smaller libraries are also implementing such systems. Special-purpose software makes this possible.

Card catalogs are being replaced for a number of reasons. The cards themselves, especially in libraries with old and heavily used card catalogs, get worn out and need to be replaced. Space in the card drawers is not infinitely expandable as collections grow in size. Searching and following cross-references to subject matter are time-consuming. Electronic catalogs using modern computer data

**Figure 9.9**     The Computerized Library: Computers have revolutionized the way patrons look for books at many libraries.

base software are easy to use and take up almost no space compared to the rooms required for traditional card catalogs. Cross-referencing is available with a keystroke or two.

Using computers, library records of borrowing and returns are easy to keep, and overdue notices can be sent out automatically. Such automation improves the control of a library's inventory and frees librarians to provide additional services. A patron can find out which branch holds a particular book as well as whether the item is currently on loan and when it is due to return. Card holders have increased access to books, periodicals, and other items, including items in other locations.

Researchers increasingly need access to electronic data base services. LEXIS and NEXIS, provided by Mead Data Central, contain 60 years of legal documentation. MEDLINE, the data base of the National Library of Medicine, contains the most up-to-date collection of medical and other health-related articles published in the world's professional journals. These are constantly being updated, with LEXIS adding new decisions and MEDLINE adding new journal articles. Libraries can make access to such systems possible to individuals nationwide. At present such access is only available in the specialized collections of law and medical school libraries and some law offices and hospitals.

In addition to computerized catalogs, books, articles, and other kinds of information are increasingly available in electronic form. This electronic material is easier to store, more compact, inexpensive to move from place to place, and easier to organize and retrieve than printed material. However, it is not feasible to retype everything ever printed. Improved scanners will help in this regard, but even they will need careful proofreading.

More and more data bases are being created on and for computers, including new dictionaries and encyclopedias. In fact, almost everything being published today is in computerized form at some if not all stages of creation and production. However, most library users are neither interested nor willing to read books or magazines through computer terminals. There is something to be said for the comfortable feeling of holding a book. Only in jest do we talk about "curling up with a good computer program."

## SOFTWARE INTEGRATION

As we've indicated, a considerable amount of applications software is available. It is often the case that users want to combine packages and share information between them. Unfortunately, in most cases files created by one package are often difficult to incorporate into files created by other packages. In some cases, transferring information between packages can resemble union/management negotiations; that is, although common ground exists, it is hard to find. Two different paths have been taken to create an environment where software is easy to use and data, including graphics, is easy to share. One approach has been to integrate or tie together software products. The other has been the development of sophisticated operating systems and work environments where stand-alone software packages easily share information. In both cases the purpose is to make computers and software easier to use.

The first approach was exemplified by the release in 1982 of Lotus 1-2-3 by Lotus Development Corp. Lotus 1-2-3 was one of the first software packages to tie business graphics and data base concepts to a powerful spreadsheet. Its easy-to-use format enables users to share information between these three high-demand tools.

On the opposite path, Apple Corp. released its Macintosh computer in 1984. The Macintosh uses a mouse for pointing and features an operating environment where pictures, or icons, indicate basic functions. Icons include file folders for creating files and a trash can for erasing files. Today, these two once-divergent paths are slowly merging.

### Integrated Environments

The Macintosh was the first inexpensive single-user computer to combine a pointing device (mouse) and icons with a graphics monitor and window-oriented software. The Macintosh's operating system is designed so that multiple software applications can be activated or run at the same time. For the user to view these multiple operations, the screen can be divided into sections, or **windows.** Each window contains a different application. Windows appear to overlap, giving the impression of papers on top of one another with the most recently activated or opened application on the top (see Figure 9.10). Many software packages designed for the Macintosh allow information or graphics visible in one window to be copied or transferred to other open windows.

Like the Macintosh, the IBM Personal System/2 also uses a window-oriented operating system and mouse. In addition, integrated operating environments are standard on the single-user workstations described in Chapter 1. These machines combine the power of minicomputers with large graphics displays and windowing software.

Even with integrated operating environments, most microcomputer packages do not share information easily. To solve this problem, three different integration approaches have been taken. **Integrated packages** combine powerful software tools such as word processing, spreadsheets, data base managers, and graphics into a single package. **Package integrators** or **window managers** provide a supervisor program to combine a number of stand-alone packages. **Families of software** create integration by designing groups of stand-alone programs that

---

**Figure 9.10**     Windows: The Apple Macintosh uses windows for multiple operations, with icons indicating basic functions.

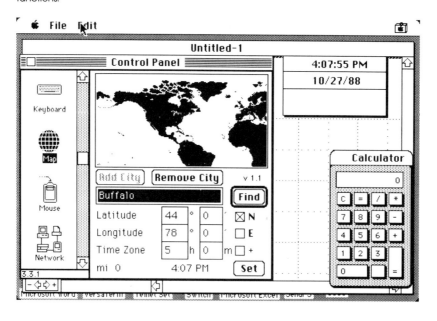

store information in a common format and use a common set of operating commands. While all of these approaches have been more or less successful, they provide at best only a fleeting glimpse of what the future holds in software integration.

## Integrated Packages

The most difficult part of using an application package is the considerable time and effort involved in learning the functions and commands. If multiple packages are used, the same learning curve is required for each package. Even when switching between packages we are familiar with, some time is spent getting up to speed and recalling how each package works. Integrated packages combine a number of different software packages into a single program. The most popular integrated packages (Lotus 1-2-3, Framework, ENABLE, and Symphony for the IBM PC; Excel and Jazz for the Macintosh) combine a word processor with a data base manager, spreadsheet, and business graphics program. Many packages include communications components, and some have added desktop aids such as note pads, calendars, and calculators. All the components of an integrated package use a common set of operating commands. For example, in ENABLE, F10 always returns the user to the menu, as does the slash in Lotus 1-2-3.

In addition to having a common command structure, integrated packages, being a single complex program, are designed to share data between component programs. Information gleaned from a data base can be transferred directly to the word processor, and graphics can easily be generated by spreadsheet data. In many packages, the connections between the components are so clearly defined that updates in the spreadsheet will be reflected in data that has been copied to a word processing report.

For convenience, most integrated packages have incorporated windows so that different components can be used simultaneously. Some packages include overlapping windows similar to those used in the Macintosh environment (see Figure 9.11). Others split the screen into two or three non-overlapping parts so that more than one operation is visible at a time. Others use function keys to switch between components that are active but not visible on the screen.

Integrated all-in-one packages are not perfect. They have a number of disadvantages. The individual components of such integrated packages are rarely as powerful or as comprehensive as their stand-alone relatives. For example, ENABLE's data base component is not nearly as versatile as the stand-alone package dBase III Plus. Also, a combined package can easily contain more components than a user requires. If only one or two components are required, why pay for more? However, the total package usually costs less than all of the components purchased independently. Last of all, integrated packages require more memory than stand-alone packages since the program is larger and more complex.

**Figure 9.11**          Workstation Windows: Integrated operating environments are standard on many workstations, including this one from Sun.

## Package Integrators

A package integrator is a program designed to combine a number of stand-alone packages so that data can be easily transferred between them. In a sense, it provides a bridge between existing applications software. The components, stand-alone packages, are selected by the user. With package integrators, the most powerful state-of-the-art tools can be combined into a single operating environment, and only those applications that are required are combined. Furthermore, component packages can be changed at any time. If, for example, a stand-alone package no longer satisfies the user's needs, it can be changed. If a stand-alone package is updated to include new features, the new version can be substituted for the old. As needs change, the combinations can change.

Package integrators allow the user to maintain the power and flexibility of stand-alone packages while making data transfer reasonable. However, such systems can be very difficult to learn. Each of the components has its own command structure, which is often incompatible with those of the other stand-alone programs. Not only must the user learn to use the individual packages, but the integrator as well. The combined cost of the stand-alone packages plus the integrator is usually considerably more than the cost of an all-in-one system.

Many package integrators are really windowing systems or *window managers*. To facilitate the transfer of data, integrators allow multiple packages to operate concurrently. Each component is placed in its own window. The user can see and transfer the data visible in one window to another. The Apple Macintosh comes with a built-in window manager. Packages such as Microsoft Windows, IBM's TopView, and X-Windows provide a similar environment on IBM PCs and their compatibles and most high-performance workstations.

## Families of Software

Both of the techniques just described are designed to combine different software components into a single unit, a super-package. A number of companies, most notably Software Publishing (the developers of the PFS Professional Family of Software), have taken a different approach. Each package in the series can stand alone and run independently of all other packages. However, each package uses the same set of commands and has the same organizational structure. In the PFS series, each package is menu-driven and the function keys perform the same tasks. The output produced by one package in the family is organized so that it can be transferred to other packages. Since all packages use the same set of commands, after one package is learned, learning additional packages is easy. In addition, users need only purchase the components they require, keeping costs down.

However, since each package is independent, most families of software do not allow more than one program to be active at a time. Without an additional integrator to ease the transfer of information, moving data from one application to another can be time-consuming.

Most software families consist of a spreadsheet, data base manager, and a word processor. Software families can focus on more specific needs. For example, a business application family can include accounting, bookkeeping, and payroll programs. Software families are usually designed to be easy to learn and very user-friendly.

Applications software turns the computer into an individualized tool, enabling us to solve problems, educate, and enjoy ourselves. As we have seen in this chapter, software brings the computer to life, transforming our world.

## SUMMARY

Computer software is divided into three categories: systems software, development software, and applications software. Systems software controls the operation of the machine. Development software consists of programs used to create, update, and maintain other programs. Applications software programs solve human problems or satisfy a human need but do not include programs that make computers work.

Specialized applications software packages focus on very specific tasks, while general-purpose applications software includes programs that focus on particular areas but can be adapted to individual needs.

In science, engineering, and mathematics, applications packages are used for data analysis and to monitor and run sophisticated experiments. Statistical packages are used to analyze all types of data. Computer-aided design is used in the development of blueprints and architectural drawings. In medicine, software assists in record keeping, disease diagnosis, medical testing, and patient care.

Computers are used as an educational aid in our schools and businesses. Administratively they maintain records, process payrolls, and control inventory. They reinforce the classroom by helping all students learn at their own rate. Simulations allow students to manipulate a model of a real-world event and study how changes affect the system. Simulation programs are used in the schools and to train doctors and pilots. Computers themselves have become a topic of study.

The largest consumer of applications software is business. Companies make use of general-purpose software such as word processors and data base systems as well as more specialized software to manage records, prepare payroll, produce accounting reports, and analyze business finances. Software also controls industrial robots and factory machinery.

In the home, computers are used for recreation and entertainment, word processing, personal record keeping and money management, educational support, and maintaining a safe, comfortable environment.

The five building block programs currently used on computers are: word processing, electronic spreadsheets, data base management systems, computer graphics, and communication packages.

Word processing software is a tool for manipulating words, sentences, and paragraphs before they go on paper. Desktop publishers are used to produce printed matter that is almost identical to typeset material.

Electronic spreadsheets manipulate numbers and formulas that are presented in the form of rows and columns. Spreadsheets are most frequently used to solve business and financial problems but can be used for any task that involves computation.

A computerized collection of information is called a data base. Data base software is used to organize data so that it can be stored, searched, sorted, and retrieved easily.

The most popular form of computer graphics is the design of graphs and charts for analysis of data. Alternatively, object-oriented graphics packages create images by placing symbols, shapes, and textures on the screen.

Communication software and specialized hardware connect computers and computer hardware over distances ranging from across the room to around the world. Such networks use telephone lines to share equipment and information.

Software integration works toward the development of computer products that share information easily and are user-friendly. Two approaches are available. One approach has been to tie together independent software products. The other is the development of sophisticated operating systems and work environments where stand-alone software can easily share information.

## Key Words

As an extra review of the chapter, try defining the following terms. If you have trouble with any of them, refer to the page number listed.

applications software  *(223)*
computer-assisted instruction (CAI)
    *(226)*
data base  *(234)*
data base management system
    (DBMS)  *(234)*
development software  *(223)*
expert system (knowledge-based system)  *(238)*
families of software  *(242)*
file management system  *(234)*

general-purpose applications software  *(223)*
heuristics  *(238)*
integrated package  *(242)*
operating system  *(222)*
package integrator (window manager)  *(242)*
specialized applications software  *(223)*
systems software  *(222)*
word processing  *(231)*

## Test Your Knowledge

1. Define *systems software.*

2. What is the difference between specialized applications software and general-purpose applications software?

3. List two medical uses of applications software.

4. List three educational uses of applications software.

5. What is CAI?

6. List four kinds of software used in business.

7. What is recreational software?

8. List five uses of computer software in the home.

9. What is a word processor? How is it used?

10. What is an electronic spreadsheet? How is it used?

11. What is data base software? How is it used?

12. Describe two common uses for graphics software.

13. What is an expert system?

14. Name three expert systems and indicate what they do.

15. Give three advantages to the computerization of library card catalogs.

16. How are specialized electronic data bases changing our libraries?

17. List the kinds of information these data bases contain.

18. What is integrated software?

19. How does an integrated environment differ from other forms of software integration?

20. List the three software integration approaches and briefly describe each.

## Expand Your Knowledge

1. Interview someone you know who works with computers. Have this person describe the tasks he or she performs on the computer and the kind of software used to help with these tasks. Write a short report on this interview.

2. Go to your local computer store. Discuss with a salesperson the kinds of software the store sells and what packages are the most popular. List the 10 most popular packages. Include the name, manufacturer, and retail price (if available).

3. Contact your computing center and identify the 10 most popular microcomputer packages used on campus. List these packages. For each package, indicate its name and manufacturer and whether it is used primarily for instruction, research, or administration.

4. Write a short research paper on one of the expert systems listed in this chapter. Use at least three different sources. Indicate what the expert system does, who uses it, and how the system was developed.

5. Go to your campus library and identify those areas where computers are used. Explain how the computer is used (automated card catalog, data base search, microcomputer lab) and who has access to the system. Ask the librarian if additional computer applications are planned for the library. List them.

# 10

# Word Processing

**Chapter Outline**

Changing the Way We Write

What Can a Word Processor Do?

Word Processing Hardware
    Keyboard • Display Screen • Printer

Types of Word Processing Programs
    Text Editor/Text Formatter • What You See Is What You Get (WYSIWYG)

How Does Word Processing Work?
    Entering Text • Editing Text (Inserting Text; Replacing Text; Deleting
    Text; Correcting Text)

Text Formatting
    Page Layout • Character Adjustment

Advanced Features
    Search and Replace • Moving Blocks of Text • Additional Capabilities
    (Mail-Merge; Spelling Checker and Thesaurus; File Merging)

Desktop Publishing

Problems and Pitfalls
    Editing Problems • Search and Replace • Spelling Checkers • Loss of
    Text • Special Effects

Computers have changed the way many people write and think about writing. When we speak we often break some of the structural rules of our language, yet we are still understood. In fact, we often say very little but communicate a great deal through our facial expressions and gestures. Written communication, by comparison, must be very specific.  We must write exactly what we mean and we must use correct sentence structure if we are to be understood.

Some people become so concerned with spelling and sentence structure when they write that they have difficulty putting their ideas down on paper. Most of us have experienced the frustration of correcting written errors, making changes, and then having to retype our letters and reports. However, if adding, deleting, and generally changing words and paragraphs could be made easier, then writing might become almost as easy as speaking. This is the power of word processing.

After studying this chapter, you will be able to:

- Describe what a word processor does.

- Explain the function of the keyboard, display screen, and printer when used with word processing software.

- Distinguish between the two types of word processing programs.

- Describe how text is entered, changed, and deleted using a word processor.

- Explain the functions of text editing and formatting.

- Trace the development of desktop publishing.

## CHANGING THE WAY WE WRITE

Writing with a computer is known as **word processing**. Programs for word processing make it possible for words and individual characters to be added, removed, and switched around anywhere within any piece of written work. Entire paragraphs can be moved freely. Changes can be made and a clean and neat copy produced without the entire document having to be retyped.

When words can be changed so easily, writers are freer to experiment with ideas. For some, this may lead to a brainstorming or free-writing approach to composing text. The flow of ideas is simply entered into the computer as it occurs. After the ideas are on paper they can be reorganized, expanded, or deleted. Many people feel that this freedom expands their creativity, and this is the main advantage of word processing for them. Others simply find that the main benefit is the removal of the drudgery of revising and correcting their work.

## WHAT CAN A WORD PROCESSOR DO?

A word processor can do everything a typewriter can do and more. Everyone has to write. Anything we put in writing—letters, reports, tables, and lists—can easily be developed and printed using word processing software. Whenever written work must be changed or corrected, word processing is appropriate. Word processing is especially useful for individualizing form letters or making multiple original documents. Now with the aid of the computer, even poor typists and spellers can produce professional-quality work. Word processing software makes this possible; but before we look at the software more closely, let us examine what hardware is needed.

## WORD PROCESSING HARDWARE

All word processing programs require a keyboard, a display screen, and a printer. Some programs require additional hardware, such as a mouse, touch screen, or joystick, making them easier to operate for people who are not experienced typists.

### Keyboard

The primary device for getting words into a computer is the keyboard. A keyboard for computer word processing looks like that of a typewriter, with the usual letters, numbers, and standard special characters such as +, %, $, and @. In addition to the traditional keys, most computer keyboards include special function keys and keys with unique symbols. Two of the most common extra keys are CTRL (control) and ALT (alternate), which are struck in combination with other keys to perform specific tasks. Some keyboards contain a separate numeric pad, which is a set of numbered keys organized like a calculator and used for entering numeric data. In addition, most keyboards have arrow and direction keys, including Page Up and Page Down, which direct the movement of the cursor on the screen. These are often called **screen management keys**. Many systems, such as the Apple Macintosh, Commodore Amiga, and IBM Personal System/2, use a mouse to control the cursor on the screen and make changes in the text. They do not require screen management keys, although such keys are often available.

### Display Screen

All word processors require a monitor where entered text is displayed. The monitor serves the same function as the paper in a typewriter. It is smaller than a standard 8 ½ by 11-inch sheet of paper, though, so only about one-third to one-half of a typed page of text can be displayed at one time. The remaining text is stored in the computer's memory. By moving the cursor up or down on the screen, the full text can be viewed one section at a time. The cursor can reach and change every character in the text. This is **full-screen editing**. On a standard typewriter, you can backspace, move the typehead forward on a given line, or move the roller to change the position of the paper. It is much faster to move a cursor around a computer screen than to reposition the paper in a typewriter. In addition, characters typed on paper cannot be easily changed, and letters or words cannot be made to neatly fit in between material that has already been typed.

### Printer

No word processing program can do its job without a printer. While a person may find it wonderful to create and change text, the document so carefully constructed and stored in the computer's memory is worthless if it can not be transferred onto paper. Since word processing is designed to substitute for typing, most word processing systems are attached to a letter-quality or near letter-quality printer. As we saw in Chapter 5, laser printers are increasingly substituting for the slower daisy wheel printers. Many systems also include fast dot matrix printers for draft copies of documents and to print charts and diagrams.

Word processing systems can print an error-free document in a fraction of the time it used to take to type, correct, and retype a document, even by the most experienced typist.

## TYPES OF WORD PROCESSING PROGRAMS

Regardless of the design of the system, all word processing software packages have two parts. The front end is concerned with entering and editing the text itself. This part controls the actual writing, as well as changing of the text. Paragraphs can be indented by setting tabs. Lines can be skipped or left blank.

The back end of a word processor is concerned with the layout, or **format**, of the text. This part controls the way the text will appear when it is printed. Formatting includes spacing, margin requirements, centering, underlining, boldfacing, and any other visual adjustments. Formatting may affect the entire document, as in line spacing, or only a single word, as in underlining.

Software manufacturers have taken two different approaches in designing word processing packages. With **text editor/text formatter** packages, the document seen on the screen contains the same text as the final document, but the layout on the screen is not what the printed version will look like. **What You See Is What You Get (WYSIWYG)** packages display the text on the screen exactly as it will appear when printed.

## Text Editor/Text Formatter

Using text editor/text formatter software, text is entered without paying attention to how it will appear on the page. When the text is being entered and edited, it is not necessary to be concerned with line length or spacing requirements. The user can add to and change the text until the words and content are completely as desired.

As text is being entered, or afterward, special formatting commands are also entered. These commands will appear throughout the text and can be seen as letters, numbers, or other symbols on the screen. When you are ready to print your document, these commands will be read by the formatting portion of the word processor. They are instructions to the formatter and will affect the final layout of the document.

In most text editor/text formatter systems, format commands sit on a line by themselves at the left-hand margin. They usually begin with a period or dot, and for this reason are called **dot commands**. They precede the text they are to affect. Dot commands indicate when paragraphs should begin, where underlining is to appear, what spacing is used between lines, and all other information necessary to produce the desired-looking document. In Figure 10.1, dot commands precede the document, and two others indicate the beginning of paragraphs.

---

**Figure 10.1**   Dot Commands: Portion of the Gettysburg Address using the text editor/text formatter NROFF on a minicomputer.

```
.ll 65   {line length 65}
.ad      {adjust right margin}
.in 12   {indent 12}
.pp      {paragraph}
Four score and eight years ago our fathers
brought forth a new nation.
Conceived in liberty, and dedicated to the proposition
that all are created equal.
.pp
Now we are engaged in a great war, testing whether
tha5t new nation, or any nation so conceived and so dedicated
can long indure. We are met on the bttlefield of that
great war. We have come to dedicate a portion of that field as
a final resting place of that great war.
.pp
It is although fitting and
proper that we should do this. . . .
```

After the text and the formatting commands have been entered and edited as necessary, the second stage of the processing begins. The formatter is a program that takes the typed text as input, follows the embedded instructions indicated by the dot commands, and produces the document in ready-to-print format. The document in this form can either be stored in memory or sent directly to a printer.

Text editor/text formatter systems are popular on mainframes and are available for microcomputers. They contain more complex formatting commands and make it easier to adjust margins and spacing than many "what you see" word processors. However, the variety of commands makes them difficult to learn, and many people find that seeing dot commands on the screen interferes with their train of thought. Furthermore, in order to see what a document looks like, the user must leave the editor portion of the program and run the formatter portion. Once in the formatter, further changes to the document cannot be made directly.

### What You See Is What You Get (WYSIWYG)

As the name indicates, a WYSIWYG (pronounced *wizzy-wig*) word processor merges editing and formatting. As with the text editor/text formatter systems, text entered into a system can be immediately corrected and adjusted. However, when a formatting command is issued, it doesn't just appear as a code on the screen. Instead, it is immediately acted upon and the text on the screen is moved around to reflect the command. If a sentence or phrase is to be underlined or centered, the operation is done right then and there. The end result is a document that appears on the screen almost exactly as it will appear in print.

## HOW DOES WORD PROCESSING WORK?

A word processor electronically processes words or, more accurately, characters. The first step involves getting the words into the computer. With a typewriter, characters appear directly on paper as they are typed. With a word processor, the characters appear on a screen as the keyboard keys are pressed. At the same time, they are stored as electronic patterns in the computer's memory. Remember, however, that when the computer is turned off or the flow of electric current is halted, information stored in main memory will be lost. For this reason, it is essential to copy the information into computer files on long-term storage devices such as floppy or hard disks. Computer files, like their paper counterparts, are given names that, to some degree, describe the contents of the file.

Some word processing programs require that you give your computer file a name before you begin entering text, while others have you name your file after it has been entered. The names you give to your files are used to call up, or

**access**, documents any time you want to work on them. Many computer file names are limited in length to eight characters with a three-character extension. However, even names made up of eight characters can be meaningful. While the computer will have no trouble distinguishing between files named junk1 and junk2, we will almost immediately forget what each file contains. File names such as budget90 or housing let for housing letter will help us remember their meaning over time.

## Entering Text

Most word processors display important information as you enter text. This includes the position of the cursor on a given line, the current line number, the name of the file being used, and any special features in use such as insertion or caps lock (for typing capital letters). The line where this information appears on the screen is called the **status line**. It reflects the current status of the word processor. Some systems call this the **ruler line** and use a ruler image to reflect the position of the cursor as well as any tab settings. Figure 10.2 shows the status line from PFS: First Choice. The word processor is set for inserting text and the position of the cursor (line 1, column 1) and margins are clearly indicated.

---

**Figure 10.2**     The Create/Edit Screen from PFS: First Choice. Margins, insert mode, and the cursor location appear on the ruler line.

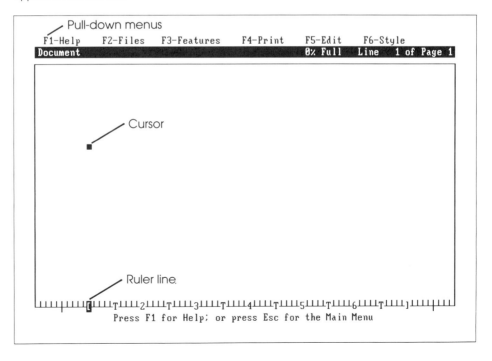

In most systems, text is entered into the word processor in much the same way a typewriter would be used to put it on paper. First, a blank screen appears. Text appears on the screen as it is typed. If the text is satisfactory when entered it can be saved on a disk and later printed. It is more likely that some changes are necessary, however. Words may have been misspelled, and other revisions may be required. The text can be revised immediately or stored on disk and revised at a later time.

When text is entered at a typewriter, the carriage, containing the paper, moves to the left as characters are typed. When the last character on a line has been typed, the typist strikes the Carriage Return key or pushes a lever to move to the next line. Word processors do not require that the Return key be struck at the end of every line. The system sets up margins marking the maximum length of every line. When a word crosses this invisible boundary, it automatically moves to the next line. This is called **word wrap**, since the words move, or wrap around, from one line to another. When we use a word processor, then, we can keep typing without paying attention to where lines begin and where they end. We simply type, and the software breaks lines at the appropriate places. Word wrap improves efficiency, letting ideas flow faster and typing speeds increase.

## Editing Text

Changing or manipulating text is called **editing**. All word processors include the most important text editing features. These are inserting, replacing, and deleting words or characters within existing text. Prior to word processing, a draft of a document produced on a typewriter was corrected or adjusted as needed and the entire report or letter had to be retyped.

For example, at the top in Figure 10.3 the document clearly requires changes, which have been entered by hand.

Making such changes on a typewriter would require retyping the entire document. Important documents were often corrected and retyped many times. This process is very time-consuming, so it is easy to see why documents may not always have been revised as often as necessary. Using a word processor to edit text enables us to make text adjustments without having to retype the unchanged portion of the document.

**Inserting Text**    Using a word processor, characters or words are easily inserted into existing text. A command informs the word processor that until further notice all characters typed are to be inserted into the existing text at the present location of the cursor. With many systems, this command is activated by striking the Ins (insert) key on the keyboard. Other programs, such as WordStar, use the CTRL (control) key together with another character, such as CTRL-V. Repeating the command, striking the insert key twice, cancels the command. (Hitting a key more than once to turn it on and then off is called **toggling**.) As the additional text is entered and the cursor moves to the right, the existing text appears to be

**Figure 10.3**    Editing and Formatting: The upper document is a hand-edited version of the Gettysburg Address. The lower document is the corrected and formatted version.

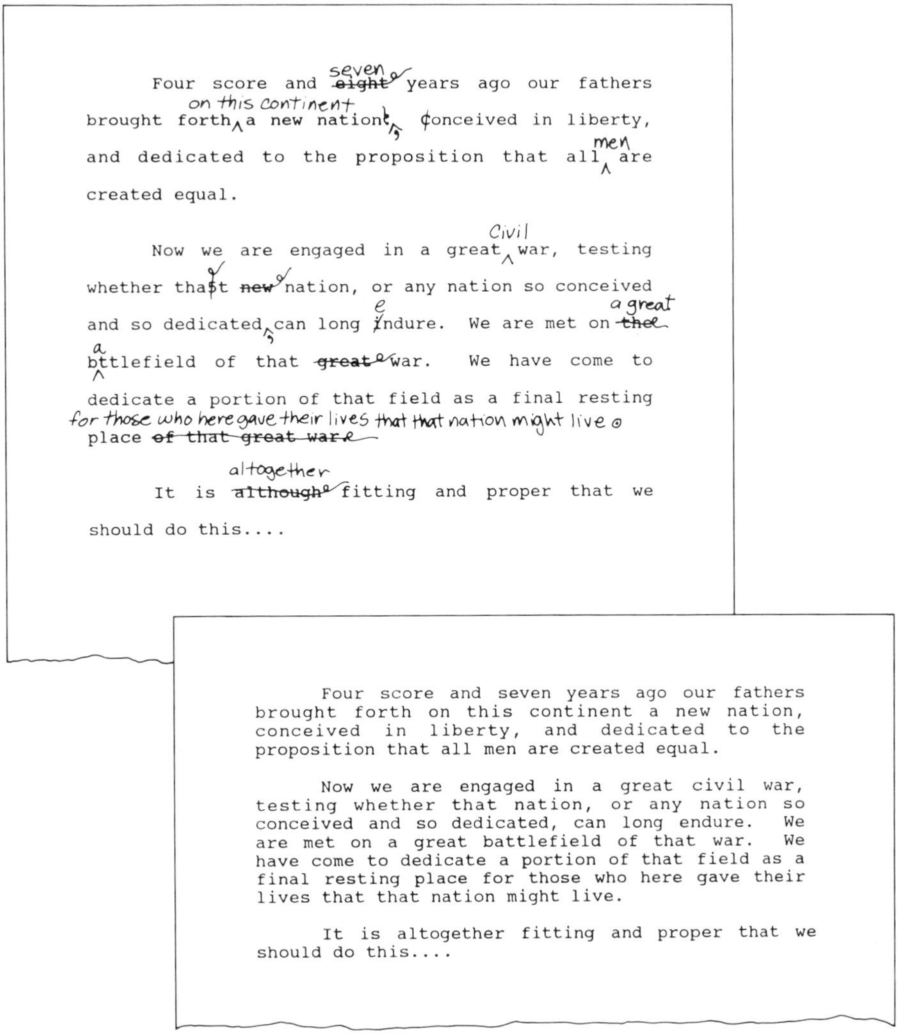

pushed to the right, making room for the additional characters. For example, in Figure 10.3 the phrase

```
"all are created equal"
```

omits the word *men* between the words *all* and *are.* To make the adjustment, the cursor is moved to the space between the two words. The insert command is then issued and the word *men* is typed. (Notice that a space also must be typed to separate the words properly.) As this happens, the remainder of the text, "are created equal," is pushed to the right to make room for the entered word.

```
"all men are created equal"
```

**Replacing Text**   Occasions arise where we want to replace existing text instead of inserting additional text. For example, while entering text we might have typed the word *the* as *teh*. The easiest and fastest correction technique is simply to move the cursor to the *e* (in *teh*) and type the correct letters right over the incorrect ones. While this could be done by deleting the existing characters and inserting new information, it is easier and simpler to enter the correct characters directly over the existing ones. Looking at our document again, in the first phrase the word *eight* should be replaced by the word *seven*.

```
"Four score and eight years ago"
```

As with a simple spelling correction, it is easy to replace a word or phrase with another word or phrase of the same length. Simply move the cursor to the location where the correction is to be made and type the new information directly over the existing information. As the new characters are typed, the old ones simply disappear from the screen.

```
"Four score and sevht years ago"
```

We continue to type over the existing text until the new text totally replaces the old.

```
"Four score and seven years ago"
```

Typing over letters is generally referred to as **overwriting**. Care must be taken when using this replacement technique, since text usually cannot be recovered once it has been replaced. Overwriting works well as long as the corrected text contains exactly the same number of characters as the text it is replacing. If, however, our phrase had been:

```
"Four score and six years ago"
```

replacement alone would not be sufficient to make the correction. If we type the word *seven* directly over the word *six*, we will immediately run into trouble because the change *(seven)* has two more characters than the original word *(six)*.

```
"Four score and sevenears ago"
```

The *seven* not only overwrites the *six*, but also the space between words and the *y* in *years*. Clearly a combination of replacement and insertion, or deletion and insertion, would be required here.

**Deleting Text**   The third component in editing with word processing software is the ability to remove, or **delete**, unwanted characters. Deleting characters is the opposite of inserting characters. To delete, the cursor is moved so that it is positioned directly at the first unwanted character. A command informs the word processor that the user wishes to delete a character, and the character disappears from the screen. Many word processing programs make use of the Del (delete) key for this purpose. Whenever the key is pressed, the character under the cursor disappears. As each character is deleted, the text moves one space to the left. Other systems, such as WordStar, use a special command involving the CTRL (control) key and another character, such as CTRL-G.

When a character or group of characters is deleted, the word processor automatically closes up the line where the character was, joining words together if necessary. For example, in our document the following line appears.

```
"testing whether tha5t new nation"
```

The word *new* should be removed and obviously the 5 does not belong in the word *that*. First the cursor is positioned at the 5, which is then deleted. Then the cursor is moved to the word *new* and, character by character, the word and the space that follows it are removed. The result is an adjusted phrase looking like this:

```
"testing whether that nation"
```

Recognizing that words, sentences, and groups of sentences are often removed from documents, most word processors include commands not only to delete individual characters but to delete whole words, sentences, and larger sections or blocks of text as well.

**Correcting Text**    Correcting text involves combinations of inserting, deleting, and replacing. There is no recommended technique. The commands are used in whatever order seems most appropriate. Using a word processor, our hand-edited version of the Gettysburg Address would now look like the document at the bottom of Figure 10.3. In all cases, once a document has been entered and corrected it must be saved on disk.

## TEXT FORMATTING

The purpose of all word processors is to create clear, error-free printed documents with ease. With a what-you-see-is-what-you-get system, the printed version is essentially what was seen on the screen, even though you still see only part of the document on the screen. With a text editor/text formatter the printed form will reflect the embedded commands. Text editor/text formatter systems do have commands that will let you examine the document on the screen as it will appear on paper.

Word processing systems make some assumptions about the kinds of documents we are most likely to print. Most systems assume that standard 8 ½ by

11-inch paper will be used in the printer. They preset the side margins and the amount of white paper to be left at the top and bottom of the page. These and other preset features are called **default parameters** or **default settings**. The system will automatically use these defaults unless told otherwise. These settings can be easily changed. As you can see in Figure 10.4, PFS: First Choice presets all the margins and the number of lines of text that will appear on a given page.

In addition, default settings usually exist for the number of pages to be printed, the number of copies to be made, the line spacing of the document, and other options. Changing system defaults is an easy process. When you are ready to print, a screen showing the default settings can be displayed. You are asked to review the settings and make whatever changes are appropriate.

Most word processing systems allow the user to choose options from a list, or **menu**. The menu may be viewed by striking a particular key or pulling down the list with a mouse. Selections are then made by pointing to an item with the mouse or arrow keys, or typing in the number or letter that corresponds to the selection. Figure 10.5 shows a menu used in PFS: First Choice. On some systems, commands are issued directly, avoiding the need for a menu. Of course, such systems assume that the user will know the required command. Usually, menus are available just in case they are needed.

---

**Figure 10.4**    The Margins and Page Length Menu from PFS: First Choice.

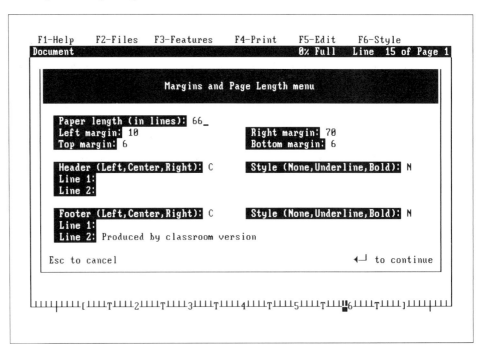

**Figure 10.5**    The Features Menu from PFS: First Choice.

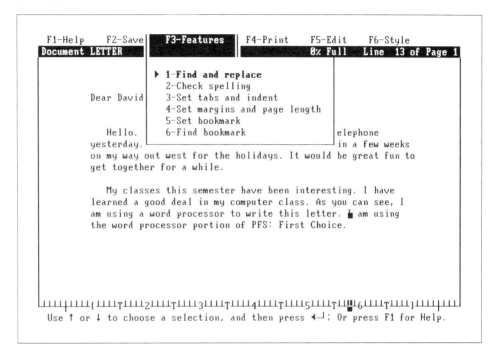

Regardless of the type of word processor being used, the way the document looks is completely under our control. We control the page layout as well as the characters in the text.

## Page Layout

The formatting portion of word processing programs allows us to adjust the number of lines on a page and paragraph indentation. It also lets us make right margins that are even, or **justified**, as they are throughout this textbook or un-even, or ragged, as they are in this paragraph. All printed documents are left-justified, meaning that the print starting at the left margin is even. Profession-ally typeset matter is often right-justified as well. Traditional typewriters cannot produce right-justified copy. Now any document typed with a word processor can be right-justified.

Margins can be adjusted to suit the document. For example, when a letter is typed, sometimes the last few lines or words and the signature may have to go on a second sheet of paper. By narrowing the side margins and reducing the top and bottom margins, the entire letter may fit on a single page. Using a word processor, the settings can simply be adjusted and the letter reprinted. Not a single word need be retyped.

Word processors also let us place information at the top and bottom of each page. Information at the top is known as **header**, and at the bottom, a **footer**. Chapter titles are often headers, while page numbers are often footers. The word processor adjusts the page so this information fits. Some systems can also make adjustments for footnotes. The footnote information is entered and the word processor types it on the appropriate page and adjusts the amount of text on that page so it fits properly.

## Character Adjustment

Word processors allow the user to adjust not only the way text fits on a page, but the way the text appears as well. Information can be centered on a line, and entire sections of text can be indented. Individual characters, whole words, phrases, or sentences can be made to stand out through underlining, overprinting, or boldfacing. Some software packages, especially those that run on the Apple Macintosh, can change the shape of individual letters. Such changes are used to highlight individual words or phrases. Not only can words be italicized, but the letters in headings and titles can be printed in a different type style, or **font**. Many word processing programs, including WordStar and MacWrite, allow the use of subscripts (characters, usually numbers, below the line) and superscripts (characters, usually numbers, above the line). This feature is very important in mathematical and scientific documents and simplifies the use of standard footnotes. Figure 10.6 illustrates the use of subscripts and superscripts.

Any feature entered with a word processor can be easily removed or changed without retyping the document. If underlining is no longer necessary, it can be removed. A word can be italicized or a superscript can be added at any time. If an entire paragraph needs to be indented, the margin for that paragraph can be adjusted after the paragraph has been created. When margins or other space changes are made, the word processor adjusts the rest of the text automatically. Word processors take the drudgery out of writing, rewriting, and printing.

---

**Figure 10.6**   Subscripts and Superscripts.

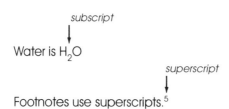

*subscript*

Water is $H_2O$

*superscript*

Footnotes use superscripts.[5]

## ADVANCED FEATURES

We have seen that word processing software makes it easy to create, edit, and print a document. In addition to the editing features we've discussed, most software includes two advanced features that make revisions even easier.

### Search and Replace

Documents stored in memory can vary in size from short notes to very long reports. While it may be possible to display the entire contents of a short note on the computer screen, most larger documents would require several screens to be viewed in their entirety. In many cases, corrections are made on a printout or hard copy of the document. These corrections must then be entered at the keyboard. Locating the place in a document where a correction is to be made by looking through the document can be tedious and time-consuming.

Most word processing systems include a **Search** command. Using this command, you type the word or phrase you are looking for, and the computer will do the looking for you. Computers can search a document, even a long one, in moments. For example, in our original version of the Gettysburg Address in Figure 10.3, we misspelled the word *battlefield*. We can use the search command to send the cursor directly to the misspelled word.

How does a search work? The first step is to move the cursor to the beginning of the document. This ensures that the system will look through every word. The search command is then issued. In WordStar, CTRL-QF would be typed. In most other systems, one of the special function keys (F1 through F10) is pressed. The system then asks the user what to search for. Using our example, we would type *bttlefield* in response to the question. After a brief wait, the system will place the cursor on the word or phrase sought. Then we can make the necessary corrections.

Many systems take this process one step further. After being told what to search for, the system will ask for the correction before it searches the document. Then when it finds the requested word, it immediately replaces it with the corrected or changed word or phrase. This process is called **Search and Replace**. In our example, when the system asked what to search for the answer would be *bttlefield*. When the system asked what to replace it with, the answer would be *battlefield*. This time-saving technique can be very valuable when working with a large document.

The Search and Replace procedure just described works for a single substitution. It often happens that a given substitution must be made in more than one place. For example, a word or a name may have been consistently misspelled. Using a **Global Search and Replace**, every occurrence of the word or phrase will be replaced by the specified correction. The computer quickly performs this otherwise tedious task. Global Search and Replace can be used to replace initials or abbreviations throughout a document. When writing a document, it is easier to use abbreviations for such things as long corporate names, book titles, names of legal cases, and complex scientific or medical terms than it is to enter the entire phrase repeatedly. When the document is complete, a Global Search and Replace can be used to replace these abbreviations with the full name. The full name only has to be typed once.

### Moving Blocks of Text

Using the editing commands already discussed, we can add or delete entire sections of text as easily as we can change a single word. Often, however, we want to change the location of an entire sentence or paragraph within our document. We could delete the words where they occur and reenter them in the new location. But it is much easier to simply move or rearrange the existing text.

Word processing systems call the portions of the text to be moved a **block**. The first step in moving a block from one place to another is to mark or identify the block. To do this, the cursor is advanced to the beginning of the block to be moved. A command is issued informing the system that a block is to be marked for moving. Then we move the cursor through the text until we reach the end of the block to be moved. In most systems, this highlights the appropriate text and identifies the block. When a mouse is available, we use the mouse to drag the cursor through the text to identify and highlight the block (see Figure 10.7). On other machines, the cursor control keys are used.

The next step is to move the cursor to the block's new location. Another command is issued, and the system automatically moves the block of text. The space created when the block is removed is automatically filled in as the rest of the text moves up, just as space is automatically made for the block in its new location. Any necessary page or line adjustments are also made automatically.

### Additional Capabilities

As word processing software has been used for an increasing variety of writing tasks, systems have added a number of additional advanced features.

**Mail-merge**   The **mail-merge** feature enables the word processing system to combine a list of names and addresses, such as a mailing list, with a form letter. This can produce a series of individualized letters, each of which looks specially typed. As the form letter is entered, it is marked in each location where an item from the mailing list will be placed. The mailing list and the form letter are entered into two separate files. Then both lists are processed together using special merge commands.

**Spelling Checker and Thesaurus**   Many word processors include an additional program that compares the words in a document with words in an electronic dictionary. Such dictionaries contain as many as 100,000 words, and addi-

**Figure 10.7**    Moving a Block of Text: A Macintosh screen with text to be moved.

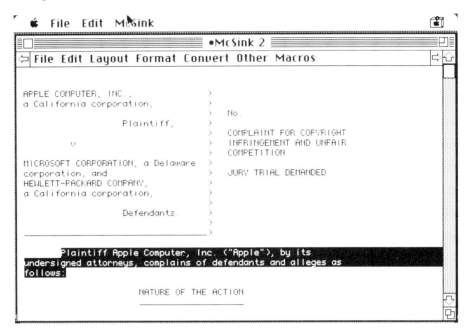

tional words usually can be added by the user. The spelling checker runs through the document, comparing each word to the words in the dictionary. If a match is found, it moves on to check the next word. If it does not find a match, the spelling checker either marks the word for later correction or asks the user to correct the error immediately. Some programs even offer suggested corrections, guessing at what the word is supposed to be. Spelling checkers have limitations. If *are* was typed instead of *art,* the spelling checker will not catch the error because both are legitimate words.

Some systems include a thesaurus. Having used a word often in a document, we may want to replace it with another word of the same meaning. By issuing a command and identifying the word, a list of synonyms will appear on the screen. The user then selects an alternative word with the same meaning to be placed in the document.

**File merging**    Word processors increasingly contain features that make it possible to combine information on files from other applications software. Charts and tables created with spreadsheets and other packages can be combined with text created with a word processor. The result is a complete document that may incorporate work done with a number of different software packages.

# On Line

## HYPERTEXT—A NEW WAY OF READING

Ever since the invention of written language, text has been read from beginning to end.

A new way of reading and processing information has been made possible by computers, however. With this new way, called **hypertext**, readers can move back and forth from one related idea to another at will.

To understand hypertext's connections, imagine you are browsing in the library. You are attracted to a book on Mozart. After reading a few pages, you learn that Mozart was an 18th century composer. Curious about who else composed music in the late 18th century, you go to the card catalog, locate a book on famous composers, and find it in the stacks. Then you read about Mozart's contemporaries. This book also discusses piano concertos, so you go to the library's record collection and listen to a Mozart piano concerto. While listening, you are struck by the quality of the background orchestra and look up the instruments that made up an 18th-century orchestra. Your browsing could go on until your interest is satisfied or until the library closes.

You could do the same thing with a hypertext system. While reading about Mozart at your terminal, you become curious about other 18th-century composers. You mark the text and request more information. A list of articles about other 18th-century composers appears in a window on your screen and you select one. The process continues just as before, only this time you remain seated and the computer brings the material to you.

Hypertext allows users to browse through linked information in any order. When links include sound, video, and graphics as well as text it is considered **hypermedia.**

Hypertext is in its infancy yet it is gaining in popularity. The most common microcomputer systems include OWL International's Guide designed for the IBM PC-AT and compatibles, and Apple's HyperCard. To encourage the use of its HyperCard system, Apple includes the software with every Macintosh.

HyperCard is based on the idea of note cards similar to what you'd use to take research notes in the library. Each card can hold text, graphics, electronic mail messages, or any other unit of electronic information. A group of cards forms a "stack." Cards within a stack are linked together, and links can be created between cards in other stacks.

OWL's Guide starts with a document such as a book and links items within the document. The links of hypertext connect one portion of the book to another, display references related to marked text, or lead to more detailed information about a marked section of the document. OWL's Guide is designed for exploring existing documents rather than creating information in the HyperCard mode.

All hypertext systems use large amounts of memory. Microcomputer users have complained that even with careful use it is easy to fill a hard disk with linked information.

Hypertext has the potential for becoming an important information-management and research tool. The release of NeXT's powerful workstation, with its massive optical memory and built-in hypertext software, is the newest step in this new direction.

*Source:* Paul Saffo, "What You Need to Know About Hypertext," *Personal Computing,* vol. 11, number 12, Dec. 1987, pp. 166–173. Jane M. Tazelaar, "Hypertext," *Byte,* vol. 13, number 10, Oct. 1988, p. 234.

Increasingly, word processors are including a variety of additional special features. They may contain calculator programs for simple on-line arithmetic and telecommunications software to transmit documents or mail messages over telephone lines (see Chapter 14). In addition, word processing software is the basis for the production of high-quality printed material used in a relatively new phenomenon called desktop publishing.

## DESKTOP PUBLISHING

Word processing has changed the way we think about writing as well as the way we write. It has also brought us to the doorstep of a another revolution. With the advanced technology of today's microcomputers and low-cost laser printers, text can be combined with graphics and photographs to create documents at our desks that in the past would have required the services of artists and typesetting equipment. Word processing and graphics software packages enable users to access and adjust any image stored in the computer's memory. Laser printers print entire pages of text at once. This combined technology allows us to do page processing on our desktops.

Small businesses, university departments, and organizations of all kinds now can produce documents, including newsletters and reports, that are camera-ready and can be directly duplicated either on a copier or phototypesetting machine. This is **desktop publishing**.

The concept of page processing using microcomputers is a natural outgrowth of the software and hardware capabilities of the Apple Macintosh. The Macintosh includes as standard equipment a high-resolution graphics monitor and a mouse. To make use of these features, Apple developed software to create pictures on the screen. Apple software such as MacDraw uses the mouse as a pencil or paintbrush along with built-in shadings and shape (circle, square, line, and curve) generators. With some practice, anyone can create pictures and diagrams (see Chapter 13). In addition, the formatting features of Macintosh word processors, such as MacWrite, and MicroSoft WORD can change the **font** or shape of characters and their size as well, within limits. Using advanced formatting software programs such as PageMaker, the Macintosh can combine pictures, diagrams, and text into cohesive documents that can be printed using dot matrix technology.

However, the print quality on most dot matrix printers is not as clear and sharp as documents typed or typeset by traditional methods. Indeed, these documents *look* like they've been produced by a computer. However, with the development of high-resolution, relatively inexpensive laser printers this has changed (see Chapter 5). By adding a microprocessor to photocopying technology, the Macintosh can now produce documents that look as though they had been professionally typeset, but at a fraction of the cost.

**Figure 10.8**    Desktop Publishing: High-quality software means that businesses now can produce documents that look almost as if they had been professionally typeset. Shown are a microcomputer, graphics display, mouse, scanner, and laser printer.

While Apple was the first to popularize desktop publishing, high-quality software is available for most other microcomputers, including the IBM Personal System/2, IBM PCs, and PC-compatibles. With the availability of such software, organizations with IBM or compatible equipment already in place are making good use of desktop publishing (see Figure 10.8).

Many of the desktop publishing features now available on microcomputers have been available for some time on mainframe computer systems using sophisticated laser printers. These large systems with their larger memory have more fonts, specialized symbols, and many other features that microcomputers cannot support. However, the cost of such systems can be quite high. Furthermore, these systems cannot realistically be called desktop because they are too large to sit on a desk.

Many computer professionals believe that page processing will have as revolutionary an effect on society as the microcomputer itself has had. Any individual or organization can now produce high-quality newsletters and documents at a reasonable cost. The ability to gather, assemble, and distribute information is no longer limited to large organizations. It is back in the hands and on the desktops of all of us.

## PROBLEMS AND PITFALLS

Up to this point, word processors have been helpful friends who have made the work of writing easier. But there are hidden pitfalls. We can avoid them, however, if we know where they are hiding. The following are some common word processing problems and some suggested solutions.

## Editing Problems

There is a danger of losing data due to *overwriting*. Care should be applied when correcting text using the overwrite feature. While typing over a character or word may appear easier than inserting and deleting, text that has been over-typed cannot be recovered. When correcting more than a word or simple phrase, it is often better to insert the new text and carefully examine the old text before it is deleted. A phrase or sentence that you replace may be useful elsewhere in the document, and you can easily move it to another position. Once it has been overtyped, it is lost.

Test also may be lost because of *hasty deletes*. Think carefully before deleting any block of text. Deleted text cannot be easily retrieved. Instead of deleting blocks of text that seem unnecessary at the moment, move them to the end of the file. Then you will be able to review them later and decide whether they contain valuable information. At the very least, hard copies of all deleted blocks should be made just in case they prove valuable later. Once text is deleted it is gone.

## Search and Replace

Users must beware of *ambiguous word use* when searching. Care must be used when asking the computer to search for a particular word, portion of a word, or a phrase. The same word may appear in more than one place within the text. For this reason, the word or phrase being searched for should be unique enough to identify the specific item being sought. This is particularly critical if the automatic replacement feature is being used. For example, if you wish to change the word *auto* to *car*, the computer will search the file for the first occurrence of the set of characters *auto* and replace it with the characters *car*. Unfortunately, the first occurrence of auto may be in the word *automatically*, which will then get changed to *carmatically*—not exactly what you intended. There are two ways to prevent this from happening. You can use the Search without the Replace and enter the correction directly when the cursor finds the word. Or you can be very explicit in specifying the word being sought. In our example, if the set of characters the computer was searching for was *auto* (including the space before and after the letters), the computer would not confuse it with the same letters that were part of a word.

There is also a danger of *unwanted changes* using Replace. Use Global Search and Replace with caution, since all occurrences of the word or phrase will be replaced. With this feature, it is possible that a change will be made where it is not wanted. A Global Search and Replace is fast, but it may save time in the long run to make changes one at a time.

### Spelling Checkers

Spelling checkers compare words in a document with words in an electronic dictionary. As a result, they cannot identify a word that is used incorrectly, such as *there* instead of *they're*. They also will not locate typing errors that happen to form real words. If *then* rather than *them* is typed, a spelling checker will not read this as an error. Furthermore, a spelling checker is only as good as its dictionary. A correctly spelled word may be flagged as incorrect if it is not included in the dictionary. This is particularly likely to happen with people's names or technical terms.

### Loss of Text

Any file created by any software package that makes use of a computer's main memory can be lost if there is an interruption of power. This is especially true of word processors, most of which store the text being processed in main memory until told to copy it onto a disk. It is wise to save text at regular intervals, either every 15 minutes or whenever anything significant has been written. In this way, if the power fails or something goes wrong with either the hardware or software, most of your work is protected. Another good working procedure is to make a printout of everything you write with a word processing system, even if it is only a very rough draft. Hardware failures do occur, and disk files can be destroyed. Work that exists as a hard copy can be retyped if necessary. Retyping is easier than recreating ideas.

### Special Effects

Special printing effects such as different fonts, boldfacing, overprinting, and underlining should be used sparingly. They are intended to enhance a document by making words or phrases stand out for emphasis. Overused, these effects can make a document hard to read or confusing.

Word processing can be a help to professional writers and to all of us who even occasionally need to put words on paper. Studies involving the use of word processors in writing classes find that students are more likely to adjust and revise their work when a word processor is available than when work is handwritten or typed. Presumably, the editing and block move features of word processors make document adjustments easy. Students who learn word processing in computer classes report that they regularly use their word processing skills once the class is over.

Just as students benefit when word processing is available, office productivity studies find that word processors considerably decrease the time needed to prepare printed documents. Furthermore, organizations of all sizes are using desktop publishing techniques to improve the appearance and timeliness of documents, while saving money.

## SUMMARY

Word processing makes it possible to add, remove, and change characters, words, and phrases within a document. All word processing programs require a keyboard, a display screen, and a printer.

Word processing packages have two parts. The front end is concerned with entering and editing the text. The back end controls the way text will appear when it is printed.

With text editor/text formatter software, text is entered without regard to how it will look on the printed page. Along with the text, dot commands are entered. These commands are read by the formatter portion of the word processor and affect the final layout of the document.

The what you see is what you get (WYSIWYG) type of word processor merges the editing and formatting features of the software. When a formatting command is issued, it is immediately acted upon and the text on the screen is moved to reflect the command.

When entering text into a word processor, the status line reflects the current status of the system, indicating the line number and position of the cursor. Special features are also indicated. Word processors do not require that the Return key be struck at the end of every line. Using word wrap and preset margins, the software breaks lines at the correct place.

All word processors include editing features that allow inserting, replacing, and deleting words or characters within existing text.

The way a document produced by a word processor looks is completely under the user's control. The formatter portion of word processing programs controls the number of lines per page, paragraph indentation, justification, and the use of headers and footers. Characters can be underlined, boldfaced, and overprinted. Many systems can change the font and size of individual characters. Sections of text can be indented, margins can be adjusted.

Using search and replace commands, information embedded within a document can be located by the software and adjusted as needed. Portions of text, or blocks, can be moved from one place to another within a document.

Most current systems include mail-merge, spelling checkers, and file-merging capabilities.

Desktop publishing combines sophisticated software, microcomputers, and laser printers to produce camera-ready documents. Advanced formatting software combines pictures, diagrams, and text into cohesive documents that can be printed at relatively low cost.

Word processing requires care. Text can be lost due to overwriting or hasty deletes, and electronic search and replace procedures can produce unexpected results.

## Key Words

As an extra review of the chapter, try defining the following terms. If you have trouble with any of them, refer to the page number listed.

access  *(255)*
block  *(264)*
default parameters (default settings)
    *(260)*
delete  *(258)*
desktop publishing  *(267)*
dot commands  *(253)*
editing  *(256)*
font  *(262)*
footer  *(262)*
format  *(252)*
full-screen editing  *(252)*
global search and replace  *(263)*
header  *(262)*
hypermedia  *(266)*

hypertext  *(266)*
justified  *(261)*
mail-merge  *(264)*
menu  *(260)*
overwriting  *(258)*
screen management keys  *(251)*
search  *(263)*
search and replace  *(263)*
status line (ruler line)  *(255)*
text editor/text formatter  *(252)*
toggling  *(256)*
what you see is what you get
    (WYSIWYG)  *(252)*
word processing  *(250)*
word wrap  *(256)*

## Test Your Knowledge

1. List the three pieces of hardware, in addition to a computer, necessary for a word processing system.

2. What is editing?

3. What is formatting?

4. Explain the differences between what you see is what you get word processing systems and text editor/text formatter systems.

5. What are dot commands? When are they used?

6. What is word wrap? Why is it useful?

7. What information usually appears on the status line?

8. Using a word processor, how would you correct the word *cna* so that it is spelled *can*? Be specific. What commands would you use?

9. Using a word processor, how would you correct the word *tha5t* so that it is spelled *that*? Be specific. What commands would you use?

10. How does *insert* differ from *replace*?

11. When formatting a document, what are default parameters?

12. Define *justification* as applied to the appearance of a document.

13. Most word processors allow you to make adjustments to individual characters. What kinds of adjustments can be made?

14. Explain how the Search and Replace command works. Why is this useful?

15. What is a Global Search and Replace?

16. What is a block move? Why is it useful?

17. What is mail-merge?

18. How does a spelling checker work?

19. What is page processing? How has page processing contributed to the rise of desktop publishing?

20. Why should the Search and Replace command be used carefully?

## Expand Your Knowledge

1. Go to a local computer store and make a list of the word processing programs in stock. What system(s) do each of these packages run on? What do they cost? Check out integrated packages as well as stand-alone software. What is the most popular package for the IBM Personal System/2? What is the most popular package for the Macintosh? What other computer systems do they carry? What is the most popular word processing package on each of them?

2. Using the word processor available to you, enter the following passage from the Declaration of Independence. Use margins of your choice.

When in the course of human events, it becomes necessary for one people to dissolve the political bonds which have connected them with another, and to assume, among the powers of the earth, the separate and equal station to which the laws of nature and of nature's God entitle them, a decent respect to the opinions of mankind requires that they should declare the causes which impel them to the separation.

We hold these truths to be self-evident, that all men are created equal; that they are endowed by their Creator with certain unalienable rights; that among these, are life, liberty, and the pursuit of happiness. That, to secure these rights, governments are instituted among men, deriving their just powers from the consent of the governed; that, whenever any form of government becomes destructive of these ends, it is the right of the people to alter or to abolish it, and to institute a new government, laying its foundation on such principles, and organizing its powers in such form, as to them shall seem most likely to affect their safety and happiness.

(a) Right-justify your passage.
(b) Print out the passage single spaced.
(c) Adjust your passage and print it out double spaced.

3. Write a short (three to five page) research paper discussing the advantages and disadvantages of desktop publishing. Examine the use of Macintosh, IBM, and IBM-compatible equipment. Include at least three references.

4. Write a short (three to five page) research paper discussing the use of electronic thesauruses. What software packages contain them? How popular are they? How do they work? Who uses them? Resources can include magazine articles or interviews with computing-center or local computer-store staff.

5. The following paragraph has *highlighted* errors. Identify what is wrong with each highlighted error and indicate how it should be corrected. Using the word processor available to you, enter and print the paragraph, double spaced, as you have corrected it.

Though many devices have an edge over the *moose* in specific areas, nothing matches the electronic rodent for overall versatility. *Amd reversability* matters, because desktop *desktop* publishing encompasses a *hiodge podge* of tasks: drawing and *and* drafting, *writeing,* editing, cutting and pasting, *layingout,* and designing. Without the mouse, I, for one, would spend most of the day plugging and unplugging various devices to support a succession of activities.

*Source:* Paul Saffo, "Desktop Publishing: Alternative Input Devices," *Personal Computing,* May 1988, p. 59.

# 11

# Spreadsheets

**Chapter Outline**

What Is an Electronic Spreadsheet?

Common Spreadsheet Features

Planning a Spreadsheet

Building a Spreadsheet
    Design the Spreadsheet • Enter the Data • Save the Data

What If

Programming Tools
    Inserting and Deleting • Copying Cells • Formatting Data •
    Mathematical Functions

Pitfalls, Problems, and Solutions

Spreadsheet software is the electronic equivalent of the accountant's green pad, with its long columns and rows filled with numbers. Spreadsheets, in pencil-on-paper form, have long been used in business by accountants, financial analysts, bankers, and bookkeepers. Spreadsheet software has brought new power to the numbers games of these professionals. It has also given the rest of us control over the numbers in our lives. Spreadsheets, especially the electronic variety, are not just for accountants any more. Just as word processing has revolutionized writing, electronic spreadsheets have revolutionized computation. Spreadsheets are for everybody. This chapter looks at spreadsheets in depth.

After studying this chapter, you will be able to:

- Describe an electronic spreadsheet.

- Discuss planning and designing a spreadsheet.

- Explain the use of formulas in spreadsheets.

- Discuss the use of what-if statements with spreadsheets.

- Identify spreadsheet programming tools.

- Understand common spreadsheet problem areas.

## WHAT IS AN ELECTRONIC SPREADSHEET?

During the spring of 1978 Dan Bricklin, a graduate student at the Harvard Business School, was confronted with a homework assignment that required the use of business worksheets, or spreadsheets. In such problems, a single numeric change typically could affect many values on the spreadsheet, requiring significant, tedious recalculations. Bricklin realized that there had to be a better way. Sophisticated in the use of computers from his undergraduate days at the Massachusetts Institute of Technology (MIT) and prior work experience, he wanted to find a way to have a computer do the repetitive, predictable work. It occurred to him that he needed something like a word processor specifically designed to work with numbers in tables—an **electronic spreadsheet**.

Despite the skepticism of his Harvard professors, Bricklin collaborated with Robert Frankston, a computer-programmer friend from MIT, to develop and release the first electronic spreadsheet in 1979. It ran on an early Apple II computer and was called VisiCalc (for VISIble CALCulator). This program was designed to automate the calculations and recalculations customarily required on paper spreadsheets.

VisiCalc and its more recent and powerful cousins, such as Lotus 1-2-3, SuperCalc3, EXCEL, and QUATTRO, have revolutionized the way we can deal with numbers. Any problem that can be solved with pencil, paper, and a calculator can be solved more quickly and accurately with spreadsheet software and a computer. Information, formerly hidden under mountains of unorganized numeric data, can be at the fingertips of anyone using an electronic spreadsheet.

With this software, data is organized into tables. Relationships among the data are established and calculations such as sums and averages can be performed. As input data changes, new sets of answers can be easily computed.

While spreadsheets are most often used to solve business and financial problems, they can be easily applied to other problems that involve mathematical calculations. Balancing a checkbook, calculating student grades, and computing the values on a tax return are easily accomplished using spreadsheet software.

## COMMON SPREADSHEET FEATURES

An electronic spreadsheet is an automated accountant's pad or ledger. In format it is a table consisting of vertical columns and horizontal rows. The columns and rows intersect to form a complex grid or matrix. Each of the boxes created by the intersection of a given column and a specific row is called a **cell**. Each cell is uniquely identified, in much the way as an individual seat in a large theater. Each cell is identified by the letter or number labels for the column and row that define it (see Figure 11.1).

In packages such as Lotus 1-2-3, SuperCalc3, and ENABLE, each column is named with a letter, while each row is identified with a number. When the spreadsheet requires more than 26 columns, double letters such as AA and BD are used. Just as with theater seats, cells are then named by a letter or letters

**Figure 11.1**      Diagram of a Spreadsheet.

COLUMNS

| ROWS | A (C1) | B (C2) | C (C3) | D (C4) | E (C5) |
|---|---|---|---|---|---|
| 1 (R1) | A1 | | | | |
| 2 (R2) | A2 | | | | |
| 3 (R3) | (R3C1) | | (R3C3) | D3 | |
| 4 (R4) | | | | | |
| 5 (R5) | | | | D5 or (R5C4) | |
| 6 (R6) | | | | | |
| 7 (R7) | | | | | E7 |
| 8 (R8) | | | | | |

followed by a number representing the column and row whose intersection creates the cell. A cell formed by the intersection of column A and row 1 would be labeled A1. Other cells would have names such as A25, D3, and E19.

Other software packages use other schemes for identifying cells. For example, in Multiplan and PFS: First Choice, cells have names such as RxCy for Row x and Column y. What would be cell D5 in a Lotus spreadsheet would be named R5C4 (for row 5, column 4) in Multiplan. Regardless of the naming scheme, each cell has a unique name that clearly identifies its location in the spreadsheet.

Let us transform our spreadsheet for a moment. Instead of looking at a pad or monitor with lines creating boxes, imagine that you are standing in the mail room of a large high-rise apartment building. In front of you is a wall of mailboxes neatly arranged in rows and columns. Each mailbox has a name and a number printed on the outside. Does the name or number on the mailbox tell us anything about the contents of the box? Of course not. The name on the box is just a means of identifying to whom the box belongs. What is inside the box depends on what the U.S. Postal Service has delivered that day, if anything. The same is true for a spreadsheet. Each cell has a name, such as A3, S17, or R45C17, but the name tells us no more about the contents of the cell than the names on our mailboxes tell us about their contents (see Chapter 3).

Mailboxes can contain letters, bills, magazines, and other items that qualify as mail. Spreadsheet cells can contain three types of data: values or numbers, formulas, and labels.

The numbers placed directly in a spreadsheet's cells are frequently known as **values**. Most spreadsheets allow values to be displayed in many different forms. Values can be whole numbers, or integers (123); real numbers (0.456 or 1245.68); and dollars and cents ($1234.56). Some software packages allow the use of scientific notation.

**Formulas** are mathematical statements or sets of instructions. Formulas are associated with a specific cell and are used to calculate the value of that cell. This numeric result is then displayed in the cell. Formulas contain the names of specific cells, such as A1, C23, or D16. The cell names used in spreadsheet formulas refer to the contents of the indicated cells. These contents are used in calculations. A formula can be stated in a simple way, such as A1+A2+D4. This means add the contents of cell A1 and cell A2 and cell D4. A formula can be more complex, such as @SUM(D3..D23). This means calculate the sum of all the values in the cell D3 through D23. In each case, the value resulting from the calculation is placed in the cell where the formula appeared (see Figure 11.2).

**Labels** are words, titles, or text that are used to form row and column headings. They usually describe what is happening within the spreadsheet. For example, Employee Name, Gross Income, Dollar Amount, and Tax Amount could be used as column or row headings. Labels are also used to provide textual data. The names found under the heading Employee Name would be considered labels. Labels cannot be used in calculations. A label that begins with a number

**Figure 11.2**    Spreadsheet Formulas: This spreadsheet contains checking account data. Some cell formulas are identified.

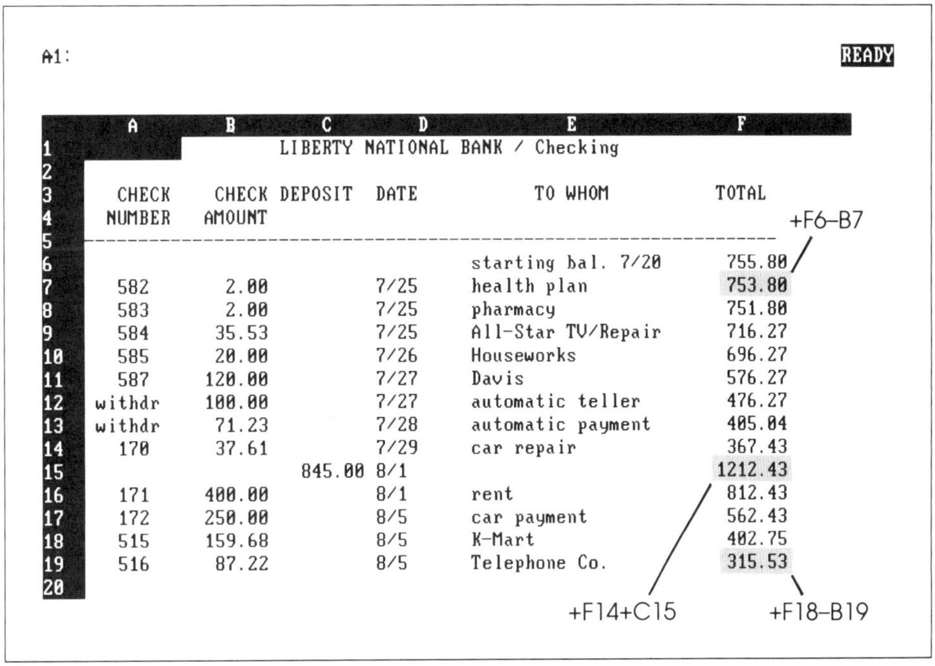

```
A1:                                                                    READY

        A        B        C        D           E              F
1                        LIBERTY NATIONAL BANK / Checking
2
3     CHECK    CHECK  DEPOSIT   DATE         TO WHOM         TOTAL
4     NUMBER   AMOUNT                                                +F6–B7
5  ---------------------------------------------------------------  /
6                                         starting bal. 7/20   755.80/
7      582      2.00            7/25       health plan         753.80
8      583      2.00            7/25       pharmacy            751.80
9      584     35.53            7/25       All-Star TV/Repair  716.27
10     585     20.00            7/26       Houseworks          696.27
11     587    120.00            7/27       Davis               576.27
12   withdr   100.00            7/27       automatic teller    476.27
13   withdr    71.23            7/28       automatic payment   405.04
14     170     37.61            7/29       car repair          367.43
15                      845.00  8/1                           1212.43
16     171    400.00            8/1        rent                812.43
17     172    250.00            8/5        car payment         562.43
18     515    159.68            8/5        K-Mart              402.75
19     516     87.22            8/5        Telephone Co.       315.53
20
                                    +F14+C15            +F18–B19
```

must be entered in a specific way to distinguish it from a value or formula. A very common example includes social security numbers or phone numbers. You would not want the social security number 399-11-6424 to be evaluated as 399 minus 11 minus 6424. Even though they are numbers, social security numbers, phone numbers, check numbers, or student ID numbers are not used in calculations. As a result, they are stored in spreadsheet cells as labels.

A spreadsheet is a tool that can be used to solve problems. Using a spreadsheet requires no knowledge of programming. Nor is a high level of skill in mathematics necessary. To use a spreadsheet effectively requires planning and enough math sense to properly define the necessary formulas. A spreadsheet presents solutions to problems. The more care and attention paid to planning the spreadsheet, the faster problems will be solved and the more direct the solutions will be.

## PLANNING A SPREADSHEET

Planning saves time; it also avoids mathematical errors. As with any computer application, spreadsheet results are only as accurate and reliable as the information given to the machine. Formulas that reference incorrect cell positions or have mistyped values will result in wrong answers. *Garbage in* produces *garbage out (GIGO).*

When designing a spreadsheet, it is important to take the time to lay it out on paper first. Identify the column headings and row headings needed. Your spreadsheet design should reflect the problem you need to solve. There is no standard spreadsheet format. Put the information in whatever order seems to best solve the problem. The following five steps will prove very useful.

1. *Understand the problem.*

2. *Specify the results.* Determine what information you need to compute. (OUTPUT)

3. *Specify the input.* Gather and organize the initial data if it is available. If not, locate the necessary data. (INPUT)

4. *Determine the formulas.* These formulas will transform the INPUT into the OUTPUT.

5. *Design the spreadsheet on the computer.* Label the columns and rows. Insert the values and formulas into their appropriate cells.

This list has a very familiar ring. We identified a similar procedure in Chapter 6 when designing an algorithm. A spreadsheet is merely a tool to assist in problem solving.

If you use a spreadsheet frequently to solve similar problems, you should consider designing a template. A **template** is the outline of a spreadsheet with only the key labels and formulas set in the appropriate places. This spreadsheet outline can be stored on a disk and used as a starting point whenever you have a similar spreadsheet problem to solve. For example, an instructor who is teaching three classes can use a spreadsheet to keep track of student grades, calculate final grades, and compute test and class averages. Each class requires a separate spreadsheet to contain students' names and grades. Yet all three will have the same major labels and formulas. It would be a considerable waste of time to retype this essential information when a single template can be used as a starting point for each class and reused next semester as well (see Figure 11.3).

**Figure 11.3**    The Template: A spreadsheet outline, a template contains only key labels and formulas. This template was created for a class/grade-average spreadsheet. Too large to run across the page, the template is divided into two sections, (a) and (b).

(a)

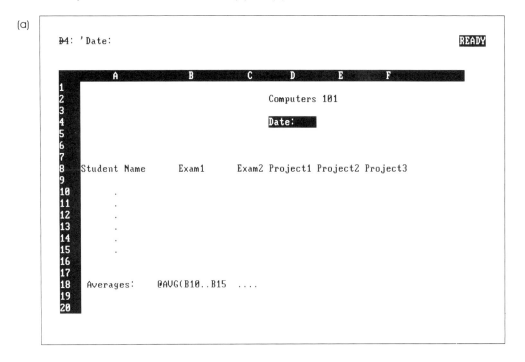

(b)

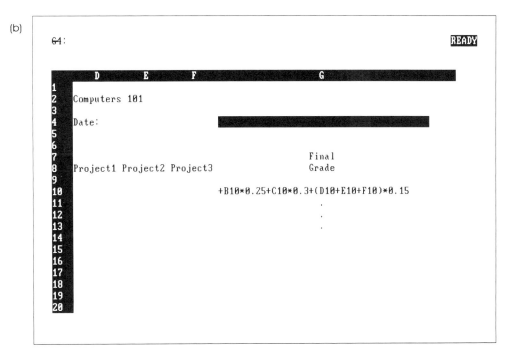

# On Line

## SPREADSHEETS AND TAX RETURNS

Preparing federal tax returns seems to require endless numeric entries and calculations. But there is a way to make this annual headache much easier—with a spreadsheet. Stand-alone applications software for tax preparation is available, but most popular tax software uses templates that build on existing spreadsheet software such as Lotus 1-2-3, VP-Planner, or EXCEL.

Unlike stand-alone packages, templates allow the user to easily adjust formulas to meet individual needs. Templates are also relatively inexpensive, because they do not include the price of a powerful spreadsheet. Updates that reflect changes in the tax codes cost a fraction of the template's original cost. Many companies make state tax templates available at a nominal fee to people who buy federal tax return software.

The simplest tax templates provide a worksheet with pre-entered labels and formulas. The preparer fills in the appropriate data by moving the cursor to the required cell location. The more powerful templates automatically move the cursor and provide on-line help screens.

Some systems are menu driven, making the package easy to use. Effective programs provide step-by-step support so the preparer doesn't have to relearn the software every year or adjust to changes in the law.

Flexible spreadsheet templates allow the preparer to begin working with any one of the multiple forms usually required. Calculated totals move easily from form to form, and changes in one line are reflected throughout. These features allow the user to test tax calculation strategies and to choose the best one.

The majority of tax template packages print forms. The Internal Revenue Service (IRS) will accept computer output for schedules and supporting forms that document calculations, but any form that requires a taxpayer's signature must look exactly like the IRS standard.

Some packages print data on a transparent overlay that can be placed on top of an IRS form and photocopied. Laser printers can also be used to produce IRS-compatible forms.

*Source:* Tom Badgett, "Taxes as Easy as 1-2-3," *Personal Computing,* Vol. 11, Number 12, December, 1987, pp. 70–74.

## BUILDING A SPREADSHEET

When you first set out to learn to use a spreadsheet package, choose a problem you understand completely. In this way you can focus on the spreadsheet layout and formula development instead of having to unravel a difficult problem. Learning to use a spreadsheet does not happen in a flash of light. It is more like learning to ride a bike; it takes time, careful attention to details, and a sense of balance. In the beginning, the sheet may fall flat, giving incorrect results. However, if you pick up the sheet, check the formulas, and head out again you're sure to get the hang of it.

## Design the Spreadsheet

Let us build a simple spreadsheet, using as our model the data generated by a small but attentive class taking a computer course. At the beginning of each semester, the instructor receives a class list containing the names and social security numbers of all students registered in the class. During the first class meeting, the instructor hands out an outline describing the grading policy, project and report deadlines, and the dates of the exams. A spreadsheet would be an ideal way for the instructor to keep track of the students' scores on exams, papers, and projects and calculate a numerical grade for each student. The following steps apply the spreadsheet plan listed earlier in this chapter to produce a grade book:

1. *Understand the problem.* The problem is to design a spreadsheet to record student scores and calculate appropriate grades and averages.

2. *Specify the results.* The results that are needed are the average grade for each of the exams and projects, the final grade for each student, and the average final grade for the entire class.

3. *Specify the input.* The input will be the student names, two exam scores, and three project scores.

4. *Determine the formulas.* Exam 1 is worth 25 percent of the grade, Exam 2 is worth 30 percent of the grade, and each project is worth 15 percent of the grade. The formulas are:

   FINAL GRADE = (exam1 * 0.25) + (exam2 * 0.30) + (proj1 + proj2 + proj3) * 0.15

   EXAM AVERAGE = sum of all scores on a given exam / number of scores

   PROJECT AVERAGE = sum of all scores on a given project / number of scores

   CLASS AVERAGE GRADE = sum of all numeric grades / number of grades

5. *Design the spreadsheet.* First, gather all the available data and determine the desired results. Next, sketch a quick layout, including appropriate labels for columns and rows. Now you can review the entire sheet for overall usability. Identify the cells in which formulas and results will be located (see Figure 11.4).

**Figure 11.4**          Sketch of a Spreadsheet Layout.

Computers 101

| Student Name | Exam 1 | Exam 2 | Project 1 | Project 2 | Project 3 | Final Grade |
|---|---|---|---|---|---|---|
| Penny A. Day |  |  |  |  |  |  |
| Bjorn Tolouse |  |  |  |  |  |  |
| . |  |  |  |  |  |  |
| . |  |  |  |  |  |  |
| . |  |  |  |  |  |  |
| S. Lee Zee |  |  |  |  |  |  |
| Averages |  |  |  |  |  |  |

Now that the spreadsheet has been designed on paper, you are ready to key it into the computer. Enter the labels for the column headings. Then reexamine the sheet, keeping in mind its overall usefulness. If you see ways to improve on the layout, do so.

## Enter the Data

Next, enter the data into this initial spreadsheet. Include all available data (student names) and the labels to indicate values that will be computed by the formulas (see Figure 11.5).

Now enter the formulas. Notice that the formulas that appear for each student under the heading Final Grade are similar. Additionally, the formulas to compute the averages for exam grades, project grades, and the final grade are also similar (see Figure 11.6). In each case, formulas are adjusted to reflect the appropriate cells.

Now that the spreadsheet has been initialized, it is ready to receive data as it becomes available. In this example, student grades will be gathered and entered over the course of a semester. As each grade is entered, the final grade will automatically be recalculated. Final grades have little meaning until all of the grades have been entered. Therefore, the interim final grades that a spreadsheet will display should be viewed as temporary, representing the result of the work completed to date. Figure 11.7 represents a completed spreadsheet that displays the semester's grades and the resulting final grade.

The ability to immediately recalculate all formulas when a data value is changed is one of the benefits of spreadsheet software. Most electronic spreadsheets allow you to activate or deactivate this automatic recalculation to facilitate the entry of large amounts of data. The automatic recalculate feature can be turned off until all of the required changes have been made. When deal-

**Figure 11.5**       Spreadsheet with Initial Data.

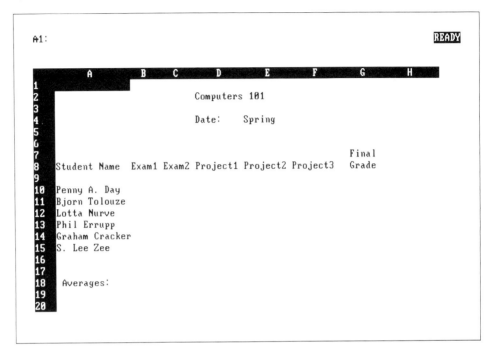

ing with complex spreadsheets, temporarily turning off the recalculation feature increases data-entry speeds, since the sheet is not recalculating formulas after each entry. When all the data has been entered, a command is issued and the spreadsheet performs all calculations at once.

### Save the Data

When working with an electronic spreadsheet or any other software package, it is necessary to periodically save or backup your work on disk. Information stored in primary memory can be lost through software problems or a momentary loss of power. After entering data into a spreadsheet, the few moments required to save the data protects it from possible loss. This is especially important prior to making major changes in the spreadsheet. Such backups ensure that if changes or adjustments to the spreadsheet do not produce the desired results, it is easy to return to the original spreadsheet by retrieving it from mass storage. Saving or backing up data guarantees its continued availability.

**Figure 11.6** Spreadsheet with Initial Data and Formulas. The spreadsheet is divided into two sections, (a) and (b).

(a)

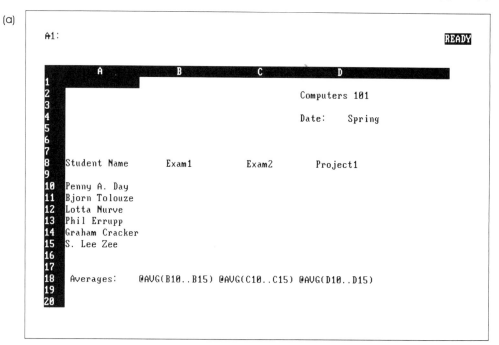

(b)

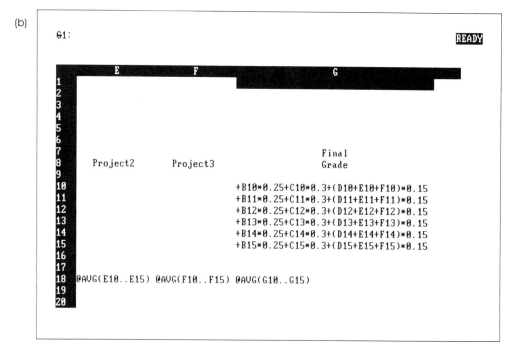

**Figure 11.7**    Final Spreadsheet with Averages and Final Grades.

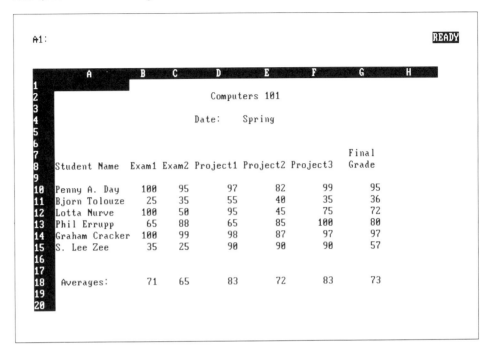

A1:                                                                    READY

|   | A | B | C | D | E | F | G | H |
|---|---|---|---|---|---|---|---|---|

Computers 101

Date:    Spring

|  | | | | | | Final | |
| Student Name | Exam1 | Exam2 | Project1 | Project2 | Project3 | Grade | |
| Penny A. Day | 100 | 95 | 97 | 82 | 99 | 95 | |
| Bjorn Tolouze | 25 | 35 | 55 | 40 | 35 | 36 | |
| Lotta Nurve | 100 | 50 | 95 | 45 | 75 | 72 | |
| Phil Errupp | 65 | 88 | 65 | 85 | 100 | 80 | |
| Graham Cracker | 100 | 99 | 98 | 87 | 97 | 97 | |
| S. Lee Zee | 35 | 25 | 90 | 90 | 90 | 57 | |
| Averages: | 71 | 65 | 83 | 72 | 83 | 73 | |

## WHAT IF

Students often ask faculty members, usually just before the final examination, "What will my grade in this course be if I get an 85 (or 65 or 95) on the final exam?" This is known as a *what-if* question. Using a spreadsheet, the instructor can easily answer such questions. Simply enter the value (85 or whatever) and watch what appears in the appropriate cell. By entering student scores and watching the effect such scores have on a student's final grade, instructors are able to forecast an event that has not yet occurred. In this way, spreadsheets make it possible for us to forecast or predict events in many different situations. Different scenarios for future events can be tested by typing in different values and noting their effects.

Let us see what the final grade of Penny A. Day might be by varying the final examination (Exam 2) scores. We can ask the spreadsheet, "*What* will happen *if* final exam grades (Exam 2) are 85, or 65, or 95?" By changing only the final score (Exam 2) we can forecast the future. Care must be taken to distinguish the what-if data from the real data. Only the data that is stored on disk is real data. The results are shown in Figure 11.8.

Spreadsheets have proven invaluable as forecasting tools in the business world. Companies now can test, based on correct initial assumptions, the effect

**Figure 11.8**    What If: This illustrates the result of asking the spreadsheet what would happen if Penny A. Day's final exam grade were (b) 85, (c) 65, or (d) 95. Her final grade prior to exam 2 is represented in (a).

(a)

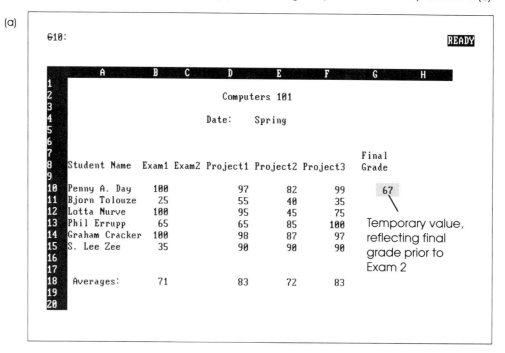

(b)

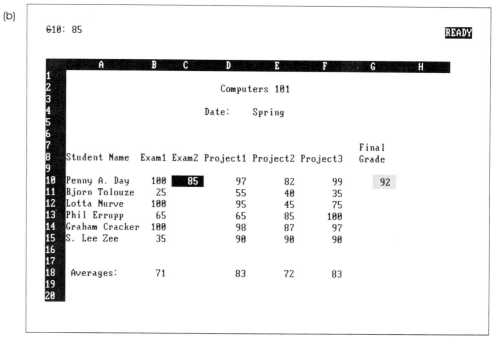

(c)

G10: 65                                                                                    READY

|   | A | B | C | D | E | F | G | H |
|---|---|---|---|---|---|---|---|---|

Computers 101

Date:    Spring

| Student Name | Exam1 | Exam2 | Project1 | Project2 | Project3 | Final Grade |
|---|---|---|---|---|---|---|
| Penny A. Day | 100 | 65 | 97 | 82 | 99 | 86 |
| Bjorn Tolouze | 25 | | 55 | 40 | 35 | |
| Lotta Nurve | 100 | | 95 | 45 | 75 | |
| Phil Errupp | 65 | | 65 | 85 | 100 | |
| Graham Cracker | 100 | | 98 | 87 | 97 | |
| S. Lee Zee | 35 | | 90 | 90 | 90 | |
| Averages: | 71 | | 83 | 72 | 83 | |

(d)

G10: 95                                                                                    READY

|   | A | B | C | D | E | F | G | H |
|---|---|---|---|---|---|---|---|---|

Computers 101

Date:    Spring

| Student Name | Exam1 | Exam2 | Project1 | Project2 | Project3 | Final Grade |
|---|---|---|---|---|---|---|
| Penny A. Day | 100 | 95 | 97 | 82 | 99 | 95 |
| Bjorn Tolouze | 25 | | 55 | 40 | 35 | |
| Lotta Nurve | 100 | | 95 | 45 | 75 | |
| Phil Errupp | 65 | | 65 | 85 | 100 | |
| Graham Cracker | 100 | | 98 | 87 | 97 | |
| S. Lee Zee | 35 | | 90 | 90 | 90 | |
| Averages: | 71 | | 83 | 72 | 83 | |

of price cuts or increases, salary increases or decreases, the hiring or laying off of employees, changes made in purchasing procedures, cuts made in overhead costs, and hundreds of other factors that constitute costs of doing business or sources of income.

## PROGRAMMING TOOLS

Most spreadsheets use essentially the same techniques for entering labels, numbers, and formulas. Each time a new spreadsheet is started, a blank ledger appears on the screen. Information is entered cell by cell, using either arrow keys or some other cursor control technique to move around the sheet.

### Inserting and Deleting

Within a spreadsheet, changes can be made almost anywhere. You do not have to add a column only to the right or rows only at the bottom of the spreadsheet. Indeed, in actual use, rows and columns often need to be added or deleted within a spreadsheet. Continuing with our grade book example, let's say the instructor decides to give three exams rather than two. To adjust the spreadsheet to allow for the extra exam scores, space must be created between column C (Exam2) and column D (Project1) for the new column, which will be headed Exam 3. Using an **insertion command**, we can place new columns or rows wherever they may be needed (See Figure 11.9).

Similarly, as needs change, spreadsheet columns or rows may need to be deleted. If Bjorn Tolouze decides to drop the course, it will be easy to delete his name and information. **Deletion commands** make it possible to remove columns and rows that are no longer necessary (see Figure 11.10).

### Copying Cells

Many tasks are repetitive. This is reflected in the design of our spreadsheets. **Copy (replicate) commands** make it possible to duplicate the contents of a cell or group of cells elsewhere on the spreadsheet (see Figure 11.11). Values, formulas, and labels can all be copied with equal ease. Sophisticated spreadsheet software automatically adjusts formulas to appropriately reflect new locations. In our grade-book example, all the averages (exam, project, grade) are calculated in the identical fashion: all the values in a given column are added and their sum is then divided by the number of values. However, each formula must be slightly different since each reflects different columns. It is possible to enter the formula once and copy it to the other cells that require the formula. For example, when we copy the formula @AVG(B10..B15) from column B to column C, the software adjusts the formula so it reads @AVG(C10..C15).

**Figure 11.9**    Inserting a New Column: A new column is being added to this spreadsheet for extra exam scores.

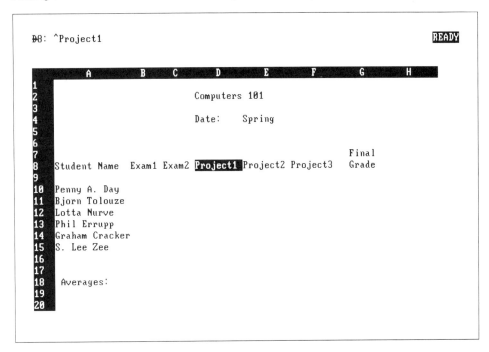

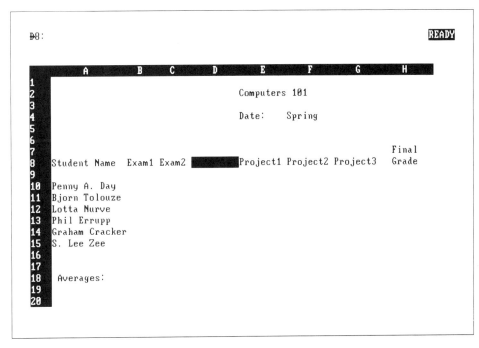

**Figure 11.9**          Continued

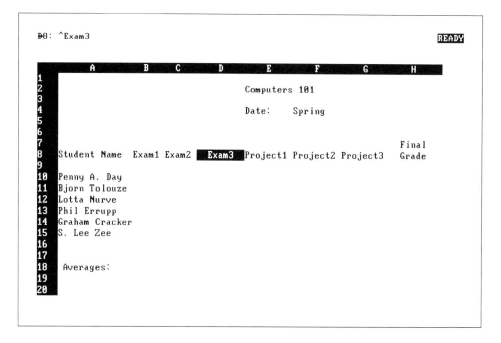

## Formatting Data

The way data are displayed on a spreadsheet is very important. The designers of spreadsheet packages recognized that to be clearly understood, a cell's contents need to be expressed in real-world terms. For example, labels such as names (alphabetic information) need to be lined up at the leftmost character, or left-justified, when they appear in columns. Sometimes it is nice to center headings over a column. When information is lined up at the rightmost character it is said to be right-justified. For numeric quantities it may also be desirable to line up, or align, numbers on their decimal points. Numeric values representing dollars and cents are more meaningful if they include a dollar sign and commas. Scientific notation can be used for very large or very small numbers. **Format commands** allow the user to justify (right, left, or center) data as necessary within a cell, display numbers in their most meaningful form, and adjust the width of columns to allow for data of varying length (see Figure 11.12).

## Mathematical Functions

Since formulas play such an important role in spreadsheets, all spreadsheets include built-in functions. **Functions** are special software routines that perform

**Figure 11.10**    Deleting a Row: Rows and columns that are no longer needed can be deleted from spreadsheets. In this case, the name of Bjorn Tolouze is being eliminated.

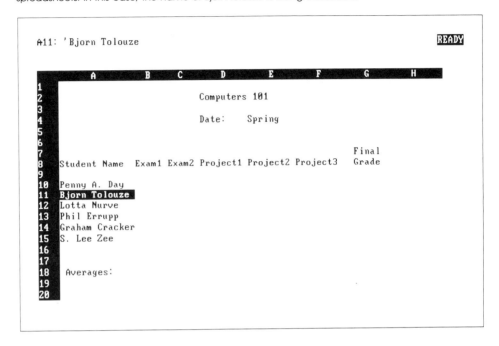

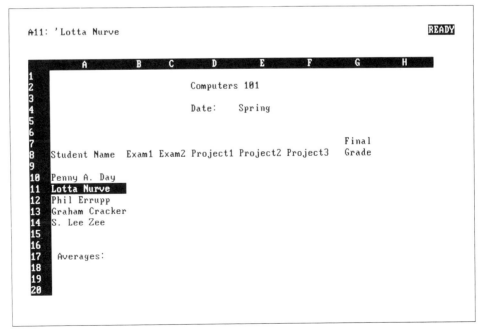

**Figure 11.11**

Copying Cells: The formula to calculate averages is copied from cell B18 into cells C18 and D18 by Lotus 1-2-3.

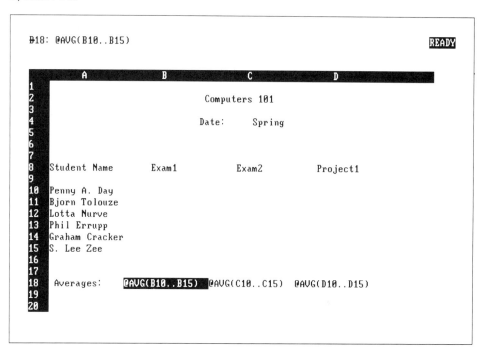

**Figure 11.12**

Formatting Data: This spreadsheet uses a number of different display formats.

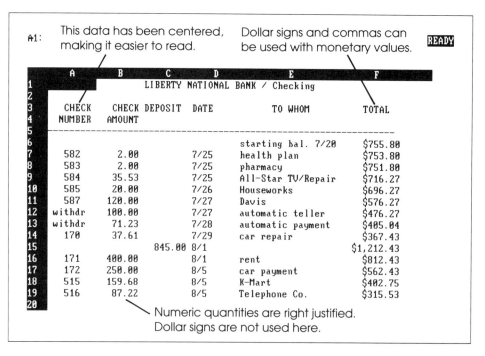

frequently needed tasks. These include such obvious routines as sum (@SUM), average (@AVG), standard deviation (@STD), and square root (@SQRT). Some functions are used to help in decision making, such as @IF for what if. @DATE is a function that gives the current date. The more complex a spreadsheet program, the more functions it provides. (The @ symbol before the function name is common to many spreadsheets, including Lotus and ENABLE.)

Many spreadsheet packages also include complex software routines that allow the user to sort columns or rows. Packages such as Lotus 1-2-3, Super-Calc3, and ENABLE also can display spreadsheet data in graphic form.

## PITFALLS, PROBLEMS, AND SOLUTIONS

Electronic spreadsheets have put more information at our fingertips. Those of us who never considered using an accountant's paper spreadsheet have found many uses for the electronic variety. Often these are uses an accountant never dreamed of. Yet, electronic spreadsheets, like all software, have their pitfalls and problems. It seems that the more sophisticated a program is, the more problems it can present.

Most spreadsheet errors are caused by carelessness. But even a careful person can run into trouble. Here are some common problems:

1. *Formula specification.* Formulas indicate how the contents of cells and data are to be combined. Incorrect formulas will produce flawed results, even if the data have been accurately entered.

2. *Rounding errors.* Spreadsheets display a cell's contents in a format that has been selected by the user. However, the value that is actually in the computer's memory and used in calculations may vary somewhat from the value displayed in the cell. For example, in a dollar-and-cents format, a value may appear as $16.54 while the value actually stored in memory might be $16.5384. Rounding occurs when there are more significant decimal digits than have been requested for display. This rounding discrepancy may be unimportant in working with one number or a single calculation. However, an accumulation of rounding adjustments can be significant when complex calculations are performed.

3. *Division by zero.* Division by zero is mathematically impossible. However, it is possible to create a situation in a spreadsheet where a formula seems to require division by zero. This can happen when a cell's contents unexpectedly become zero and a formula that references that cell expects to divide by its value. For example, consider the formula: @SUM(A1..A5)/B2. This formula is perfectly sound mathematically except in the situation where B2 is zero. If B2 becomes zero, the formula is meaningless. Since such formulas are common and the contents of cells do change, division by zero may be

encountered. Some spreadsheets automatically check for this occurrence. However, other spreadsheets simply attempt to carry out the required calculations, producing meaningless results. It is important to review spreadsheets to make sure they make sense.

4. *Formulas that don't adjust for insertions and deletions.* This is the most common of all spreadsheet problems. As data change and rows and columns are added or deleted, care must be taken to ensure that formulas continue to reflect the spreadsheet's data. In some spreadsheet software, formulas do not automatically adjust to reflect these changes. As a result, incorrect formulas produce incorrect results.

5. *Writing over cells.* A spreadsheet is only as accurate as its data and formulas. However, a cell's contents are easily changed. When a cell's contents are altered, there may be a ripple effect throughout the entire spreadsheet since cells are referenced by formulas in other cells. Equally troublesome is the situation where a value may be typed over a formula, thereby changing the meaning and content of that cell.

How can we protect the accuracy of our spreadsheet against these problems? An important concept in any computer environment is **documentation**. Spreadsheets should contain documentation, a clear written description of how the sheet is to be used. This description should specify how the formulas were derived. The documentation explains the spreadsheet in terms that can be understood by anyone who has to make use of it, including *you* at a later date. For example, how well will you recall all the considerations you made in designing your spreadsheet one year from now? It is useful to keep a record of when and where changes are made in the spreadsheet. In this way, if an error is later detected, it can be easily corrected.

Another way to reduce spreadsheet errors is to recognize the possibility of their existence. When you look at the results of key formulas, ask yourself: "Does this answer make sense?" Check the results by hand, using a calculator to validate the formula. When using complex formulas, have someone else check them for accuracy. At the very least, print out all formulas and check them over yourself, looking for possible errors.

Remember, spreadsheets can only be as accurate as the values, formulas, and labels placed in the cells. Garbage in gives garbage out. But there is no reason to throw out the spreadsheet with the garbage. Paying attention to details, taking care in designing the sheet and entering the data, and checking to see whether calculated results are reasonable will ensure an accurate spreadsheet.

## SUMMARY

In 1979, Dan Bricklin and Robert Frankston released VisiCalc, the first electronic spreadsheet. Any problem that can be solved with pencil, paper, and a calculator can be solved more quickly and accurately with an electronic spreadsheet.

An electronic spreadsheet is designed as a table consisting of vertical columns and horizontal rows. The boxes formed by the intersection of these rows and columns are cells. Some packages name their cells with a column letter followed by a row number (D6). Others use names such as RxCy for Row x and Column y.

Spreadsheet cells can contain three types of data: values or numbers, formulas, and labels. The numbers placed directly in a spreadsheet's cells are known as values. Formulas are mathematical expressions associated with a specific cell and are used to calculate the value of that cell. Labels are words, titles, or text that are used to form row and column headings or to provide textual information.

Five steps are useful in planning a spreadsheet: (1) Understand the problem, (2) Specify the results, (3) Specify the input, (4) Determine the formulas, (5) Design the spreadsheet.

What-if statements enable spreadsheet users to forecast events or test scenarios by adjusting values within a given spreadsheet and studying the changes produced.

Spreadsheet information is not static. It can be adjusted as needed. Rows and columns can be inserted or deleted to reflect changes in data. Data from cells can be copied into other cells easily. Format commands allow the user to justify (right, left, center) data as necessary within a cell, display numbers in their most meaningful form, and adjust the width of columns to allow for data of varying length.

Formulas play such an important role in spreadsheets that the most common mathematical and financial formulas come as built-in functions provided by the developer of the spreadsheet.

Most spreadsheet errors are caused by poor planning or carelessness. Common errors include incorrect use of formulas, roundoff errors, division by zero, and overwriting of information stored in cells. Attention to detail, careful entering of data, and the use of documentation can reduce these errors.

## Key Words

As an extra review of the chapter, try defining the following terms. If you have trouble with any of them, refer to the page number listed.

cell  *(277)*
copy (replicate) commands  *(290)*
deletion commands  *(290)*
documentation  *(296)*
electronic spreadsheet  *(276)*
format commands  *(292)*

formulas  *(278)*
functions  *(292)*
insertion command  *(290)*
labels  *(278)*
template  *(280)*
values  *(278)*

## Test Your Knowledge

1. Who invented VisiCalc? What computer did it first run on? How long ago was it invented?

2. Define *cell*.

3. Describe two cell-naming conventions.

4. List the three types of data that can be stored in spreadsheet cells.

5. What is a formula?

6. What does GIGO stand for?

7. List the five steps in planning a spreadsheet.

8. When is it useful to design a spreadsheet template?

9. How are what-if statements used with spreadsheets?

10. Using the data found in Figure 11.7, what would Bjorn Tolouze's final grade be if he had gotten a grade of 90 on his last exam rather than a 35? Use the formula shown in Figure 11.6 to assist you.

11. Describe how a row is inserted into an existing spreadsheet.

12. Why is it sometimes necessary to delete rows and columns from existing spreadsheets?

13. How does a copy or replicate command work?

14. List the three ways data can be aligned in a cell.

15. What is a spreadsheet function?

**Figure 11.13**

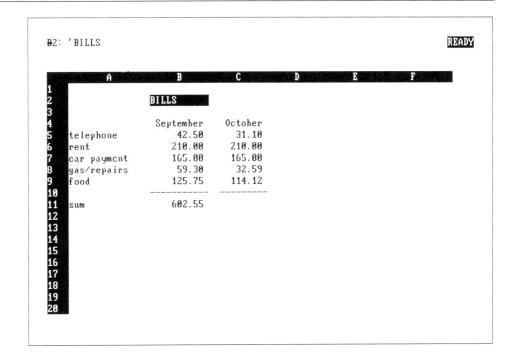

16. In the spreadsheet shown here in Figure 11.13, the formula used to total (sum) September's bills is @SUM(B5..B9). This formula is copied from cell B10 to cell C10. What will the formula in cell C10 read?

17. List three common problems associated with electronic spreadsheets.

18. For the three problems identified in Figure 11.13, describe how each problem can be either avoided or corrected.

19. Describe spreadsheet documentation.

20. Fill in the missing blank in this sentence. A spreadsheet is to _____ what a word processor is to text.

---

## Expand Your Knowledge

1. Using a spreadsheet available to you, calculate your grade point average (GPA) using last semester's grades. Be sure to include your name and a heading for your spreadsheet. Check your formulas. A GPA is a weighted average with a three-credit course worth more than a one-credit course. Use

labels that make your spreadsheet's contents easily understood and readable.

2. Many electronic spreadsheets include analysis graphics (see Chapter 13). Research one spreadsheet package that contains analysis graphics. Write a short paper including the following:

   (a) List the kinds of graphics the package provides.
   (b) Describe each type of graph and the nature of the data required to produce it.
   (c) Is special hardware required to view the graphs on a monitor?
   (d) Is special hardware required to print these graphs?

3. Electronic spreadsheets are very popular in business. Write a short (3 to 5 page) paper explaining the use of spreadsheets in business. Include a discussion of financial forecasting. Use at least three sources of information.

4. A student organization kept the following financial information on paper for a three-month period:

| | September | October | November |
|---|---|---|---|
| Starting balance | 83.00 | | |
| | | | |
| Dues | 110.00 | 25.00 | 50.00 |
| Fund raising | | 112.63 | 53.97 |
| | | | |
| Paper & supplies | 127.62 | | |
| Photocopying | 12.00 | 5.00 | 15.00 |
| Advertising | 6.00 | 6.00 | 6.00 |
| Postage | 20.00 | | 20.00 |
| Food | 37.00 | 37.00 | 12.20 |
| Plates, cups, etc. | 11.50 | 2.25 | 9.75 |
| | | | |
| Ending balance | | | |

Enter this information into an electronic spreadsheet. You may want to adjust the layout to better suit your design. Using appropriate formulas, answer the following questions:

(a) Over the three-month period, how much was spent for each of the following: paper and supplies, photocopying, advertising, postage, food, and paper goods?

(b) Over the three-month period, how much was taken in through dues and fund raising?

(c) Calculate the ending balance for each month. (This is the starting balance for the following month.)

(d) Calculate the group's average monthly expenditure.

(e) Calculate the group's average monthly income.

5. Design a spreadsheet template you and your fellow students can use to calculate federal tax returns. The template should reflect the short form. Include all formulas and labels.

# 12

# Data Bases

**Chapter Outline**

What Is a Data Base?
> Paper Data Bases • Modern Data Base Systems • Microcomputer Data Base Systems

Steps in Getting Started

The Data Base in Use
> Creating a Data Base • Searching and Sorting • Changing a Data Base • Generating Reports

Complex Searches and Sorts

Using Multiple Files

Advanced Features

Pitfalls, Problems, and Solutions
> Improving Sorting Speed • Maintaining Data Integrity • Avoiding Deletion Errors • Avoiding Data Loss

Data Base Machines

A data base is an organized collection of raw facts. We use data bases, although not computerized ones, all the time. Whenever we file information in a file cabinet, use a telephone directory, a dictionary, an encyclopedia, or *any* book, we are using data bases.

All data bases, whether they are manual systems, designed for large mainframes, or available on the smallest personal computer, use the concept of files. As a starting point, think of a file cabinet (a data base) filled with file folders, each labeled with some key word (student name, ID number, course number) and ordered in some appropriate way (alphabetic, numeric, by date). Each folder is filled with information related to the key on the outside. In general, computerized data bases function in much the same way except that file folders are replaced by records in an electronic file.

In this chapter we will look at modern data base systems and their functions. We will concentrate on software that allows us to manage and manipulate data in order to process information. Until recently, access to data bases was limited to those few specialists who knew how to manipulate them. Today, access to data bases is readily available through modern data base tools. Data base software is often easier to learn than word processing or the use of a spreadsheet. While a word processor can be viewed as a glorified typewriter and an electronic spreadsheet as a computerized accountant's ledger, modern data base tools are further removed from their non-computer counterparts.

After studying this chapter, you will be able to:

- Define *data base*.

- Distinguish between file managers and data base managers.

- Discuss the steps involved in planning data base files.

- Describe how a data base is created.

- Understand searching and sorting.

- Identify how changes are made in data base files.

- Explain how data bases can make use of more than one file.

- Describe data base machines.

## WHAT IS A DATA BASE?

Some people think of a data base as "the stuff stored in computers." Some might be aware of *data banks,* such as those used by insurance companies to store statistical and financial records that go back for many years. Others may think of ominous Orwellian "Big Brother" data banks containing all sorts of personal facts about entire populations. Whether we use the current words *data base* or the somewhat older term *data bank,* all of these impressions reflect an understanding of the functions served by storing huge amounts of records or facts.

A **data base** is a set of facts or records organized so that specific items are easy to find. Data bases are usually organized around a topic, an account number, or a **key**, which is an identifier such as a last name.

## Paper Data Bases

Keeping careful records is essential in our world. A business's profits are directly linked to its ability to keep track of its clients. Schools keep records on every student, and accuracy is vital. Until recently, file rooms were the hub of every complex organization. However, as organizations grew and their work became more complex, the time needed to locate information stored in the file room increased. This made paper storage inefficient in large and complex organizations such as retail chains, universities, and banks. Paper storage became a limiting factor on the size of the organization itself. When the paperwork became too much to handle, some organizations had to restrict their growth.

The advent of computers brought an end to these limitations. Large organizations such as airlines, insurance companies, the telephone companies, utilities, the Internal Revenue Service, and universities who could afford to purchase large mainframes did so. While mainframes could perform a number of tasks, their basic purpose for these organizations was electronic record keeping. In most cases, these electronic filing systems varied little from their manual counterparts, except that more data could be stored and it could be located more rapidly.

In manual filing systems, key records such as a student's name and address were often duplicated in many files to make the processing of information easier. For example, a student's name and address might appear in the university's grade file, student billing file, and again in the general information file. Such duplication of data is clearly a waste of resources. In addition, it increases the risk of having a data base filled with unreliable data. Imagine that a student moves during a given semester. The student diligently fills out all the appropriate forms required by the university indicating the change of address. The student's address is correctly changed on the grade file and the general information file, but is unchanged on the billing file. The student receives an accurate end-of-semester grade report, but never receives a tuition bill and never pays the tuition for the next semester. As a result, the student is unable to register. After considerable frustration, the registration office discovers that the student never filed a change-of-address form, while the student correctly claims that he did. You can clearly see the problem.

Data integrity or reliability is directly related to the ability of the data base to remain current. *A data base is only as reliable as its data.* If information is updated incorrectly or inconsistently—if data is corrected in one file and not in another—then the integrity of the entire data base is in doubt. Maintaining the integrity of the data within a data base is not a trivial matter.

## Modern Data Base Systems

To make the most efficient use out of a data base, it is necessary to plan the way in which the data are organized. Data needs to be organized so it can be retrieved, or located and viewed, easily. Historical organization patterns must be carefully examined. Data should not be organized in a particular way simply because it has always been done this way. Whenever possible, duplicated data needs to be eliminated and retrieval times minimized. The goal is to make all data quickly and easily available to all who need access to it, while maintaining data integrity.

Mainframe data bases are designed to ensure high retrieval speeds. As a result, the structure of these data bases makes updating and changing complicated. Data base specialists are often required when working with such systems.

In modern microcomputer data bases, data are stored and their files are structured differently from their mainframe counterparts. Specialists are not usually available to micro users. As a result, software must make it easy to create, update, and change a data base. Of course, there are some trade-offs: microcomputer data bases are easier to use than their larger cousins, but they take more time to search and sort. However, these data bases do not have to process the huge amounts of data stored on larger systems. As a result, retrieval speeds are still reasonable.

A data base is an ideal aid for decision making. When you use a data base, you can ask the computer to find individual items or sets of items that meet specific criteria. An individual query might be to find the grade report for Frank N. Stein. A search for a set of items might be a list of all juniors or seniors who have gotten an A in Computer Science 101 or an alphabetical list of all graduate students who have high school teaching experience. The data retrieved from the data base is then used to make decisions.

A hand search through paper files in a large university's filing cabinets seeking all the grade reports for a single individual (Frank N. Stein) could take a considerable amount of time. It would take even longer to locate and list the set of graduate students who have high school teaching experience. Computerizing a data base is appropriate whenever the amount of data to be searched or sorted is too large to reasonably process by hand.

## Microcomputer Data Base Systems

Most microcomputer data base systems use *files* designed as tables to store information. Tables are composed of rows and columns. Each row or *record* contains related information such as a student's name and address. Each column or *field* contains a specific type of information such as last name, first name, or zip code. In Figure 12.1, Penny Lofer's information forms a record, while the address column is a field.

The simplest kind of data base packages are **file managers**, or file management systems. These are patterned after an index-card file. The records, reflect-

**Figure 12.1**     Fields and Records.

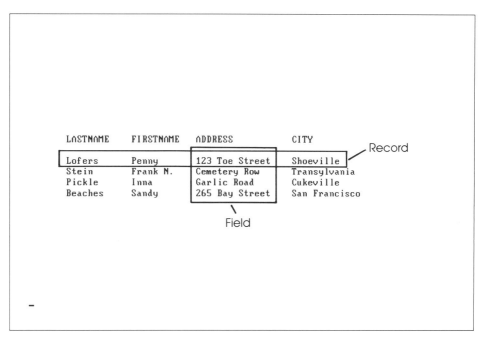

ing individual index cards, can be searched and sorted on any of the fields in the record. File managers are usually menu-driven, since the user selects the required task from a list. Reports organizing data from many records can be easily created. Many file managers can perform simple calculations on gathered information. File managers usually deal with data contained in one file at a time. As a result, records in a file may contain fields that are only slightly related. File managers are excellent for manipulating simple data files such as mailing addresses, appointments, and lists of phone numbers. However, besides dealing with only one file at a time, they usually do not reorganize data to produce new data files, produce involved reports, or perform complex searches and sorts.

The more complex **data base managers** or data base management systems can do all this and more. The best known of these packages are dBASE III Plus, Revelation, and R: Base 5000.

Sophisticated data base managers have two modes. Like simpler data base software, they can be menu-driven. This mode helps new users learn the software and start entering data. As the user becomes more familiar with the package, the menus can be turned off and the software becomes **command-driven**. In this mode, commands can be directly given to the machine. Files can be created containing groups or lists of commands that are frequently used together. Such files are called **command files**. By calling on this file, a single command can set in motion a whole series of commands. Command files allow data base managers to incorporate many of the essentials of a programming language into their structure. The advanced user can create screens that request data in a specific order, display output in a useful format and customize reports that are tailored to specific needs. Data base managers have more flexibility and can organize data in a greater variety of ways than file managers. However, their complexity makes them harder to learn, harder to use, and much more expensive.

## STEPS IN GETTING STARTED

Whatever type of data base is used, the data must be entered into the system before anything can be done with it. Certainly, it is possible to enter data into a microcomputer data base without thinking about how it will be used. But such a haphazard approach would result in more time being needed to retrieve the data later on. Planning before the data is entered will save hours of frustration later while we wait for the system to gather the data items we request. The following six steps will help us to plan now to save time later. These steps are very similar to those used to design an algorithm (Chapter 6).

1. *Understand the problem.* Identify the kind of queries we expect to make of the data base. If a paper system is currently used, what questions are asked and what information is regularly requested?

2. *Identify the output.* Determine the kind of output reports the data base will generate. What kind of reports are created by the manual system currently in use? Are there any other types of reports that should be produced? Specify exactly the information to be contained in these reports.

3. *Identify the input.* The input to a data base is directly determined by the output. We cannot get something out of the data base if we haven't put it in. What data do we need to produce the desired reports? What data is currently being used?

4. *Organize the data.* Plan your files. Does it make sense to place all the data in a single file? Or does the information logically break down into a series of files? Determine what information is needed and decide its order in the records.

5. *Test and revise your data base.* Enter sample data and use it to test the data base. Can the required reports be created? Expect to find that revision is necessary. Recognize assumptions and reorganize the data base to reflect needs.

6. *Enter the data.* Once the data has been entered, reports that previously took weeks to gather are almost instantly available.

# On Line

## PUTTING THE BYTE ON CRIME

Police detectives are handing over more and more of their investigative duties to computers.

New crime detection software is allowing computers to take over a number of tedious and often time-consuming tasks such as ruling out suspects and keeping records. As a result, detectives have more time to plan investigations, locate and interview witnesses, question suspects, and search for evidence. All it takes is $5000 for a personal computer and the necessary software.

Specific software applications were originally designed to meet the needs of individual police departments. Some of them now are being purchased, licensed, and exchanged. A police user group has even been formed.

Among other things, the software allows computers to compile lists of wanted criminals, stolen cars and credit cards; put together data on crime incidences and the modus operandi of criminals; compile lists of aliases, fingerprints, and criminal histories; and analyze movement and telephone calls.

Although police departments are generally enthusiastic about the software's potential, some people are concerned that it endangers the individual's right to privacy. Opponents fear that innocent people may be categorized as associates of criminals. Law enforcement officials say they are aware of such potential problems and that they are taking care to restrict access to the systems and the data bases.

*Source:* Jack Bologna, "Software Applications Put the 'Byte' on Crime," *Computerworld*, Dec. 14, 1987, p. 85.

## THE DATA BASE IN USE

Planning, however, is only the beginning stage in using your data base as a problem-solving tool. Somehow all the required information must get into the machine. This data will then be searched, sorted, and extracted to suit particular needs and generate reports. To be effective, data base software must help the user to do all of the following:

1. Create the data base.

2. Search the data base for specific items.

3. Sort the data by key.

4. Add, delete, and update the data base.

5. Report the results.

Data base software for microcomputers is designed to be quickly and easily understood by users. For this reason, the basic procedures are fairly similar in all major packages. Most packages use words or phrases from common speech as commands. Create, List, Browse, Show, Edit, Sort, and Delete are common data base commands. These commands and all the data base examples used in this chapter are from dBASE III Plus.

## Creating a Data Base

Creating the data base itself is a fairly straightforward task. Every data base from the simplest to the most complex has a structure. Microcomputer data bases put few restrictions on how data are to be entered.

Let us create a data base containing general data about students in a computer science class. We must first determine the data that we want in our file. What data items will we need to search for? For this example, we want each student's name, address, and year in school. The software needs to know the nature or *type* of the data to be entered. Each student's name consists of letters, but the student's address is a more complicated matter. If an entire address— 1210 Main Street, Downhome, Texas, 12345—were stored as a single data item, it would be impossible to use any parts of the address in a search. Suppose we wanted to gather data about all Texans in the class. We would not be able to search for Texas since the student's home state is combined with other information.

Data entered into a data base must be divided into as many different *fields* as is appropriate. The number of fields will be determined by the categories for which we will need to search. We might want to search addresses in as many as four categories. Therefore, we set up four fields: street, city, state, and zip code. Using the address just mentioned, 1210 Main Street would be stored in the street field, Downhome would go into the city field, Texas into the state field, and 12345 into the zip code field. How many fields do we need for the student's name? It is likely that we would want the last name separated from the first name, so each of these would go in different fields. We would then need two fields: lastname and firstname. If we had a reason, we might even want the middle name to have a third, separate name field.

When creating a data base, the software will ask for a file name. As with all software, the file name should reflect the contents of the file. Our student data base could be called studinfo. The software will also ask questions that help to define the data base's structure. Before any data can be entered into the system, we need to specify the order and type of information we expect to enter. In response to queries from the software, we tell the system what specific fields will be needed, the names of the fields, what kind of data to expect (letters, numbers, or both), and how wide (how many characters) the field should be. No data have been entered into the data base yet. But we have made a reservation for the data that will be entered.

The data base file structure for our student list could look like this:

| | field name | type | width | dec |
|---|---|---|---|---|
| 1 | LASTNAME | Char/text | 10 | |
| 2 | FIRSTNAME | Char/text | 10 | |
| 3 | STREET | Char/text | 20 | |
| 4 | CITY | Char/text | 15 | |
| 5 | STATE | Char/text | 2 | |
| 6 | ZIP | Char/text | 5 | |
| 7 | YEAR | Numeric | 4 | 0 |

Field names should be chosen so that their contents are obvious. An individual field's contents can be of various types. The type can be made up of characters, such as a student's last name, numbers intended for use in calculations, dates, or logicals (true or false).

In addition to type, we need to tell the machine the size of each field. For example, we need to specify that LASTNAME will occupy 10 spaces. Similarly the zip code (ZIP) will be exactly five spaces. The zip code can be stored as either a group of characters or as a numeric field since it is made up of digits. A numeric field can be used in calculations. However, we never perform calculations on zip codes. They are not mathematically manipulated in any way. As a result, it makes more sense to store the zip code as a character field. If a field is numeric, the software asks for the number of necessary decimal places. All these specifications merely set up the environment in which our data base will live. No one has moved in yet. No data have been entered or stored.

Obviously, a data base is only as effective as the data in it. Once the structure has been defined, the data items or *records* are entered one at a time, one field at a time, until all the required information has been entered. In Figure 12.2, the data for our general student file would be entered one student (record) at a time.

Just as we created a general file for our computer class, we can create another file in our data base containing other information about our class. Figure 12.3 contains the semester's grades in a file called crsgrade, for course grade. The file also contains each student's social security number. Our data base now consists of two files containing information about our students.

## Searching and Sorting

We will want to search or sort our files so that they provide the information we require. *Searching* means that the software will look through the stored data to find those items that satisfy particular criteria, much like the search function on a word processor. In Figure 12.4a, the student file (studinfo) was used to list the names and home towns of all students from Wisconsin and to list the names and addresses of all freshmen. Similarly, in Figure 12.4b we searched the grade file (crsgrade) to get a list of the names of all the students who received A's on their

**Figure 12.2**    Student Information File: Data for this general student file is entered one student at a time.

```
studinfo

RCD# LASTNAME  FIRSTNAME   STREET               CITY          STATE ZIP   YEAR

   1 Lofers    Penny       123 Toe Street       Shoeville     WI 53777    FRSH
   2 Stein     Frank N.    Cemetery Row         Transylvania  PA 34567     JR
   3 Pickle    Inna        Garlic Road          Cukeville     NY 12345    FRSH
   4 Beaches   Sandy       265 Bay Street       San Francisco CA 67890    SOPH
   5 Errupp    Phil        1020 Station Road     Gasville      NJ 23890     SR
   6 Nomial    Polly       456 Equation Circle  Triangle Park NC 23421    SOPH
   7 Mint      Said A.     Dirt Road            Diggersville  CO 97531    FRSH
   8 Itis      Senior      College Circle       Madison       WI 53706     SR
   9 Long      Harry A.    Main Street          Slowtowne     KA 55667     JR
  10 Ferma     Terry       789 Earth Avenue      Boston        MA 44668    SOPH
  11 Grahm     Telly       5325 Western Union   New York City NY 11101     JR
  12 Maykitt   Willie      56 Main Street       Tryhard       FL 65432     SR

—
```

**Figure 12.3**    Semester Grade File: This file contains the semester grade and social security number of each student.

```
crsgrade

RCD# LASTNAME  FIRSTNAME   SSNUM        MIDTERM   FINAL PAPER LGRADE
   1 Lofers    Penny       123-45-6789    100       95 A       A
   2 Stein     Frank N.    998-87-7654     25       45 C       F
   3 Pickle    Inna        555-55-5555    100       25 D       D
   4 Beaches   Sandy       098-76-5432     85       75 B       B
   5 Errupp    Phil        192-83-8475     85       69 B       B
   6 Nomial    Polly       999-88-7777     95       99 A       A
   7 Mint      Said A.     445-67-5678     75       80 C       C
   8 Itis      Senior      987-98-9876     85       65 D       D
   9 Long      Harry A.    234-56-7890     99       98 B       A
  10 Ferma     Terry       678-78-5678     95       80 B       B
  11 Grahm     Telly       666-11-1515     45       80 A       B
  12 Maykitt   Willie      777-00-8733     65       59 D       D

—
```

**Figure 12.4**    Searching a File: The software has sorted the file to find (a) all students from Wisconsin and all freshman, and (b) all students who received A's on their papers and those who scored 70 or less on the midterm.

(a)

```
USE STUDINFO
LIST FOR STATE = 'WI' FIRSTNAME, LASTNAME, CITY, STATE

    RCD#  FIRSTNAME  LASTNAME  CITY        STATE
       1  Penny      Lofers    Shoeville   WI
       8  Senior     Itis      Madison     WI


LIST FOR YEAR = 'FRSH' FIRSTNAME, LASTNAME, CITY, STATE, ZIP

    RCD# FIRSTNAME  LASTNAME  STREET          CITY         STATE ZIP
       1 Penny      Lofers    123 Toe Street  Shoeville    WI    53777
       3 Inna       Pickle    Garlic Road     Cukeville    NY    12345
       7 Said A.    Mint      Dirt Road       Diggersville CO    97531




    -
```

(b)

```
USE CRSGRADE
LIST FOR PAPER = 'A' FIRSTNAME, LASTNAME

    RCD# FIRSTNAME  LASTNAME  PAPER
       1 Penny      Lofers    A
       6 Polly      Nomial    A
      11 Telly      Grahm     A


LIST FOR MIDTERM < 70     {if no field names are specified all are listed}

    RCD# LASTNAME   FIRSTNAME  SSNUM        MIDTERM FINAL PAPER LGRADE
       2 Stein      Frank N.   998-87-7654       25    45 C     F
       7 Mint       Said A.    445-67-5678       75    80 C     C
      11 Grahm      Telly      666-11-1515       45    80 A     B
      12 Maykitt    Willie     777-00-8733       65    59 D     D




    -
```

paper and again searched the file for the names and grades of all those with scores of 70 or less on the midterm.

*Sorting* reorders or rearranges the records in a data base file either alphabetically, numerically, or by date. To sort, one or more fields in the data base are used. For example, we might want to sort the grade file into social security number order and then list the grade report without student names. This would allow the professor to post the grade report and protect the identity of the students. In Figure 12.5, crsgrade is sorted by social security number. The resulting file is first listed with all fields showing, including each student's name. The file is then listed without student names.

Sorting a data base file is not done in quite the same way we would sort a stack of index cards. If we sorted a stack of index cards, the card file itself would change. With most microcomputer data base systems, when a data base file is sorted the original file is not affected. A copy of the file is created in the specified order. In Figure 12.5, the crsgrade file is sorted by social security number, and the reordered version is stored in a new file called sortssn.

## Changing a Data Base

The information stored in most data bases needs to be changed or added to regularly as changes take place in the real world. As we have seen, a data base is only as reliable as the data stored within it. As people move to new addresses, new employees join a company, and students take another examination, the appropriate files must be adjusted.

Adjustments to an existing file can be made in a number of ways. An entire record can be deleted when it is no longer needed, and new records can be added. When we delete a record by using the Delete or Remove command, the software removes it from the data base file. All the records that follow it will automatically be renumbered. Adding information to a data base file is just as easy as deleting. Most systems have commands such as Add or Append that ask the user to enter the data into the data base according to the specifications made when the data base was created. This ensures that the new data conform to the style used when the original data were entered.

Stored data also may need to be corrected. For example, if a student has moved, the new address must replace the old one in the data base. Data can be corrected by using editing features built into the data base software. Editing features in a data base are similar to those in simple word processing software. Using the editor, entire fields can be changed or simple typing errors can be corrected.

One of the most important adjustment features common in data bases for microcomputers is the ability to add fields to existing records. It often happens that after a data base has been designed and entered, new uses for the data become apparent. For example, after using our general student file, we might want to send special announcements to all students over 30 or to all students

**Figure 12.5**    Sorting a File: The student information file has been sorted by social security number. The original file is shown in (a), the sorted file in (b).

(a)

```
USE CRSGRADE
SORT ON SSNUM TO SORTSSN

USE SORTSSN
LIST
      RCD# LASTNAME    FIRSTNAME    SSNUM          MIDTERM FINAL PAPER LGRADE
         1 Beaches     Sandy        098-76-5432         85    75 B     B
         2 Lofers      Penny        123-45-6789        100    95 A     A
         3 Errupp      Phil         192-83-8475         85    69 B     B
         4 Long        Harry A.     234-56-7890         99    98 B     A
         5 Mint        Said A.      445-67-5678         75    80 C     C
         6 Pickle      Inna         555-55-5555        100    25 D     D
         7 Grahm       Telly        666-11-1515         45    80 A     B
         8 Ferma       Terry        678-78-5678         95    80 B     B
         9 Maykitt     Willie       777-00-8733         65    59 D     D
        10 Itis        Senior       987-98-9876         85    65 D     D
        11 Stein       Frank N.     998-87-7654         25    45 C     F
        12 Nomial      Polly        999-88-7777         95    99 A     A

      -
```

(b)

```
LIST SSNUM, MIDTERM, FINAL, PAPER, LGRADE

      RCD# SSNUM         MIDTERM FINAL PAPER LGRADE
         1 098-76-5432        85    75 B     B
         2 123-45-6789       100    95 A     A
         3 192-83-8475        85    69 B     B
         4 234-56-7890        99    98 B     A
         5 445-67-5678        75    80 C     C
         6 555-55-5555       100    25 D     D
         7 666-11-1515        45    80 A     B
         8 678-78-5678        95    80 B     B
         9 777-00-8733        65    59 D     D
        10 987-98-9876        85    65 D     D
        11 998-87-7654        25    45 C     F
        12 999-88-7777        95    99 A     A

      -
```

turning 18 as a reminder to register to vote. We need to add a date of birth field to each record. Without a date of birth field, such searches would be impossible. Most sophisticated data base systems allow the user to modify or change the structure of the data base itself. By adding a date field called BIRTHDATE we have essentially altered the nature of the data base. Every record in the file is altered by the addition of a new field. Of course, as when we created the data base, no information has been entered into the file. We have reserved a place for each person's birth date. Now we have to enter the data using the editing features available.

## Generating Reports

All of the features discussed so far call for interactive communication between the user and the data base. The user and the computer talk directly to each other. The user gives a command, and the response appears on the screen. The user enters data, which appear on the screen and are stored in the computer's memory. However, the most effective use of a data base is to reproduce the results of searches, sorts, and changes in a more permanent form.

Data base reports can simply be paper or disk copies of summaries sent to the screen. Examples include a list of all students living in New York or of students with a course grade of B or better. But most systems also have various report-generating features. These make it possible to print reports with titles and column headings. They specify how many columns are to be printed and their order, and they indicate column spacing and margins. Many systems provide totals and subtotals of numeric fields where appropriate.

While most systems send these reports to a printer, some systems store them as disk files. Many systems can do both. These disk files are stored on disk in a form readable by other software packages. They also can be read and adjusted by the data base itself.

As data base software becomes more sophisticated, solving even more complex tasks is possible. Several fields acting together can be used for searching and sorting. Specified numeric data can be subjected to statistical analysis. More than one file can be searched, and programs can be written using command files. These are just some of the advanced features available on current data base software.

## COMPLEX SEARCHES AND SORTS

Suppose we want to identify those students whose grades on the final exam were between 65 and 75. If we used the comparisons of less than (<), greater than (>), equal to (=), and combinations of all three, we would still not get the necessary information. People often need to search a file to locate records that share several criteria. For this reason, most data base packages include the logical operations of AND, OR, and NOT. These provide additional ways to make use of data bases. Figure 12.6 shows a search of the course grade file for the students with final grades between 65 and 75.

We can also sort by multiple fields. For example, if we sort a large file alphabetically by last name, we will find that all the Smiths are together, but that they are not listed in alphabetical order by first name. Figure 12.7a shows what happens to our student data file when we sort alphabetically by last name only. The file is alphabetized correctly by last name, but Rocky Beaches follows Sandy Beaches and Frank N. Stein appears before Bere Stein. Two independent sorts will not do the trick; if we were now to sort by first name the results would not be in last name order. We must do a sort within a sort to get what we want. Figure 12.7b demonstrates such a complex sort—by two fields at the same time—producing the correct result.

---

**Figure 12.6**    Complex Searches: The course grade file has been searched for students with grades between 65 and 75.

```
LIST FOR FINAL >= 65 .AND. FINAL <= 75

    RCD# LASTNAME  FIRSTNAME  SSNUM        MIDTERM FINAL PAPER LGRADE
       4 Beaches   Sandy      098-76-5432       85    75 B     B
       5 Errupp    Phil       192-83-8475       85    69 B     B
       8 Itis      Senior     987-98-9876       85    65 D     D




    _
```

**Figure 12.7**     Sorting by Multiple Fields: (a) A file sorted by last name and (b) a complex sort of two fields at the same time.

(a)

```
SORT ON LASTNAME TO LAST

    RCD# LASTNAME  FIRSTNAME   STREET                CITY           STATE...
       1 Beaches   Sandy       265 Bay Street        San Francisco  CA
       2 Beaches   Rocky       262 Stone Avenue      Rockville      MD
       3 Errupp    Phil        1020 Station Road     Gasville       NJ
       4 Ferma     Terry       789 Earth Avenue      Boston         MA
       5 Grahm     Telly       5325 Western Union    New York City  NY
       6 Itis      Senior      College Circle        Madison        WI
       7 Lofers    Penny       123 Toe Street        Shoeville      WI
       8 Long      Harry A.    Main Street           Slowtowne      KA
       9 Maykitt   Willie      56 Main Street        Tryhard        FL
      10 Mint      Said A.     Dirt Road             Diggersville   CO
      11 Nomial    Polly       456 Equation Circle   Triangle Park  NC
      12 Pickle    Inna        Garlic Road           Cukeville      NY
      13 Stein     Frank N.    Cemetery Row          Transylvania   PA
      14 Stein     Bere        Happy Road            Milwaukee      WI


    -
```

(b)

```
is139


SORT ON LASTNAME, FIRSTNAME TO BOTH
    RCD# LASTNAME  FIRSTNAME   STREET                CITY           STATE...
       1 Beaches   Rocky       262 Stone Avenue      Rockville      MD
       2 Beaches   Sandy       265 Bay Street        San Francisco  CA
       3 Errupp    Phil        1020 Station Road     Gasville       NJ
       4 Ferma     Terry       789 Earth Avenue      Boston         MA
          .
          .
          .
      11 Nomial    Polly       456 Equation Circle   Triangle Park  NC
      12 Pickle    Inna        Garlic Road           Cukeville      NY
      13 Stein     Bere        Happy Road            Milwaukee      WI
      14 Stein     Frank N.    Cemetery Row          Transylvania   PA




    -
```

## USING MULTIPLE FILES

The main value of an electronic data base is to give fast and easy access to information. The more logical the organization of the data, the faster it can be retrieved. Data that naturally seem to go together should be contained in the same file. However, the same records should not appear in more than one file. Advanced data base systems allow different but related files within a data base to be linked together. In this way, information stored in one file is accessible to other files. This helps to avoid unnecessary duplication. It also greatly improves the integrity of the data, since changes need to be made to fewer fields. Files that can be linked together provide tremendous flexibility in gathering information.

Recall that our student data base consists of two files. One contains general student records and the other contains course grades. For most purposes these files will be processed independently, since they contain different kinds of information. For example, letters about tuition changes will go to all students listed in the general file. On the other hand, a search for students doing poorly on the midterm in our computer class would use only the grade file. However, if letters are to be sent to all students doing poorly on the midterm, then mailing-address data from the general file would be needed as well.

The major difference between file managers and data base systems is that data base systems are able to deal with more than one file simultaneously. Advanced systems such as dBASE III Plus allow the use of 10 files or more. In systems that work with multiple files, the different files are linked together by matching fields that contain common information.

Fields that are shared by different files are called **key fields** or **keys**. Typical keys are social security, student, and employee numbers. However, any field that the files hold in common can be used. In our example data base, both the grade file and the general file have LASTNAME and FIRSTNAME in common. While either of these could be used as a key, it seems more logical to use LASTNAME to relate the files together. However, common last names, such as Smith, Brown, and Stein, that belong to two or more students could cause confusion when files are linked together. For this reason, it is better to choose a field that is unique for all records, such as social security numbers.

By using the appropriate features of our data base, we could search the grade file for the names of all students receiving grades lower than 75 on the midterm. This would be the result:

> Frank N.    Stein
> Telly       Grahm
> Willie      Maykitt

By linking together our files using LASTNAME, we could search the grade file for the required student names and extract their addresses from the general file.

| | | | | | |
|---|---|---|---|---|---|
| Frank N. | Stein | Cemetery Row | Transylvania | PA | 34567 |
| Telly | Grahm | 5325 Western Union | New York City | NY | 11101 |
| Wille | Maykitt | 56 Main Street | Tryhard | FL | 65432 |

## ADVANCED FEATURES

People who make extensive use of data bases require software packages that are simultaneously fast, easy to use, and able to perform even more complex tasks than those we've already discussed. A wide range of advanced features is now available, although not all of them are in all systems.

- *Command flexibility.* The software can be run by selecting items from an on-screen menu or by issuing commands. Software that is both menu-driven and command-driven gives the novice an easy introduction to data base operations and still offers the advanced user greater flexibility.

- *Programming language features.* Many features of programming languages are built into the software. Statements for decision making, such as IF/THEN/ELSE, and looping statements such as WHILE, CASE, and GOTO are included. These, too, give advanced users greater flexibility.

- *Individualized command files.* Users can develop individualized command files, which are really programs. These can include the passing of data (parameters) between different command files.

- *Debugging aids.* Debugging aids designed to simplify the use of programming tools have been added to a number of systems (Chapter 7).

- *Information transfer.* The ability to transfer data base information to a word processor has become fairly common. Now, data bases may also transfer data to and from other standard packages, such as Lotus 1-2-3. Data also can be filed, transferred, and stored in binary format (PFS: Professional File) or in the more standard ASCII format.

- *Artificial intelligence.* The techniques of artificial intelligence using natural language tools are gaining in popularity, making data bases easier to use and understand.

- *Calculators and statistical functions.* In addition to being able to calculate totals and subtotals on numeric fields, advanced systems contain the mathematical capabilities of a calculator. Many have statistical functions including square root, natural log, and exponentiation as well.

## PITFALLS, PROBLEMS, AND SOLUTIONS

Despite all that modern data bases can do, or perhaps *because* of their increased capabilities, they are often mastered more by trial and error than by formal instruction. Even experienced people, including programmers, may find problems in getting data base software to do what they want when they want it. Some typical problems can be solved by careful advance planning and attention to detail. Other problem areas may be avoided if they can be anticipated. Let's turn to several common problems and pitfalls.

### Improving Sorting Speed

Microcomputer data bases were designed primarily to be easy to use. As a result, their structure may be efficient for entering data but not so efficient in retrieving records. Sorting through data base files can be time-consuming even for a computer. To improve sorting speed, most data base packages include a feature called **indexing**. As each record is entered, it is given a number indicating the order of its entry into the data base. This is the record number. When sorting, an **index file** containing the fields being used in the sort and the corresponding record number is created.

When we do an indexed sort, the index file and not the original file is sorted. The records remain in the data base in the order in which they were entered. Since the index file contains much less information, it can be sorted through more quickly. The actual records can then be pulled from the original file in the specified order. This technique significantly improves the time involved in sorting. In addition, a given file can be indexed on any number of fields with a considerable saving of space.

### Maintaining Data Integrity

A data base is only as reliable as the information it contains. All fields containing the same data must be updated at the same time. Data bases in which files are linked together should be designed so that as few fields as possible are duplicated. The less duplication there is in a data base, the easier it will be to update and keep accurate. In addition, when files contain data that logically belong together, it is easier to keep track of the data.

### Avoiding Deletion Errors

To keep data up-to-date, it is obviously necessary to remove unwanted or outdated items. But once a record has been removed or a field overwritten, the previous data are gone. They cannot be retrieved. Some systems do not remove records as soon as the Delete command is used. Such records are marked for deletion but not removed altogether. They are unavailable for searching and sorting purposes, but they remain in the data base until a second command is given to complete the deletion. This gives the user a chance to make sure records are no longer needed before they are eliminated. In Figure 12.8, records 4 and 9 are marked with an asterisk (*) for deletion.

### Avoiding Data Loss

Commands that change the structure of files or reports must be used with considerable care. Even simple changes in the spelling of a field name can lead to loss of data. In some data base systems when the name of a field is changed from LNAME to LASTNAME, for example, all data in that field is removed. This is because when the data base is recopied using the new structure, only those fields whose field names have remained constant are copied. The system assumes that a new name implies new data. Data base field names should not be changed unless new data accompanies the change.

Changes in field width can cause similar problems. For example, if we wanted to have the information in our general student file printed out one record per line, the length of a number of fields (including LASTNAME) would require shortening. Such changes do not become a problem until the general student file and course grade file need to be linked together using LASTNAME as a

---

**Figure 12.8**    Records Marked for Deletion.

```
crsgrade

RCD# LASTNAME    FIRSTNAME   SSNUM          MIDTERM   FINAL PAPER LGRADE
   1  Lofers      Penny       123-45-6789     100     95 A      A
   2  Stein       Frank N.    998-87-7654      25     45 C      F
   3  Pickle      Inna        555-55-5555     100     25 D      D
   4 *Beaches     Sandy       098-76-5432      85     75 B      B
   5  Errupp      Phil        192-83-8475      85     69 B      B
   6  Nomial      Polly       999-88-7777      95     99 A      A
   7  Mint        Said A.     445-67-5678      75     80 C      C
   8  Itis        Senior      987-98-9876      85     65 D      D
   9 *Long        Harry A.    234-56-7890      99     98 B      A
  10  Ferma       Terry       678-78-5678      95     80 B      B
  11  Grahm       Telly       666-11-1515      45     80 A      B
  12  Maykitt     Willie      777-00-8733      65     59 D      D


-
```

key. When the system was asked to display the names and addresses for all students with poor midterm grades, there was no problem in displaying the names. However, when the system tried to find the addresses in the general file, blanks were displayed. The reason for this is not obvious. The LASTNAME field in the general student file has been reduced in width for printing. The effect was that the computer was asked to compare an 8-character LASTNAME with a 10-character LASTNAME in the linked file. When linking two fields together, the system looks for *exact* matches. Eight characters do not match exactly with 10 characters. To avoid this problem, key fields must be defined in identical ways.

## DATA BASE MACHINES

Data base systems hog computer resources: they demand large amounts of CPU time, disks are filled with the necessary files, and considerable constraints are placed on main memory whenever a request is processed. Such considerations are of little concern on microcomputers, on which data base systems run independently of other programs. However, this is an important issue in large organizations in which computer resources and data base information are shared among several people. The resource demands of large system data bases have, in part, been addressed by increasing the primary and secondary storage capacity of the computer systems on which they run. In addition, software manufacturers have worked very hard to improve the performance of their programs. However, these improvements are little more than a Band-Aid on a serious wound. In the last few years, data base machines have appeared on the market. A **data base machine** is a special-purpose peripheral device added onto an existing computer system. It is designed to perform data base operations exclusively, independent of the main system CPU. Data base machines are designed either to speed up the transfer of information in and out of memory or decrease the time it takes to perform search operations. Those that speed up search operations use parallel processors to perform the highly repetitive searches common in data bases. Such specialty devices hold the potential for bringing the user-friendly aspects of microcomputer data bases to large multi-user systems.

Data bases provide users with the access to information necessary for making decisions in a complex world. Microcomputer data bases are relatively easy to use. However, we may have to adjust our outlook and move away from the paper and pencil world to make effective use of them. Once learned, data base systems can simplify our lives by making information more accessible.

## SUMMARY

A data base is an collection of facts organized around a key. Data needs to be organized so that it can be retrieved, or located.

A data base is only as reliable as its data. Data integrity or reliability is directly related to the ability of the data base to remain current.

Microcomputer data base systems use files designed as tables to store information. Each row or record contains related data, and each column or field contains a specific type of data.

There are two kinds of data base packages. File managers are patterned after an index-card file, with records reflecting individual cards. They are menu-driven and commonly use one file. Searches, sorts, reports, and simple calculations can be performed on that file. Data base managers are more sophisticated. They are both menu- and command-driven. They can organize data in a greater variety of ways than file managers.

Planning a data base will improve the retrieval of data. Six planning steps should be followed: (1) Understand the problem, (2) Identify the output, (3) Identify the input, (4) Organize the data, (5) Test and revise the data base, and (6) Enter the data.

Data base software must help the user to do all of the following: (1) Create the data base, (2) Search the data base for a specific item, (3) Sort the data by key, (4) Adjust the data base, and (5) Report the results.

Current data base systems allow for complex searches using AND, OR, and NOT, and complex sorts using more than one field. Data base managers can manipulate multiple files and contain decision-making statements such as IF/THEN/ELSE.

Sorting through use of an index file, containing the fields being used in the sort and record numbers, greatly improves the speed of microcomputer data base sorts.

Data base machines have been developed as special-purpose peripheral devices that speed up the transfer of data in and out of memory or decrease the time it takes to perform search operations by employing parallel processing.

## Key Words

As an extra review of the chapter, try defining the following terms. If you have trouble with any of them, refer to the page number listed.

command-driven  *(307)*

command file  *(307)*

data base  *(305)*

data base machine  *(323)*

data base managers  *(307)*

file managers  *(306)*

index file  *(321)*

indexing  *(321)*

key field (key)  *(319)*

## Test Your Knowledge

1. What is a data base?

2. Define *data integrity.*

3. Define *file, record,* and *field.*

4. How do file managers and data base managers differ?

5. How is a menu-driven data base system different from a command-driven system?

6. How do numeric and character data differ? Give examples of each.

7. If a social security number is made up entirely of digits, why is it most often stored in a character field?

8. What is a data type? List the four different field data types.

9. How are data types used when defining the structure of a file?

10. When entering student addresses in a data base, why should each part of the address be entered in a separate field?

11. What kind of adjustments can be made to existing data base files?

12. Define *searching.*

13. Define *sorting.*

14. What is a data base report?

15. Define *key field.*

16. What data is used to index a file?

17. Explain the difference between an indexed sort and a standard sort.

18. What are the advantages of using an advanced data base system, which allows multiple files, over the simpler file-management system?

19. Why must the key used to link two data base files be identical?

20. What is a data base machine?

## Expand Your Knowledge

1. Many people fear that the rapid expansion of large data base systems is a threat to personal freedom. Is this a valid concern? If so, what can be done to minimize the effects? Research and write a five-page paper on this question.

2. Using a data base system available to you, create a file of your record/tape collection. Include at least 15 records and tapes. Fields should include artist, title, type (CD, tape, record), condition, and cost.

   (a) Perform one search on your data base, such as a list of all CDs in your collection by a particular artist. Print out the results.
   (b) Perform one complex sort of your data base on two fields. For example, create an alphabetical list of your collection by artist and title. Print out the result.

3. Using a data base system available to you, create a special-occasion file of your family members. Include name, birthday data, anniversary data, and address for each family member. Plan your fields carefully so you can gather the information you need from your data base.

   (a) Perform one search on your data base, such as a list of all family members with birthdays in September. Print out your results.
   (b) Perform one complex sort of your data base on two fields. For example, create an ordered list by birth-month and birth-day of all family members. Print out your results.

4. Read George Orwell's *1984*. In a short (three to five page) paper, discuss the role of computers and data bases in the book.

5. Medical researchers urge the development of a nationwide medical data base. Research and write a short (three to five page) paper on how such a system could facilitate organ transplants and general medical research.

# 13

# Computer Graphics

## Chapter Outline

Creating Images

Hardware

Boards and Monitors (Monochrome Displays; Color Displays) • Graphics Input Devices (Digitizer; Digitizing Camera; Light Pen; Mouse) • Graphics Output Devices (Printers; Plotters; Other Hard Copy Devices)

Software

Analysis Graphics • Presentation Graphics • Computer-Aided Design • Creative Graphics

The Computer as an Artistic Medium

Computer graphics is the creation of visual images using computers. If we close our eyes and think about computer graphics, what do we see? The images that frequently come to mind are the fast-moving creatures encountered in computer games or the dramatic special effects found in movies. Through computer graphics, we can display DNA molecules, view the frontiers of space, and experience the dog-fighting spacecraft of the future. While these creations are the most dramatic of the computer-generated images, they represent only a tiny segment of the computer graphics in use today.

Despite the incredible graphics displays used in the entertainment industry, the most common forms of human communication are spoken and written words. While we use pictures and other visual images to assist us, language remains the most fundamental and pervasive form of communication. Still, researchers studying memory have rediscovered that "a picture is worth a thousand words." Studies indicate that information presented graphically is remembered longer and with greater accuracy than equivalent information presented in written form. Using computers to create clear, easy-to-understand visual images that convey meaningful information is within our reach.

After studying this chapter, you will be able to:

- Identify how computer graphic images are created.
- Distinguish between the different types of graphics monitors.
- List the types of graphics input devices.
- Understand the graphics output devices that produce hard copy.
- Understand the computer graphics used to analyze and present information.
- Identify the important features in computer-aided design (CAD).
- Explain how computers are used to produce creative images.
- Discuss computer art.

## CREATING IMAGES

Most artists do not use computers. Their creative images are composed of solid lines, shapes, and shaded areas. The artist places the pen, paintbrush, or chalk on a medium and with a series of strokes or dots of color creates an image. Computer images are not composed of strokes. They are created either out of thousands of points of light called **pixels** (for picture elements) or straight-line segments **(vectors)** placed close together. In both cases the human eye sees the image as continuous even though it is not. Newspaper photographs, television, and some modern motion pictures are all generated using pixel-like technologies.

Most computer-graphics technology uses pixel-generated images. The computer screen is composed of thousands of light-sensitive locations, each of which can be lit independently. The more pixels that make up the screen, the higher the resolution of the image and the clearer the picture. **Resolution** is a measure of pixel density on a screen. Low-resolution monitors have 60,000 pixels (300 across and 200 down), while current high-resolution screens have more than one million pixels (1024 horizontally and vertically). Using graphics software to link each pixel to a specific memory bit or set of bits is called **bit-mapping** (each pixel "maps" onto a bit). Controlling the simultaneous lighting of thousands of pixels to create meaningful images requires complex software. Multiple colors further complicate the process. Modern computer workstation-based graphics systems use special memory and processor chips to control the display screen.

## HARDWARE

Unlike other applications software, such as spreadsheets and data base packages, computer graphics require specialized hardware as well as sophisticated software.

In this section we will examine the hardware required to generate computer graphics. In addition to the specialized input and output devices, graphics software requires significant computation power and memory.

### Boards and Monitors

As was discussed in Chapter 5, today's computers are equipped with a monitor for displaying information. While graphics play an increasingly important role, most computer-generated information continues to be in the form of words and numbers. One-color, or **monochromatic**, monitors designed to display high-resolution text were not designed to display graphic images. Until recently, the reverse was also true: graphics monitors were not designed to display clear text. With the introduction of high-resolution graphics monitors it became possible to display both clear, readable text and graphics on a single monitor.

A monitor, however, is not a stand-alone device. One cannot simply replace a monochromatic monitor with a color graphics monitor. The picture elements (pixels) on a monochromatic monitor and on a graphics monitor are controlled differently. Each monitor requires a different set of computer chips to operate. In other words, for a graphics monitor to run on a computer, a special internal **graphics board** is required. More to the point, until the recent development of inexpensive high-resolution color monitors, clear, readable text could only be produced on a monochromatic monitor. Color graphics required a different monitor and a different board. If both graphics and text were required for a particular application, a complete computer system either had two monitors and two monitor boards or the user settled for the grainy, unclear characters produced when text was displayed on a graphics monitor.

A number of microcomputers, such as the Macintosh II, the Commodore Amiga, and the IBM Personal System/2, now include a high-resolution color graphics monitor as standard equipment (see Figure 13.1). This reflects the impact graphics has had on the microcomputer market.

We will examine the four most popular types of monitors. While more specialized monitors exist, they are very expensive and not widely available.

**Monochrome Displays**    Monochrome displays use lighted pixels of a single color to produce images on a dark background. Monitors with green, amber, or white images are popular. Monitors with amber characters on a dark gray background have been found to cause less eyestrain than other combinations and are now standard on some systems. Monochrome monitors are designed to produce high-resolution characters, having a pixel density of 720 by 350.

In response to the demand for graphics and high-resolution text, Hercules Computer Technology developed an inexpensive monochrome graphics board that could produce high-resolution characters and shaded display graphics on a

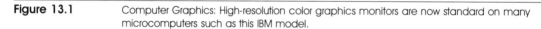

**Figure 13.1**    Computer Graphics: High-resolution color graphics monitors are now standard on many microcomputers such as this IBM model.

monochromatic monitor. The **Hercules board** became the standard for mono-chromatic graphics.

**Color Displays**    Most color monitors use a red-green-blue **(RGB)** format. When these three colors of light are mixed, white light is produced. Monitors using color combinations other than RGB are popular with computer artists. Color monitors are more expensive than monochromatic monitors, requiring more complex hardware. Each color requires independent yet integrated hardware to light the different-colored pixels in the desired combinations. In addition, keep-ing track of and controlling the more complex hardware requires more memory. As the price of memory has dropped, color monitors with increased resolution and correspondingly higher-quality graphics have become more affordable.

**Color graphics adaptor (CGA) monitors** usually use the red-green-blue com-bination to create white light. They are considered low-resolution systems, hav-ing a pixel density of 640 by 200 pixels. Despite the resolution, the addition of color so dramatically increases the visual effect of graphics that many users pre-fer CGA monitors to the higher-resolution monochrome systems for graphics. However, when used for displaying large amounts of text, as in word processing applications, CGA monitors with their low resolution produce fuzzy characters that can cause eyestrain.

**Enhanced graphics adaptor (EGA)** monitors are similar to CGA systems ex-cept they produce more clearly defined images. Their higher resolution is pro-duced by having a density of 640 by 350 pixels. Character resolution close to that produced by monochromatic monitors makes such systems useful for both text processing and graphics. The EGA board is an internal component that de-termines both the resolution and the number of colors available. As much as 256K of RAM is required on the graphics board to operate the monitor. This RAM is dedicated to color control.

**Video graphics adaptor (VGA)** monitors are very high-resolution systems (640 by 480 pixels) that produce remarkably lifelike images. Such systems can display hundreds of colors easily. This higher resolution requires additional memory and support hardware resulting in a price often four times that of EGA monitors.

## Graphics Input Devices

In Chapter 5, we discussed general input and output devices, including the digi-tizer, light pen, and mouse. Many of the keyboard alternatives discussed were originally designed as graphics input devices. Clearly they are not limited to such use.

Many graphs, charts, and designs are stored as a series of mathematical coor-dinates rather than as bit-mapped pictures. Coordinate information requires far less memory. Graphics input devices and their associated software transform images either into sets of coordinates or into a bit-mapped duplicate of the original image.

**Digitizer**    A digitizer, often called a graphics tablet, is a flat pad-like attachment to a computer. A stylus or "pen" is connected to the tablet and is used for drawing (see Figure 13.2). Where the stylus touches the tablet a circuit is completed. Digitizers function in two ways. In conjunction with the attached stylus, the tablet can be used to create freehand drawings or it can be used to trace predrawn diagrams. In either case, the tablet converts the drawings into digital form.

**Digitizing Camera**    The **digitizing camera** is a camera-like device that scans an existing diagram or picture and converts the image into digital form. The diagram or picture is converted into a complex collection of dots that can be represented as pixels on a computer screen. These pixels are then mapped onto memory, at least one bit per pixel, to create bit-mapped graphic images. The more pixels per inch, the better the resolution of the image. Color images require multiple bits per pixel to store colored images.

**Figure 13.2**    The Digitizer: Used with a stylus, the digitizer converts freehand or predrawn diagrams into digital form. A CalComp DrawingBoard is shown.

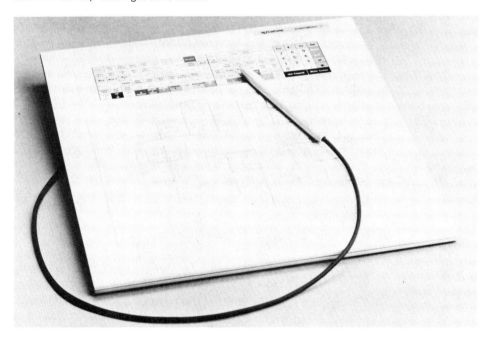

**Light Pen**    A light pen is a pointing device designed to interact with a special-ized monitor. Where electrical circuitry is the basis of digitizing tablets, photo-electric cells create the connection between the light pen and the screen. An image drawn with a light pen is digitally stored as a series of points. Light pens are used to enter drawings, correct or alter previously stored images displayed on the screen, or simply point to information presented in the form of a menu (see Figure 13.3).

**Mouse**    The mouse is a pointing device whose movement on any flat surface is reflected in the movement of the cursor on an associated monitor. Software con-verts the mouse's movement around the screen into graphic images. The cursor's changing position is recorded, creating a digital record.

### Graphics Output Devices

Monitors are combination devices. In association with a mouse or light pen they are input devices. When displaying visual information they are output devices. In this section, the output devices are limited to those that produce hard copy.

---

**Figure 13.3**    The Light Pen: Similar to a touch-sensitive screen, the light pen such as this one from Koala Technologies lets users interact with the computer image.

**Printers**    All graphics printers use dot matrix technology (see Chapter 5). As with text, the denser the concentration of dots the higher the quality of the picture. Dot matrix printers can directly translate screen pixels into hard copy images. Of the four varieties of dot matrix printers—impact, thermal, inkjet, and laser—the most dramatic images are created by laser printers because of the very high density of dots they can produce. However, most laser printers are limited to black marks on a white surface. Color laser printers are very expensive, resulting in limited use. Most color graphic images are produced on either thermal or inkjet printers. While thermal color printers are less expensive to purchase, their operating costs are high. They require special paper and the ink colors are limited. Inkjet printers use three primary ink colors that combine to form a large number of other colors.

**Plotters**    Plotters create graphic images by coordinating the movement of as many as four colored pens and paper. They can be used to draw almost any shape and can even shade areas. They are predominantly used to create engineering drawings, maps, and charts. Using perspective, they can create the impression of three-dimensional images in two dimensions. Two basic varieties are popular. The **flatbed plotter** holds the paper still while the pens move across the page. **Drum plotters** position the paper over movable drums that rotate as the pens move. Drum plotters can produce more complex designs since both the paper and the pens can rotate. In addition, they can handle very large pieces of paper. Drum plotters are more expensive and more versatile than flatbed plotters.

**Other Hard Copy Devices**    A number of devices can reproduce the images displayed on graphics monitors onto 35mm slides or color transparencies. The 35mm slides then can be converted into photographs using standard photographic equipment.

## SOFTWARE

While specialized hardware is required to generate computer graphics, it is the graphics software that allows us to transform data into information and art.

We have already learned that computers play a significant role by assisting us in examining and analyzing data. Computer graphics provide an additional way for us to communicate what we have discovered. Currently, computer graphics used in this way fall into four categories:

- analysis graphics
- presentation graphics
- computer-aided design
- creative graphics

## Analysis Graphics

As the name implies, **analysis graphics** are visuals used to analyze large amounts of data. A graph, chart, or picture can condense lists of numeric data and reveal relationships and trends. Analysis graphics software is widely available for all types of computers, with microcomputer use representing the largest component. Mainframe packages are used to analyze weather data, producing not only the traditional weather maps used on the evening news, but detailed maps of hurricanes and other storms in motion. In addition, graphics software is used to analyze data transmitted from exploratory space vehicles and in the study of earthquakes, volcanoes, and the atomic structure of life.

The heaviest user of microcomputer analysis graphics is business. Software designed to support such use is often called **business graphics**. Microcomputer analysis graphics take the form of line and bar graphs, scattergrams, and pie charts. Such graphics identify trends, reveal relationships, and assist in locating patterns.

**Line graphs** are used to look for trends. The upward or downward direction of the lines reflect the trend. For example, if we plotted gasoline prices against time, we'd notice that despite some decreases the overall trend is toward an increase in pump prices. In Figure 13.4, the number of students enrolling in programming courses over the last five years has been plotted. The graph indicates an increase and then a leveling off of total enrollment.

**Scattergrams** show the distribution among a set of values. To show the distribution of student grades, exam scores could be plotted. Depending on the individual scores, they may cluster around specific points or scatter throughout the entire range. Looking at a scattergram of raw data often provides valuable insights to relationships that may not be apparent in lists of numbers.

**Bar graphs** are used to show the differences within a single set of data and to compare the relationships between different sets of data. In Figure 13.5a, a bar graph is used to compare one class's average grades on three different exams. By using multiple bars on a single graph, different classes can be compared on the same three exams (see Figure 13.5b).

**Pie charts** are used to show proportional relationships in a given set of data. For example, within a given class they can demonstrate the relationship between A's, B's, C's, D's, and F's (see Figure 13.6). This type of graph is most commonly used in portraying budgets. For example, it can display the proportion of the federal budget that goes to military spending as opposed to social programs.

Many spreadsheet and data base packages include analysis graphics. All stand-alone analysis packages are designed to incorporate the data stored in spreadsheets and data bases. Analysis graphics software is relatively inexpensive and easy to use. Its popularity as a decision-making tool is growing rapidly.

**Figure 13.4** The Printer: This line graph of student enrollment in programming courses was created with a printer.

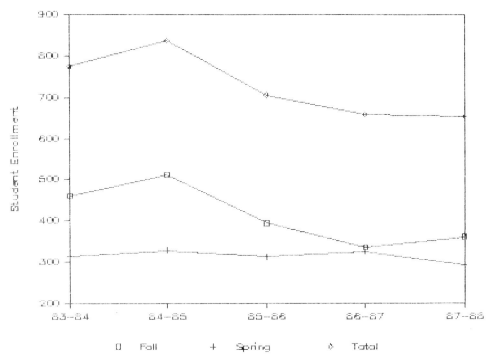

### Presentation Graphics

Analysis graphics and presentation graphics are very similar. While analysis graphics provide insight into collected data, **presentation graphics** are designed to assist in presenting these insights to others (see Figure 13.7). Both types of software produce similar graphics, such as line and bar graphs and pie charts, and are heavily used in business. As with analysis graphics, most presentation packages accept data from existing spreadsheets and data bases, and both are used to study and visualize data. Presentation graphics, however, are designed for "pizazz."

The graphics produced by analysis packages are more than adequate for identifying trends and analyzing data. When giving presentations, remember that audiences usually have limited time and quickly waning interest. The attention-getting features of presentation packages are often as critical to getting the information across as the content itself. Presentation graphics packages create dramatic effects by adding brilliant colors, three-dimensional diagrams, easily

**Figure 13.5**     Bar Graphs: Printers can also create bar graphs, such as these (a) indicating one class's average exam grades and (b) the grades of three different classes on the same exam.

(a)

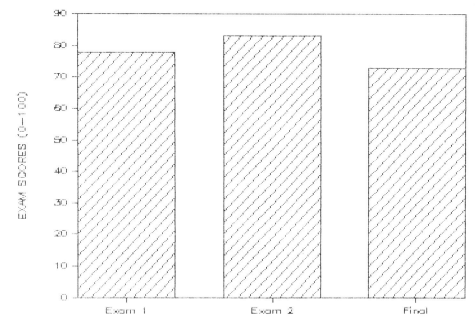

(b)

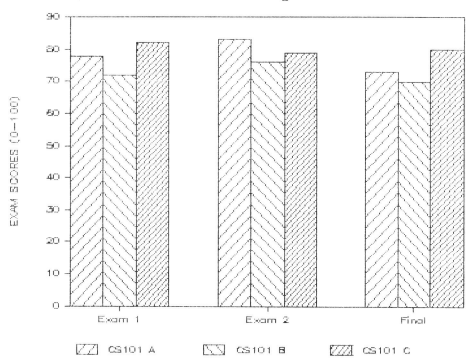

**Figure 13.6**  Pie Charts: Pie charts show proportional relationships, such as this one of the grade distribution within a class.

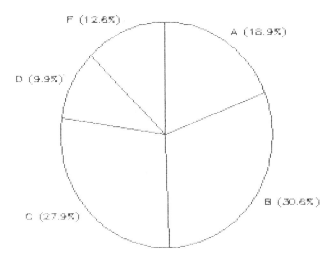

**Figure 13.7**  Presentation Graphics: Used heavily in business, presentation graphics present data with pizazz.

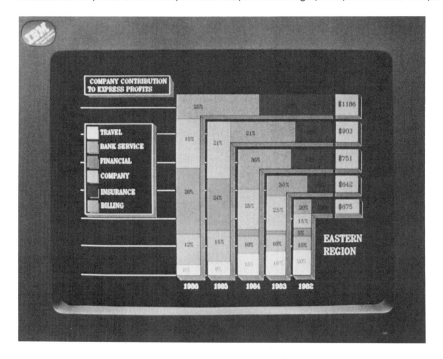

recognized symbols, and a variety of letter fonts to analysis graphics. Most current presentation packages are designed to:

- Enhance the graphics produced by other programs such as Lotus 1-2-3. In addition to making these graphics more visually appealing, such graphics can be reduced or blown up as needed for inclusion in reports. Additional explanatory information also can be added to clarify the graph.

- Create graphs, diagrams, pictures, and charts from data entered at the screen.

- Create charts and diagrams from stored graphic symbols such as pictures, lines, curves, circles, and rectangles. The user, assisted by the software, acts as an artist combining pictures, lines, and words to create the desired visual.

- Create color transparencies, slides, and hard copy visuals from on-screen displays. Specialized hardware attachments, such as a camera with color slide film, are required.

Until recently, the presentation materials just described were created by graphic artists and illustrators. Through the use of presentation software, those preparing a presentation now have closer control over the graphics they will use. Graphics that previously took days or weeks to produce by professional artists can be created in minutes with presentation software without a reduction in quality. Since time is no longer a factor, software-generated graphics can be tailored to specific audiences and can reflect up-to-the-minute changes in information.

## Computer-Aided Design

The application of computer graphics to the design, drafting, or modeling of devices or structures is called **computer-aided design (CAD)**. CAD designs have traditionally been used to create tools and machine parts, buildings, aircraft, and cars (see Figure 13.8). More recently, computer chips have been designed using CAD. Perhaps the most unique use of CAD software has been in the development of special effects for the motion picture industry.

Historically, CAD has been a mainframe or minicomputer application. Such systems were predominantly used by engineers, architects, and draftsmen. However, state-of-the-art CAD work environments are powerful single-user workstations. These workstations include a small minicomputer, a high-resolution color graphics monitor equipped with a pointing device such as a digitizer or lightpen, and a keyboard (see Chapter 1). Specialized software that supports two-dimensional and three-dimensional graphics is required. Such workstations are often connected to larger systems, where data bases of existing drawings are stored.

**Figure 13.8**     Computer-Aided Design: Computer-aided design is used to create buildings, aircraft, and cars.

There are two stages in using the computer as a design tool. In the first stage, a geometric model of the machine part, aircraft, or building is designed on the graphics monitor. The designer creates all the lines, curves, and shapes that the diagram requires. With the assistance of CAD software, shading, perspective, and color are added, converting the design from a flat, two-dimensional diagram into a seemingly three-dimensional image called a **solid model**. This solid model can be rotated and viewed from any angle. It can be examined as a unit, enlarged, or reduced. It can be broken into its component parts, each of which can be further examined. Designs can be examined from the outside as well as from the inside. In a building model, for example, the outside walls can be stripped away, leaving the supporting structure visible.

In the second stage, the model can be tested and analyzed as if it had already been constructed. In addition to the structural design, the physical constraints and limitations inherent in construction materials are also entered into the computer. Simulated stress tests then can be performed on the model. These stress tests evaluate the model's performance under specific conditions. The design is

# On Line

## CAD IN CRYSTAL

Computer-aided design (CAD) isn't just for designing spacecraft and futuristic cars.

On their personal computers, business people are using it to create scale-model steam engines, to map chemical processes, and to plot the placement of equipment in factories. A buyer for a Seattle, Washington, jeweler even used it to design a crystal pattern.

Ray Fair, the watch and giftware buyer for Weisfield's Jewelers, wanted a special crystal pattern to sell for Valentine's Day. He contacted Galway, the Irish crystal maker. Galway's president agreed to send him a sample in 10 days if Fair could design a pattern and wire it to the company.

There wasn't time for a professional artist to create a hand-drawn design, so Fair turned to his IBM PC and his CAD package. He created an outline of a faceted crystal flute and tried out a variety of patterns before settling on a row of identical hearts encircling the top. He created the pattern in just a few hours, printed it on a color printer, and wired it to Galway.

Fair's crystal went on sale in Weisfield's 80 West Coast locations in time for Valentine's Day.

Since then, Fair has used his CAD program for other projects, including creating a diagram of how watch links fit together for his company's newsletter. He considers the $100 he spent for the program, called Generic CADD, a good investment.

"I bought Generic CADD as a toy, but it is by no means a toy. It's a full-featured professional tool," Fair said. Generic CADD has the precision and zooming capabilities that are lacking in paint and draw programs. Changing angles and closing gaps are also more difficult with paint and draw programs, he added.

*Source:* Christine Strehlo, "Ideas Etched in Glass," *Personal Computing,* vol. 12, number 4, April, 1988, p. 116.

studied for structural flaws. Using the results of these tests, the engineer can adjust or redesign the model to eliminate indicated problems. This type of pretesting is far less expensive than building a physical model and testing it for flaws, while netting the same results. Furthermore, revisions can be made more quickly and more accurately to CAD designs than to physical models.

Once CAD designs are complete, two-dimensional versions can be produced on paper in the form of extremely detailed blueprints. Alternatively, the design can be used directly in the development of the items.

In most cases, CAD designs are stored as **digitized models** (binary versions of the design) in memory and can be retrieved and used whole or in part as the foundation of future drawings. Such CAD data bases reduce the cost and time involved in the development of new products.

While most CAD software operates on workstations or on larger systems, the increase in processing power and storage capacity of today's microcomputers has made high-quality CAD software available on these machines. Microcomputer CAD products are relatively inexpensive and they contain large libraries of drawings that are easy to modify. Microcomputer CAD has found its way into the design of clothing, jewelry, and thousands of other products.

## Creative Graphics

Computer graphics are finding use in business and education where drawings, pictures, diagrams, and charts are important. In many cases, software-generated graphics are replacing paper-and-pencil drawings with clearer, more colorful results.

Just as word processors and spreadsheets manipulate text and numbers, **graphics editors** manipulate images by lighting and unlighting thousands of pixels. Graphics editors, often called paint packages or computer easels, can create freehand sketches using a mouse, digitizer, light pen, or other pointing device. In addition, graphics editor software includes preprogrammed graphics primitives such as circles, squares, points, curves, and lines, which can be entered on the screen and manipulated along with freehand drawings. Colors and shadings selected from a menu are applied to computer images in much the same way an artist selects colors from a paint palette and applies them to a canvas. Using software similar to CAD, two-dimensional sketches can be made to appear three-dimensional and the impression of texture can be added (see Figure 13.9).

Graphics editors can edit or adjust screen images. Sections of drawings can be erased or moved to other locations on the screen (similar to block moves with a word processor), enlarged, and reduced in size. Software can simulate the thin lines drawn with a pencil point or the thicker lines and shading made with a paintbrush. The computer artist can even duplicate the effect produced by paint from a spray can.

At present, most graphics editors run on microcomputers and workstations. On single-user systems, both the processor and large amounts of memory can be dedicated to the tasks of drawing pictures. Manipulating individual pixels requires a large amount of dedicated memory. In the single-user environment, the computer can instantly respond to the artist's actions on the screen. In multi-user environments, graphics editor users must contend with noticeable delays between the time an image is drawn on the screen and its actual appearance.

CAD packages routinely contain graphics editors as part of their modeling software. However, until Apple released its Macintosh, stand-alone graphics editors were not widely available. Initially, Macintosh images were limited to black and white. Despite this limitation, pictures generated on the Macintosh and

**Figure 13.9**    Paint Packages: These computer easels can create freehand sketches or use preprogrammed graphics primitives such as rectangles and lines.

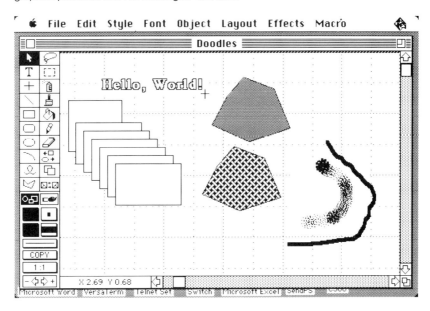

printed on a laser printer could rival sophisticated pen-and-ink drawings. Current microcomputer software is not limited to the Macintosh, and color packages are popular.

## THE COMPUTER AS AN ARTISTIC MEDIUM

As we've already seen, the dominant use of computer graphics is to analyze and present information. However, computer graphics are also being used as tools for creative expression. Computer artists use the computer as a tool to create art (see Figure 13.10).

The motion picture industry is the most obvious place where computer graphics have altered our perceptions. Computers generate most of the dramatic special effects currently used on television and in the movies. A graphics system called Pixar produces computer-generated visual effects that cannot be distinguished from natural photography. Pixar was developed by Lucasfilms. Unlike photography, however, Pixar graphics need not reflect the real world. They re-

**Figure 13.10**        Computer Art: Often dramatic, colorful, and detailed, computer art may not appeal to everyone.

flect the artist's imagination. Pixar has been purchased by NeXT Corp. (NeXT's president is Stephen Jobs, cofounder of Apple Computer.) NeXT machines contain remarkable graphics capabilities.

While graphics editors are the most popular means of producing artistic images on a computer screen, two additional techniques are available. Some computer artists write programs that mathematically describe the images they wish to create. Equations describe the shapes, sizes, and colors of objects on the screen. Such programs are extremely complex and require considerable programming expertise. The second technique uses a digitizing camera to convert a drawing or photograph into a computerized copy in binary form (digitized). The copy is then stored in memory. This binary information is next converted into lit or unlit pixels on a computer monitor. This digital image can then be manipulated using graphics software.

Computer art is often dramatic, colorful, and incredibly detailed. Its images range from the real to the surreal. As with any form of art, it may not appeal to everyone.

As the cost of graphics hardware decreases and computer users become more aware of the benefits of computer-generated graphics, the demand for high-quality computer graphics will continue to increase. However, while computer graphics are viewed as an attractive and even dramatic use of computers, they are not yet commonly thought of as a tool for presenting information. Just as computers have altered the way we approach writing, calculating, and storing information, so too will computer graphics change our image of information.

## SUMMARY

Computer graphics is the creation of visual images using computers. Computer images are created out of points of light called pixels or segments of straight lines called vectors.

The more pixels that make up the screen, the higher the resolution of the image. Using graphics software to link each pixel to a specific memory bit or set of bits is called bit-mapping.

For graphics to be displayed on a computer monitor, a special internal graphics board controlled by a special processor and dedicated memory is required. Monochromatic monitors are usually used to display high-resolution text. A Hercules board is an inexpensive monochromatic monitor board that can display high-resolution graphics as well as text.

Color monitors are usually of the RGB format. Color monitors are more expensive than monochromatic monitors, requiring more complex hardware. Each color requires independent yet integrated hardware to light the different-colored pixels. Color monitors include CGA monitors, which are low-resolution systems; EGA monitors, which produce higher-resolution images and acceptable text resolution; and VGA monitors, which are very high-resolution systems that produce remarkably lifelike images.

Graphics input devices include the digitizer, the digitizing camera, the light pen, and the mouse. Graphics output devices include printers, plotters, and devices to produce 35mm slides and color transparencies.

Graphics software can be used to examine and analyze data or create art. Analysis graphics use visuals to analyze large amounts of data. Presentation graphics add dramatic effects to analysis graphics for use in presenting information.

Computer-aided design (CAD) applies computer graphics to the design, drafting, or modeling of devices or structures. Currently, CAD software operates on powerful single-user workstations that combine a minicomputer, color graphics monitor, and a pointing device with sophisticated modeling software.

Graphics editors manipulate images by lighting and unlighting pixels. They combine preprogrammed graphics primitives with freehand drawing. Images can be enlarged, reduced, and adjusted at the screen.

Computer art's most popular application is in the motion-picture industry. Pixar generates computer visuals that look like photographs.

## Key Words

As an extra review of the chapter, try defining the following terms. If you have trouble with any of them, refer to the page number listed.

analysis graphics *(335)*
bar graph *(335)*
bit-mapping *(329)*
business graphics *(335)*
color graphics adaptor (CGA) monitor *(331)*
computer-aided design (CAD) *(339)*
digitizing camera *(332)*
digitized model *(342)*
drum plotter *(334)*
enhanced graphics adaptor (EGA) monitor *(331)*
flatbed plotter *(334)*
graphics board *(329)*

graphics editor *(342)*
Hercules board *(331)*
line graph *(335)*
monochromatic *(329)*
pie chart *(335)*
pixels *(328)*
presentation graphics *(336)*
RGB *(331)*
resolution *(329)*
scattergram *(335)*
solid model *(340)*
vectors *(328)*
video graphics adaptor (VGA) monitor *(331)*

## Test Your Knowledge

1. Define *pixel.*

2. How do pixel and vector graphics differ?

3. Define *resolution.*

4. What is the relationship between computer monitors and monitor boards?

5. How does a monochromatic monitor differ from a color monitor?

6. Explain the differences between CGA, EGA, and VGA color monitors.

7. List and describe the four most common graphics input devices.

8. Describe how color graphics printers produce pictures.

9. Describe how plotters work.

10. How are drum plotters different from flatbed plotters?

11. List the types of graphics used to analyze information.

12. How does presentation graphics differ from analysis graphics?

13. What is computer-aided design?

14. Explain solid modeling.

15. What is a graphics editor and how does it work?

## Expand Your Knowledge

1. Visit a local computer store and discuss the different types of graphics monitors available on personal computers. Write a short three-page paper explaining the differences between the monitors. Include current prices and system requirements.

2. Write a five-page paper on microcomputer CAD. Include a section explaining the differences between microcomputer CAD and the software that runs on larger systems.

3. Write a short paper (three to five pages) on Pixar graphics.

4. Using software reviews found in computer magazines such as *Personal Computing,* compare three presentation graphics packages. Include current prices where available.

5. Using analysis software available at your school, design a graph or chart that compares your exam grades in a course. Use proper titles and labels.

# 14

# Computer Communications and Networking

### Chapter Outline

Making the Connection
    Modems • Channels

Communication Media
    Twisted-Pair Copper Wire • Coaxial Cable • Microwave Signals • Fiber
    Optic Cable

Software
    Protocols • Microcomputer Software

Networking
    Early Connections • Local Area Networks • Wide Area Networks •
    Bulletin Boards • Academic Computer Networks • Corporate/Business
    Networks (Transportation Industry; Hotel and Motel Industry; Electronic
    Banking; Retail Industry) • Information Networks

An information explosion is occurring all around us. Keeping track of even critical information is increasingly difficult. More medical reports are generated, court cases decided, discoveries made, research published, and news reported in print and on the airwaves than can possibly be assimilated. Hotel, airline, and theater reservations are made without leaving home. Banking is available 24 hours a day. Computers are making just about all information more accessible.

The transmission of information over long distances is called **telecommunication**. This information can be in the form of computer-generated data, the spoken word as in telephone conversations, or video in the form of television. The media used to transmit this information vary widely, including telephone wires, fiber optic cable, radio signals, and satellites.

Before computers became popular, the world was already "wired." Friends across the country or around the world could and still can be contacted by picking up and dialing the telephone. Television brings almost instantaneous images of events occurring on Earth and in space. Telecommunication is usually thought of in terms of computers and telephones. However, the wiring of America began in the 1840s with the invention of the telegraph. The telegraph transmitted digital signals, sets of dots and dashes, like the zeros and ones used by modern computers. In the early 1900s, telegraph signals were replaced by voice signals with the invention of the telephone. Voice signals are not digital and for a while digital communications all but disappeared. Computers, however, have reintroduced digital communication.

The exchanging of information between computers and computing devices over communication lines is called **telecomputing**. These "conversations" can be simply the transfer of information from one place to another or they can involve considerable amounts of processing. The bulk of information transferred and processed does not come from computer professionals but from businesses, service organizations such as travel agents, and individuals.

After studying this chapter, you will be able to:

- Understand the different kinds of modems and their uses.
- Describe the different types of communication media.
- Define communication channels.
- Identify the role of software in computer communications.
- Describe local area networks.
- Identify the different types of wide area networks.
- Describe the services offered by academic networks.
- Identify the uses of wide area networks by business and industry.
- Describe the information utilities.
- Understand information networks.

## MAKING THE CONNECTION

The simplest way to get computers and computing devices to communicate is to connect them by wires capable of transmitting digital signals (see Figure 14.1).

Computers connected in this way can share information and peripheral devices such as printers, disk drives, terminals, and color graphics equipment. Machine size is irrelevant. Large machines can be connected as easily as a microcomputer sitting on a desk is connected to a nearby printer.

Unfortunately, as the distance between computing devices increases, the reliability and strength of the signal decreases. While it is possible to have a memo printed on a printer down the hall, using one in the next building requires that the signal between the computer and printer be boosted, or enhanced. Even with the addition of such devices, direct-connection distances are limited.

As the demand to connect more and more computing devices over longer and longer distances grew, it became obvious that an alternative to directly wiring equipment together was needed. Furthermore, users of different computers in distant locations wanted to exchange information and share ideas and resources. The telephone became the obvious solution. Information and ideas had long been shared in this way. Offices, businesses, and homes nationwide and even worldwide were already connected by millions of miles of copper wire. Repeaters and signal boosters were in place. Using the telephone to transmit computer-generated information seemed only logical.

**Figure 14.1**    Connected Computers: Computers and computing devices communicate with one another by transmitting digital signals over wires.

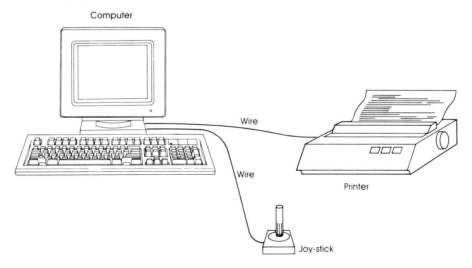

## Modems

Unfortunately, computers do not speak the same language as telephones. Computers and computing devices produce **digital signals**, or high and low electrical pulses representing ones and zeros. The telephone system, on the other hand, was designed to transmit the human voice as a continuous **analog signal**. In order for a computer to "talk" over traditional telephone lines, its digital signal had to be converted into an analog equivalent.

The solution came in the form of a device called a **modem** (MOdulate/DE-Modulate). A modem converts, or modulates, digital signals into corresponding analog signals so they can be carried over existing phone lines. The same device also converts incoming analog signals, or demodulates them, into their corresponding digital signals so they can be understood by a receiving computer. For two computers to "talk" over the telephone two modems are required, one connected to each computer, to code and decode the digital message (see Figure 14.2).

By combining the existing telephone infrastructure with modems, computers and computing devices anywhere in the world can communicate.

Just as there are different kinds of computers, different kinds of modems are available. The two most popular modems plug directly into telephone jacks and are called **direct-connect modems**. One type consists of a special circuit board that is inserted into an expansion slot in most desktop machines. These boards are included in many portable machines. Such modems are called **internal direct-connect modems** because they are placed inside the box housing the computer and they use the computer's power supply.

**External direct-connect modems** are stand-alone modems housed in a self-contained box. They plug into both the computer (or terminal) and the phone jack. Such modems are not designed to fit into a particular computer model and are used with a wide variety of computers and terminals. However, they do require their own power supply and cost more than the internal variety.

**Figure 14.2**    The Modem: Computers "talk" with one another over telephone lines through the use of modems.

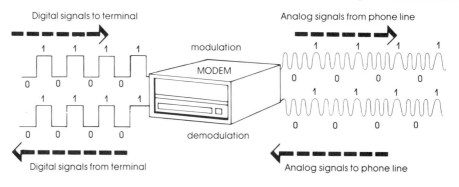

Not all modems are direct-connect models. In an early modem design called an **acoustic coupler**, the telephone receiver (handset) was cradled in a pair of rubber cups located on the modem. The digital signals produced by the computer were converted into audible sounds that were then "spoken" into the telephone receiver. Similarly, the audible sounds produced by the telephone were converted by the modem into digital signals. Audible signals transmitted across the air space between the telephone receiver and the acoustic cups produced slow and often unreliable signals. Background noises could interfere with the data flow, producing transmission errors. Acoustic couplers are still used with telephones that do not have modular connections, such as pay phones and many hotel systems.

Since modems are computer devices, intelligent models with built-in microprocessors are very popular. These **intelligent modems** can be programmed to automatically dial and answer the telephone and disconnect from the phone system when a "conversation" is complete. The more intelligent a modem, the more it can do when combined with sophisticated communications software. Several different kinds of modems are represented in Figure 14.3.

The demand for the transmission of digital signals is rapidly increasing. Wherever possible, telephone companies are converting their lines to transmit digital signals directly. Such lines transmit data faster than their analog counterparts. This is critically important to organizations that transmit large amounts of computer data over long distances. Increasing transmission speeds decreases the cost of long-distance communication. In addition, when digital lines are used, modems are not required since no translation is necessary. However, since the bulk of residential conversations will continue to be via the spoken word, residential phone systems are unlikely to change. Computer conversations involving machines in homes and many offices will continue to require modems.

## Channels

Computers can process data at incredible speeds. Transmission lines send and receive information at varying speeds, however, depending on their design. Transmission channels or data communication circuits are the roadways computers use to send data from place to place. Automobile roads vary in width from one-lane country roads to six-lane superhighways, reflecting the speeds our cars can go. Similarly, computer channels come in narrowband, voiceband, and broadband varieties, reflecting data-transmission speeds. Just as roads, modern data circuits are usually bi-directional, with a sending and a receiving channel both open at the same time. A channel's **bandwidth** reflects the amount of data that can be transmitted in a given block of time. The wider the bandwidth the faster data can be transmitted, so more data can be sent in a shorter amount of time. A car driving on the highway can be an analogy. The car covers more ground in 10 minutes at 55 MPH than at 30 MPH.

**Figure 14.3**   Types of Modems: (a) A Hayes internal direct-connect modem, (b) a Hayes external direct-connect modem, and (c) an acoustic coupler by Lexicon.

(a)

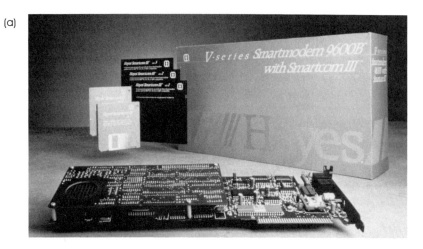

(b)

(c)

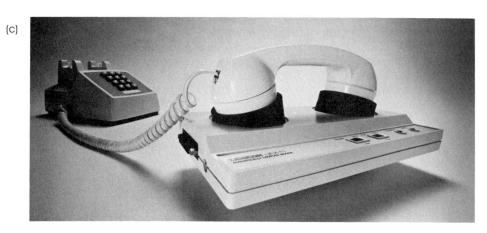

Computers transmit information in terms of bits, 10 of which usually are required to represent a single character. A modem transmitting at 300 bits per second (bps) sends 30 characters per second (cps). Since people read at approximately 120 cps, 1200 bps modems are more popular than the 300 bps models. Demand is increasing for modems that transmit at 2400 bps and faster modems.

**Narrowband channels** transmit at rates less than 30 characters per second and are rarely used for the transmission of computer data. Telegraph and teletype machines transmit over narrowband channels. **Voiceband channels** were originally used for the transmission of sound. Standard telephone lines are voiceband channels. Such channels can transmit digital data at between 30 and 960 characters per second. Voiceband is frequently used to transmit computer-generated data. **Broadband channels** transmit at rates of more than one million characters per second. Such channels are obviously used for transmitting large amounts of data.

## COMMUNICATION MEDIA

Communication channels can use copper wire, radio waves, or glass to transmit data. Different media support different transmission speeds and therefore have different uses.

### Twisted-Pair Copper Wire

The most common, least expensive, and easiest-to-install communication medium is **twisted-pair copper wire**, used with telephones. These standard telephone wires run throughout our homes, offices, and cities and were designed to carry audio transmissions. Together with modems, they can be used for computer communications. Not being designed for digital transmission, twisted-pair copper wires are relatively slow and are easily affected by electromagnetic interference, which reduces the reliability of the transmission.

### Coaxial Cable

Like twisted-pair copper wire, **coaxial cable** uses two conductors, but one of them is cast like a shell around the other (see Figure 14.4). This nearly eliminates electromagnetic interference. While far more expensive than standard twisted-pair copper wire, coaxial cable can be used to transmit data at very high speeds. In most cases, the high transmission speeds offset the added cost of installation.

**Figure 14.4**     Coaxial Cable: Casting one conductor like a shell around another reduces electromagnetic distortion in coaxial cables. A cross-section is shown.

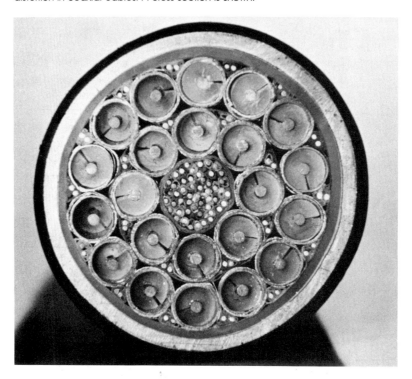

## Microwave Signals

**Microwave signals** are extremely high-frequency radio waves that can be used to transmit data at high speeds. Microwaves are used to transmit computer data and both television sound and pictures. Radio waves travel along straight lines or lines of sight. When used across the surface of the planet, repeater stations placed approximately 30 miles apart are required to compensate for the curvature of the Earth. In large cities, microwave transmission dishes are often placed on rooftops to capture data sent from one location to another within the city. Many universities use such dishes to send data between campuses.

Microwave signals are also beamed to orbiting satellites thousands of miles above the Earth, which then relay the signals back to Earth stations in distant locations (see Figure 14.5). Microwaves are high-volume, high-speed links in the communication system.

**Figure 14.5**    Satellite Transmissions: Microwave signals are transmitted from Earth to a relay satellite, which then sends that signal back to Earth.

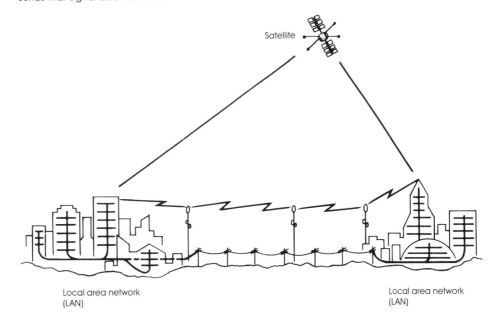

Local area network
(LAN)

Local area network
(LAN)

### Fiber Optic Cable

The newest link in our communication system is **fiber optic cable**. Fiber optic cables are composed of hair-thin, perfectly clear glass or plastic fibers packed in a protective casing (see Figure 14.6). These cables conduct laser light rather than electricity. Lasers produce a single-frequency light, which does not separate into colors when transmitted over any significant distance.

Light provides an extremely broad channel for the transmission of data. Fiber optic cable can transmit vast amounts of data very quickly. Light sources can be turned on and off more rapidly than electricity, producing faster transmission speeds. In addition, fiber optic cable is lightweight and not subject to electrical interference, which causes transmission errors. It also breaks when wiretapped, an important data-security feature. This type of medium is so useful for the transmission of computer and voice data that the communications industry expects as much as one-third of the nation's communications links will be fiber optic by the early 1990s.

**Figure 14.6**   Fiber Optic Cable: Laser beams transmit data through fiber optic cables made of glass or plastic. A cross-section is shown.

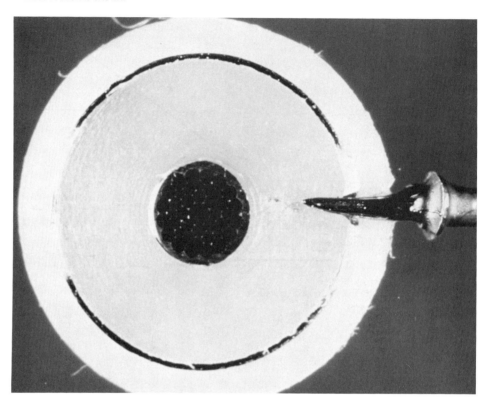

## SOFTWARE

Judging from the information discussed thus far, it might appear that computers and computing devices require nothing more than wires to communicate. Such is not the case. While hardware connections are critical, software is required to organize and interpret the signals.

### Protocols

When government leaders meet to discuss affairs of state, there are rules governing how the conversations between them will take place. These rules include who speaks and in what order, how one interrupts another speaker, and even how far apart participants stand. These rules are called **protocols**. Similar protocols are as necessary when computers communicate as when people communicate. Computers that use different communication protocols cannot talk to each other. Protocols control transmission speeds, the direction of transmission, error detection and correction, and interruption techniques to name a few. As communication between machines becomes more and more important, standard telecommunication protocols are developing.

### Microcomputer Software

Microcomputer communication software serves two purposes. First, the software allows the microcomputer and the modem to function in a coordinated way. Software provides the instructions for dialing telephone numbers, establishing connections, and breaking connections when conversations are complete. Second, the software allows the user to set and change the protocols necessary for data communication. On the simplest level, microcomputer communication software converts a microcomputer into a dumb terminal capable only of sending and receiving information from another computer (see Chapter 5). More commonly, the software allows the microcomputer to act both as a terminal and as a processor. By setting transmission speeds, direction, and establishing error-correction techniques, communication is established between devices. The software allows for data to be captured on a disk from which, if required, it can later be sent to a printer. This process is called **downloading**. Similarly, files stored on a microcomputer can be sent over the communications link to another machine, which is called **uploading**.

Without software, the links could not be established and data could not be transmitted between machines. Clearly, computers and computing devices can communicate at widely varying speeds, using a wide variety of media

---

## NETWORKING

A **computer network** is frequently defined as a group of computers and computer devices linked together over transmission lines so that information and resources can be shared. Computer networks, especially those that span the continent, are electronic "old-boy/girl networks," connecting people with similar interests in a given industry, field, or discipline. At the physical level, computer networks link machines. At the user level, computer networks link people to people, and people to the information they seek.

Computer networks link computers and peripherals for a specific purpose. These purposes can be very simple: a small office may have two microcomputers that need to share a printer or an extra hard disk. They can be as complex as a national airline reservation system or a research network for supercomputer users and other researchers such as NSFnet. How the network is organized, what equipment is used, and how connections are made depend on the distances and devices involved as well as the needs of the users. Let us examine how networks are designed.

## Early Connections

While the term *networking* has only been recently applied to computers, simple forms of computer networks have existed since the early 1950s. Prior to the microcomputer revolution, a computer-using organization purchased a multiuser machine, either a mainframe or a minicomputer, and connected terminals, printers, card readers, and other peripherals to it. Such a machine was called a **host computer**. The host computer and its associated devices were located close together. Distances between devices were limited, and connections consisted of coaxial cables. Transmission speeds were high. Both equipment and access were centralized, so the cost of resources was spread over a number of users. Within organizations, computing centers with specialized staffs were given the task of locating information stored in the central computer. Pertinent information was requested from the computing center, and the results were provided hours or days later.

In the early 1980s, the host-computer model was radically altered. With the introduction of the microcomputer, computing power became available to everyone. The model shifted from a highly centralized host computer to individual stand-alone machines. Nowhere was this more evident than in offices and on college campuses. In offices, microcomputers appeared where no computer connections existed before. On college campuses, rooms previously filled with terminals were replaced by rooms full of stand-alone personal machines. The microcomputer model had several advantages over the centralized model:

- Distance was not a limitation. A microcomputer could be placed anywhere, since it did not require a connection to anything else.

- Microcomputers were easier and "friendlier" to use than multiuser systems.

- Specialized software, such as spreadsheets and word processing programs, increased productivity.

Unfortunately, the stand-alone model had disadvantages as well. While it did increase access to computing power, it also isolated its users. In the centralized model all information was shared and access was limited. In the decentralized model access was widespread but information was limited to what was stored on each individual machine. People working together on a project could not share their results. Information was often duplicated on many machines, increasing the risk that one or more of these copies was inaccurate. Furthermore, the stand-alone model made it difficult to share expensive peripherals such as laser printers and plotters.

Computer networks are the outgrowth of these two divergent models. Along with the awareness that neither the host model nor the stand-alone model was ideal came technological advances. Connection devices and communication software make networking possible.

## Local Area Networks

When computers, printers, storage devices, and other peripherals are linked together so they can communicate in any combination, a network is formed. The most common network, called a **local area network (LAN)**, covers a limited geographic area such as a series of offices, an entire building, a number of nearby buildings owned or operated by a single organization, or a college campus. This limited-area network shares resources and information among a variety of users. LANs connect many devices simultaneously over a common communications channel.

The connections between the devices in local area networks are continually undergoing change. Coaxial cable systems, for example, may be replaced by fiber optic systems. However, all LANs consist of communications channels and specialized systems software that enable the hardware to communicate. Currently, the most popular LANs use Ethernet. Developed by Xerox in association with Intel Corp. and Digital Equipment Corp., Ethernet is a LAN in which all computers and devices are connected to a single coaxial cable. Specially designed communications software is used to control transmission. Sharing a common high-speed channel results in rapid communication. Complex systems often require signal boosters to ensure accurate transmission of data. Slower speed LANs, such as AppleTalk, can be operated on twisted-pair copper wire.

## Wide Area Networks

We have seen that direct computer connections (point-to-point) can be made between two computing devices, regardless of distance, by using modems. In addition, groups of computers and peripherals can communicate over limited distances using LANs. Such computers linked together provide a unique environment for the sharing of resources, such as sophisticated laser and color printers, as well as the sharing of ideas.

Connecting LANs over long-distance communications lines with modems or other forms of digital communication creates **wide area networks**. In addition to the LANs, individuals using desktop computers can call into these networks using modems and standard telephone lines. A wide area network environment enables computer users everywhere there is a telephone to share information, ideas, and computer resources. Through such networks, time and distance cease to separate people. This sounds like a futuristic vision, but it is not. It exists today.

A wide range of national and international wide area networks is currently available. Some, such as Dow Jones and MEDLINE, allow subscribers to search huge data bases for the latest up-to-the-minute information. Some make our daily lives easier by allowing for worldwide air, hotel, and automobile reservations. Others permit the purchase of tickets to shows, concerts, and sporting events from our homes. Still others link academic institutions in the United States to their counterparts in dozens of countries around the world. Others, sponsored by the U.S. government, enable researchers to share ideas and equipment.

Networks have developed so that resources, ideas, and information can be shared. Such sharing improves productivity and stimulates creativity. Distance and time zones cease to be problems for collaborative efforts, and expensive resources become available to those who need them.

Wide-area networks fall into four general groups: bulletin boards, academic computer networks, corporate/business networks, and information networks.

## Bulletin Boards

The simplest wide area network is the electronic bulletin board. Everyone is familiar with the concept of a bulletin board. At home they consist of important papers, phone numbers, coupons, and other items secured to some type of board for safe keeping. In grocery stores they announce garage sales, advertise services such as house painting and baby sitting, and offer discount coupons on grocery items. The classified pages of college and local newspapers often have sections in which people can leave personal messages, such as "Happy Birthday Dad" or "Male 21 interested in blonde female," and advertise services and products. **Electronic bulletin board systems (EBBS or BBS)** serve the same purpose as their non-electronic counterparts. Instead of thumbtacks and tape, electronic BBSs use computers, modems, and the telephone. To connect to the bulletin board, the board's computer is called on the telephone by another computer. Messages are left and information is exchanged over this electronic connection.

Hundreds of thousands of computer owners use their computers as a means of developing electronic relationships. Bulletin boards facilitate the exchange of all kinds of information from stock quotes and telephone numbers to programs and user-written software called **shareware**. Chatting electronically with others, discussing hardware and software problems, or simply socializing with electronic friends are popular bulletin board pastimes.

Computer bulletin boards take two forms: public boards and commercial boards. Most public BBSs are free. They are maintained by an individual or a group, or they are sponsored by an organization such as a business or university. Such systems are usually limited to one machine type (Apple, IBM, Amiga, Macintosh), although some can be reached by any microcomputer. Most systems have on-line help facilities to assist new users. Just as information posted with a thumbtack on a grocery store bulletin board is available to anyone who passes by, so information posted electronically is available to anyone who gains access to a given electronic board.

Commercial bulletin boards are components of larger commercial data base services. Bulletin boards such as The Source and CompuServe are available only to subscribers. Fees are based on the length of time a subscriber is connected to the service. Commercial bulletin boards include news services, access to special publications or stock market reviews, and electronic mail services as well as entertainment, hotel, and restaurant information. Software can be exchanged, free classified ads posted, and electronic shopping or banking is available.

Bulletin boards provide users with an easy and convenient means of communicating. Through the telephone and microcomputers, they link interesting people throughout the country.

## Academic Computer Networks

Within the last five years, every major American university has become connected to a variety of academic computer networks. All of these are interconnected so that messages and files can be electronically sent anywhere within the American academic community. The purpose of **academic computer networks** is to provide an environment where geographically separated faculty members, researchers, administrators, and students can communicate, share ideas and resources, and work jointly on projects. Access and use of computer networks has produced a noticeable increase in the productivity of computer scientists and other scientists and researchers.

Wide area academic computer networks offer a number of services. These include electronic mail, file transfer, and access to remote systems.

Electronic mail, introduced in Chapter 1, is the most commonly used service on all computer networks. Often called *E-mail*, it is a computerized version of the U.S. Postal Service. Each user has an electronic mailbox on a host computer. Just as with a home or office mailbox, others can leave messages in the mailbox for later reading.

An E-mail user creates a message on a local computer. This message can range from a multi-page report to a few lines such as: "Hello, I expect to be visiting your university in March. Can you make the necessary local arrangements for me?" The writer supplies the local electronic mail system with the computer address of the person to whom the message is going. This is an electronic address having any number of forms similar to `buffalo!kershner` or `kershner@buffalo.edu`. The local mail system sends the message across the network to the address specified, where it appears in the appropriate electronic mailbox. The receiver can then respond when it is convenient.

Electronic mail is much faster and more reliable than postal services. Messages are transmitted in minutes rather than days. Since messages wait until the receiver has the opportunity to read them, they are not subject to the typical game of "telephone tag," often played when trying to reach busy people by telephone. (A phone call is made to a colleague who is not in. A message is taken. The colleague returns the call only to find the original caller is now not

## *On Line*

# *"TALKING" OVER E-MAIL*

Long-distance relationships are always difficult. Letter writing takes too long and people just aren't themselves on the telephone.

Electronic mail, or E-mail, has come to the rescue for many people. E-mail provides an entirely new mode of communication. Over long-distance networks, campus-wide networks, and corporate electronic mail systems, people correspond, share secrets, ideas and reports, trade gossip, and ask for information. Over E-mail people communicate.

While there are no formal rules governing what to write or not to write using E-mail, an etiquette does exist. Users are warned not to "cc," or copy, messages to too many others so that the messages do not wind up on the wrong screens. Saturating the network with classified ads or political announcements is frowned upon. Some companies, such as 3Com, have developed informal rules. 3Com's E-manners, for example, warn against "flaring," or using E-mail to solve personal problems rather than talking things over in person.

Real communication involves emotion. The E-mail equivalent of yelling is typing in capital letters, while writing messages entirely in lower case is considered mumbling. Most remarkable is the freedom people feel when using E-mail. Experts feel that E-mail can contain very open conversations where participants really let their hair down. E-mail has been used to make romantic dates, plan parties, and just blow off steam.

Many executives resist using E-mail because they feel that typing is for those lower on the corporate ladder. Brian Blackmarr, a Dallas-based office-automation expert, told *Newsweek* about one manager who was so frustrated at having to use a keyboard that he sent an obscene message to the information-processing director. The message was signed "Anonymous." Unfortunately for the executive, his E-mail system automatically attached information identifying him as the sender.

Privacy on E-mail is always a problem. While messages are supposed to be secret, it is easy enough to send a copy of another person's message. Federal law makes intercepting E-mail a crime, but many networks are rumored to have message graveyards where messages can be read by anyone with the correct access code. The sheer volume of E-mail on most systems may make this concern unnecessary.

The benefits of E-mail outweigh any of the risks. With E-mail, students can leave messages for instructors; reports, papers, and ideas can be shared over long distances; and friends can keep in touch whenever they have a moment. David Ferris, a computer consultant, told *Newsweek* that E-mail results in "fewer people wandering around the corridors, nudging each other. It saves time—and it encourages workers of all ranks to change the rigid hierarchical nature of communication." Besides, sending and receiving E-mail is fun.

*Source:* Barbara Kantrowitz, Nadine Joseph, and Susan Agrest, "A New Way of Talking," *Newsweek*, March 17, 1986, p. 71.

in. A message is left and the tag cycle continues.) E-mail is a rapid, easy way for people to communicate. Time zones and meetings no longer interfere with communication and the sharing of ideas.

With file transfer, files can be transferred between any two computers attached to the network. Files can contain papers, computer programs, computer graphics, and anything else that can be represented electronically. The ability to transfer such information makes collaborative efforts easy. A paper can be drafted in one location and reviewed, corrected, and commented on in another location on the same day. A program with a bug can be sent across the country to be debugged. Using a computer network, joint projects are not limited to a single location. They can involve individuals across the nation and in other parts of the world.

Through a network, a scientist can connect, or **log in**, to a distant computer without disconnecting from the local computer. In other words, using high-speed computer links, a scientist connected to a mainframe at one university can also connect and run programs, for example, on a supercomputer located at a distant university. Compared to using a modem and standard telephone lines, such a system provides a high-speed, relatively inexpensive means of communicating. Of course, the user must have the right to gain access to all the computers upon which connections are made.

While all academic networks provide similar services, their goals and constituencies are different. The following are two examples of academic computer networks.

BITNET (Because It's Time NETwork) is currently a cooperative network begun between City University of New York and Yale University in 1981. It is a discipline-independent network serving more than 400 colleges and universities in the United States with connections in 21 countries, including Canada, Israel, Japan, and most European nations. The goal was to create a network connecting all higher educational institutions. Through BITNET, faculty members, administrators, and students can communicate, share ideas, exchange electronic mail, and transfer files. Everything from research papers and financial reports to personal chats and career advice is sent over the network. Connections are made over leased telephone lines paid for by individual institutions. Reasonable membership fees are charged to support services.

NSFnet is a network in the process of creation. In 1984 the National Science Foundation (NSF) established the Office of Advanced Computing, whose task it was to provide both supercomputers and access to them to researchers nationwide. Two projects resulted. One project is charged with creating supercomputing centers across the country. The other originally established a national network connecting the scientists to the supercomputers. Currently, NSFnet has links to about a dozen mid-level networks in addition to the supercomputer centers. These mid-level networks have developed regionally or statewide with the support of the National Science Foundation, local governments, and universities. Eventually, NSFnet expects to develop into a hierarchy of networks: a national backbone with worldwide links, dozens of mid-level or statewide networks, and about 500 campus-level networks.

## Corporate/Business Networks

As might be expected, if the academic community has found networking to be an invaluable tool that increases productivity, the business community would find it useful in much the same way. Most of the networks used by businesses provide benefit in two areas:

1. *Intra-organizational services and productivity.* Local area networks are used to improve intra-organizational services and productivity. Using corporate networks, ideas, information, and resources can be shared within a company. Such networks improve decision making by giving executives the data needed to make decisions. In addition, networks improve access to the expertise available within an organization. Furthermore, expensive computer resources can be effectively shared at a substantial saving.

2. *Consumer services.* Wide area networks provide new consumer services simply not available prior to their development. Such services include electronic banking, advanced hotel and transportation reservation systems, and improvements in customer service within large retail chains.

While local area networks are playing an increasing role in the daily working of America's corporations, they have had only limited impact on the everyday lives of American citizens. On the other hand, wide area corporate networks are increasingly evident around us.

**Transportation Industry**   Anyone who has visited a travel agent; taken a trip by plane, ship, or train; or rented a car has seen first hand the effect of computers on the transportation industry. What is not as obvious is that the services provided are available because of wide area networks. The oldest of these networks is SABRE, the airline reservation system developed by American Airlines. Using such networks, agents can reserve and cancel seats, check flight schedules, print tickets and boarding passes, arrange for special meals, as well as provide services for the handicapped and children traveling alone. SABRE and similar networks operated by other airlines include information on all flights (see Figure 14.7). System access is not limited to travel agents. Airline networks allow individuals to call the airlines and make reservations or check flights. The networks contain a large data base of information including, weather reports, landing schedules, and pricing structures. Similar services are available on the networks serving other modes of transportation, such as trains and buses.

**Hotel and Motel Industry**   Just as individuals and travel agents can make transportation arrangements by connecting with industry-wide reservation systems, so too can hotel and motel reservations and services be arranged. The

**Figure 14.7**    Computerized Travel: Using wide area networks such as SABRE, travel agents can make reservations, print tickets, and arrange for special airline services.

largest hotel and motel chains, including Holiday Inn (Holidex) and Hilton Hotels, have their own chain-wide computer network. By calling a central number, usually toll free, and speaking with a reservation clerk or connecting a microcomputer directly, rooms can be reserved, and special services such as cribs and handicapped facilities can be arranged. These systems also maintain customer billing, automated wakeup services, inventory controls, and forwarding of messages.

**Electronic Banking**    The largest, most comprehensive industry-wide network exists in the banking industry. The motivation for establishing such a network came from the Federal Reserve System. Trillions of transactions are carried out annually between the Federal Reserve and its member banks. In order to handle the volume of transactions and the amount of funds transferred between banks, the Federal Reserve established FEDWIRE. Using this system, funds are transferred electronically between banks. Effective, accurate accounting is maintained without any cash or formal paperwork leaving member banks. This system has proved so effective that independent cooperative systems have sprung up worldwide to serve other thrift organizations. These **electronic fund transfer (EFT)** systems have made national and international banking quicker, safer, easier, and substantially less expensive.

As banking became more computerized and networking became a more common procedure between banks, the idea of banking networks was extended to the bank customer as well. With the establishment of automated teller machines (ATMs), local area networks designed specifically for routine bank transactions became available to the public.

**Retail Industry**     As was discussed earlier, cash registers don't simply store money anymore. In most large retail stores and an increasing number of smaller stores as well, cash registers are modified computer terminals or **point-of-sale (POS) systems**. While these systems still handle cash transactions, they also print customer bills, check a customer's credit, and keep track of inventory. These terminals are the end-points of local area networks established within a given retail organization. The majority of these networks serve individual stores within a specific region, such as western New York or southeastern California. The large chain stores, such as Sears and J.C. Penney, have national networks connecting individual stores with centralized warehouse and credit facilities.

## Information Networks

We use computer networks almost daily. These links provide access to information and services unheard of 10 years ago.

The information explosion has prompted the establishment of electronic data bases to store the massive amounts of information being generated. Some of these data bases are limited to specific types of information, such as journal articles and abstracts in the fields of medicine (MEDLINE) and law (LEXIS). Other data bases gather information and organize it for easy access. Sources include newspaper and magazine articles, movie reviews, stock quotes, and corporate reports. Initially, such information was available only to a few selected organizations. Connections often required specialized equipment and software, and high membership fees where charged.

In recent years, however, many of these data base organizations or **information utilities**, have "gone public," making the information available to any microcomputer owner willing to subscribe to the service. Fee structures reflect the needs of the utilities' users. Just as with long-distance telephone charges, fees are higher during working hours than late at night or on weekends. Those individuals and businesses that require up-to-the-minute information during the work day pay higher fees for the service. Those for whom time is not quite as critical make alternative arrangements.

Access to information utilities is a limited form of networking that is basically the sharing of resources. Through these networks, individuals across the nation and the world can tap into the information available.

A number of information utilities have taken the data base retrieval model and advanced it considerably, offering additional services to subscribers. These utilities, called **information networks**, offer subscribers the kinds of services that the academic networks provide their users. Information networks give users access to data base information and bulletin boards. They make electronic mail available and easy to use, and often provide travel and shopping opportunities. In a sense, they are full-service networks whereby subscribers share resources as well as ideas.

Many such networks now exist (see Figure 14.8). The three most popular are The Source, operated by Reader's Digest; CompuServe, a division of H&R Block; and Dow Jones News/Retrieval Service, operated by Dow Jones & Co., publishers of the *Wall Street Journal*. Subscribers to these services can send electronic mail to other network subscribers; catch up on the day's news, weather, and sports; and search extensive data bases for information ranging from the condi-

---

**Figure 14.8**     Information Network: Subscribers to full-service networks such as CompuServe have access to data base information, bulletin boards, and electronic mail services.

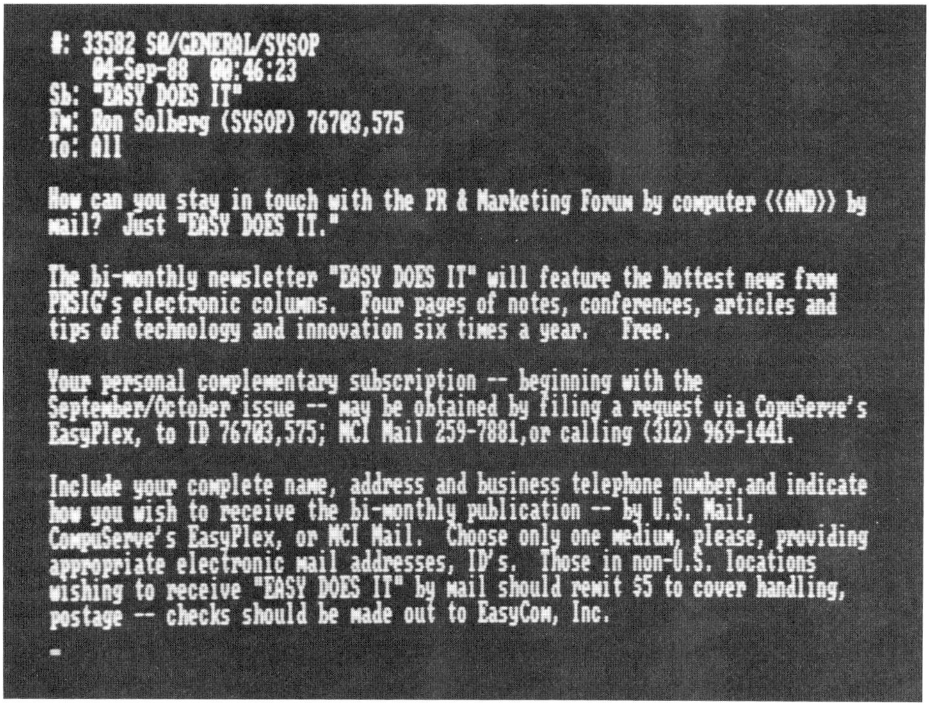

tion of the dollar on international markets to computer crime. The most frequent search is for financial data, including information on stocks, bonds, and investments. Portfolio analysis is often available, and historical information on corporate America is maintained.

Special-interest groups use the bulletin boards provided by these information networks to share ideas ranging from medical treatments to the solutions to complex computer games. Subscribers can check airline schedules, buy tickets, and shop in electronic catalogs. Some services, such as Dow Jones, focus more on business people, while still providing a full range of services.

Information networks provide their subscribers with access to ideas, information, and people to an extent never before imagined. Just as academic networks have reduced the barriers that separate researchers, students, and administrators, information networks are making time, distance, location, and politics irrelevant to individual and corporate subscribers.

As computers have become more important in our lives, we have come to realize that while their isolated use has its advantages, isolation in any form has disadvantages as well. Networking provides us with a means of sharing information, ideas, and resources without reducing the benefits stand-alone systems provide. Networking has the potential to help unify the planet and its people despite time and distance.

## SUMMARY

The transmission of information over long distances is called telecommunication. This information includes data transmitted by telephone and television, as well as computer-generated data. Telecomputing is the exchange of information between computers and computing devices over communication lines.

The simplest way to connect computers and computing devices together is to connect the equipment with wires. Such direct connections operate only over limited distances.

Computers can communicate over telephone wires through the use of a modem. Telephone wires transmit analog rather than digital signals. Modems are used to code and decode messages and computer data for transmission.

Transmission channels are the pathways used to send computer data from one place to another. They are usually bi-directional. A channel's bandwidth reflects the amount of data that can be transmitted in a given block of time. The wider the bandwidth, the faster the transfer of data.

Communications channels use twisted-pair copper wires, coaxial cable, microwave signals, and fiber optic cable to transmit information.

Software is required to organize and interpret the signals transmitted between devices. Telecommunication protocols control transmission speeds, the direction of transmission, error detection and correction, and interruption techniques. Microcomputer communication software allows the microcomputer to act as both a terminal and a processor. Uploading and downloading of information are facilitated.

A computer network is a group of computers and computer devices linked together over transmission lines so that information, resources, and ideas can be shared. Computers linked in a limited geographic area are called a local area network (LAN). Connecting LANs and other computers using long-distance communication lines and modems creates a wide area network. Wide area networks provide universities, industries, government, and individuals with access to data base information, electronic mail (E-mail), file transfer, and remote log in. Networking allows people to share ideas, information, and resources despite time and distance.

## Key Words

As an extra review of the chapter, try defining the following terms. If you have trouble with any of them, refer to the page number listed.

academic computer network  *(363)*  
acoustic coupler  *(353)*  
analog signal  *(352)*  
bandwidth  *(353)*  
broadband channels  *(355)*  
coaxial cable  *(355)*  
computer network  *(359)*  
digital signals  *(252)*  
direct-connect modem  *(352)*  
downloading  *(359)*  
electronic bulletin board (EBBS or BBS)  *(362)*  
electronic fund transfer  *(368)*  
external direct-connect modem  *(352)*  
fiber optic cable  *(357)*  
host computer  *(360)*  
information network  *(369)*  

information utility  *(368)*  
intelligent modem  *(353)*  
internal direct-connect modem  *(352)*  
local area network (LAN)  *(361)*  
log in  *(365)*  
microwave signals  *(356)*  
modem  *(252)*  
narrowband channels  *(355)*  
point-of-sale (POS) systems  *(368)*  
protocols  *(358)*  
shareware  *(362)*  
telecommunication  *(350)*  
telecomputing  *(350)*  
twisted-pair copper wire  *(355)*  
uploading  *(359)*  
voiceband channels  *(355)*  
wide area network  *(361)*

---

## Test Your Knowledge

1. Define *telecomputing.*

2. How is telecommunications different from telecomputing?

3. What is the simplest way to connect computing devices?

4. What does a modem do?

5. List the three types of modems.

6. What is a communication channel?

7. Define *bandwidth.*

8. How do narrowband, voiceband, and wideband channels differ?

9. List four kinds of communications media.

10. Why is fiber optic cable popular as a transmission medium?

11. What is a computer communication protocol?

12. Why is software important in microcomputer commuenciations?

13. What is a computer network?

14. What does LAN stand for?

15. What is a wide area network?

16. How does E-mail work?

17. List the industries that are currently making extensive use of wide area networks.

18. What is an information utility?

19. How does an information network differ from an information utility?

20. Name the three most popular information networks.

---

## Expand Your Knowledge

1. Contact a representative of your computing center. Discuss your campus network. What transmission medium is most popular? Are all computers and computing equipment connected to the network? What academic networks are available to researchers on your campus? Can anyone use E-mail? Write a short (three to five page) paper detailing your information.

2. Automated libraries are gaining popularity on college campuses. Increasingly, such library automation systems are connected to campus-wide networks. Research such library/campus-network connections. Write a short paper on the services such interconnections provide.

3. In addition to BITNET and NFSnet, other academic networks are common. Write a short paper on the history and use of one of the following networks: CSnet, ARPAnet, UUCPnet, BITNET, or NSFnet.

4. Investigate the public bulletin boards available in your local area. Compile a list of these bulletin boards. Include phone numbers, services, fees if any, and contacts. Sources can include books in your local or campus library, local computer-user groups, your local paper, and computer stores.

# 15

# Evaluating Computers and Software

## Chapter Outline

Buying a Computer—Know Your Needs
Steps in Purchasing a Computer • Purchase Sources (Computer Stores; University and College Buying Programs; Mail-Order and Catalog Sales)

Protecting Your Purchase
Surge Protectors • Insurance Riders

Buying Software
Necessary Software • Steps for Purchasing Software

Learning and Support
Documentation • Information and Self-Education • Courses and Training • User Groups

*So, You want to buy a computer! What do you need it for?* While this may seem like a strange introduction to a chapter dealing with the purchase of computers and software, it is a singularly important question. Buying a computer with all of its associated peripherals and software is expensive. Research indicates that computers are often the third most expensive purchase made by an individual during his or her lifetime. The gold and silver medals go to the purchase of a house and a car. If you cannot instantly identify your reasons for purchasing a computer, you don't need one. Furthermore, answers such as, "It will help me in school," "It will make me more organized," or "I'll use it to balance my checkbook and pay bills" are not sufficiently compelling reasons to purchase a computer.

In recent years, most of the cheapest computers (costing less than $500) have disappeared from the market. The computer market has evolved rapidly. Consumers are more sophisticated and more demanding than first thought. Computers that were merely sophisticated toys lost their appeal. Today's consumers want computers that are easy to operate, run a wide variety of software, and can produce graphics.

If you are still interested in buying a computer, let me not discourage you. They are valuable tools and can be lots of fun. They are expensive, however, and their varied use makes them different from other consumer purchases. When you buy a toaster, you know or think you know what it does. When you buy a car, assuming you know how to drive, you expect to be able to sit down and immediately drive the car away. While a new car does come with an owner's manual, it is infrequently used.

After studying this chapter, you will be able to:

- List the steps required to successfully purchase a computer.
- Describe the primary sources of computer purchases.
- Identify the types of protection computers require.
- List the steps in purchasing appropriate software.
- Discuss the methods available to learn how to use hardware and software.
- Understand the purpose of user groups.

---

## BUYING A COMPUTER—KNOW YOUR NEEDS

The new owner of a computer can expect to spend many often frustrating hours sitting in front of the machine learning how it operates. Learning to use a computer can be compared to owning and learning to drive a pre-Model T automobile. A lazy drive down a country lane implied hours of driving in circles before the vehicle was actually under human control.

Since computers are not like other consumer products, a more careful approach to their purchase is required. The same care that is used when purchasing a house or a car should be used when purchasing a computer. When purchasing a house or a car, needs are analyzed. With a house, such considerations as the number of bedrooms needed and garage space are examined. With a car, seating capacity is examined, as are the number of doors and engine size.

Once needs have been assessed, affordability is determined and shopping begins. While this approach is time-consuming, in most cases it leads to satisfying purchases. The same measured approach is necessary when buying a computer. Just as with a home, a computer should serve your needs for some time.

## Steps in Purchasing a Computer

There are nine important steps involved in a successful computer purchase.

*Step 1: Analyze your needs.* The more carefully you determine what you are going to do with the computer, the more satisfied you are going to be with the machine you eventually buy. Personal computers are used for widely varying tasks from entertainment to serious research, from word processing to electronic shopping. The most common uses include:

- word processing
- entertainment
- business finance
- personal finance
- record keeping
- general education
- telecommunications
- programming

Buying a computer requires considerable homework. Make a wish list in general terms of the kinds of tasks you expect to do with your computer (see Figure 15.1). Next refine your list. Be specific. Your list might look like this, for example: (1) Write papers and reports and check spelling, (2) Maintain detailed information on record or slide collections, (3) Play computer games or chess, (4) Communicate with other computers from home or work.

Make sure to consider *who* will use the computer. Is it an individual or family purchase? If it is a family machine, everyone should be involved in developing the wish list. If the computer is expected to perform multiple tasks, order your list. The most pressing needs will have the highest priority.

*Step 2: What can I afford?* Deciding how much you can afford to spend is not trivial. A complete computer system, including software, can cost thousands of dollars. A system that is too small to meet your needs cannot perform the identi-

**Figure 15.1**          (a) Home record keeping and (b) entertainment are just two of the many uses of computers today.

(a)

(b)

fied tasks. On the other hand, funds are always limited. If you cannot afford a system that meets your primary needs, a computer is not appropriate at this time. While you can rethink your priorities, you may regret purchasing a machine under adjusted priorities, since it might not meet expectations.

*Step 3: Analyze your software needs.* Determine the software (the specific computer tools) that will meet the needs identified in Step 1. Information is critical. Most consumer products perform a single task. Computers, given the proper software, can perform multiple tasks. Software can be used as a classification tool, since each program performs a specific task or group of tasks. Some software focuses on very specific problems, such as calculating income taxes or maintaining a business inventory. Other packages, such as word processors, data base systems, and communications software, are more general. Carefully identified needs are required if appropriate software is to be located. While it is possible to write your own software, this should be considered only by very experienced programmers.

As an initial phase in your software analysis, match the goals you identified in Step 1 with the available software. For example, writing papers and checking for spelling errors requires a word processor with a spelling checker. Maintaining and accessing information about a record or slide collection can easily be performed by data base software, and communicating with other computers requires communication software.

*Step 4: Research the available software.* Having identified the general software needed, you need to identify the specific packages or the specific features a software package must contain to suit your needs. Remember, not all software packages or languages are available for all microcomputer systems. For example, Apple has the best selection of pre-college educational software, while the financial, record-keeping, and word processing software most frequently used by businesses, such as Lotus, dBASE III Plus, and WordStar, run on IBM and compatible equipment.

The task of researching software can seem overwhelming, but it need not be. Start by talking to people who own computers. What kinds of software and hardware do they have? Are they satisfied with their purchases? What software is used at your school? What packages have you heard about? Software must be determined *before* hardware can be selected. Many software packages, including games, spreadsheets, data base systems, and desktop publishers, require specialized hardware. Many packages have memory requirements.

Now, go to the library. The library is an outstanding source of information about computers and software. Increasingly, public and university libraries are providing access to computers and software. Such computer sites provide an ideal unpressured way to experiment with computers and software. Public and college libraries carry a wide variety of computer magazines, many of which regularly review computer products. Magazines such as *Byte, Family Computing,*

**Figure 15.2**      Computer Magazines: Numerous computer magazines are on the newsstands to help buyers choose a computer and software.

*Personal Computing,* and *Consumer Reports* give advice to the consumer about computer hardware and software (see Figure 15.2).

In addition to using friends, neighbors, and the library as information resources, computer courses are available at schools and community centers. Learning about computers and software makes intelligent consumers. Once you know what kind of software you need, you are ready to visit computer stores.

*Step 5: Shop for software and identify hardware requirements.* Software will determine the amount of memory and peripheral equipment you need. Plan on visiting a number of computer stores. Individual stores will sell different brands of computers and have salespeople with varying hardware and software experience. Use the salespeople as resources. Let them try to sell you a machine by demonstrating software packages that suit your needs. However, you are "just shopping." At this stage you are not yet prepared to buy anything. Leave your checkbook at home. Some stores will pressure you to "buy a computer today!" Do not let the salespeople snow you with computer buzzwords. Be skeptical. If the salesperson is confusing you or refuses to answer your questions, shop elsewhere. Computer stores abound and most have staffs that are competent, easy to work with, and understanding.

While identifying software packages that satisfy your needs, take careful notes. What hardware and peripherals do the packages require? For example, communication packages require a modem, word processors require a printer if you intend to get a hard copy of your written product, and many games require a color monitor to be effective. Many packages have memory requirements.

Ask questions—the more you ask, the happier you will be with the product you eventually buy. Consider these questions: What machines do the packages you're interested in run on? When the package you liked was demonstrated, did the machine have any special hardware? Will you need that hardware to use the program? What does the software cost? What does the hardware cost? If you buy everything together in a package, can you get a discount?

*Step 6: Identify the computer that suits your individual needs.* Think carefully about the software packages you have seen demonstrated. List the packages you preferred in one column. Next to each package list the hardware it requires. Weigh the following:

1. *Compatibility.* Is compatibility important to you? Do you want to share files with others? If so, you must have a compatible machine.

2. *Expandability.* Is the computer system you've identified expandable? As your computing needs and expectations grow can your computer grow with you? As your needs change you may need to add more memory or peripherals. For example, future software may require a voice synthesizer or a modem.

Adjust your lists to reflect these considerations. Be sure to include in your software list packages you have used in school or in the office. The more familiar you are with software packages the quicker you will put your purchase to effective use. Prioritize both lists and check to see that the packages and hardware you've outlined satisfy the needs listed in Step 1.

*Step 7: Go shopping again.* You have undoubtedly seen more than one machine that could satisfy your needs (see Figure 15.3). This should not make you nervous. If you were shopping for a car you would expect to find more than one suitable vehicle. A car would be selected, at least in part, on price, overall design, and available options. Select your computer the same way. Comparison shop, but price should not be the sole factor in your selection. Service and customer support, including setup, instruction, and a willingness to answer questions before and after your purchase should play a considerable role. To some degree, you get what you pay for. Computers can be purchased through the mail. While such purchases can save you money, customer support is essentially unavailable. It is very difficult to explain a problem to a sales representative over the telephone. Similarly, if you purchase your computer from a local organization, select one that will help you "get up and running." While you should not expect weeks of one-on-one instruction, some hand-holding is reasonable.

**Figure 15.3**   Computer Shopping: Selecting a computer from the vast array available, such as these from IBM, can be difficult.

*Step 8: Purchase your machine and arrange for support and service.* When you've located the machine you want, spend some time with the sales representative arranging for support. Many computer stores will assemble the computer and provide some initial instruction on its operation. Be sure to understand all warranties and guaranties. Computers do break down. Discuss service with the salesperson. Different levels of repair services are available. Repairs done in your home or business, called **on-site service**, can be very expensive. Repair service pick up or customer drop off are more reasonable alternatives for microcomputers. Ask about the availability and cost of loaner equipment while your machine is being repaired. As with a car, once you've gotten used to having a computer around, its absence can prove very inconvenient.

*Step 9: Enjoy your machine.* Take time to learn how to use your machine effectively. Lessons may be appropriate. Initially, learning to use a computer can be frustrating. But it will also be a source of fascination and fun. If you shopped carefully, your computer will satisfy your needs and you will find uses for your computer system that you neither considered nor envisioned.

## Purchase Sources

Computers can be purchased in a number of different ways. The three most popular are computer stores, university and college buying programs, and mail-order sales.

**Computer Stores**   Local computer stores sell a wide variety of hardware and software (see Figure 15.4). Some specialize in specific brands while others sell

**Figure 15.4**     The Computer Store: Some computer stores sell specific brands, others offer a variety of products.

machines from many manufacturers. Sales representatives are usually knowledgeable and helpful. Unfortunately, staff turnover is high, and not all representatives are equally trained. Many computer stores have a service department and can trouble shoot hardware problems. They also provide advice and some instruction on hardware and software products they sell. The cost of these services is included in the price charged for hardware and software. Such local support can be invaluable to new and experienced customers alike.

**University and College Buying Programs**     Many colleges and universities have arrangements with major microcomputer manufacturers to sell computers to students, faculty, and staff at substantial savings. Manufacturers find such arrangements attractive, since they can count on a large number of sales to a constantly changing population. The university community benefits because up-to-date equipment is available at a considerable discount. Standard manufacturer warranties apply to such sales, and many schools pre-test the hardware prior to delivery. Some schools provide inexpensive and convenient on-campus repair facilities. While such programs are economical, most schools cannot provide the type of user support found at local computer stores.

# *On Line*

## COMPUTERS FOR CADETS

The three U.S. military service academies—the Air Force Academy, the Naval Academy, and the Military Academy—have joined a host of other colleges and universities across the country in requiring entering freshmen to purchase microcomputers.

Cadets are buying Zenith Z-248 personal computers, an IBM PC/AT compatible costing approximately $1500 each. The Zenith systems include two external disk drives and 512K of internal memory. Peripheral devices and software are tailored to the needs of individual academies.

All three academies have computing facilities available to all students. However, academy officials agree that the number of hours of academic work assigned to each cadet essentially demand that each cadet have a dedicated machine. Access to computers is critical, and shared facilities cannot meet the students' needs. James L. Moss, director of computing services at the U.S. Naval Academy, recently told *The Chronicle of Higher Education* that "We want to create an information-technology environment so they (the cadets) use the computers in the simplest and most routine jobs." Such an environment can only be provided by cadets owning their own machines.

*Source:* "3 Service Academies Require Students to Buy Computers," *The Chronicle of Higher Education*, p. 42.

**Mail-Order and Catalog Sales** Computers, software, and peripheral devices, like most other products, can be purchased through the mail. Mail-order purchases are usually the least expensive way to buy computers and associated products. Mail-order purchases can reduce costs by as much as 50 percent, although buyers should watch for extra fees connected to shipping and handling that may significantly increase the purchase price. While manufacturers' warranties remain in force with such purchases, customer support is non-existent. A product that does not operate properly under warranty must be returned to the manufacturer in the original box. Once the warranty has expired, users are on their own. However, items that require no user support, such as ribbons, paper, disks, and computer games, are excellent mail-order purchases for the novice.

## PROTECTING YOUR PURCHASE

Today when a personal computer is purchased, all of the components necessary for operation, such as a keyboard, a monitor, internal and external memory, and some sort of operating system, are included. All that is needed to turn this machine into a problem-solving tool is carefully selected software. But two other factors are important as well, surge protectors and insurance riders.

### Surge Protectors

Chapter 5 identified many of the peripheral devices available for today's machines. However, software often dictates a system's hardware. Although computer usage is very individualized, no desktop computer should be purchased without a **surge protector**. This inexpensive and easily overlooked device can save the computer owner hundreds if not thousands of dollars in repairs. A surge protector, costing between $25 and $100, restricts or limits the amount of electrical current passing through an electrical outlet. If line current were constant and never interrupted, a surge protector would be unnecessary. After power failures and, to a lesser degree, when a device is turned on, power surges through lines into electrical devices. Such power surges can be so strong that chips burn out. Surge protectors safeguard electrical equipment from such burnouts at a relatively insignificant cost (see Figure 15.5).

**Figure 15.5**      The Surge Protector.

While surge protectors should always be used with computers, they can provide protection for other devices as well. TVs, VCRs, and microwave ovens contain computer chips that can be damaged by power surges.

### Insurance Riders

Another form of protection recommended for computers is insurance. Many home owner and renter insurance policies do not cover repairs to or replacement of damaged or stolen computers. This is especially true if the computer is partially used for business purposes. Special computer riders available from insurance companies can be added to standard homeowners and renters policies at a nominal cost.

Given the cost of today's computers, peripherals, and software, surge protectors and policy riders are worth the expense.

## BUYING SOFTWARE

When buying a computer system, it is difficult if not impossible to separate the purchase of software from the purchase of hardware. As stated earlier, the more carefully you analyze your computer needs and the more carefully you search for appropriate software to satisfy those needs, the happier you will be with your computer selection. Searching for appropriate software is not trivial. Within each application area, there can be hundreds of packages performing essentially the same task but in somewhat different ways. While many packages are well written and easy to use, this is not always the case. Success in using a program is often a reflection of your computer experience. Packages such as PFS: First Choice are designed for the new user. Other packages, such as Lotus and dBASE, require more experience.

### Necessary Software

Chapter 9 identified the five building block programs: (1) word processing, (2) spreadsheet, (3) file or data base management, (4) communication, and (5) graphics.

While these packages constitute a fairly complete set of problem-solving computer tools, everyone does not need to purchase software from each of these groups. Packages are only as good or as useful as the person using them. A spreadsheet program is an inherently useful program. However, it is valueless to the computer owner who has no interest in using the computer for personal or business finance. A data base program is an extremely valuable tool for organizing information, whether recipes, information about a stamp collection, or tax records. However, entering the data into a data base is a very time-consuming task. Without the necessary time commitment to data entry, a file or data base program is worthless. Programs are only useful if they are used.

## Steps for Purchasing Software

Software needs and interests change, and computer owners purchase additional software to satisfy these needs. Just as careful planning is needed when purchasing a computer, so planning is necessary whenever software is purchased. The following six steps contribute to successful software purchases. They are applicable for initial as well as for future software purchases.

*Step 1: Analyze your needs.* Determine the type of software necessary to meet these needs. Create a list of the features you require. Imagine yourself using the package. What are your expectations? Adjust your list to reflect your expectations.

*Step 2: Identify packages that suit your needs.* Since software packages vary considerably in the features they contain and their ease of use, learn as much as possible about what is available. Read software reviews. Talk to other users. Test available software. Experiment with the software used by your friends, available at school, or in the library. Do not overlook local computer stores. They often have software you can test prior to purchase.

When reading software reviews, remember that, just like a movie, software appeals differently to different individuals. Just as a movie critic can pan a movie you absolutely loved, a software reviewer can praise a package you find hard to understand and difficult to use. It is often helpful to read several different reviews. Different reviewers will focus on different package features. By reading a number of reviews, a clearer picture of a package's advantages and disadvantages will emerge.

While it is possible to develop software to satisfy your needs, good software requires considerable programming skill and is very time-consuming to write. Programmers can be hired to write software tailored to specific needs, but such programs are very expensive.

*Step 3: Assess your hardware.* Different packages often have different memory and hardware requirements. Before purchasing any program, be sure it will run on your machine or be prepared to purchase the additional hardware required.

*Step 4: Determine what you can afford.* Price differences between packages can be significant. Be careful to purchase a package that will satisfy your present and anticipated needs. Avoid software extras you will never use.

*Step 5: Comparison shop.* Once you've determined which package you want, compare prices. Shop around. Just as you would look for the best price for a TV or VCR, do the same for software. Different computer stores sell the same software packages at different prices. Do not overlook mail-order software firms. Ordering software by mail can result in considerable savings. However, do not

**Figure 15.6**    Software: Comparison shopping for software can result in savings for the customer.

shop by price alone. Just as with the purchase of hardware, user support can mean the difference between a package that meets your needs and one that is worthless. When you are learning to use a new package, being able to show an experienced user a problem and to ask about specific features can be vital. Many manufacturers provide toll-free customer support telephone lines. While price is important, user support can turn confusion into insight (see Figure 15.6).

*Step 6: Purchase only what you need.* Learning to effectively use software requires time. It is easiest to learn one package at a time. New packages are constantly being developed, and existing software is always being improved, refined, and made easier to use. Prices change. Buy only what you need at the moment. Don't buy software that may sit on the shelf and gather dust.

Carefully selected software will transform the computer from a confusing machine to a problem-solving tool.

## LEARNING AND SUPPORT

Learning to use a computer requires time and attention. Unlike a television set, it cannot simply be plugged in and turned on.

### Documentation

All hardware and software come with use and operating instructions called **documentation**. In most cases, documentation consists of written instruction manuals that try to explain everything from installation and general use to the trouble shooting of errors. Unfortunately, most documentation is written by the people who developed the hardware or software and understand its operation. Pages are often filled with buzz words and jargon the novice has yet to learn. Most new users find documentation anything but user-friendly. It is a valuable resource once you know how a package works, but as an initial learning tool it leaves much to be desired.

### Information and Self-Education

It is very difficult for a novice to learn to use a computer and make effective use of software simply by reading the accompanying documentation. For some, learning by experimentation, sometimes called **useful hacking**, is a rewarding experience. For most, more formal techniques are required. Computer books designed to assist in understanding software can be found in most bookstores. These are not textbooks. Rather, they are how-to guides written by people who are writing about software they have mastered. Such books are filled with examples and sample problems readers can follow as they work on their computers. Error messages are explained, common errors are examined, and possible solutions provided.

In addition to books, dozens of computer magazines are available at newsstands. Many of these include reviews and reports explaining how to make better use of both software and hardware. Many local newspapers and computer magazines include question-and-answer columns in which experts provide solutions to computer problems.

### Courses and Training

For many, however, such self-help approaches are inadequate. Computers require hands-on instruction. Two forms of hands-on instruction are popular, tutorials and courses.

A number of manufacturers include self-teaching materials, or **tutorials**, along with their printed documentation. This material includes a series of lessons a user can follow while sitting at the computer. Each lesson is designed to provide instruction on the operation of a small portion of the software. *Hands-on* is the key. Such learning is self-guided and self-paced. Lessons can be provided on disk, as part of the printed documentation, or both.

Self-teaching material can be very useful, but it does not allow the learner to ask questions. Furthermore, it is often inflexible. For many, the quickest and easiest way to learn to use hardware and software is to enroll in a short course. Such courses are widely available. Some are provided by computer stores to assist and encourage customers. Short and semester-long computer courses are offered by local colleges and school districts. While the costs of such courses vary, most are quite reasonable.

On the more expensive side, private organizations offer weekend classes designed to teach a specific software package very quickly. These course can be very effective and very expensive. In addition, private lessons can provide an effective way to learn to use computers and software.

## User Groups

All over the nation and in many foreign countries, computer users have formed clubs or groups called **user groups**. User groups form around particular types or models of computers. For example, Apple groups are distinct from Macintosh groups even though both machines are built by Apple Computer Corp. Groups exist for IBM PCs and compatibles, Apples, Ataris, Amigas, and many others, including machines that are no longer manufactured. (Machines are called **orphans** if they are no longer being manufactured.) These groups provide their members with many types of support ("No, you are not crazy if you think the documentation for that package was written by a Martian") as well as hardware and software information. Members share ideas and problem-solving tips. User-written programs, or **shareware**, are made available to members. Shareware is public-domain software that is available for free distribution and has not been protected under U.S. Copyright laws. Many groups maintain large software lending libraries where members can try out software prior to purchase.

Some individuals join users groups for the hands-on support available from more experienced users. Others appreciate the social atmosphere where ideas and information can be easily shared. Many user groups have monthly or weekly meetings and include speakers and discussion on hardware and software.

Buying computers and software requires planning and a careful assessment of one's needs. Support, information, and training are readily available to those who seek them out. Carefully chosen and supported, a computer can be a fascinating and fun tool.

## SUMMARY

Nine steps are important in making a successful computer purchase. They are: (1) Analyze your needs, (2) Determine affordability, (3) Analyze software needs, (4) Research available software, (5) Shop for software and identify hardware requirements, (6) Identify the appropriate computer, (7) Shop again, (8) Purchase the machine, and (9) Put the machine to use.

The most popular ways to purchase computers are through computer stores, university and college buying plans, and mail order.

Surge protectors and insurance riders added to homeowner or renter policies are important safeguards for desktop computers.

Careful planning is needed when purchasing software. Six steps contribute to successful software purchases. They are: (1) Analyze your software needs, (2) Identify packages that suit your needs, (3) Assess your hardware needs, (4) Determine what you can afford, (5) Comparison shop—look for the best price, and (6) Purchase only what you need.

Documentation is the use and operating instructions that manufacturers provide with hardware and software.

Books, magazines, and newspapers provide people with information and advice on hardware and software use. Tutorials and courses can provide hands-on experience with computers and software.

User groups are clubs formed around a particular model or type of computer. These groups provide their members with support; access to software, including shareware; and problem-solving tips.

## Key Words

As an extra review of the chapter, try defining the following terms. If you have trouble with any of them, refer to the page number listed.

documentation  *(389)*          surge protector  *(385)*
on-site service  *(382)*         tutorials  *(389)*
orphans  *(390)*                 useful hacking  *(389)*
shareware  *(390)*               user group  *(390)*

## Test Your Knowledge

1. What is the first step needed for the successful purchase of both hardware and software?

2. Name the nine steps in buying a computer system.

3. Briefly describe each of the nine steps involved in buying a computer system.

4. Why is it necessary to identify software needs prior to a hardware purchase?

5. What role does the library play in buying a computer?

6. Why should compatibility and expandability be considered when purchasing a computer?

7. List the three popular sources for computer purchases.

8. What is a surge protector? Why is it useful?

9. Name the five building-block software packages.

10. Name the six steps in buying software.

11. Define *documentation.*

12. What types of self-education materials are available to computer owners?

13. Explain the two types of hands-on instruction available to educate users about computers and software.

14. What is a user group?

15. Define *shareware.*

## Expand Your Knowledge

1. Contact your computing center and learn if your school participates in a computer buying program. If it does, gather material about the plan, including the hardware available and current price lists. Write a short paper instructing fellow students how to purchase a computer through your school.

2. Identify your computer needs. Using available resources, identify the software you would require and the hardware needed. In three columns list your needs, available software, and required hardware.

3. Using a local computer store and three computer magazines, compare prices for three printers and five software packages of your choice. How much can you save buying by mail? In your opinion, is buying by mail worth it?

4. Contact a local user group. Attend a meeting and write a short paper on the organization. Include the kind of support the group provides, meeting days and times, and location.

# 16

# Issues and Responsibilities

## Chapter Outline

Computers, An Agent of Change

Computers and Crime

Hacking

Theft, Piracy, and Plagiarism
   Protecting Intellectual Property • Plagiarism

Privacy

Computer Matching

Throughout this text the tool called the computer has been examined and discussed. A *tool* sounds innocuous; it is merely an aid humans use that is incapable of influence or effect. Yet, tools do indeed make a difference. They do more than provide assistance. Their use can alter the very nature of the human experience. The harnessing of fire changed life for ancient man, as did the invention of the wheel, the steam engine, and other traditional tools. Written language, number systems, and mathematics helped make sense out of an increasingly complex world. Tools enabled people to travel across the seas, build magnificent structures, and empowered us to reach for the stars. The printing press put the world in our hands, and the invention of the steam engine and the harnessing of electricity not only altered the nature of work, they irreversibly changed our daily lives.

After studying this chapter, you will be able to:

- Identify common computer crimes.
- Describe destructive hacking.
- Discuss intellectual property.
- Understand copyright law as it applies to computer software.
- Discuss software plagiarism.
- Understand how computers can affect personal privacy.
- Describe computer matching.

## COMPUTERS, AN AGENT OF CHANGE

It is perhaps too early to tell if the computer will have as powerful an effect on modern humanity as the taming of fire did on our ancient ancestors or as profound an effect on our lifestyles, employment, and behavior as the steam engine. But by any account, the effects of the computer on humanity are not and will not be trivial.

Changes that alter the structure of society are never simple or easy. Growth and progress always cost something. "There is no free lunch," the saying goes. Or, as Clarence Darrow exclaimed: "Unless a fellow moves ahead, he's left behind." While progress and change may inevitably alter the course of humanity, the direction and effects of such change are under our control. Significant changes in how we live require, perhaps even demand that we reexamine the ethical, moral, and human underpinnings of our society. The computer is affecting society and will not go away, any more than other inventions that caused societal disruptions. The computer is here to stay. As its use becomes more pervasive, it will affect us more, not less. Its potential to benefit humanity is incredible. Its potential to negatively affect each of us and society is equally real.

As were the tools of the Industrial Revolution before it, the computer is just a tool, a machine. The potential for positive or negative effects rests not with the computer but with humanity. We, the people, must decide how, where, in what ways, and for what purposes this machine will be used. The opportunity and the responsibility rest with each of us.

Earlier chapters in this text focused on the opportunities computers provide. This chapter will examine the issues and conflicts the use of computers has caused. Included are threats to personal privacy, the value of intellectual property, plagiarism, computer crime, and civil rights, to name a few. The problems caused by the introduction of the computer into our lives are complex, the solutions elusive. The changes wrought by the computer require that we reexamine how we behave toward each other and society. We as individuals must take responsibility for the computer—now and in the future.

## COMPUTERS AND CRIME

*Computer crime* has an aura of mystery. The criminal is cracking a complex safe filled with unusual, hard-to-describe, and valuable property (information). No blood is spilled, no fingerprints are left behind, nothing is visibly broken, no one has been hurt. Or so it appears.

For the mass media, crimes involving computers have a certain magic. In reality, the computer is only the most modern tool in the criminal's arsenal. The crimes are as old as "civilized" man: theft, fraud, destruction of private property, breaking and entering, and vandalism. However, there is a difference between computer crime and its equally serious counterparts on the streets. Computer crimes are harder to trace, easier to get away with, and are infrequently prosecuted. Little evidence is left behind to point to the perpetrator. The crime can be carried out without physically coming into contact with the victim, his or her office, or home.

The following facts are frightening:

- The American Bar Association surveyed a wide cross-section of companies and public agencies and found that more than 25 percent of these organizations had experienced incidences of crime against their computer systems in a one-year period. The financial losses in one year approached a billion dollars.

- Surveys have found that a considerable portion of computer crime goes unreported. Organizations fear that reporting such crimes will publicize the fact that their computer systems are vulnerable, their on-line security lax, thus making the organization a target for further abuse.

- Studies indicate that approximately 80 percent of all computer crime is committed by people with an insiders' knowledge of the computer systems. In other words, computer crime is committed by employees against their own employers.

While it is easy to claim that no one is hurt in such crimes since there is no blood, the reality is quite different. The direct cost in stolen revenue, compromised equipment, and lost files is quite high. The indirect costs, measured in repair and programmer time to correct debilitated machines and programs, are significant. These losses are directly passed on to consumers. What might these crimes look like?

- An employee is fired or laid off. Before leaving, the employee adds a few "innocuous" instructions to the company's payroll program. When the system attempts to delete the disgruntled employee, the program instructs the system to delete all other employees as well. While we may be sympathetic to the fired employee, is the damage to the company's records insignificant? What about the considerable inconvenience to the other employees whose paychecks may be delayed?

- A bank programmer adjusts the rounding portion of the program that calculates interest. Every time any account has its interest rounded down for posting, such as from 25.321 to 25.32, these fractions of pennies are placed in the programmer's account. Given the vast number of accounts processed and sufficient time, the programmer's account can accumulate to a tidy sum. Who is being hurt? Each customer loses only a tiny amount. Is a little theft from a lot of people a less significant crime?

- An insurance agent invents a client, has the accounts activated, makes regular changes and adjustments to the client's policies to give them a normal appearance, and eventually cashes in or makes claims against the policy. If your insurance rates are rasied by the number of claims made, is no one hurt?

- A teenager breaks into a hospital's computer system to look around, just to prove it could be done. Nothing is stolen and no one is hurt—or so the youngster claims. However, if the program entered contains the chemotherapy records of cancer patients, apparently insignificant, unanticipated changes can be critical. If the system that is breached monitors intensive care patients, even a momentary interruption could be deadly. Is no one hurt when such risks are involved?

- The father of a teenager arrested for breaking into a number of computers across the country says he is proud of his son. The father claims the son is practicing skills that will prove useful in the future. Would he feel the same way if his son were found breaking into and entering his neighbor's house? Is there a difference?

All of these crimes involve computers. However, people committed them. The computer was merely a tool. People are responsible. Unfortunately, the most frustrating and preventable of computer crimes are often committed by youths between the ages of 12 and 17.

## HACKING

Breaking and entering, eavesdropping, harassment, vandalism, destruction of private property, possession of stolen goods, theft—in anybody's book these are crimes. However, when the property damaged, stolen, or lost is electronic information, the "place" broken into is a computer, and the perpetrators are bright youngsters, the crimes appear to be taken less seriously by much of society, though not by the victims.

One dictionary's definition of a **hacker** is "someone who intentionally breaks into other computer systems, whether maliciously or not." Unfortunately, hackers are usually computer-competent teens, many of whom have used their home

---

**Figure 16.1**    Hacking: Computer hackers, who break into other computer systems, are violating the privacy of individuals and organizations.

computers to commit the crimes like those just described (see Figure 16.1). Some merely enter large computer systems, unauthorized, to prove it could be done. No harm is intended, they're merely looking around. They read electronic information and mail and in some cases make copies of the information, leaving the original intact. They have no interest in the information they find, since the thrill is in breaching the electronic security of the system. However, they *are* committing the electronic equivalent of voyeurism. The privacy of individuals and organizations is being violated.

Most unsettling is the lack of support that victims and law enforcement officials get from society, not to mention the parents of these young hackers. Cries of "No one has been hurt" or "It's the company's fault for not having better security systems," or even a feeling that the invaded computer system somehow benefits because security weaknesses have been uncovered, are all common.

These same people who find such crimes insignificant would not feel the same if surface mail were being read or the break-ins were to nearby houses. Hackers usually see nothing wrong with such snooping. Why should they, if so many around them see little wrong? Yet the organizations and individuals victimized feel the same as if the crimes had occurred on the streets. Certainly where sensitive information is involved, can we afford to believe that nothing has been changed even by accident? More to the point, we have the right to expect our property to be protected, regardless of its form. Someone must take responsibility. Hacking youths need to know that what they are doing is wrong.

What is even more frightening is that not all hacking is this benign. The highly publicized Milwaukee 414ers (named after their area code) broke into dozens of computer data bases on supposedly secure machines just to look around. These included the Sloan Kettering Cancer Institute and Los Alamos National Laboratories as well as computers at the Defense Department. Other hackers have broken into credit card and credit bureau data bases such as TRW, copied information, and made purchases or harassed people they didn't like with this stolen information. Others have broken into school computers and changed or deleted grades and other "offensive" information. Satellite communications have been interrupted, mailing lists and other electronic information have simply been erased.

To make matters worse, hackers often feel compelled to provide others with evidence of their ill-gotten information. It is not enough to break into a system, a hacker needs to tell others about the exploit. Hacker bulletin boards often include telephone numbers one can use to charge long-distance phone calls without a trace. Such free phoning is called **phreaking** and has long-distance phone companies alarmed. Bulletin boards also list credit card information, as well as passwords and computer phone numbers needed for breaking into unsuspecting systems. Until 1986, it was illegal to obtain and use such information, but not illegal to make it public. Would you like your credit card information posted?

Are hackers pranksters or criminals? It is as much a question of law as a question of morality. Even if no one is physically hurt, does that make computer

# On Line

## COMPUTER VIRUSES CAN MAKE YOU SICK

Computer viruses are seemingly innocuous programs disguised as normal software. Their sole purpose, however, is to destroy programs and data on the computers of unsuspecting users.

Virus programs are commonly downloaded from computer bulletin boards where users can exchange public-domain software. Unsuspecting users select the virus program, advertised on the bulletin board as a useful program or utility. When the program is executed, it proceeds to destroy any available information.

Virus programs can ruin all of the programs and data stored on a microcomputer's hard disk in less time than it takes to bring up the system. All of the computers on a large network can be "infected" in less than a minute and a multiuser system can be crashed in less than five minutes. Operators of computer bulletin boards have become so outraged by virus programs that they are warning board users by circulating a list of the disk-killing programs that have been identified. Computing center officials on college campuses and large businesses and organizations are warning users of the potential threat from virus programs.

Viruses come in two varieties. The simplest variety is exemplified by Egabtr. Claiming to be an innocent program to enhance screen graphics, it contained disk-destroying code. Such programs are fast and deadly. They immediately destroy information stored on disks. Software viruses can be even more treacherous. Such programs stay hidden for weeks or months, infecting hard disks and floppies alike. Then at a predetermined moment all contaminated software is disabled. Barry M. Simon, a professor at California Institute of Technology, told *The Chronicle of Higher Education* that "People who write viruses like to brag. They usually leave some clue that they've done something." Unfortunately, when their messages appear it is usually too late. Egabtr displays the words "Arf, Arf! Gotcha!" after it has destroyed disk information.

Computer pranksters have existed on college campuses for years. Unfortunately, the threat is no longer limited in scope. Viruses can affect computers everywhere. Any user that connects to a bulletin board, is part of a computer network, or shares disks with others is vulnerable. Some have suggested "computer celibacy" as a solution. However, such a solution eliminates one of the major advantages of modern computers: sharing of ideas and information. A less radical approach seems best. Program disks should be write-protected and backups should always be made. All programs received from acquaintances, bulletin boards, or networks should be tried with hard drives turned off and backup copies of the operating system available. Be vigilant. Programs making incredible claims may turn out to be quite different.

Solutions other than celibacy exist. A number of programs, including Data Physician, C4Bomb, and Disk Defender, have been designed to pretest software for viruses. However, no program can guarantee protection against all viruses. Vigilance and backup copies of software and critical data are the only guarantees against computer viruses.

*Source:* Judith A. Turner, "Worries Over Computer 'Viruses' Lead Campuses to Issue Guidelines, *The Chronicle of Higher Education*, March 2, 1988, p. A15.

eavesdropping right? When bright youngsters violate society's codes should they be held less responsible than their street-wise counterparts? The actions are basically the same and should be considered just as illegal.

Computer ethics must be as much a part of learning about computers as learning to program or using software. Respect for another's rights and computer property are important values, as important as proper treatment of equipment. We must actively teach responsibility along with computer usage, or youthful hacking will continue to be a problem.

Law enforcement groups realize that not all computer break-ins are committed by young hackers. Every computer system that is accessible to others by telephone and every computer bulletin board could be a target for the not-so-funny antics of vandals. Bulletin boards, university and corporate systems, and, increasingly, home systems are being purposely crashed or erased by unknown computer vandals.

Until the mid-1980s, most states and the federal government had no formal statutes focusing on computer crime. Most computer criminals were charged with illegal use of phone lines. In 1984, at least partially in response to the computer invasions caused by the Milwaukee 414ers, the Federal Computer Fraud and Abuse Act was passed, making it illegal to tamper in any way with the federal government's computer systems. The act was expanded in 1986 to include computer crimes against most private computers. In addition, the 1986 Electronic Communications Privacy Act was passed, making it illegal to intercept electronic information including bank transactions and electronic mail. This law also made it a federal crime to transfer information obtained through computer break-ins. Passing on computer information such as phone numbers, passwords, and the like became the equivalent of trafficking in stolen goods.

## THEFT, PIRACY, AND PLAGIARISM

Unfortunately, anything that is valuable has the potential for being stolen. Computer software and hardware are no exception to the rule. The legal rules that apply to computer hardware are identical to those on any other physical product. The physical machine is clearly property and its removal without the owner's permission constitutes theft. Similarly, reproducing a computer's hardware without the permission of its inventor/owner carries legal consequences. While lawsuits involving hardware may take considerable time to resolve, the laws that apply are easily understood.

### Protecting Intellectual Property

Computer software is a totally different story. Copyright law has been extended, to some degree, to protect software in much the same way a book or musical score is protected. However, computer software differs dramatically from books and sheet music. Two books can discuss the same topic, using different words, without really being the same. However, two different programs can be written that produce the identical or very similar output. Is the second program violating the copyright of the original program? Copyright law is unclear with respect to the protection of ideas or, as software is often called, *intellectual property.* In fact, there is no clear definition, legal or otherwise, for the term *intellectual property.* The issue in question is whether ideas can be copyrighted and, if so, to what degree?

Software authors and software companies contend that the *idea* upon which the program is based constitutes the intellectual property since any number of different programming paths can be used to produce the same results. Classroom programming assignments exemplify this. One assignment can result in multiple versions of the same program. Most have somewhat unique features, yet they all produce the same results. This is quite different from the papers that result from an assignment in a composition class. Just as with the programming assignment, each student in the writing class is given the same charge. However, the ideas presented and the results produced by students differ significantly. The programming assignment produces different paths to the same result while the writing assignment produces different paths to different results.

Therein lies the problem. Software authors, just like authors of the printed word, justifiably feel that what they have written is their intellectual property. It is the work of their minds, requiring considerable time and effort. Both software and print authors hope and expect to get reimbursed for their work (see Figure 16.2).

Unfortunately, this issue of copyright protection for intellectual property is more complex than it may first appear. It is in everybody's best interest to protect the efforts of software authors if we expect such people to continue writing the applications programs that are so useful on modern computers. However, when an idea becomes private property, it essentially becomes off limits unless permission is obtained for its use. Such limitations would stifle creativity since new ideas usually spring from the seeds of other ideas. If ideas are private property, they cannot be used as the building blocks for improvements on existing products or the development of new ones.

Some middle ground needs to be found so that the property of software authors is protected without dramatically restricting the creative processes of others.

## Plagiarism

No one would argue that it is unethical to directly copy someone else's book, article, or program and put your name on it as the author. But what about using another's work as a starting point for your own creation? With a few things changed, the revised version is presented as an original work. If the changes are

| **Figure 16.2** | A Software Licensing Agreement: Copyright agreements such as this one accompanying IBM's Easywriter software protect software by restricting its use. The purchaser "agrees" to the contract by breaking the package seal. (Reproduced by permission of IBM.) |

International Business Machines Corporation  Boca Raton, Florida 33432

**IBM Program License Agreement**

YOU SHOULD CAREFULLY READ THE FOLLOWING TERMS AND CONDITIONS BEFORE OPENING THIS DISKETTE(S) OR CASSETTE(S) PACKAGE. OPENING THIS DISKETTE(S) OR CASSETTE(S) PACKAGE INDICATES YOUR ACCEPTANCE OF THESE TERMS AND CONDITIONS. IF YOU DO NOT AGREE WITH THEM, YOU SHOULD PROMPTLY RETURN THE PACKAGE UNOPENED; AND YOUR MONEY WILL BE REFUNDED.

IBM provides this program and licenses its use in the United States and Puerto Rico. You assume responsibility for the selection of the program to achieve your intended results, and for the installation, use and results obtained from the program.

**LICENSE**

You may:

a. use the program on a single machine;

b. copy the program into any machine readable or printed form for backup or modification purposes in support of your use of the program on the single machine (Certain programs, however, may include mechanisms to limit or inhibit copying. They are marked "copy protected.");

c. modify the program and/or merge it into another program for your use on the single machine (Any portion of this program merged into another program will continue to be subject to the terms and conditions of this Agreement.); and,

d. transfer the program and license to another party if the other party agrees to accept the terms and conditions of this Agreement. If you transfer the program, you must at the same time either transfer all copies whether in printed or machine-readable form to the same party or destroy any copies not transferred; this includes all modifications and portions of the program contained or merged into other programs.

You must reproduce and include the copyright notice on any copy, modification or portion merged into another program.

YOU MAY NOT USE, COPY, MODIFY, OR TRANSFER THE PROGRAM, OR ANY COPY, MODIFICATION OR MERGED PORTION, IN WHOLE OR IN PART, EXCEPT AS EXPRESSLY PROVIDED FOR IN THIS LICENSE.

IF YOU TRANSFER POSSESSION OF ANY COPY, MODIFICATION OR MERGED PORTION OF THE PROGRAM TO ANOTHER PARTY, YOUR LICENSE IS AUTOMATICALLY TERMINATED.

**TERM**

The license is effective until terminated. You may terminate it at any other time by destroying the program together with all copies, modifications and merged portions in any form. It will also terminate upon conditions set forth elsewhere in this Agreement or if you fail to comply with any term or condition of this Agreement. You agree upon such termination to destroy the program together with all copies, modifications and merged portions in any form.

**LIMITED WARRANTY**

THE PROGRAM IS PROVIDED "AS IS" WITHOUT WARRANTY OF ANY KIND, EITHER EXPRESSED OR IMPLIED, INCLUDING, BUT NOT LIMITED TO THE IMPLIED WARRANTIES OF MERCHANTABILITY AND FITNESS FOR A PARTICULAR PURPOSE. THE ENTIRE RISK AS TO THE QUALITY AND PERFORMANCE OF THE PROGRAM IS WITH YOU. SHOULD THE PROGRAM PROVE DEFECTIVE, YOU (AND NOT IBM OR AN AUTHORIZED PERSONAL COMPUTER DEALER) ASSUME THE ENTIRE COST OF ALL NECESSARY SERVICING, REPAIR OR CORRECTION.

Continued on inside back cover

merely cosmetic we would consider this *plagiarism*. However, how much has to change before the work can be considered original? In courses involving programming this is a major issue. A student would never consider handing in a photocopy of an English paper written by a friend (with the name changed of course), yet receiving essentially identical programs containing perhaps a few changes in variable names and spacing is not uncommon. Individual assignments are not intended to become group projects. There is a clear difference between sharing ideas and helping others, and turning in identical programs. However, the time involved in writing and debugging programs, as well as the rigorous approach to problem solving that is required, sometimes causes students to collaborate rather than work alone. Individual programming assignments, as with any other written work, are expected to be done by the individual student. Anything else is plagiarism.

This problem is not limited to college campuses, and for this reason copyright protection for software is necessary. It is illegal to duplicate a book on a copy machine. It violates the author's copyright. To possess a copy of a printed work, we must pay for it. The author is entitled to just compensation for the work. Of course, it makes very little sense to duplicate a book on a copy machine since the cost of copying a book is often more than the purchase price. Furthermore, even the most sophisticated books are relatively affordable. Books rarely cost more than $50. With software, however, the reverse is true. Software is usually inexpensive to copy but has a purchase price of hundreds of dollars. Is the violation different? Should our wallets affect our integrity? Unfortunately, such software duplication is widespread, even though unethical and usually illegal.

## PRIVACY

One of the cornerstones of our behavior as Americans is a deep and abiding belief that as individuals we have a right to privacy. This means that no organization, person, or government agency has the right to invade the solitude of our minds. The First Amendment protects freedom of religion, speech, press, and assembly and the right to petition the government. The Fourth Amendment protects "the right of the people to (be) secure in their persons, houses, papers and effects against unreasonable search and seizure." The Constitution has granted us and all future generations the right to be left alone. According to *Webster's Dictionary*, **privacy** is "the quality or state of being apart from company or observation." Things that are private are "not known or intended to be known publicly; unsuitable for public mention, use or display."

The computer is a powerful tool, and because it is invaluable for collecting, organizing, storing, and retrieving information, it has the potential to put our privacy at risk if misused. Businesses, organizations, and the government have always collected information about their constituencies and their adversaries. We pay taxes, take out insurance, purchase items on credit, use checking accounts, go to school, see our doctors, and license or register an incredible number of things every day. Computerized data bases have proven invaluable tools for making it easy to find and use this information, which in most cases has been freely given. For example, computerized medical records save lives, and computerized business records save time and money. However, it was not our intent that information freely given in one instance should be available to other organizations or individuals without our consent. Our right to be private individuals means that only those who have a "need to know" should have access to the intimate details of our lives and that *we* determine who has a need to know.

Think about all the different kinds of information that has been collected about us. Every time we fill out a form, for any reason, we are supplying information to others about ourselves. We fill out job applications, tax returns, credit card applications, we open bank accounts, give the post office and census bureau information about persons living in our homes, and have telephones connected in our homes and businesses (see Figure 16.3). While this information may not be given totally voluntarily, especially in the case of tax returns, we are

**Figure 16.3**    Personal Data: Every time we fill out a job application, open bank accounts, or complete our tax forms we are consciously supplying personal information that is entered into various data bases.

conscious that we are giving out personal information. Yet other information is collected about us of which we are often less aware. For example, every long-distance call we make is recorded, as is every check we write regardless of the amount. Every loan payment we make for such things as cars, homes, and educational loans is recorded. Every credit card purchase and payment we make, every school we ever attended, every class we ever took, every grade we ever got, every interaction we have ever had with the police, from traffic tickets to complaints, have been recorded someplace. The more we think about it the longer the list grows.

Without anyone intentionally watching, almost every action we take in our daily lives has been recorded. This realization can seem incredibly ominous. It would not be an impossible task for the government or any other organization that wished to do so to gather up all of this information and place it in a single massive, centralized computer data base. If this occurred, "Big Brother" would indeed be watching. How would we feel? How would we act? What would have happened to our freedom? Even if the government did nothing more than collect the data, its very collection could affect they way we live our lives.

Before this picture gets too bleak, we need to recall that such a centralized data base does not exist and is unlikely to come into being. However, we should not lessen our vigilance. In the early 1970s, Congress passed legislation clarifying our rights and responsibilities regarding collected information. In 1970 the Fair Credit Reporting Act and the Freedom of Information Act guaranteed us access to and the right to correct the information government agencies and credit organizations collect about us. In 1973, the Crime Control Act was passed requiring that police agency records contain not only arrest information but the outcome of the case as well. An arrest does not imply guilt. The most important piece of legislation passed was the Federal Privacy Act of 1974. Partly in response to the Watergate scandal, this act limits the kind and nature of the information the government can collect. Information must be "relevant and necessary." Gossip and secondhand information cannot be collected. This act further reinforced our rights to see and correct information that is collected. It also prohibits the collection of information about our religious or political activities.

As long as the data collected about us is decentralized and we are conscious of our rights, computerized data bases are tools that benefit each of us. In most cases, information collected about us cannot be released without our consent, which is as it should be if our privacy is to be protected. Many people feel that the current controls are not strong enough. They feel that no information should be given out about us without our first reviewing that information and then giving our informed consent. While such an idea has merit in principle, in practice it would make transacting the nation's business almost impossible. In some cases such consent would make information inaccessible, even to those with a "need to know," and could threaten our lives. For example, if you were injured in an accident and doctors could not gain access to your medical records, critical information would not be available and your life would be at risk. On the other hand, we don't want our medical histories to become public knowledge. A delicate balance must be created between privacy and the need to know.

## COMPUTER MATCHING

Ask even an experienced computer programmer what computer matching is and either a long dissertation on how to compare two lists using a computer will be given or the newest computer dating service will be described. Actually, **computer matching** uses a computer to compare two files or lists of information, seeking the same item on both lists. A computerized dating service is indeed an excellent example of how computer matching works. Every person who purchases a membership answers a series of questions about himself or herself and specifies the qualities necessary in a prospective date. Then each client is compared with every other client. Those whose requirements match are given each others' names, addresses, phone numbers, and other important information so they can arrange to meet. While this may not seem romantic, such electronic matchmaking does take some of the trauma out of first dates. Such computer matching is done with the wishful consent of all the parties involved. Every client knows that he or she will be compared over and over again and willingly participates.

However, each of us unknowingly participates in electronic matching without our consent on a regular basis. Information we gave willingly for a particular purpose is being matched against other collected information without our knowledge or consent by federal, state, and local governments. The government uses matching for a number of seemingly altruistic purposes. For example, the State of New York and other states as well compare the names and social security numbers of all persons getting income tax refunds against a list of individuals convicted of failing to pay child support. If a match is found (and many are), the income tax check is withheld and the funds are used as partial payment for the unpaid child support. Another example is the comparison of motor vehicle registrations against tax records to find persons living in one state who register their cars in another state to avoid fees or taxes on their vehicles. Still another example is the comparison of federal tax records against military draft-registration records to locate young men who have not registered for the military draft (see Figure 16.4).

At first glance, such matching may seem reasonable. However, it could be easily argued that matching violates our civil rights. Matching assumes guilt without due process of law. Our private records are compared without our permission. We may not have committed a crime and yet we are suspect as if we had criminal records. It would be all too easy to match for membership in questionable organizations where the individuals in power determined the definition of *questionable*.

**Figure 16.4**     Computer Matching: Some state tax departments use computer matching to compare the names of people receiving tax refunds with people convicted of failing to pay child support.

Perhaps Big Brother is watching or at least matching. There is considerable risk to our civil rights in matching. It is arguable that matching, as it is currently called, is in the interest of both citizens and the government. However, where are the checks and balances? Who watches over the shoulders of the government agencies involved in matching to ensure that the rights of the individual are protected?

As we have seen, computer crime, hacking, software piracy, computer matching, and protecting our general privacy are complex issues brought on by our success at integrating computers into our daily lives. Harnessing the power of computers carries problems with it. But these problems provide us with the opportunity to examine the way we live and allow us to choose the best path to our future.

To protect our privacy and reduce computer crime, each of us must assume responsibility for our actions. We must act ethically, whether there is a law to compel us or not. We must educate ourselves and future generations in both the pitfalls and the vast benefits that computers can bring. Computers are machines;

tools for modern man. How we use them determines their effects. If they are harmful, it is because we employ them without caring for our fellow men and women. If they are beneficial, it is only because we strive to make them so. We can use these incredible tools wisely or foolishly. The future is up to each of us.

## SUMMARY

The computer is the most modern tool used by the criminal. Crimes committed using computers include theft, fraud, destruction of private property, breaking and entering, and vandalism. Computer crimes are hard to trace and often go unreported.

A hacker is someone who intentionally breaks into other computer systems, whether maliciously or not. Hacking, the electronic equivalent of breaking and entering, is often committed by youths aged 12 to 17. In many cases, hackers do not intend to do damage. Hacking using long-distance phone lines and charging the calls to unauthorized numbers is called phreaking. The 1986 Electronic Communications Privacy Act makes it illegal to intercept electronic information.

Copyright law has been extended to protect computer software. Software authors and companies consider intellectual property to be the ideas upon which software is based. However, the law is unclear with respect to the protection of ideas.

Americans believe in a right to privacy, which is the right to be left alone. Businesses, organizations, and the government collect vast amounts of information about people daily. The gathering of this collected information into a centralized data base could threaten our civil rights. A number of laws passed in the 1970s, including the Federal Privacy Act, address this issue.

Computer matching uses a computer to compare two files or lists of information, seeking the same items on both lists. A number of states use computer matching to seek individuals violating the law. Matching may violate our civil rights since it assumes guilt without due process of law and uses collected information without a person's permission.

## Key Words

As an extra review of the chapter, try defining the following terms. If you have trouble with any of them, refer to the page number listed.

computer matching  *(406)*            phreaking  *(398)*
hacker  *(397)*                        privacy  *(403)*

## Test Your Knowledge

1. Why are computer crimes bloodless crimes?

2. Why are many computer crimes not reported to the police?

3. What is a hacker?

4. Define *phreaking.*

5. Who were the 414ers? How did they get their name?

6. What is the Electronic Communications Privacy Act? Why is it important?

7. How do software authors define intellectual property?

8. Define *plagiarism.*

9. Is software copyrightable?

10. Americans believe that as individuals they have a right to privacy. Why?

11. Define *privacy.*

12. How can computer data bases threaten this right to privacy?

13. Name three laws that protect privacy rights.

14. Define *computer matching.*

15. List two areas where computer matching benefits society.

## Expand Your Knowledge

1. In a three-page paper, defend the position: "No one is hurt by computer crime." Use at least three sources to support your conclusions.

2. If computer matching may violate our civil rights, why is it used? In a short (three to five page) paper examine computer matching. Compare the "greater good" theory with the risk to our civil rights. Use at least three information sources.

3. Research hacking. Write a short (three to five page) paper on hacking. Include the kinds of crimes that are committed by hackers, machines that have been compromised, and the outcome of legal prosecution or identification of hackers. Include at least four information sources.

4. Many students feel that there is nothing wrong with duplicating copyrighted computer diskettes. How do you feel? Using two information sources, write a three-page paper defending your viewpoint.

5. Lotus Corp. recently brought a lawsuit against two of its competitors, VP-Planner and The Twin, for copyright infringement. Write a short (three to five page) paper on this lawsuit. What charges did Lotus make? How did VP-Planner and The Twin respond? In your paper, explain how this suit addresses the issue of intellectual property. Has the case been resolved? If so, how? Use at least four information sources.

# Photo Credits

## Chapter 1

1.2(a) Apple Computer, Inc.; 1.2(b) ETA Systems, Subsidiary of Control Data; 1.3(a) Boeing Company; 1.3(b) NASA; 1.4(a, b) International Business Machines Corporation; 1.5 Raytheon Company; 1.6 Motorola Inc.; 1.8(a) International Business Machines Corporation; 1.8(b) Apple Computer, Inc.; 1.9 Apple Computer, Inc.; 1.10 Radio Shack, Division of Tandy Corporation; 1.11 Toshiba America, Inc.; 1.12 COMPAQ Computer Corporation; 1.13 Digital Equipment Corporation; 1.14 International Business Machines Corporation; 1.15 SUN Microsystems, Inc.; 1.16 International Business Machines Corporation; 1.17 Photo, Paul Shambroom/Courtesy, Cray Research, Inc.

## Chapter 2

2.2 Dr. E. R. Degginger; 2.3(a) Portrait by Philippe de Champaign/The Bettmann Archive; 2.3(b) Smithsonian Institution Collection; 2.4(a) The Bettmann Archive; 2.4(b) IBM Archives; 2.5(a) The Granger Collection; 2.5(b) IBM Archives; 2.6(a) Smithsonian Institution Collection; 2.6(b) Courtesy Joan and David Slotnick; 2.7 BBC Hulton Picture Library/The Bettmann Archive; 2.8(a) IBM Archives; 2.9(a) IBM Archives; 2.9(b) Burroughs Corporation; 2.10(a, b) Iowa State University Information Service; 2.11 The Granger Collection; 2.12 Cruft Photo Lab, Harvard University; 2.13 University of Pennsylvania Archives; 2.14 The Institute for Advanced Study, Princeton, NJ; 2.15 Sperry Corporation; 2.16 International Business Machines Corporation; 2.17 International Business Machines Corporation; 2.18(a, b) AT&T Archives; 2.19 International Business Machines Corporation; 2.21(a, b) International Business Machines Corporation; 2.22 Digital Equipment Corporation; 2.23 Motorola Inc.; 2.24 Bill Gallery/Stock, Boston; 2.25 COMPAQ Computer Corporation; 2.26 Apple Computer, Inc.

## Chapter 3

3.5(a, b) International Business Machines Corporation; 3.6 International Business Machines Corporation.

## Chapter 4

4.2(a, b) 3M Company; 4.5 Seagate Technology; 4.8(a) BASF Corporation Information Systems; 4.9 Seagate Technology; 4.10 SONY Corporation of America.

## Chapter 5

5.2(a) International Business Machines Corporation; 5.2(b) Digital Equipment Corporation; 5.2(c) Apple Computer, Inc.; 5.3 Apple Computer, Inc.; 5.4(a) Apple Computer, Inc.; 5.4(b) Microsoft Corporation; 5.5 International Business Machines Corporation; 5.6 Applicon; 5.7(a) Hewlett-Packard Company; 5.7(b) International Business Machines Corporation; 5.8 International Business Machines Corporation; 5.9 Koala Technologies; 5.10(a) Ford Motor Company; 5.10(b) Department of Neurology, University of Wisconsin; 5.11 Panasonic Industrial Company; 5.13 Epson America, Inc.; 5.14 International Business Machines Corporation; 5.15 Hewlett-Packard Company; 5.17 Hewlett-Packard Company; 5.18 Hewlett-Packard Company; 5.19 Burroughs Corporation; 5.20 SUN Microsystems, Inc.; 5.22 Hank Morgan/Rainbow; 5.23 Worlds of Wonder; 5.26 Recognition Equipment, Inc.; 5.28 Kurzweil Computer Products, A Xerox Company; 5.29 American Petroleum Institute; 5.30 NCR Corporation; 5.31 NCR Corporation.

## Chapter 9

9.1 National Oceanic and Atmospheric Administration; 9.2 Boeing Aerospace Company; 9.3 Chrysler Corporation; 9.4 International Business Machines Corporation; 9.8 Apple Computer, Inc.; 9.9 Carnegie-Mellon University; 9.11 SUN Microsystems, Inc.

## Chapter 10

10.8 Hewlett-Packard Company.

## Chapter 13

13.1 International Business Machines Corporation; 13.2 CalComp Display Products, Division of Lockheed; 13.3 Koala Technologies; 13.7 International Business Machines Corporation; 13.8 International Business Machines Corporation; 13.10 Dicomed Corporation.

## Chapter 14

14.3(a, b) Hayes Microcomputer Products, Inc.; 14.3(c) Lexicon, Inc.; 14.4 AT&T Bell Laboratories; 14.6 AT&T Bell Laboratories; 14.7 American Airlines; 14.8 CompuServe, Inc.

## Chapter 15

15.1(a) Apple Computer, Inc.; 15.1(b) Microsoft Corporation; 15.2 Jeffrey Mark Dunn; 15.3 International Business Machines Corporation; 15.4 Julie Houck/Stock, Boston; 15.5 Radio Shack, Division of Tandy Corporation; 15.6 Kindra Clineff/Picture Cube.

## Chapter 16

16.1 Carnegie-Mellon University; 16.3 SEC Corporation; 16.4 International Business Machines Corporation.

# Glossary

**abacus** an ancient calculating device invented in China around 5000 B.C. on which calculations are performed by manipulating strings of beads (Ch. 2)

**ABC** acronym for *Atanasoff Berry Computer* (Ch. 2)

**aborted (bombed)** a program that does not produce the desired results (Ch. 7)

**academic computer network** a computer network that enables geographically separated faculty members, researchers, administrators, and students to communicate, share ideas and resources, and work jointly on projects (Ch. 14)

**access** to call up a document or file on the computer (Ch. 10)

**access arms** movable arms similar to the playing arm of a phonograph that read information from disks (Ch. 4)

**acoustic coupler** an early modem that cradled a telephone receiver in rubber cups and translated digital signals into audible signals that could be transmitted over telephone lines (Ch. 14)

**Ada** a computer language named after Ada Lovelace that was commissioned by the Department of Defense to be an all-purpose computer language capable of doing all computer-related tasks, is highly structured, and is capable of communicating directly with computer hardware (Ch. 8)

**address** a number or code that describes the location in memory where data or instructions are stored (Ch. 3)

**addressable** a characteristic of data stored on magnetic disks; each data record has its own unique address or location in memory (Ch. 4)

**ALGOL** a computer language designed for scientific programming (Ch. 8)

**algorithm** a problem-solving procedure consisting of a step-by-step set of instructions (Ch. 6)

**ALU** acronym for *arithmetic and logic unit* (Ch. 3)

**American Standard Code for Information Interchange** see *ASCII* (Ch. 3)

**analog computer** a computer that manipulates measurable data such as voltage, pressure, and rotation (Ch. 1)

**analog signal** a continuous signal used in telephone line transmissions (Ch. 14)

**analysis graphics** visuals, such as graphs or charts, used to analyze large amounts of data by revealing relationships and trends (Ch. 13)

**Analytical Engine** a steam-powered, general-purpose computing device designed in 1833 by Englishman Charles Babbage that included the five components found in modern digital computers (Ch. 2)

**applications software** programs that allow the computer to perform particular tasks or solve specific problems (Ch. 9)

**arithmetic and logic unit (ALU)** the part of the CPU that contains circuitry responsible for performing addition, subtraction, multiplication, and division and can make simple decisions by choosing between two alternatives using the

**ALU** *(continued)* mathematical operations of less than (<), greater than (>), and equal to (=) (Ch. 3)

**ASCII (American Standard Code for Information Interchange)** a seven-bit code used to store computer characters that is the standard code for most minicomputers and microcomputers (Ch. 3)

**assemblers** see *assembly languages* (Ch. 8)

**assembly languages (assemblers)** mnemonic, low-level computer languages whose individual instructions correspond directly with machine language instructions and that must be translated into machine-readable form; each type of computer has its own individual assembly language (Ch. 8)

**Atanasoff Berry Computer (ABC)** an early prototype for an electric computer invented in 1942 by John V. Atanasoff with the help of student Clifford Berry that included a memory drum and arithmetic unit (Ch. 2)

**ATM** acronym for *automated teller machine* (Ch. 5)

**automated teller machines (ATMs)** computerized banking machines that are available 24 hours daily and can be used to make deposits and withdrawals and to transfer funds between accounts (Ch. 5)

**backup** duplicate copies of information stored in memory (Ch. 4)

**bandwidth** the amount of data a communication channel can transmit in a given block of time; the wider the bandwidth the faster the data can be transmitted (Ch. 14)

**bar codes** groups of black bars of varying thickness, such as those found on supermarket products, used in optical character recognition (Ch. 5)

**bar graph** a graph used to show the differences within a single set of data or to compare the relationships between different sets of data (Ch. 13)

**BASIC** a computer language invented as a tool to teach programming (Ch. 8)

**Bernoulli Box** a removable hard disk system used on certain microcomputers released in the mid-1980s (Ch. 4)

**binary number system** a number system using base 2 (Ch.1)

**bit** the symbols 0 or 1 (Ch. 1)

**bit mapping** using graphics software to link each pixel to a specific memory bit or set of bits (Ch. 13)

**BITNET** a discipline-independent wide area academic computer network serving many colleges and universities in the United States and having connections in foreign countries (Ch. 14)

**block** see *physical record* (Ch. 4); also portions of text to be moved in a word processing system (Ch. 10)

**bombed** see *aborted* (Ch. 7)

**broadband channels** communication channels that transmit at rates of more than one million characters per second (Ch. 14)

**bubble memory** a non-volatile data storage system that uses cylinders of magnetic material resting in a magnetic film on garnet chips (Ch. 3)

**bug** any error in a computer program (Ch. 7)

**Burroughs' Adding/Listing Machine** the first practical adding and listing machine, unique because it used a paper printing device for output; patented in 1888 by William Burroughs (Ch. 2)

**business graphics** analysis graphics used in business (Ch. 13)

**byte** a group of bits (usually eight) that represents one character of data (Ch. 1)

**C** a modern form of assembly language that has syntax structures of a high-level language along with the ability to communicate directly and easily with computer hardware (Ch. 8)

**CAD** acronym for *computer-aided design.* (Ch. 13)

**CAI** acronym for *computer-assisted instruction* (Ch. 9)

**cathode ray tube (CRT)** a type of terminal monitor (Ch. 5)

**cell** the intersection of a given column and a specific row on a spreadsheet (Ch. 11)

**central processing unit (CPU)** the electronic circuitry within the computer that changes or processes data (Ch. 1)

**CGA** see *color graphics adaptor monitor* (Ch. 13)

**clones** IBM look-alikes that can use IBM hardware and software (Ch. 2)

**coaxial cable** a high-speed data-transmission medium that consists of two conductors, one cast like a shell around the other, and virtually eliminates electromagnetic interference (Ch. 14)

**COBOL**   a high-level language invented during the second generation of computers and designed exclusively to assist businesses; well suited for creating and processing large files and generating reports (Ch. 8)

**color graphics adaptor (CGA) monitor**   a low-resolution color monitor that has a pixel density of 640 by 200 (Ch. 13)

**color graphics (multi-color) monitors**   monitors that can produce multicolored displays (Ch. 5)

**COLOSSUS**   the first practical single-purpose electronic computer, developed by the British during World War II with the help of Alan Turing used exclusively to break German codes (Ch. 2)

**command driven**   a mode in which the menus of a data base manager's menus are turned off and the user gives commands directly to the machine (Ch. 12)

**command files**   files that contain groups or lists of commands frequently used together (Ch. 12)

**compatibles**   computers that can do most of what an IBM PC can do, including run its software (Ch. 2)

**compiler**   a program that takes as input a high-level language and translates it in a single operation, producing a machine-readable code as output (Ch. 7)

**computer-aided design (CAD)**   the application of computer graphics to the design, drafting, or modeling of devices or structures (Ch. 13)

**computer-assisted instruction (CAI)**   self-paced instructional software that gives students immediate reinforcement when learning or reviewing material (Ch. 9)

**computer (punched) card**   an 80-column paper card for storing computer data and instructions that uses one or more holes punched in each column to represent digits and uppercase letters (Ch. 4)

**computer matching**   a procedure in which a computer is used to compare two files or lists of information, seeking the same item on both lists (Ch. 16)

**computer network**   a group of computers and computer devices linked together over transmission lines so that information and resources can be shared (Ch. 14)

**computer virus**   a seemingly innocuous program disguised as normal software whose sole purpose is to destroy programs and data on the computers of unsuspecting users (Ch. 16)

**control unit**   a component of the CPU whose circuitry controls the internal activities of the computer and that manages the flow of data throughout the machine based on the instructions it receives from programs (Ch. 3)

**copy (replicate) commands**   spreadsheet commands that make it possible to duplicate the contents of a cell or group of cells elsewhere on the spreadsheet (Ch. 11)

**core**   see *magnetic core memory* (Ch. 3)

**CPU**   acronym for *central processing unit* (Ch. 1)

**crash**   a breakdown of computer equipment (Ch. 4)

**CRT**   acronym for *cathode ray tube* (Ch. 5)

**cursor**   a flashing light most often in the shape of a rectangle, underscore, or an arrow that indicates on the screen where the next character will appear (Ch. 5)

**daisy wheel**   the typing element on a letter-quality printer closely resembling spokes on a bicycle wheel that transfers characters onto paper when a hammer strikes each spoke (Ch. 5)

**data**   raw facts collected from any number of sources that are the basis of information (Ch. 1)

**data base**   raw facts usually organized around a topic, account number, or key to make specific items easy to find (Chs. 9, 12)

**data base machine**   a special-purpose peripheral device exclusively designed to perform data base operations that is added onto an existing computer system (Ch. 12)

**data base management systems (DBMS)**   complex data base systems able to search, sort, and report easily that are used to manipulate multiple files at once (Chs. 9, 12)

**data integrity**   reliability, directly related to the ability of the data base to remain current (Ch. 12)

**DBMS**   acronym for *data base management systems* (Chs. 9, 12)

**debugging**   finding and correcting errors in programs (Ch. 7)

**default parameters (default settings)**   settings that a computer system will use unless directed otherwise (Ch. 10)

**default settings**   see *default parameters* (Ch. 10)

**delete**  to remove unwanted characters (Ch. 10)

**deletion commands**  spreadsheet commands that make it possible to remove columns and rows that are no longer necessary (Ch. 11)

**desk checking**  see *hand simulation* (Ch. 7)

**desktop portable**  a personal computer designed like a small suitcase that has the capabilities of a standard desktop microcomputer (Ch. 1)

**desktop publishing**  the production of camera-ready documents on a microcomputer that can be directly duplicated either on a copier or a phototypesetting machine (Ch. 10)

**development software**  programs used to create, update, and maintain other programs (Ch. 9)

**diagnostic messages**  error messages produced when a program is being translated that assist the programmer in diagnosing program problems by locating syntax errors that made statements impossible to translate (Ch. 7)

**Difference Engine**  a special-purpose computing device designed in 1822 by Englishman Charles Babbage to solve polynomial equations (Ch. 2)

**digital computer**  a device that manipulates data, performs arithmetic, and assists in problem solving by organizing data into countable units or digits (Ch. 1)

**digital signal**  high and low electrical pulses used to represent ones and zeros produced by computers and computing devices (Ch. 14)

**digitized model**  a binary version of a CAD design that is stored in memory (Ch. 13)

**digitizer (graphics tablet)**  an electronic drawing device that employs a special pen to sketch directly on the surface of a tablet and then transmits the sketch simultaneously onto the screen (Chs. 5, 13)

**digitizing camera**  a camera-like device that scans a diagram or picture and converts the image into digital form (Ch. 13)

**direct-connect modem**  a modem that connects directly into a telephone jack (Ch. 14)

**direct OCR**  see *direct optical character recognition* (Ch. 5)

**direct optical character recognition (direct OCR)**  a system that can read printed characters that are not written with special ink (Ch. 5)

**diskette**  see *floppy disk* (Ch. 4)

**disk pack**  2 to 12 disks stacked together on a single spindle, similar to phonograph records (Ch. 4)

**documentation**  a written description of how a program or software package is to be used (Chs. 11, 15)

**dot commands**  format commands in most text editor/text formatter systems that sit on a line by themselves in the left margin and usually begin with a period or dot (Ch. 10)

**dot matrix printer**  printers whose characters are made up of a pattern or matrix of dots (Ch. 5)

**download**  to transmit a file as a unit from a larger computer to a smaller one (Chs. 5, 14)

**drum plotter**  a plotter that positions the paper over movable drums that rotate as the pens move (Ch. 13)

**dumb terminal**  a terminal that can be used only for entering data or viewing output and must be connected to a large computer (Ch. 5)

**EBBS or BBS**  see *electronic bulletin board* (Ch. 14)

**EBCDIC (Extended Binary Coded Decimal Interchange Code)**  an eight-bit code used to store characters on IBM mainframes (Ch. 3)

**editing**  changing or manipulating text (Ch. 10)

**EDSAC**  the first computer to incorporate a stored program, using letters as input and converting them to binary digits by means of a primitive assembler; built in 1949 at Cambridge University in England (Ch. 2)

**EDVAC**  a stored-program machine built in 1951 that used a unique binary code developed by von Neumann (Ch. 2)

**EFT**  acronym for *electronic fund transfer* (Ch. 14)

**EGA**  see *enhanced graphics adaptor monitor* (Ch. 13)

**electronic bulletin board (EBBS or BBS)**  the simplest wide area network, which is called on the telephone by another computer so users can leave messages and exchange information (Ch. 14)

**electronic fund transfer (EFT)**  transferring funds electronically between banks (Ch. 14)

**electronic mail (E-mail)**  the process by which computer users exchange electronic messages over telecommunication media (Ch. 1)

**electronic spreadsheet**  software designed to be an automated accountant's pad or ledger that can manipulate rows and columns of numbers (Ch. 11)

**electrostatic printers**   non-impact printers whose tiny wires induce a chemical reaction in the paper's chemical composition when electrically charged and produce dot matrix characters (Ch. 5)

**E-mail**   see *electronic mail* (Ch. 1)

**embedded computers**   computers built into other devices, including missiles, automobiles, and hospital intensive care unit equipment (Ch. 8)

**enhanced graphics adaptor (EGA) monitor**   a high-resolution color monitor useful for processing text and graphics and having a pixel density of 640 by 350 (Ch. 13)

**ENIAC**   the first general-purpose electronic computer, which was room-sized, contained 18,000 vacuum tubes, could perform several mathematical operations at once, and had limited memory capacity; developed in 1946 by John Mauchly and Presper Eckert at the Moore School (University of Pennsylvania) (Ch. 2)

**EPROM**   acronym for *erasable and programmable read only memory* (Ch. 3)

**erasable and programmable read only memory (EPROM)**   PROM chips that can be erased by removing them from the computer and specially treating them (Ch. 3)

**Ethernet**   a LAN in which all computers and devices are connected to a single coaxial cable and that uses specially designed communications software to control data transmission (Ch. 14)

**E-time**   see *execution time* (Ch. 3)

**execute**   to process a program using a computer (Ch. 3)

**execution time (E-time)**   the time required to execute an instruction (Ch. 3)

**expert system (knowledge-based system)**   a collection of rules used by human experts written as a computer program that attempts to duplicate the ways in which professionals make decisions (Ch. 9)

**Extended Binary Coded Decimal Interchange Code**   see *EBCDIC* (Ch. 3)

**external direct-connect modem**   a stand-alone modem housed in a self-contained box that plugs into both the computer (or terminal) and the phone jack (Ch. 14)

**families of software**   software that is integrated by designing groups of stand-alone programs

that store information in a common format and use a common set of operating commands (Ch. 9)

**fiber optic cable**   thin, clear plastic or glass wires that use lasers to transmit vast amounts of data very quickly (Ch. 14)

**field**   a data item (Ch. 4), or a column in a data base that contains a specific type of information such as last name or first name (Ch. 12)

**file**   combinations of records that are read and processed as a single unit (Ch. 4)

**file managers**   the simplest kind of data base packages, usually menu-driven, able to process only one file at a time, and able to search and sort records on any of the fields in the record (Ch. 12)

**firmware**   another name for read-only memory (Ch. 3)

**first-generation computers**   the first commercial computers, which used vacuum tubes, computer (punched) cards for input and output of data and instructions, had magnetic core memory, and were programmed using machine language; included UNIVAC I and the IBM 650 (Ch. 2)

**flatbed plotter**   a plotter in which the paper is held in one place while the pens move across the page (Ch. 13)

**floppy disk (diskette)**   a small, removable magnetic disk used mostly with microcomputers (Ch. 4)

**flowchart**   a pictorial method of depicting an algorithm in which the focus is on the program's logical flow (Ch. 6)

**font**   a type style (Ch. 10)

**footer**   information at the bottom of a page (Ch. 10)

**format**   the layout of text (Ch. 10), or spreadsheet commands that allow the user to justify (right, left, or center) cell data (Ch. 11)

**format commands**   commands that allow the user to justify data as necessary within a spreadsheet cell, display numbers in their most meaningful form, and adjust the width of columns to allow for data of varying length (Ch. 11)

**formulas**   mathematical statements or sets of instructions associated with a spreadsheet cell and used to calculate the value of that cell (Ch. 11)

**FORTRAN**   a high-level language invented during the second generation of computers for

**FORTRAN** *(continued)*  processing complex mathematics that is still popular in mathematics and engineering (Ch. 8)

**fourth-generation computers**  modern digital computers based upon large-scale integration and microprocessors (Ch. 2)

**full backup**  a complete copy of all the data stored in memory at a given time (Ch. 4)

**full-screen editing**  editing whereby every character in the text can be adjusted as needed by moving the cursor up or down on the screen (Ch. 10)

**function**  special spreadsheet software routines that perform frequently needed tasks, including sum, average, standard deviation, and square root (Ch. 11)

**function keys**  special additional keyboard keys found on intelligent terminals and personal computers that can be programmed to perform special tasks (Ch. 5)

**general-purpose applications software**  software programs that focus on particular areas but can be adapted to individual needs (Ch. 9)

**general-purpose computer**  a computer designed to solve a variety of problems (Ch. 1)

**global search and replace**  a word processing command that tells the computer to replace every occurrence of a particular word or phrase with a specified correction (Ch. 10)

**graphics board**  a set of chips that allow a graphics monitor to run on a computer (Ch. 13)

**graphics editors**  graphics software that includes preprogrammed graphics primitives, such as circles, squares, points, curves, and lines, that can be entered on the screen and manipulated along with freehand drawings; also called paint packages or computer easels (Ch. 13)

**graphics tablet**  see *digitizer* (Ch. 13)

**hacker**  someone who intentionally, maliciously or not, breaks into other computer systems (Ch. 16)

**hand-held portable**  a tiny, light portable computer with limited memory, cassette-tape storage, and a one-line display (Ch. 1)

**hand simulation (desk checking)**  using pencil and paper to go through each program instruction to identify the step or steps that are producing errors (Ch. 7)

**hard copy**  computer output printed on paper (Ch. 5)

**hard disk**  see *magnetic disk* (Ch. 4)

**hardware**  the set of physical components that combine to make up a computer system (Ch. 1)

**Harvard MARK I**  a general-purpose computing device developed by Harvard professor Howard Aiken in association with IBM that used electromagnetic telephone relays, punched paper tape, and could perform addition or subtraction in 0.3 second, yet is not often considered a computer because it did not have a memory (Ch. 2)

**header**  information at the top of a page (Ch. 10)

**Hercules board**  a monochrome graphics board that produces high-resolution characters and shaded display graphics on a monochromatic monitor (Ch. 13)

**heuristics**  written or unwritten rules of thumb used when people evaluate situations or make decisions (Ch. 9)

**high-level languages**  English-like programming languages, such as Pascal, BASIC, FORTRAN, COBOL, Modula 2, and Ada, designed for easy problem solving that do not require an in-depth knowledge of the computer's internal structure but need a compiler to translate instructions into machine readable form (Ch. 8)

**Hollerith's Census Machine**  an early calculating device that automated the tabulating of census information and could be used to keep track of large amounts of similar data (Ch. 2)

**home computer**  a microcomputer designed for use in the home (Ch. 1)

**host computer**  a multiuser machine, either a mainframe or a minicomputer, with terminals, printers, card readers, and other peripherals connected to it (Ch. 14)

**hybrid computer**  a computer that combines the input/output design of an analog computer with the digital computer's ability to store instructions and perform highly accurate mathematical calculations (Ch. 1)

**hypermedia**  hypertext whose links include sound, video, and graphics as well as text (Ch. 10)

**hypertext**  software that allows users to browse through linked information in any order (Ch. 10)

**IBG**  acronym for *interblock gap* (Ch. 4)

**IBM 650**  the first computer designed specifically for the business community (Ch. 2)

**IC**  acronym for *integrated circuits* (Ch. 2)

**icons**   on-screen pictures that represent common computer tasks (Ch. 2)

**impact printers**   printers whose characters are formed by tiny hammers striking paper through an inked ribbon (Ch. 5)

**information**   the result of changing data in some way so that meaningful conclusions can be drawn (Ch. 1)

**index file**   a file containing key data and record numbers that is used in indexing to improve sorting speed (Ch. 12)

**indexing**   a data base feature in which the index file is sorted rather than the original file (Ch. 12)

**information**   the result of changing data in some way so that meaningful conclusions can be drawn (Ch. 1)

**information networks**   private computer networks that offer subscribers access to data base information, bulletin boards, and electronic mail service, as well as travel and shopping opportunities (Ch. 14)

**information utilities**   electronic data bases, some of which offer specific information such as medical journal articles, available to any microcomputer owner willing to subscribe (Ch. 14)

**inkjet printers**   non-impact printers frequently used to produce color graphics that squirt microscopic dots of ink on the surface of paper to form dot matrix characters (Chs. 5, 13)

**input**   the initial or raw data entered into the computer for processing (Ch. 1)

**input device**   a piece of computer hardware designed to transmit data to the CPU (Ch. 5)

**insertion command**   a spreadsheet command used to place new columns or rows wherever needed (Ch. 11)

**instruction time (I-time)**   the time required to interpret an instruction (Ch. 3)

**integrated circuits (IC)**   chips of a semiconductor material, usually silicon, etched with miniaturized electronic circuitry (Ch. 2)

**integrated packages**   powerful software tools such as word processors, spreadsheets, data base managers, and graphics combined into a single package (Ch. 9)

**intelligent modems**   modems that contain a multi-processor chip and can be programmed to automatically dial and answer the telephone and dis-

connect from the phone system when a conversation is complete (Ch. 14)

**intelligent terminal**   a computer terminal with its own built-in microprocessor that is capable of performing limited processing tasks independent of the computer to which it is attached (Ch. 5)

**interblock gap (IBG)**   a section of blank tape that separates blocks on magnetic tape (Ch. 4)

**internal direct-connect modem**   a modem inside the computer housing that uses the computer's power supply (Ch. 14)

**interpreter**   a special program that translates and executes a program one statement at a time (Ch. 7)

**interrecord gap (IRG)**   a piece of blank tape used to separate logical records for processing on magnetic tape (Ch. 4)

**IRG**   acronym for *interrecord gap* (Ch. 4)

**I-time**   see *instruction time* (Ch. 3)

**Josephson Junction**   an electronic switch invented in the early 1980s that could change states from 0 to 1 at least 10 times faster than devices in use at the time (Ch. 4)

**joystick**   a keyboard alternative used almost exclusively with home computers and video games to move the cursor around the screen (Ch. 5)

**justified**   margins that are even or straight (Ch. 10)

**key**   see *key field* (Ch. 12)

**key field (key)**   a field shared by different files in a data base (Ch. 12)

**keyboard**   the traditional means of putting information into a computer from a terminal, containing standard typewriter keys, a number pad, and special keys such as CTRL, ESC, and BREAK used to communicate with the computer (Ch. 5)

**knowledge-based system**   see *expert system* (Ch. 9)

**labels**   words, titles, or text within a spreadsheet that are used to form row and column headings (Ch. 11)

**LAN**   acronym for *local area network* (Ch. 14)

**laptop portable**   a computer designed to fit comfortably into a briefcase and having a typewriter-sized keyboard and monitor (Ch. 1)

**large-scale integration (LSI)**   the technology by which thousands of circuits are squeezed onto large-scale integration *(continued)* computer chips, reducing machine size and improving speed (Ch. 2)

**laser printers**   non-impact printers that combine lasers with copy-machine technology to produce dense dot matrix characters (Ch. 5)

**Leibniz's Multiplier**   a calculating device invented in 1673 by Gottfried Wilhelm Von Leibniz that expanded upon Pascal's calculator and could add, subtract, multiply, and divide (Ch. 2)

**letter-quality printers**   printers that produce type indistinguishable from that formed by an electric typewriter by printing a completely formed character with each strike of a hammer (Ch. 5)

**light pen**   a hand-held pen with a light-sensitive point, connected to the computer by a narrow cable, used as an input device in association with a keyboard and CRT (Chs. 5, 13)

**line graph**   a graph that reflects trends by the upward or downward direction of its lines (Ch. 13)

**line printer**   a printer that types an entire line of output at once (Ch. 5)

**linkage editor (link/load program)**   a program that automatically links programs being translated for use by a computer (Ch. 7)

**link/load program**   see *linkage editor* (Ch. 7)

**LISP**   the dominant language for artificial intelligence programming that is designed to manipulate lists of non-numeric information (Ch. 8)

**local-area network (LAN):**   a computer network that covers a limited geographic area such as a series of offices or an entire building and is owned or operated by a single organization or college (Ch. 14)

**logical records**   combinations of related fields on magnetic tape (Ch. 4)

**logic error**   a program error produced when a program executes completely but either no output or incorrect output results because the algorithm or logic of the program is incorrect (Ch. 7)

**log in**   to connect to a computer (Ch. 14)

**LOGO**   an interactive programming language developed to teach programming to children through the use of on-screen graphics to develop and reinforce problem-solving skills (Ch. 8)

**LSI**   acronym for *large-scale integration* (Ch. 2)

**machine dependent**   usable by only one brand of computer (Ch. 8)

**machine-independent**   a computer language or program that operates on any computer for which an appropriate translator program exists (Ch. 8)

**machine languages**   the lowest level of computer languages that uses instructions in the form of combinations of 1's and 0's and can be understood and interpreted directly by the machine's internal circuitry; each type of computer has its own individual machine language (Ch. 8)

**magnetic core memory (core)**   a non-volatile storage medium used with early computers that consisted of tiny (1/100 inch) iron oxide (ferrite) rings with several wires threaded through each ring that could be magnetized to represent 1 or 0 (Ch. 3)

**magnetic disk (hard disk)**   a direct access storage device, first marketed by IBM in 1956, both sides (surfaces) of which are coated with a magnetizable compound able to store data and instructions as magnetized dots (Ch. 4)

**magnetic ink character recognition (MICR)**   a system designed to automate check processing in which a machine similar to a card reader reads numbers containing iron oxide particles printed at the bottom of a check (Ch. 5)

**magnetic tape**   a strong plastic tape coated on one side with an iron oxide on which computer data and instructions can be stored as microscopic magnetized dots (Ch. 4)

**mainframe**   a large, very fast, 32- to 64-bit multiprocessor-based multiuser computer (Ch. 1)

**mail-merge**   a word processing feature that combines a list of names and addresses with a form letter (Ch. 10)

**memory (storage)**   the electronic circuits that store data and the results of processing (Ch. 1)

**menu**   a list of options (Ch. 10)

**MICR**   acronym for *magnetic ink character recognition* (Ch. 5)

**micro**   see *microcomputer* (Ch. 1)

**microcomputer (micro)**   a single-user computer whose CPU is a microprocessor (Ch. 1)

**microprocessor**   a chip containing a central processing unit (CPU) and its associated memory and often called a computer on a chip (Ch. 1)

**microwave signals**   very high-frequency radio waves that can be used to transmit data at high speed, including computer data and television sound and pictures (Ch. 14)

**mini** see *minicomputer* (Ch. 1)

**minicomputer (mini)** a multiuser digital computer that is smaller, less expensive, and has less data-handling capability than a mainframe but is more expensive and more powerful than a microcomputer (Ch. 1)

**modem** a device that converts, or modulates, computer-generated digital signals into corresponding analog signals so they can be carried over phone lines (Ch. 14)

**Modula-2** an improved version of Pascal with the ability to control system hardware and that is designed to support the development of large programs through the careful use of subprograms (Ch. 8)

**monochrome monitor** a computer monitor designed to display high-resolution text using lighted pixels of a single color to produce images on a dark background and whose characters have a pixel density of 720 by 350 (Ch. 13)

**mouse** a palm-sized pointing device for a computer used in association with a keyboard (Ch. 5)

**multiprocessor** a CPU designed to perform multiple tasks simultaneously (Ch. 1)

**multiuser system** a computer system designed to handle more than one user at a time (Ch. 1)

**narrowband channels** communication channels that transmit at rates of less than 30 characters per second and are rarely used for the transmission of computer data (Ch. 14)

**natural language processing** a research area within artificial intelligence investigating the ability of computers to process information received by the computer in a natural (human) language such as English (Ch. 5)

**non-impact printers** printers that use heat, electricity, lasers, photography, or ink sprays to print dot matrix characters (Ch. 5)

**NSFnet** a wide area network created by the National Science Foundation initially intended to provide both supercomputers and access to them to researchers nationwide. (Ch. 14)

**number crunching** the solving of complex problems that involve vast amounts of mathematical manipulations (Ch. 1)

**object code** see *object program* (Ch. 7)

**object program (object code)** the translated machine-language version of a program (Ch. 7)

**OCR** acronym for *optical character recognition* (Ch. 5)

**OMR** acronym for *optical mark reader* (Ch. 5)

**on-site service** computer repairs done at the location of a computer (Ch. 15)

**operating system** software that coordinates or oversees the tasks performed by the computer by integrating the instructions of a specific program with the actual wiring of the computer's hardware and that also provides communication between the user and the programs (Ch. 9)

**optical character recognition (OCR)** computer recognition of printed information in the form of bar codes or the direct recognition of printed characters (Ch. 5)

**optical mark readers (OMR)** an input device designed to read hand-written pencil marks on specially designed forms that are commonly used for analyzing multiple choice tests and survey questions (Ch. 5)

**orphans** computers that are no longer being manufactured (Ch. 15)

**output** information that is the result of computer processing (Ch. 1)

**output device** computer hardware that communicates computer output to people (Ch. 5)

**overwriting** typing over letters in word processing (Ch. 10)

**package integrator (window manager)** a program designed to combine a number of stand-alone packages so that data can be easily transferred among them (Ch. 9)

**parallel computing** computers containing more than one CPU, each with its own primary memory, executing multiple instructions simultaneously (Ch. 3)

**parity (check bit)** an extra bit added to ASCII and EBCDIC codes to ensure accurate transmission of data (Ch. 3)

**partial backup** a copy of data items that have changed over a given period of time (Ch. 4)

**Pascal** a computer language named after the mathematician Blaise Pascal that is a general-purpose teaching language emphasizing top-down design (Ch. 8)

**Pascal's Calculator** the first adding machine, invented in 1642 by Frenchman Blaise Pascal and consisting of a series of gears or wheels that could perform addition and subtraction when manipulated (Ch. 2)

**PC**  acronym for *personal computer* (Chs. 1, 2)

**peripheral devices**  see *peripherals* (Ch. 5)

**peripherals (peripheral devices)**  the physical devices attached to the computer's CPU (Ch. 5)

**personal computer (PC)**  a flexible and memory-rich microcomputer (Ch. 1), and the name coined by IBM for its single-user microcomputer (Ch. 2)

**phreaking**  free phoning using telephone numbers that hackers have obtained by illegally breaking into computer systems (Ch. 16)

**physical record (block)**  a group of logical records that are read and processed at once (Ch. 4)

**pie chart**  a graph used to show proportional relationships in a given set of data (Ch. 13)

**Pixar**  a computer graphics system that produces computer-generated visual effects that cannot be distinguished from natural photography (Ch. 13)

**pixels**  points of light on a computer screen used to create graphic images (Ch. 13)

**point-of-sale (POS) systems**  computer systems that process business transactions at the location (point) where the sale occurs and are commonly found in supermarkets, department stores, and restaurants (Ch. 5)

**portable**  the ability to move programs from machine to machine with only minor changes required (Ch. 8)

**portable computer**  a complete microcomputer designed to be carried from place to place (Ch. 1)

**preprogrammed**  having program instructions directly built in (Ch. 1)

**presentation graphics**  analysis graphics designed to assist in presenting insights to others (Ch. 13)

**primary memory**  memory associated with the CPU that stores instructions and data while a file or program is being processed (Ch. 3)

**privacy**  the right to be left alone (Ch. 16)

**program**  the step-by-step set of instructions, written in a computer language, that directs the computer to perform specific tasks and solve specific problems (Ch. 1)

**programmable read only memory (PROM)**  special ROM chips on which user-written programs can be stored and that can be programmed only once (Ch. 3)

**programming language**  a language that people use to communicate with computers (Ch. 8)

**PROM**  acronym for *programmable read only memory* (Ch. 3)

**protocols**  computer communication rules that control transmission speeds, the direction of transmission, error detection and correction, and interruption techniques (Ch. 14)

**pseudocode**  a written method that uses English phrases and formulas in outline form to indicate the step-by-step instructions necessary for solving a problem (Ch. 6)

**punched paper tape**  a one-inch-wide continuous strip of paper on which computer data instructions can be stored as a unique pattern of holes punched across the tape's width (Ch. 4)

**RAM**  see *random access memory* (Ch. 3)

**random access memory (RAM)**  user-programmable, general-purpose memory that stores program instructions, initial data, and intermediate and final results from programs (Ch. 3)

**read only memory (ROM)**  pre-programmed or manufacturer-defined memory that utilizes non-volatile, primary memory chips and contains vital operational instructions for the computer (Ch. 3)

**read/write head**  a tiny electromagnet that can create, read, or erase the magnetic dots that store information on the surface of a magnetic disk (Ch. 4)

**records**  combinations of fields that form larger units of meaningful information (Ch. 4), or a row in a data base that contains related information such as a student's name and address (Ch. 12)

**register**  very fast, mini-memory devices directly embedded in the CPU that are used to hold a data item, an instruction, or a piece of information (Ch. 3)

**resolution**  a measure of pixel density on a computer screen (Ch. 13)

**RGB**  the red-green-blue format used by most color monitors (Ch. 13)

**ROM**  acronym for *read only memory* (Ch. 3)

**ruler line**  see *status line* (Ch. 10)

**run-time error**  error message produced when a program is executed and stops processing (Ch. 7)

**scattergram**  a graph that shows the distribution among a set of values (Ch. 13)

**screen management keys** arrow and direction keys, including Page Up and Page Down, that direct the movement of the cursor on the screen (Ch. 10)

**search** a procedure in which the computer will examine stored data to find items that satisfy particular criteria (Ch. 10)

**search and replace** the process by which a computer searches for a designated word or phrase and replaces it with a corrected word or phrase (Ch. 10)

**secondary memory** memory outside the processor that is used for semi-permanent storage (Chs. 3, 4)

**second-generation computers** computers based on the transistor that could be programmed in either assembly language or a higher-level language such as FORTRAN or COBOL, and whose solid-state technology made them smaller, faster, and more reliable than first-generation machines (Ch. 2)

**seek time** the time it takes to find information on a disk (Ch. 4)

**semiconductor memory** the current memory technology in which thousands of microscopic integrated circuits are etched on a silicon chip (Ch. 3)

**shareware** user-written or public-domain software that is available for free distribution and has not been protected under U.S. copyright laws (Chs. 14, 15)

**silicon chips** tiny integrated circuits packed onto chips of silicon (Ch. 2)

**slide rule** a device invented in 1621 by William Oughtred that has two rulers that slide against one another and are marked so that the distances of the markings from the ends are mathematically proportional (Ch. 2)

**soft copy** computer output sent to a video screen (Ch. 5)

**software** programs used for problem solving or that direct the operations of the computer (Ch. 1)

**solid model** a seemingly three-dimensional model produced by CAD software (Ch. 13)

**solid state** a tiny electronic switch built with no moving parts (Ch. 2)

**sorting** a data base procedure that reorders or rearranges the records in a data base file either alphabetically, numerically, or by date (Ch. 12)

**source code** see *source program* (Ch. 7)

**source program (source code)** the high-level language version of a program (Ch. 7)

**special-purpose computer** a computer that is designed to solve a specific problem and has program instructions built directly into its hardware (Ch. 1)

**specialized applications software** applications software that focuses on a very specific task or group of tasks (Ch. 9)

**speech recognition** a computer input device that focuses on specific voices or understands natural language (Ch. 5)

**status line (ruler line)** the line on a word processing screen where information about the file appears, including cursor location, the amount of text entered, and the file name (Ch. 10)

**storage** see *memory* (Ch. 1)

**stored program concept** a theoretical program design developed by mathematician John von Neumann in the late 1940s in which program instructions are stored as numeric codes directly in the machine's memory (Ch. 2)

**subprogram** a division of a large, complex program that solves a specific part of the problem (Ch. 8)

**supercomputers** ultra-fast computers designed to process hundreds of millions of instructions per second and store and retrieve millions of data items (Ch. 1)

**superconduction** the condition in which the resistance and heat associated with the flow of electricity is virtually eliminated (Ch. 4)

**supermini** minicomputers that perform like mainframes (Ch. 1)

**surge protector** a peripheral device designed to safeguard electrical equipment by restricting or limiting the amount of current passing through an electrical outlet (Ch. 15)

**syntax** the set of rules that define how words and mathematical expressions can be combined within a computer language (Ch. 7)

**syntax errors** errors made in the use and structure of programming language (Ch. 7)

**systems software** software that controls the operation of the computer, receives input, produces output, manages and stores data, and carries out or executes the instructions of other programs (Ch. 9)

**telecommunication**   the transmission of information over long distances using communication lines, including computer-generated data, telephone conversations, or video in the form of television (Ch. 14)

**telecomputing**   the exchanging of information between computers and computing devices over communication lines (Ch. 14)

**template**   the outline of a spreadsheet with only the key labels and formulas set in the appropriate places (Ch. 11)

**text editor/text formatter software**   two-phase word processing software whose text contains special formatting or dot commands that provide instructions to the formatter; to see what a document looks like, the user must leave the editor portion of the program and run the formatter portion (Ch. 10)

**thermal printers**   non-impact printers whose tiny, heated wires react chemically with special paper to produce dot matrix characters (Ch. 5)

**third-generation computers**   computers that used integrated circuits with electronic circuitry etched onto small silicon chips and were smaller, more reliable, and less expensive than second-generation machines (Ch. 2)

**toggling**   hitting a key more than once to turn it on and then off (Ch. 10)

**top-down analysis**   a technique for breaking down problems into subtasks that can be further divided until each subtask can be solved directly (Ch. 6)

**touch screen**   a user-friendly computer terminal designed so that the user makes choices or activates commands by pointing to and touching information displayed on the screen (Ch. 5)

**touch tablet**   an input device with a 4 ½-inch square pad that combines features of a mouse with a touch screen and was developed by Koala Technologies Corp. for use with home and personal computers (Ch. 5)

**transistor**   a tiny electronic switch or semiconductor device that controls the flow of electricity between two terminals (Ch. 2)

**transmission channels**   data communication circuits that computers use to send data from place to place (Ch. 14)

**tutorials**   self-teaching materials that include a series of lessons a user can follow while sitting at the computer (Ch. 15)

**twisted-pair copper wire**   the most common, least expensive, and easiest-to-install communication medium (Ch. 14)

**UNIVAC I**   the first computer built for data processing rather than military or research use (Ch. 2)

**Universal Product Code (UPC)**   a bar code adopted by the grocery industry in 1973 whose bars contain information uniquely identifying each grocery item (Ch. 5)

**UPC**   acronym for *Universal Product Code* (Ch. 5)

**upload**   to transmit a file as a unit to a larger computer (Ch. 14)

**useful hacking**   learning to use a computer or software by experimentation (Ch. 15)

**user-friendly**   a term used to describe software or computer hardware that is designed to be easy to use and is intended for people with little technical expertise (Ch. 5)

**user groups**   computer clubs formed around particular types of computers to provide members with software and hardware support (Ch. 15)

**utility programs**   programs that control input, output, and critical processing tasks such as disk access (Ch. 7)

**values**   the numbers placed directly in a spreadsheet's cells (Ch. 11)

**VDT**   acronym for *video display terminal* (Ch. 5)

**vectors**   closely placed, lighted straight-line segments used to create screen images and characters (Ch. 13)

**very large-scale integration (VLSI)**   the technique whereby hundreds of thousands of transistors and circuits are packed onto silicon chips (Ch. 2)

**video display terminal (VDT)**   the most common means of communicating with a computer, consisting of a keyboard attached to a monitor (Ch. 5)

**video graphics adaptor (VGA) monitor**   a very high-resolution color monitor that produces remarkably lifelike images and has a density of 640 by 480 pixels (Ch. 13)

**VisiCalc**   the first electronic spreadsheet, developed by Dan Bricklin and Robert Frankston in

1979 to run on an early Apple II computer (Ch. 2)

**VLSI**    acronym for *very large-scale integration* (Ch. 2)

**voiceband channels**    communication channels that were originally used for the transmission of sound (telephone lines) and that can transmit computer data at between 30 and 960 characters per second (Ch. 14)

**voice synthesis**    a computerized voice output device that either records words and phrases, stores them in the computer's memory, and later builds sentences from them, or records phonemes (the finite sounds that comprise a spoken language) and uses them to construct words and sentences (Ch. 5)

**volatile**    requiring continuous current to retain stored information (Ch. 3)

**von Neumann Computer**    a theoretical computer designed in the early 1950s by John von Neumann that was based on the concept of storing a program in memory, that received instruction entered as a numeric code, and whose hardware was organized into components, each of which performed a specific task and could be called upon in series repeatedly to perform its function (Ch. 2)

**what you see is what you get (WYSIWYG)**    word processing software in which entered text can be immediately corrected and adjusted, formatting commands are immediately acted upon, and the text on the screen is moved around to reflect the command (Ch. 10)

**wide area network**    computers and computing devices connected over long-distance communications lines (Ch. 14)

**Winchester disk**    a magnetic disk system invented by IBM in which the disks, access arms, and read/write heads are sealed in an airtight container (Ch. 4)

**window manager**    see *package integrator* (Ch. 9)

**windows**    overlapping screen images in which the computer user can view multiple computer operations at once (Chs. 1, 9)

**word**    the number of bits that can be processed at one time (Ch. 1)

**word wrap**    an automatic carriage return feature in which the software sets up margins marking the maximum length of every line, and when a word crosses this invisible boundary, it automatically moves to the next line (Ch. 10)

**word processing**    writing with a computer; characters, words, and phrases can easily be added, removed, and changed within a document (Chs. 9, 10)

**workstation**    the physical layout of furniture and computer equipment designed to make using computers both comfortable and efficient, or a highly sophisticated desktop minicomputer including a large graphics monitor, a pointing device, and software that enables the user to run several programs at the same time (Ch. 1)

**WYSIWYG**    acronym for *what you see is what you get* (Ch. 10)

# Index

Abacus, 32–33
ABC (Atanasoff-Berry Computer), 44
Academic computer network(s), 363, 365–366
Access arms, 95–96
Accumulator, 72
Acoustic coupler, 353
Ada, 214
Address, 78
Address register, 73
Aiken, Howard H., 45–47
ALGOL, 212
Algorithm, 158
Altair 8800, 60
American Standard Code for Information Interchange (ASCII), 75, 76
Analog computers, 9
Analog signal, 352
Analysis graphics, 335
Analytical Engine, 39
Applications software
    business use, 227–229
    communication, 236–238
    data base, 234
    defined, 223–224
    education and training, 225–227
    expert systems, 238–239
    graphics, 234–236
    home use, 229–231
    medicine, 224–225

science, engineering, math, 224
spreadsheets, 232–234
word processing, 231–232
Arithmetic and logic unit (ALU), 71–72
ASCII. *See* American Standard Code for Information Interchange
Assemblers. *See* Assembly language
Assembly language, 202
Atanasoff, John V., 44
Automated cash register, 145–147
Automated teller machines (ATMs), 147–149

Babbage, Charles, 36–39
Backup, 102
Bandwidth, 353
Bardeen, John, 53
Bar graphs, 335
BASIC, 207–209
Bernoulli Box, 101–102
Berry, Clifford, 44
Binary number system, 7–8
Biological chips, 84
Bit, 8
Bit-mapping, 329
BITNET, 365
Block. *See* Physical record
Brattain, Walter, 53
Bricklin, Dan, 276

Broadband channels, 355
Bubble memory, 83–84
Bug(s), 180–181, 190
Bulletin boards, 362–363
Burroughs, William, 41–43
Byte, 8

C, 214
Cartridge tape, 93
Cassette tape, 93
Cathode ray tube (CRT), 122
Cell, 277
Census, 40–41
Central processing unit (CPU), 5, 70–71
    arithmetic and logic unit, 71–72
    control unit, 72
    registers, 72–73
Channels, 353–355
Clones. *See* Compatibles
Coaxial cable, 355–356
COBOL, 212
Color graphics adaptor (CGA) monitors, 331
Color graphics monitors, uses of, 122–123
COLOSSUS, 45
Command-driven, 307
Command files, 307–308
Communication media, 355–358
Communication software, 236–238, 358–359

Compatibles, 61
Compiler, 179, 181
Computer(s)
    analog, 9
    in art, 343–345
    basic components, 5
    binary number system, 7–8
    and change, 394–395
    connections, 351
    crime, 395–397
    development, 43–52
    digital, 9
    first-generation, 53
    fourth-generation, 58–59
    hacking, 397–400
    hybrid, 9–11
    learning and support, 389–390
    networks, 359–370
    purchase sources, 382–384
    purchasing, 376–382
    second-generation, 53–55
    third-generation, 55–58
    viruses, 399
Computer-aided design, defined,
    339–342
Computer-assisted instruction
    (CAI), 226
Computer (punched) card, 91–92
Computer matching, 406–408
Computer Museum, 63
Computer network. *See* Net-
    work(s)
Control unit, 72
Copy (replicate) commands, 290
Copyright law, 400–401
Corporate/business networks,
    366–368
Crash, 102
Cylinder method, 99

Daisy wheel printers, 125–126
Data, 3–4
Data base(s), 234, 304–305
    advanced features, 320
    complex operations, 316–318
    data base management system
        (DBMS), 234, 307

file management system, 234
    manual, 305
    microcomputer systems,
        306–308
    modern, 305
    multiple files, 319–320
    pitfalls and problems, 321–323
    planning, 308
    software, 234
    in use, 309–316
Data base machine, 323
Data base management system
    (DBMS), 234, 307
Debugging, 180, 190–192
Deletion command, 290
Desk checking. *See* Hand simula-
    tion
Desktop portables, 18
Desktop publishing, 267
Development software, 223
Diagnostic messages, 181
Difference Engine, 37–39
Digital computers, 9
Digital Equipment Corp. (DEC),
    19
Digital signals, 352
Digitized models, 341
Digitizer, 117–118, 332
Digitizing camera, 332
Direct-connect modems, 352
Direct optical character recogni-
    tion (direct OCR), 143–144
Disk pack, 95
Documentation, 389
Dot commands, 253
Dot matrix printers, 126–127
Download(ing) 134, 359
Dumb terminal, 132

EBCDIC. *See* Extended Binary
    Coded Decimal Interchange
    Code
Eckert, J. Presper Jr., 47, 50
Editing, 256
EDSAC (Electronic Delay Storage
    Automatic Calculator),
    49–50

EDVAC (Electronic Delay Vari-
    able Automatic Computer),
    50
Electronic bulletin board systems
    (EBBS or BBS), 362
Electronic fund transfer (EFT), 368
Electronic mail (E-mail), 23,
    363–365
Electronic spreadsheet, 276
Electrostatic printers, 127–128
Embedded computers, 214
Enhanced graphics adaptor
    (EGA) monitors, 331
ENIAC (Electronic Numerical In-
    tegrator and Calculator),
    47–48
EPROM. *See* Erasable and pro-
    grammable read only mem-
    ory
Erasable and programmable read
    only memory (EPROM), 83
Ethernet, 361
Execution time  (E-time), 80
Expert systems, 238–239
Extended Binary Coded Decimal
    Interchange Code
    (EBCDIC), 75, 76
External direct-connect modems,
    352

Fair, Ray, 341
Federal Reserve System, 367–368
FEDWIRE, 367–368
Fiber optic cable, 357–358
Fields, 90
File management system, 234,
    306–307
Files
    organization, 90–91
    naming, 178
Floppy disk (diskette), 99
Flowchart, 158
Font, 267
Format, 252
Format commands, 292
Formulas, 278
FORTRAN, 206–207

Frankston, Robert, 276
Functions, 292–295

General-purpose computers, 11
General-purpose register, 73
Global Search and Replace command, 263
Graphics board, 329–330
Graphics hardware, 329–331, 333–334
Graphics software, 234–236, 334
   analysis graphics, 335
   computer-aided design, 339–342
   creative graphics, 342–343
   presentation graphics, 336–339
Graphics tablet. *See* Digitizer
Greender, Thomas M., 237

Hacker, 397–400
Hand-held portables, 18
Hand simulation, 191
Hard copy, 122
Hardware, 7
Harvard Mark I, 45, 181
Hercules board, 331
Heuristics, 238
High-level language(s), 203–204
Hoff, Ted, 59
Hollerith, Herman, 41
Home computers, 17. *See also* Microcomputers
Host computer, 360
Hybrid computers, 9–11
Hypertext, 266

IBM (International Business Machines Corp.)
   history of, 41
   IBM PC, 17, 60–62
   IBM 650, 51–52
   IBM System/360, 55–58
Impact printers, 125–127
Index file, 321
Indexing, 321

Information, 4, 90–91
Information networks, 368–370
Information utilities, 368
Inkjet printers, 128
Input, 5
Input devices
   defined, 112
   digitizer, 117–118
   joystick, 115–116
   keyboard, 113–115
   light pen, 117
   mouse, 116
   print recognition, 140–144
   speech recognition, 136–138
   touch screen, 119–121
   touch tablet, 121–122
Input/output devices, 132
Insertion command, 290
Instruction time (I-time), 80
Insurance riders, 386
Integrated circuits, 55–57
Integrated packages, 242–243
Intel Corp., 59, 60
Intelligent modems, 353
Intelligent terminal, 132–134
Interblock gap (IBG), 93
Internal direct-connect modems, 352
Interpreter, 179–180
Interrecord gap (IRG), 93

Jacquard, Joseph, 36
Jobs, Steven, 60, 74
Josephson Junction, 105–106
Joystick, 115–116

Kemeny, John, 207
Keyboard, 113–115
Key fields, 319
Keys. *See* Key fields
Knowledge-based system. *See* Expert system
Koala Technologies Corp., 121
Kurtz, Thomas, 207
Kurzweil reading machine, 144

Labels, 278
Laptop portables, 18
Large-scale integration (LSI), 57
Laser printers, 128–130
Leibniz (von), Baron Gottfried Wilhelm, 35
Letter-quality printers, 125–127
Libraries, 239–241
Light pen, 117, 333
Line graphs, 335
Line printers, 127
Linkage editor, 179
Link-load program. *See* Linkage editor
LISP, 212–213
Local area network (LAN), 361
Logic error, 189–191
Logical records, 93
Log in, 365
LOGO, 213
Lotus Development Corp., 241
Lovelace, Lady Ada Augusta, Countess of, 39, 214

Machine-dependent, 201. *See also* Machine language
Machine-independent, 204
Machine language, 201–202
Macintosh, 62, 241–242, 267
Magnetic core memory, 80
Magnetic (hard) disk, data organization, 95, 97–99
Magnetic ink character recognition (MICR), 141–142
Magnetic tape, 93–95
Mail-merge, 264
Mainframes, 23–24
Mauchly, John W., 47, 50

McCarthy, John, 212
Memory
   addresses, 78
   as bytes, 8
   defined, 5
   new technologies, 83–84
   primary, 73, 80–83

secondary, 73
Microcomputers (micros)
    defined, 14–19
    development, 60–62
    home computers, 17
    personal computers, 17
    portable computers, 17–19
Microprocessor, 14, 59, 60
Microwave signals, 356–357
Milwaukee 414ers, 398
Minicomputers (minis), 19–21
Modems
    acoustic coupler, 353
    defined, 352–353
    direct-connect, 352
    intelligent, 353
Modula-2, described, 214–215
Monochromatic, 329
Monochrome displays, 330–331
Mouse, 116, 333
Multiprocessor, 23. *See also* Main-
    frames

Narrowband channels, 355
National Science Foundation
    (NSF), 365–366
Natural language processing,
    204–205
Network(s)
    defined, 359–360
    history, 360–361
    local area network, 361
    wide area network, 361–370
NeXT Corp., 74, 103, 344
Non-impact printers, 127
NSFnet, 365–366

Object code. *See* Object program
Object program, 179
On-site service, 382
Optical character recognition
    (OCR), 142–143
Optical mark readers (OMR), 141
Optical memory, 102–103
Orphans, 390
Oughtred, William, 33

Output, 5
Output devices
    defined, 112
    monitors, 122–123
    plotters, 130–132
    printers, 123–130
    voice synthesis, 139

Package integrators, 242, 244–245
Papert, Seymour, 213
Parallel computing, 84
Parity, 77
Pascal, 209–211
Pascal, Blaise, 33–35
Pascaline, 34–35
Peripherals (peripheral devices),
    112
Perpendicular recording, 103–104
Personal computer (PC), 17. *See*
    *also* Microcomputers
Phreaking, 398
Physical record, 93
Pie charts, 335
Pixar, 343
Pixels, 328
Plagiarism, 401–403
Plotters, 130–132
Point-of-sale (POS) systems,
    145–147, 368
*Popular Electronics*, 60
Portable, 204
Portable computers, 17–19. *See*
    *also* Microcomputers
Postal service (U.S.), 150–151
Powers, John, 41
Preprogrammed, 11
Presentation graphics, 336–339
Primary memory
    defined, 73
    magnetic core, 80
    semiconductor memory, 80–82
Printers
    daisy wheel, 125–126
    dot matrix, 126–127
    electrostatic, 127–128
    inkjet, 128
    laser, 128–130

    line, 127
    thermal, 127–128
Print recognition technology,
    140–141
    optical mark reading, 141
    magnetic ink character recogni-
        tion, 141–142
    optical character recognition,
        142–144
Privacy, 403–406
Program(s), 7, 158
    debugging, 190–192
    execution of, 79–80, 185–190
    testing, 192–196
    translation of, 179–185
Programmable read only mem-
    ory (PROM), 83
Programming language(s)
    assembly language, 202
    choosing, criteria for, 205–206
    defined, 200
    high-level language(s), 203–204
    machine language, 201–202
    natural language processing,
        204–205
    *See also* Ada, ALGOL, BASIC,
        C, COBOL, FORTRAN,
        LISP, LOGO, Modula-2,
        Pascal
PROM. *See* Programmable read
    only memory
Protocols, 358–359
Pseudocode, 158
Punched paper tape, 92

RAM. *See* Random access mem-
    ory
Random access, memory (RAM),
    82–83
Read only memory (ROM), 83
Read/write head, 96
Records, 90
Reel-to-reel tape, 93
Registers, 72–73
Resolution, 329
RGB, 331
Ritchie, Dennis, 214

Roberts, Ed, 60
ROM. *See* Read only memory
Ruler line. *See* Status line
Run-time errors, 188, 190

SABRE, 366
Scattergrams, 335
Screen management keys, 251
Search and Replace command, 263
Search command, 263
Secondary memory, 73
Sector method, 97–98
Semiconductor memory, 80–82
Shareware, 362, 390
Shockley, William, 53
Slide rule, 33, 34
Soft copy, 122
Software
    applications software, 223
    communication, 358–359
    copyright protection, 400–401
    defined, 7
    development software, 223
    families, 242, 245
    integration, 241–245
    licensing agreement, 402
    plagiarism, 401–403
    purchasing, 386–388
    systems software, 222
Software Publishing, 245
Solid state. *See* Transistor
Source code. *See* Source program
Source program, 179
Special-purpose computers, 11
Speech recognition devices, 136–138
Spreadsheets
    building, 282–287
    common features, 277–279
    pitfalls and problems, 295–296
    planning, 280
    programming tools, 290–295
    software, 232–234

Status line, 255
Storage. *See* Memory
Storage register, 73
Subprograms, 207
Supercomputers, 24–26, 59
Superconductors, 104–106
Superminis, 21
Surge protectors, 385
Syntax errors, 180, 190
Systems software, 222

Telecommunication, 350
Telecomputing, 350
Template, 280–281
Text editor/text formatter, 252–254
Thermal printers, 127–128
Top-down analysis, 160
Touch screen, 119–121
Touch tablet, 121–122
Transistor, 53
Translator program, 203–204
Turing, Alan, 45
Tutorials, 389–390
Twisted-pair copper wire, 355

UNISYS, 41
UNIVAC I, 50–51
Universal Product Code (UPC), 143
Upload(ing), 134, 359
Useful hacking, 389
User-friendly, 140
User groups, 390
Utility programs, 179

Values, 278
Vectors, 328
Very large-scale integration (VLSI), 58–59
Video display terminal (VDT), 132, 135

Video graphics adaptor (VGA) monitors, 331
Viruses, 399
VisiCalc, 60, 276
Voiceband channels, 355
Voice synthesis, 139
Von Neumann bottleneck, 84
Von Neumann, John, 48, 50

Watson, Thomas J., 41, 45. *See also* IBM
Watson, Thomas Jr., 51
What You See Is What You Get (WYSIWYG), 252, 254
What-if questions, 287
Wide area network
    academic computer networks, 363, 365
    bulletin boards, 362–363
    corporate/business networks, 366–368
    defined, 361
    information networks, 368–370
Wilkes, Maurice, 49
Winchester disk, 99–101
Window managers. See Package integrators
Wirth, Niklaus, 209, 214
Word processing, 231–232, 250
    advanced features, 262–267
    basic functions, 254–259
    capabilities, 251
    hardware, 251–252
    problems and pitfalls, 268–270
    programs, types of, 252–254
    text formatting, 259–262
Word wrap, 256
Workstation, 22–23
Wozniak, Stephen, 60

Zuse, Konrad, 44–45